The Steganographia
Books I, II, III & IV

Steganographia

SWCM - Sourceworks of Ceremonial Magic Series

Volume I – The Practical Angel Magic of John Dee's Enochian Tables - ISBN 978-0-9547639-0-9

Volume II – The Keys to the Gateway of Magic: Summoning the Solomonic Archangels & Demonic Princes – ISBN 978-0-9547639-1-6

Volume III – The Goetia of Dr Rudd: The Angels & Demons of *Liber Malorum Spirituum seu Goetia* – ISBN 978-0-9547639-2-3

Volume IV – The Veritable Key of Solomon– ISBN 978-0-7378-1453-0 (cloth) - ISBN 978-0-9547639-8-5 (limited leather)

Volume V – The Grimoire of Saint Cyprian: *Clavis Inferni* - ISBN 978-0-9557387-1-5 (cloth) – ISBN 978-0-9557387-4-6 (limited leather)

Volume VI – *Sepher Raziel: Liber Salomonis* – ISBN 978-0-9557387-3-9 (cloth) – ISBN 978-0-9557387-5-3 (limited leather)

Volume VII – *Liber Lunæ & Sepher ha-Levanah* - ISBN 978-0-9557387-2-1 (cloth) - ISBN 978-0-9557387-3-8 (limited leather)

Volume VIII – The Magical Treatise of Solomon, or *Hygromanteia* – ISBN 978-0-9568285-0-7 (cloth) - ISBN 978-0-9568285-1-4 (leather)

Volume IX – A Cunning Man's Grimoire: The secret of secrets – ISBN 978-0-9932042-7-2 (cloth) – ISBN 978-0-9932042-8-9 (leather)

Volume X – Clavis or Key to the Mysteries of Magic – Ebenezer Sibley – ISBN 978-1912212-08-8 (cloth) – ISBN 978-1912212-09-5 (leather)

Volume XI – *Ars Notoria* (Vol. 1) The Grimoire of Rapid Learning by Magic – Version A - ISBN 978-1912212-03-3 (cloth) – ISBN 978-1912212-04-0 (leather)

Volume XII – *Ars Notoria* (Vol. 2) The Method: Mediaeval Angel Magic – Version B - ISBN 978-1912212-28-6 (cloth)

Volume XIII – *The Steganographia Books I, II, II & IV*. ISBN 978-1912212378 (cloth). ISBN 978-1912212385 (leather)

For further details of forthcoming volumes in this series edited from classic magical manuscripts see www.GoldenHoard.com

Books on the Western Esoteric Tradition by Stephen Skinner

Agrippa's Fourth Book of Occult Philosophy (edited) – Askin, Ibis

Aleister Crowley's Astrology (edited) – Spearman, Ibis, Weiser

Aleister Crowley's Four Books of Magick (edited) – Watkins

Ars Notoria – Volume 1 (with Daniel Clark) – Golden Hoard, Llewellyn

Clavis or Key to the Mysteries of Magic (with Daniel Clark) – Golden Hoard, Llewellyn

Complete Magician's Tables – Golden Hoard, Llewellyn

Cunning Man's Grimoire (with David Rankine) – Golden Hoard, Llewellyn

Dr John Dee's Spiritual Diaries: the fully revised and corrected edition of *A True & Faithful Relation of what passed…between Dr John Dee…* with full Latin translation – Golden Hoard, Llewellyn

Geomancy in Theory & Practice – Golden Hoard, Llewellyn

Goetia of Dr Rudd: Liber Malorum Spirituum (with David Rankine) – Golden Hoard, Llewellyn

Grimoire of Saint Cyprian: Clavis Inferni (with David Rankine) – Golden Hoard, Llewellyn

Keys to the Gateway of Magic (with David Rankine) – Golden Hoard, Llewellyn

Magical Diaries of Aleister Crowley (edited) – Spearman, Weiser

Michael Psellus 'On the operation of Daimones' (edited) - Golden Hoard

Millennium Prophecies: Apocalypse 2000 – Carlton

Nostradamus (with Francis King) – Carlton

Oracle of Geomancy – Warner Destiny, Prism, Golden Hoard

Practical Angel Magic of Dr Dee (with David Rankine) – Golden Hoard, Llewellyn

Sacred Geometry – Gaia, Hamlyn, Sterling

Search for Abraxas (with Nevill Drury) – Spearman, Golden Hoard

Sepher Raziel: Liber Salomonis (with Don Karr) – Golden Hoard, Llewellyn

Splendor Solis (with Rafal Prinke, Joscelyn Godwin & Georgiana Hedesan) – Watkins

Steganographia (with Daniel Clark) – Golden Hoard, Llewellyn

Techniques of Graeco-Egyptian Magic – Golden Hoard, Llewellyn

Techniques of High Magic (with Francis King) – C.W. Daniels, Golden Hoard

Techniques of Solomonic Magic – Golden Hoard, Llewellyn

Terrestrial Astrology: Divination by Geomancy – Routledge

Veritable Key of Solomon (with David Rankine) – Golden Hoard, Llewellyn

Figure 1: Portrait of Trithemius.[1]

---

[1] A modern re-rendering of a classical portrait originally by Meister Hans Burgkmair created in the 4th quarter of the 15th century and currently residing in the Condé Museum, Château de Chantilly. Courtesy of Daniel Clark.

The Steganographia

by Johannes Trithemius
Abbot of Spanheim

Books I, II, III & IV

edited by
Dr Stephen Skinner & Daniel Clark

GOLDEN HOARD PRESS
2024

Published by Golden Hoard Press Pte Ltd
Robinson Road PO Box 1073
Singapore 902123
www.GoldenHoard.com

First Edition

© 2024 - Stephen Skinner
www.SSkinner.com

All rights reserved. No part of this publication may be reproduced or utilized in any form or by any means, electronic or mechanical, including printing, photocopying, uploading to the web, recording, or by any information storage and retrieval system, or used in another book, without specific written permission from the publisher, except for short fully credited extracts or quotes used for scholastic or review purposes.

UK ISBN: 978-1912212378 (cloth)

UK ISBN: 978-1912212385 (leather)

US ISBN: 978-0738779522 (cloth)

Contents

	MS page	*Printed page*
List of Figures		11
List of Tables		12
Acknowledgements		15
Introduction		19
Brief Biography of the Benedictine Abbot		46
The MANUSCRIPT		67
Manuscript Summary of the Contents of Book I	i	70
French Preface - Advice to the Reader	ii	74
Apology for the Marvellous Natural and Supernatural effects	v	77
Oath by the author on the Goodness and Honesty of this Art	xxx	92
FIRST BOOK of the *Steganographia*	1	95
Chapter 1 Parmersiel	1	97
Chapter 2 Padiel	6	103
Chapter 3 Camuel	10	106
Chapter 4 Aseliel	13	108
Chapter 5 Barmiel	16	110
Chapter 6 Gediel	19	112
Chapter 7 Asiriel	21	114
Chapter 8 Maseriel	24	117
Chapter 9 Malgaras	27	119
Chapter 10 Dorothiel	29	121
Chapter 11 Usiel	32	123
Chapter 12 Cabariel	35	126
Chapter 13 Raysiel	37	128
Chapter 14 Symiel	40	130
Chapter 15 Armadiel	42	132
Chapter 16 Baruchas	44	134
Chapter 17 **Carnesiel**	46	137
Chapter 18 **Caspiel**	50	139
Chapter 19 **Amenadiel**	51	141
Chapter 20 **Demoriel**	53	143

	MS page	Printed page
Chapter 21 Geradiel	55	145
Chapter 22 Buriel	57	147
Chapter 23 Hydriel	59	149
Chapter 24 Pyrichiel	61	151
Chapter 25 Emoniel	63	153
Chapter 26 Icosiel	64	155
Chapter 27 Soleviel	66	157
Chapter 28 Menachiel or Menadiel	68	159
Chapter 29 Macariel	69	161
Chapter 30 Uriel	71	163
Chapter 31 Bydiel	73	165
Chapter 32 Recapitulation	74	167
SECOND BOOK of the *Steganographia*	80	175
Chapter 1 Samael	81	178
Chapter 2 Anael	84	181
Chapter 3 Vequaniel	86	183
Chapter 4 Vatmiel	87	185
Chapter 5 Sasquiel	89	187
Chapter 6 Saniel	91	189
Chapter 7 Barquiel	92	191
Chapter 8 Osmandiel	94	193
Chapter 9 Quabriel	95	195
Chapter 10 Oriel	97	197
Chapter 11 Bariel	99	199
Chapter 12 Beratiel	101	201
Chapter 13 Sabathan	102	203
Chapter 14 Tartys	103	205
Chapter 15 Serquanich	105	207
Chapter 16 Jesischa	107	209
Chapter 17 Abasdarhon	108	211
Chapter 18 Zaazenach	110	213
Chapter 19 Mendrion	112	215
Chapter 20 Narcoriel	113	217

Steganographia

	Printed page MS page	
Chapter 21 Pamiel	115	219
Chapter 22 Jasguarim	116	221
Chapter 23 Dardariel	118	223
Chapter 24 Sarandiel	120	225
Chapter 25 Recapitulation	121	227
THIRD BOOK of the *Steganographia*	125	231
Preface - The Angels of Saturn	128	232
Chapter 1 – the Tables	128	234
Of the Variable Movement of the Planets, Interpretation of the Tables	135	241
Of the First Angel of Saturn - Orifiel	139	244
Of the Second Angel of Saturn - Sadael	142	248
Of the Third Angel of Saturn - Poniel	144	250
FOURTH BOOK of the *Steganographia*	150	255
Book of Sacred Numbers – First Part	151	256
Chapter 1 Of the Numbers of the Elements	153	258
Chapter 2 Of the Numbers of each Particular Being	156	260
Chapter 3 Of the Number of Beings or Uncertain Spirits	157	262
Chapter 4 Of the Number of Bad Spirits	158	263
Chapter 5 Of the Differences between Good and Bad Spirits	161	265
Chapter 6 Of the Nature of Evil Spirits	164	268
Chapter 7 Of the Differences between Good and Bad Intelligences	165	269
Book of Sacred Numbers – Second Part	166	270
Chapter 1 True ways to achieve success with the Sacred Numbers	166	270
Chapter 2 How many numbers to use when you do an Operation	167	271
Chapter 3 The Different types of Number used for the Operations	169	273
Chapter 4 What are the Numbers of Chapter 3	173	276
The Veritable Secrets	175	278
The True Way to make the Magical Bell	175	278
Warning to the Disciples	182	283
How to prepare Parchment for the Operations of our Art	185	286
Table of the Proper and Particular Movement of 10 Celestial Spheres	186	288
Table of the Proper and Particular Course of the 7 Planets	187	291

	MS page	Printed page
The Shemhammaphorashim	188	295
The Shemhammaphorash of Solomon	189	296
The First Order in the East	201	306
Twelfth Order	203	312
The Almadel	213	313
The 4 Regions of the 4 Elements	214	316
The Shemhammaphorash of Adam	215	317
The 12 Altitudes of Solomon	221	321
Making the Almadel	223	324
The Shemhammaphorash of Moses	231	330
Annotations	233	332
Appendices		335
Appendix 1. Good and Evil Aerial Spirits from the *Theurgia-Goetia*.		336
Appendix 2. Trithemius' letters embedded in the *Steganographia*.		340
Appendix 3. Planetary Hours.		341
Appendix 4. The Angelic Rulers of *De Septem Secundeis*.		342
Appendix 5. Calculating the Current Quarter Days for Timing.		344
Appendix 6. Comparison with the Spirit Register of the *Theurgia-Goetia*.		345
Bibliography		347

List of Figures

Printed page

Figure 1: Portrait of Trithemius	4
Figure 2: Title page of the Latin edition of the *Steganographia* dated 1721	16
Figure 3: A manuscript mentioning Pelagius dated 1465	25
Figure 4: A full Spirit Compass Rose from the *Theurgia-Goetia*	38
Figure 5. Johann Heidenberg (*aka* Trithemius) portrait by Durer	45
Figure 6: The 'Sponheim Closter' a historical town view	48
Figure 7: Title page of the *Catalogus Scriptorum Ecclesiasticorum*	49
Figure 8: Title page of the *Book of Eight Questions to Maximilian Caesar*	56
Figure 9: Tomb relief of Trithemius carved by Tilman Riemenschneider	61
Figure 10: A copy of the *Steganographia* made by Dr John Dee	62
Figure 11: Edward Kelly reading Trithemius	63
Figure 12: Title page of French Manuscript BPH 277	68
Figure 13: The Four Parts of the World and their Spirits	136
Figure 14: The full list of 31 Spirits as it appears in the manuscript	168
Figure 15: The Proper Movement of the Ten Celestial Spheres	287
Figure 16: The Proper and Particular Course of the 7 Planets in the Zodiac	290
Figure 17: The Ark of the Covenant guarded by two Cherubim	295
Figure 18: Figure of the Holy and Precious Almadel	314
Figure 19: Design for the Almadel of Solomon as a Table of Practice	323
Figure 20: A simple Almadel of Solomon	329

List of Tables

	MS page	Printed page
Table 1: Circular Table of Direction and Universal Map	i	73
Table 2: Table of Directions, Winds and Spirits	5	101
Table 3: The Angels of Camuel's host	11	106
Table 4: Names of the Spirits submitted to Prince Aseliel	14	108
Table 5: The Angels of Prince Barmiel's host	17	110
Table 6: The Angels of Prince Gediel's host	19	112
Table 7: The Angels of Prince Asiriel's host	22	114
Table 8: Hosts of Maseriel's Spirits by day and night	25	117
Table 9: Hosts of Prince Malagras by day and night Spirits	27	119
Table 10: Hosts of Prince Dorothiel	30	121
Table 11: Grand Prince Usiel his Princes and their sigils	33	124
Table 12: Emperor Cabariel and his 20 Princes	36	126
Table 13: Emperor Raysiel and his 50 Princes	38	128
Table 14: Emperor Symiel and his Dukes	41	130
Table 15: Emperor Armadiel with his 15 Princes	43	132
Table 16: Emperor Baruchas with his vassals	45	134
Table 17: Supreme Prince Carnesiel with his vassals	47	137
Table 18: Prince Caspiel with his vassals	50	139
Table 19: The Dukes of Amenadiel with their Counts	52	141
Table 20: The Dukes and Counts of Demoriel	54	143
Table 21: Emperor Geradiel and his hosts	56	145
Table 22: The Dukes of the Wandering Prince Buriel	58	147
Table 23: The Dukes of Hydriel, Prince of Water	60	149
Table 24: The Counts of Pyrichiel, Supreme Spirit of Fire	61	151
Table 25: The Princes, Dukes and Counts ruled by Emoniel	63	153
Table 26: The Princes, Dukes and Counts ruled by Icosiel	65	155
Table 27: The Dukes and Counts of Soleviel	66	157
Table 28: The Dukes and Counts of Menadiel or Menachiel	68	150
Table 29: The Principal Princes of Emperor Macariel	70	161
Table 30: The Dukes and Counts of Prince Uriel	71	163
Table 31: The Dukes and Counts of Prince Bydiel	73	165

Steganographia

	MS page	Printed page
Table 32: The Full Table of 31 Spirits.	75	170
Table 33: The Dukes and Counts of Samael	82	178
Table 34: The Dukes and Counts of Anael	84	181
Table 35: The Dukes and Counts of Vequaniel	86	183
Table 36: The Dukes and Counts of Vathmiel	88	185
Table 37: The Dukes and Counts of Sasquiel	90	187
Table 38: The Dukes and Counts of Saniel	91	189
Table 39: The Dukes and Counts of Barquiel	93	191
Table 40: The Dukes and Counts of Osmadiel	94	193
Table 41: The Dukes and Counts of Quabriel	96	195
Table 42: The Dukes and Counts of Oriel	98	197
Table 43: The Dukes and Counts of Bariel	99	199
Table 44: The Dukes and Counts of Berathiel	101	201
Table 45: The Dukes and Counts of Sabrathan	102	203
Table 46: The Dukes and Counts of Tartis	104	205
Table 47: The Principal Spirits of Serquanich	106	207
Table 48: The Dukes and Counts of Jefischa	107	209
Table 49: The Dukes and Counts of Abasdahon	109	211
Table 50: The Dukes and Counts of Zaazenach	111	213
Table 51: The Dukes and Counts of Mendrion	112	215
Table 52: The Dukes and Counts of Narcoriel	114	217
Table 53: The Dukes and Counts of Pamiel	115	219
Table 54: The Dukes and Counts of Jasguarim	117	221
Table 55: The Dukes and Counts of Dadariel	119	223
Table 56: The Dukes and Counts of Sarandiel	120	225
Table 57: Mansions of the Spirits in the order of the Planets	127	233
Table 58: The Punctual Table	130	236
Table 59: The Degrees of Saturn's Movements - the First Table	132	238
Table 60: Pure Motions of the Planets – the Second Table	133	239
Table 61: Movement and Pure Motion - the Third Table	134	240
Table 62: The Hours of Orifiel, Angel of the first three hours	140	245
Table 63: The Hours of Sadael, Angel of the second three hours	143	248
Table 64: The Hours of Pomiel, Angel of the third three hours	144	250

Steganographia

	MS page	Printed page
Table 65: The Olympic Spirits and their Planets	181	282
Table 66: The Proper Movement of the 10 Celestial Spheres	186	289
Table 67: The Proper Course of the 7 Planets in the Zodiac	188	294
Table 68: The Order of the seven Planetary Heavens	194	300
Table 69: The Four Elements and their presiding Angels	214	316
Table 70: Twelve Signs of the Zodiac with their Angels	214	316
Table 71: Days, colours, angels and metals of each Planet	215	317
Table 72: Good and Evil Aerial Spirits of the Compass		337
Table 73: Good and Evil Aerial Spirits (Emperors)		338
Table 74: Good and Evil Aerial Spirits (Wandering Princes)		339
Table 75: Angelic and Planetary Rulers of Trithemius' Ages		344
Table 76: The Spirits of the *Steganographia* and the *Theurgia-Goetia*.		354

Acknowledgements

We would like to acknowledge the work of Fiona Tait and Christopher Upton who made the first English translation of the *Steganographia* published in 1982 by Adam McLean as *The Steganographia of Johannes Trithemius*. That edition is regrettably out of print and rather hard to find, even second-hand. We therefore thought it worthwhile to publish a new translation, with the addition of Book II and Book IV and all the previously missing tables.

A number of commentators have provided commentary on the cryptography embedded in the *Steganographia*. Perhaps the best survey of this volume from a cryptographic point of view was done by Selenus. J.W.H. Walden of Harvard University translated part of Selenus' text, which was also included in Adam McLean's edition. Selenus provided an exhaustive explanation of the cryptographic method used by Trithemius in each of the chapters of Book I and Book II, while Jim Reeds also cracked the different codes used in Book III. We will not in this volume say much about cryptography as it has been more than adequately covered by these two authors.

We have however located a French manuscript (Bibliotheca Philosophica Hermetica MS PH277) which despite its late date (1784) seems to be much more complete than any of the earlier Latin editions. We were thus able to publish Book II and Book IV for the first time ever from this manuscript, which have never before appeared in any English edition. For copyright permission for the page illustrations drawn from that manuscript, we have to thank the Allard Pierson Museum, University of Amsterdam.

A page of the 17th century copy of the *Steganographia* which John Dee patiently copied in 1563 has been reproduced here by permission of Llyfrgell Genedlaethol Cymru *aka* The National Library of Wales.

Our thanks to Jérémie Segouin for his help with the French transcription of Book IV and corrections to the translation from French. Jérémie plans to publish a parallel French edition through Editions du Monolithe.

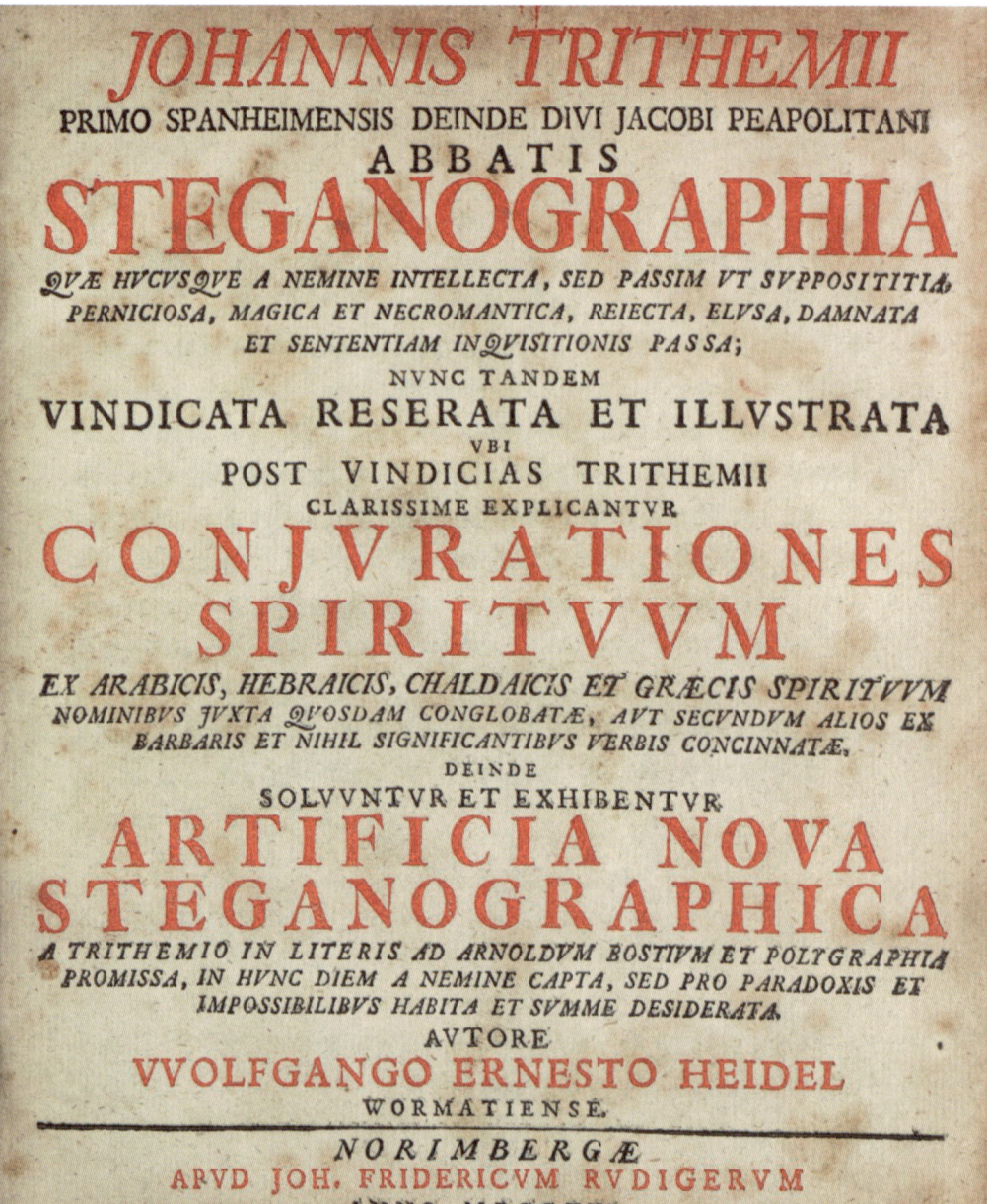

Figure 2: Title page of the Latin edition of the *Steganographia* dated 1721. This edition is one of the most complete Latin editions which includes *Clavis & Sensus,* the keys to the cryptography not present in most other editions.

[*The Latin title page:*]

Johannis Trithemii

Primo spanheimensis deinde divi Jacobi Peapolitani abbatis

Steganographia

qvae hvcvsqve a nemine intellecta, sed passim ut supposititia, perniciosa, magica et necromantica, reiecta, elvsa, damnata et sententiam inquisitionis passa; nvnc tandem vindicata reserata et illvstrata vbi post vindicias Trithemii clarissime explicantvr

Conjvrationes Spiritvvm

ex Arabicis, Hebraicis, Chaldaicis et Graecis spiritvvm nominibvs juxta qfosdam conglobatae, aut secundum alios ex barbaris et nihil significantibus verbis concinnatae. Deinde solvvntvr et exhibentvr

**Artificia Nova
Steganographica**

a Trithemio in literis ad Arnoldvm Bostivm et Polygraphia promissa, in hunc diem a nemine capta, sed pro paradoxis et impossibilibus habita et summe desiderata.

Autore

Wolfgango Ernesto Heidel

Wormatiense.

Norimbergae

apud Joh. Fridericum Rudigerum

Anno MDCCXXI.

[*Translation of the Latin title page*:]

The *Steganographia* of Johannes Trithemius, first Abbot of Spanheim, then of St James's Abbey, the Peapolitan, which here and there was understood by no one, but as suppositions, destructive, magical, necromantic, rejected, banished, condemned, and which suffered the sentence of the Inquisition; where after the vindication of Trithemius they explained most clearly the conjurations of the spirits from the Arabic, Hebrew, Chaldaic and Greek names gathered together under certain conditions, or, according to others, composed of barbarous and meaningless words. Then solve and present the new steganographic artifacts promised by Trithemius in the letters to Arnold Bostius and in the *Polygraphia*, to this day taken by no one, but considered paradoxical and impossible and highly desirable.

Author Wolfgang Ernesto Heidel of Worms.

[Printed at] Nuremberg by John Frederick Rüdiger, in the year 1721.

A book "for which a thousand crownes have been by others offred, and yet could not be obteyned; a boke for which many a lerned man hath long sought and dayly yet doth seeke; whose use is greater than the fame thereof is spred; the name thereof to you is not unknown." The *Steganographica*, "a boke for your Honor, or a Prince, so meet, so needfull and commodious, as in humayne knowledge none can be meeter or more behovefull…"

- Dr John Dee's evaluation of the value of the *Steganographia* (1563).

Introduction

Academic discussions of this book usually centre around the question of its subject. Is it a book about cryptography or about magic? Those authors who prefer to say that it is a book about magic say that cryptography is a necessary adjunct to hide the real topic, which would have been a dangerous one in the 1500s. Those who prefer to think of it as a book about cryptography suggest that it is wrapped in magic in order to deter casual readers. Of these two arguments, it seems obvious that magic is definitely the more dangerous topic of conversation for a 16th-century Abbot, and therefore it is most likely to have been the real topic, hidden within cryptography. An interest in cryptography during the time of the Inquisition would seem to be a lot more innocent than an interest in actually calling spirits.

We do not think it is a question of deciding if it is one or the other, because it is most decidedly both. In fact the essence of the cryptography in the *Steganographia* is that the spirit names are derived by using a semi-cryptographic process. This is precisely the same as Agrippa,[1] where tables are used to derive spirit names.[2] The same tables that are used to encrypt also produced the spirit names.

Instead of trying to pointlessly separate the cryptography from the sorcery, as many commentators have attempted, we should instead recognise that the cryptography was an integral part of the sorcery. The huge tables drawn up by Dr John Dee, in imitation of Trithemius and Agrippa, were designed to be used to *derive* powerful and evocable spirit and angel names. Using these tables to write letters to spies or potentates was less important, compared to this main use, especially for Dee.

I would like to suggest that this book is not about one or other of these topics, but is actually about the transmission of information by secret means, be it by code or by magic, the two halves of which, Trithemius has interwoven with consummate skill. Steganographia is usually simply translated as "secret writing" from the

---

[1] Agrippa owned a copy of the *Steganographia*. See Thorndike, Vol. V, p. 131.
[2] Book III, Chapter XXVI.

Greek στέγω, *stego*, meaning 'to cover' or 'hidden' plus γραφω, *grapho*, meaning 'to write.' Another possible derivation may be derived from στεγανός, *steganos*, which means 'water-tight', not just 'hidden' or 'covered,' hence 'water-tight writing.'

On the surface Trithemius purports to show how to send secret messages, via the agency of the angels to distant friends, effectively being a sort of 'spirit telegraph.'

Information has for many centuries been secreted in coded texts, and cryptography has for a long time taken centre stage, not just in warfare and spying, but now in everyday information transmissions like online shopping, banking, cryptocurrencies and the structure and behaviour of the internet itself. The invention of computers and the internet in the mid-20th century has effectively achieved what Trithemius was experimenting with 500 years ago, the secret and almost instantaneous transmission of knowledge in written form. However, the magical methods he used are still not well understood, so in this book, we intend to focus on that side of the question.

Although academic research on magic has accelerated in the last 30 years or so, few academics have tackled the *Steganographia* from this point of view. Conveying information via the good offices of spirits was definitely a totally new field of endeavour developed by Trithemius. Apart from the work of Peter d'Abano, it was probably the first time anyone had investigated that possibility. Although we will examine cryptography briefly, this book will concentrate on the magical side of the equation, as cryptography has now become a well-known part of our daily lives, but magic has not.

Astronomical Background

For Trithemius, astronomy, as seen in the Alphonsine Tables (which have tracked the location of the 7 classical planets in the sky since 1252 CE), must be truly linked with actual historical changes on Earth, governed by these planets. The first two planets in his historic sequence were Saturn and Jupiter, a fact which is highly significant.

If we look at the relative size and mass of these planets, and consequently their gravitational forces acting on the Earth, it becomes immediately obvious that these two planets are huge compared to their tiny compatriot planets.

Of the classical planets that have been known about since antiquity:

> Jupiter is 11 times the size of Earth and 317 times its mass.
> Saturn is 9 times the size of Earth and 95 times its mass.

These two planets also have the largest magnetospheres of any of the planets. By comparison, Mercury, Venus, Mars and the Moon are almost insignificant, as they are all smaller than the Earth.[1]

This means that in reality, the biggest *physical* planetary influences on Earth, apart from the Sun, are Jupiter and Saturn, with the rest of the planets being relatively insignificant in both physical and gravitational terms. Pursuing this line of reasoning, the strongest planetary conjunction, therefore, arrives when these two huge planets align together in the same part of the sky, or in astrological terms, are in conjunction.

Because the annual orbital period of Jupiter is 11.9 years, and that of Saturn is 29.4 years these planets only come into conjunction once every 20 years. Because of orbital mechanics, each conjunction of these two heavyweights occurs almost exactly one-third of the way around the zodiac, as they make their way around the sun. Thus three successive conjunctions trace the full 360 degrees circle of the zodiac in 60 years.

It is also fascinating that these conjunctions take place in blocks of related zodiacal signs as determined by their Element. When this conjunction occurs in Aries, Sagittarius and Leo, any astrologer will realise that the conjunctions have described a Fire triplicity or trigon. After 180 years (3 such periods of 60 years), the entire pattern migrates to the next triplicity of signs. Each triplicity in turn only relates to one Element.

The triplicities which each take 180 years to complete are:

    Fire: Aries, Sagittarius and Leo
    Earth: Taurus, Capricorn and Virgo
    Air: Gemini, Aquarius and Libra
    Water: Cancer, Pisces and Scorpio.

Finally, when all four triplicities have been covered by these conjunctions, after approximately 720 years, the whole cycle restarts. Thus we have actual planetary movements relating directly to astrological (and feng shui) time divisions and patterning.

The Chinese were perhaps the first to spot this pattern and so used the 20-year period for their basic Period or 'Age.' For Chinese astrology, and more particularly for feng shui, the 60-year and 180-year cycles mark out the length of significant periods. Chinese astrology and classical San Yuan feng shui observe these periods in their calculations, confirming that both of these practices and their measurements are strictly based on real observable physical phenomena. Of course, the slight divergence from the arithmetical perfection of the basic ingredients (i.e. 11.9 years rather than 12 years for Jupiter's orbital period) means that these absolute numbers need to be 'corrected' slightly over long periods of

---

[1] Mars is actually 1.5 times Earth, but still tiny compared to Jupiter and Saturn. I am here ignoring the non-Classical Planets like Neptune and Uranus, which are anyway much further away from Earth.

time, just as the length of the Gregorian year has to be corrected every four years by Western calendar makers, to keep it matched with the actual seasons.

Thousands of years ago, the Chinese thought this conjunction was significant and built it into their most important chronological structure of 5 Elements x 12 years, creating the 60-year Period.[1] Chinese historians have frequently been able to tie major Chinese dynastic changes into these astronomical cycles.[2] Predictions based on this enabled many, often accurate, conclusions about Chinese dynastic changes to be drawn.

The Arab astrologer Masha'allah ibn Athari also saw in this sequence of Saturn-Jupiter conjunctions a way to organise the history of the world, or at least of the Middle East. He categorised the 20-year periods as 'little conjunctions'; with the larger 180-year periods as 'middle conjunctions,' which might indicate the breaks between kingdoms or major dynasties; and the 720-year periods as 'greater conjunctions', which only ended after the full cycle of all four full triplicities had been completed. These greater conjunctions, he daringly suspected, might mark the rise and fall of major religions.

In Alexander Boxer's opinion,[3] the Jupiter-Saturn "conjunction theory of history is, without a doubt, the most significant addition to astrology since Roman times."

Astrological and Angelic Timing of History

Just as the Chinese were able to tie significant historic events into a repeating cycle of Jupiter and Saturn conjunctions, so Trithemius thought that his sequence of planetary and angelic rulerships might enable him to categorise, plot and even predict, historical events.

In Europe, this system of planetary and angelic rulerships was initially promoted by the 13th-century astrologer, philosopher and professor of medicine, Peter d'Abano,[4] from whom Trithemius drew his vision of planetary Intelligences[5] governing set periods of history.

Trithemius also thought that the 12-year gap between the conjunctions of Saturn and Jupiter was a highly significant indicator. He therefore decided upon a Grand Cycle of just over 2,480 years, which was to be successively ruled by the Angel of each of the 7 classical planets, making a single rulership period of 354 years and 4 months for each Angel.

---

[1] The 60-year period meant that the 12 years period could cycle through all the five Chinese Elements.
[2] I have shown examples of this in my book *Advanced Flying Star Feng Shui*, Singapore: Golden Hoard, 2018, pp. 37-40, and in *Guide to the Feng Shui Compass: A Compendium of Classical Feng Shui*, Singapore: Golden Hoard, 2008.
[3] Boxer (2020), p. 159.
[4] Brann (1999), p. 134.
[5] An alternative designation for angels.

The reason for this side trip into astronomy and Chinese astrology will become relevant when we examine Trithemius' efforts to tie historical events into this sequence of planetary and angelic rulerships, as outlined in his *De Septem Secundeis*.[1] In this book Trithemius attempts to embrace the whole of history from the Creation up to 1500 CE, and beyond, by showing which Angel ruled each period.[2]

Predictions

But did it work? One such correspondence between these cycles and history, which Trithemius did not live to see, was the predicted return of the 'Firey Trigon' of 1603. He was undoubtedly aware of its impending happening, as indeed was Dr John Dee, but he could not have predicted its significance for England with the end of the Elizabethan era and the death of Queen Elizabeth I which coincided with it.

One event that Trithemius did correctly declare in 1480 was that the Jews would not be truly free until the founding of their own state of Israel, or as he put it,

> "…nor will liberty be restored to the Jews before the third revolution of the spirit of Michael, and this will take place after the birth of Christ, in the year 1880, in the 8th month."[3]

Here Trithemius is depending completely on his system of Angelic rulership to make this remarkably accurate prediction.[4] Zionism, the movement that energised the return of Jews to their land of Israel, was established just a few years after this date, and the actual term 'Zionism' was later created by an Austrian Jew in 1890.

Trithemius also appeared to predict the Protestant Reformation during the period ruled by Mars which, according to his system, began in 1525. The Protestant Reformation is generally recognised to have begun slightly before that in 1517 in Germany, when Martin Luther (1483-1546) posted his ninety-five theses on the door of the church in Wittenberg, arguing that the Catholic church had to be reformed. Mars certainly seems to have ruled the subsequent wars of religion after that, which began with the German Peasant's War in 1524-1525, the largest European uprising until the French Revolution.

Similar predictions have been based on astrological configurations, such as that of the French Cardinal Pierre d'Ailly (1350-1420) who around the year 1400 wrote that the Antichrist was expected to arrive in France in the year 1789, and rule for

---

[1] See Appendix 4 which has a summary of the historic periods outlined in *De Septem Secundeis*.
[2] The beginning of the world was March 8th 2637 BC according to Chinese cultural history. But Trithemius considered 5206 years BC to be the baseline date of Creation. Ironically 2637 is close to half of 5206.
[3] Literally "…*nec restituetur Judaeis libertas ante tertiam revolutionem Michaelis spiritus, haecque fiet post Christi nativitatem anno* 1880, *mense* 8."
[4] Boxer (2020), p. 164.

10 years, based on his astrological calculations. Not a bad prediction for someone who could not have known that the French Revolution would run exactly from 1789 to 1799, during which time there was a complete upheaval of religion and the established social order in France.

Book III outlined the conditions of the Age of Saturn which began the whole cycle. It seems likely that Trithemius intended to work through all 7 Planetary Ages, rather than just Saturn, as this planet was not supposed to rule again until the year 2234. Of course, these Tables of Saturn are not relevant for the current period, calculations for which must be redone for the Age of the Sun in which we currently live, under the rulership of its angel Michael. Accordingly, the tables in Book III are simply of historical interest, not of any practical use except that they do show us the calculational method.

Trithemius and Magic

Despite his position in the church hierarchy as an Abbot, Trithemius was not slow to avow his interest in magic, nor did he always hide behind the label 'natural magic,' as many of his colleagues did. As Zambelli points out, Trithemius "had unashamedly maintained that ceremonial practices were indispensable in magic and had criticized those who, following Ficino and Pico, claimed not to go beyond 'natural' Magic." Trithemius, if he were alive today, would have had the same reaction to those who see magic as 'something done in the head,' merely a subset of psychology.

Trithemius claimed that he acquired his knowledge of magic from Libanius Gallus who visited him in Spanheim in 1495. In his autobiography, Trithemius claimed to have held Libanius in high regard, despite the literal translation of his name. Libanius in turn claimed that his knowledge of magic came from the pious Majorcan hermit Pelagius.[1]

Trithemius also claimed some of his magical knowledge came from an "ancient philosopher" called Menastor, whom he reputedly identified with the assistance of one of the planetary angels. It was Menastor apparently who discovered that "it is possible for us, by means of a special art, to make known to a friend, however distant he is, an idea in our minds - and this in twenty-four hours, without words, without books, and without a messenger, very perfectly, reconditely, and secretly."[2] That succinctly sums up the avowed objective of the *Steganographia*.

---

[1] See the manuscript mentioning Pelagius Eremita in Figure 3.
[2] Brann (1999), p. 143.

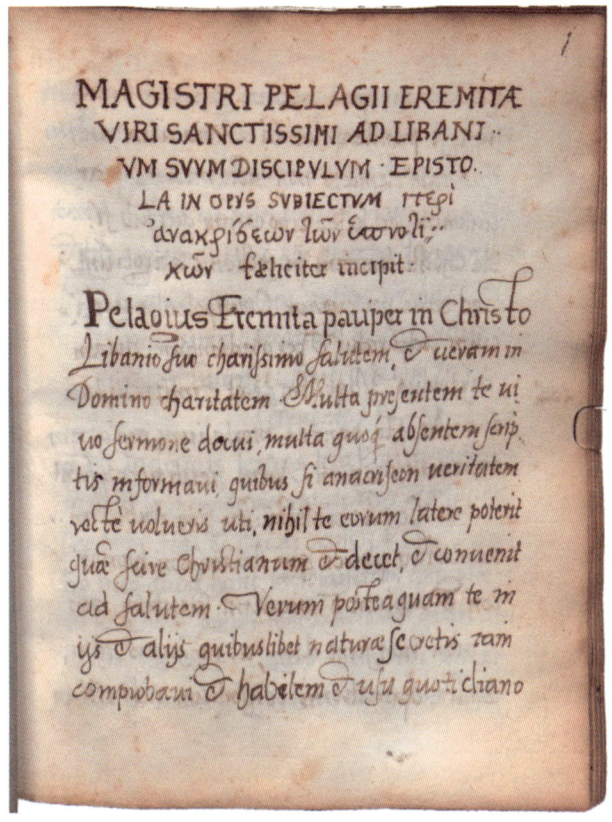

Figure 3: A manuscript mentioning Pelagius dated 1465.[1]

Rules for the Practice of the 'Spirit Telegraph'

As the spirits of this grimoire have this objective, Trithemius enunciated the rules for this practice in some detail:

1. The first key requirement is that the correct invocation is used for a particular Spirit or Angel. Likewise, the magician receiving the message must also use the same style of invocation to reply, as a violation of this rule will not only result in the failure of the operation, "but will also call down great danger upon the head of the operator."
2. Both operators should observe strict esoteric secrecy, and not discuss the operation with outsiders.
3. The operator should memorize the key differences, locations, names, orders, and Offices of the Spirits involved, together with details of their Dukes, Counts and servants under their governance. It is useful to work

---

[1] Österreichische Nationalbibliothek. Cod. 10477. Pelagius de Mallorca. *Ad Libanium Gallum de somniorum interpretatione libri tres*, 1465.

some of this detail into the words of the invocation.
4. He should be especially careful to pronounce the Spirit name correctly, and enunciate the words of the conjuration clearly, otherwise the spirits invoked will not only disobey, but will outrightly resist his commands.
5. A degree of gravity and loftiness of purpose should be preserved in all conjurations.
6. The conjurer should thoroughly know the character of the Spirits: which are good and which are bad, which are prompt and which are tardy, which are benevolent as opposed to spirits which are harsh and rebellious. He should also know the distinction between nocturnal spirits and diurnal ones, realizing that one group cannot be used for the operations appropriate to the other group. If this is not observed "he will advance only with very great difficulty, and at last succumb to stupor."
7. The usual provision that these operations should take place in solitary circumstances far from the 'madding crowd' forms the seventh rule. Trithemius notes that "all the spirits ministering to this art have been endowed with such a nature and condition that they completely detest and flee the throng of men, and hate public gatherings."
8. The operator must always use the correct notation and be careful when drawing up the special character of the particular spirit. The character is important because it enables the spirit to identify with the operation, and the spirit must perceive this character before it will act upon the operator's commands. As Trithemius said, if the spirit "does not see the impression of that character, it utterly refuses to obey the person summoning it to bear a secret message to someone else."

Register of Spirits

Another hint of the importance of magic in the *Steganographia* is that Book I and Book II are predominantly registers of spirits, an essential part of most grimoires. A number of these spirit names also occur in other grimoires, and the standard ending *'iel'* used in Book I are a well-attested indication that these entities are angels. In Book II some spirit names however have a more demonic leaning, as well as having a selection of angelic names. The 'headline' angels or spirits in each chapter have a list of other supporting spirits, and their sub-servants.

Furthermore, all of these spirits later appear in two books of the *Lemegeton*, entitled *The Arte of Theurgia-Goetia*, and the *Pauline Art* (Volume 1), both of which are definitely grimoires.[1] The *Steganographia* is certainly an important part of the

---

[1] 'Theurgia' is a word whose meaning has become corrupted, especially in the last two decades. Originally it meant the opposite of magic. Magic was the calling of gods, angels, spirits or demons to the magician. Theurgia is exactly the opposite and involves the magician rising to the level of the

evolution of these two grimoires.[1]

Direct Angel Communication – an Alternative view

Another possible key to understanding the *Steganographia* is the suggestion that the messages that were encoded to be sent by Trithemius' 'spirit telegraph' were not only meant for human recipients. The messages were maybe sometimes also meant to be sent *to* the angel concerned, not just *by* the angel, and in that case were not intended for human recipients at all.

Looked at from this point of view, the *Steganographia* simply becomes another method of evocation. Michel Scot recommends his readers attach by a cord to his copy of the *Liber Consecrationis* a paper or parchment sheet with the names of the questioned demon and its functions written upon it, when making a request, in order for there to be no mistake by the demonic recipient. This parallels the requirement in the *Steganographia* to write the name and rank of the spirit with their particular conjuration of a piece of virgin paper or parchment. Here the objective is quite clearly to communicate directly with the spirit, not with an absent friend.

To do this the message is first reduced cryptographically before being sent, as part of the magical technique itself. There is much secrecy in magic about putting the exact request or demand to the spirit or angel. Such requests have in the past been addressed in English, Latin, Hebrew or even in Enochian, with varying opinions arising as to which language was the most effective. Here Trithemius addresses the angels in a cryptographic code. There is no human 'friend' at the other end.

The magician faces the quarter of the angel, invokes the angel and submits his request, demand or prayer verbally, but this is also inscribed in code on a piece of paper directed to the spirit. The mental effort involved in encoding the request is perhaps part of the magical procedure. This request is what the magician wants the spirit to accomplish. As simple as that – there is no human messenger – there is no human recipient.

Structure of the Conjurations

When you examine the conjurations within the *Steganographia* you will see that hidden within them are the names of some of each Duke's servitors who are actually required to do the task. See for example Parmersiel (see Table 73 in Appendix 1) for the names of his servitor spirits, and match them with the names embedded in the invocations. Although these spirits are listed with their directions and seals in the *Theurgia-Goetia*, the corresponding conjurations from

---

gods. As such there are few extant rituals of Theurgia, as outlined in my book *Techniques of Graeco-Egyptian Magic*, Singapore: Golden Hoard, 2020. This distinction gradually became lost, as theurgia and magic began to be associated in the minds of both magicians and academics, until in the last few decades, theurgy began to be seen incorrectly as a synonym for magic.

[1] See David Rankine, *Grimoire Encyclopaedia* (2023), pp. 203-208 for a fuller background.

the *Steganographia* are missing from the *Theurgia-Goetia*, so you have to re-insert them in each case.[1] By combining the seals in the *Theurgia-Goetia* with the invocation, timing and direction in the *Steganographia* we arrive at the full method.

Blaise de Vigenère, who was both a cryptographer and a magician, also understood why these invocations to angels might need to be encoded. But why go to such trouble? The answer may be found in the work of a modern magician, Austin Osman Spare who understood that by 'sigilising' or encoding his requests, he was more effectively able to convey them to the spiritual creatures which would then be tasked to accomplish them. Spare did not however take into account the specific names of the angels or spirits being addressed, the timing, or the correct direction, making his method a lot less effective.

All *four* things need to be in place before this particular system works:

  i) the cryptographic conversion of the message or request to the spirit;

  ii) the correct direction to be faced – according to the 32 possible directions (Figure 4);

  iii) the correct time – as marked by either the 12 Planetary hours of the day or the 12 Planetary hours of the night;

  iv) the spirit's sigil and/or the tiny seal from Table 1.

The Lemegeton

Trithemius is a key person in the history of the *Lemegeton*, as we can say with certainty that all five parts of that book existed in 1500 and all five were known to Trithemius, and probably in his library at Spanheim, indeed he may have written two of them. The key volume mentioned by Trithemius in his *Antipalus Maleficiorum* (1508) is a work called *Composition of the Names and Characters of the Evil Spirits*. Although this book or manuscript has since been lost, it is fairly clear from the Latin title (*Liber Malorum Spirituum*) that this is most likely to have been the source not only of the names, but also of the seals of the 72 Spirits to be found in the *Goetia*. Unlike all the other manuscripts of the *Goetia*, Dr Rudd's copy is actually entitled *Liber Malorum Spirituum*, and so may in fact be closer to the original in Trithemius' library.

1. The first part, the *Goetia*, with its elaborate list of spirits and including its seals, already existed before 1508 in Trithemius' library.

2. Trithemius himself is the source of the demon names in the second (*Theurgia-Goetia*) part of the *Lemegeton*, which can be traced directly to his *Steganographia*. The second part of the *Lemegeton*, the *Theurgia-Goetia* is

---

[1] This has been done in my edition of the *Theurgia-Goetia*, as included in *The Goetia of Dr Rudd*, Singapore: Golden Hoard, 2010.

simply Book I of Trithemius' *Steganographia* recast in a more practical form with many more detailed sigils.

3. The third part of the *Lemegeton*, the *Ars Paulina* (Book 1) also comes directly from Book II of the *Steganographia*.

4. The fourth part of the *Lemegeton*, the *Art Almadel*, uses a skrying method outlined by Trithemius, who obviously knew it well. The *Almadel* attributed to Solomon was also in his library, and it appears in Book IV of the present volume. The technique involving wax tablet angel magic was something that Dr John Dee would also use almost 100 years later.

5. Finally the fifth part, the *Ars Notoria* is known in many different manuscripts, most of them missing the key illustrations or *notae*, with some dating from as early as 1225. At least one copy, probably more, was in Trithemius' extensive library.

You can see that all the separate parts of the *Lemegeton* already existed in 1508 and were most certainly all present in Trithemius' library. So Trithemius or his pupils look like the most likely persons to have brought them all together in one volume as the *Lemegeton*.

The *Steganographia* upon which were based the *Theurgia-Goetia* and the *Art Pauline* (Book 1) is concerned with cryptography, and how communication can be addressed to the spirits or angels. This also provides a useful way of seeing just how the books of the *Lemegeton* relate to each other.

a) The *Theurgia-Goetia* is concerned with direction, and it even begins with the diagram of a spirit Compass Rose (see Figure 4). Direction is here the key, as it is with Book I of the *Steganographia*.

b) The *Art Pauline* (Book 1) has spirits which are assigned to specific hours of the night and the day. Time here is the key, as it is with Book II of the *Steganographia*.

c) The angels of the *Art Pauline* (Book 2) are assigned to the 360 degrees of the Zodiac. Book III looks at the degrees of the Zodiac.

In Solomonic magic, the Planetary hours have always been of prime importance, and they are stressed in almost every grimoire. Many grimoires actually begin with tables of Planetary hours, because of their importance. In Chinese Taoist sorcery, the key is found in the compass direction in the form of the ring of 24 'Mountains,' associated with the correct timing. Chinese Taoist magicians express this knowledge by saying that just for a small timeframe, a secret door or 門 '*men*' opens, and at that time communication can be made between this world and the other, or even that things can pass from one world to the other via this doorway. One practical use of this knowledge is in the materialisation and de-materialisation of things and entities, which is a classic phenomenon associated with magic.

Such ideas have only survived in the West in mythology and in stories of children being spirited away to fairy realms, or in folk memories of the magical significance of thresholds, doors opening into fairyland or the underworld for a short period of time in a specific direction at specific times and at specific places. Much of this knowledge has been lost in the West. Of course, it is still spoken of in very general terms by saying that at Halloween the 'veil is thinned', so the concept of opening a door at a particular time has not been completely lost. But the technology for finding that door, and its time, is no longer commonly available in the West, except in the *Steganographia*. Traces of this technology are still present in the *Theurgia-Goetia's* 'spirit compass' and the Taoist 24 Mountain ring on a feng shui luopan.[1]

There is a branch of Chinese metaphysics, allied with feng shui, which deals specifically with these doors. It is called *Qi Men Dun Jia*, and it still contains a detailed knowledge of these techniques, which have sadly just become a folk memory in the West. Virtually none of those detailed techniques are presently available outside of the Chinese language, where there exists an extensive literature. In these texts the time and direction system are a lot more complex than the simple layout of the *Steganographia* or its descendant grimoires.[2]

Condemning Magical texts

Trithemius' technique for remaining safe in the face of church persecution was to condemn works of magic, whilst yet listing and promoting them. The classic example of this is Trithemius' *Antipalus Maleficiorum* which was one of the most complete and useful catalogues of grimoires dating from 1508 when Trithemius wrote it. With almost every listed title Trithemius added severely condemnatory remarks such as:

> "For filthy lies are told in this, in which all things were demoniacal, and this [book] with good reason, should be removed far from the Church of God" about the *Book Almadel*, which he later used extensively in Book IV.

> "And what it contains, is but vain, foolish, and open to invented lies, promising the workers of it all outstanding [results] and there is nothing in it, unless deception, conscience and the strong soul entirely subject to the demons?" said of the *Claviculae Salomonis*.

And so he goes on for more than 70 books, damning each in turn. Unfortunately he did not have time to so protect the *Steganographia* in this manner, and so it was that this book ruined his reputation as it began circulating before he had time to inbuild its defences or even complete it.

---

[1] See Skinner, *The Complete Magician's Tables*, Singapore: Golden Hoard, 2022, p. 104.
[2] Note that the primary conjurations are missing from the *Theurgia-Goetia* in Joseph Peterson's edition of the *Lemegeton*, but these are supplied in *The Goetia of Dr Rudd*, Singapore: Golden Hoard, 2007, pp. 215-306.

This is a technique that he passed down to his students and his student's students. His best-known student, Cornelius Agrippa, used the same technique when he published *The Uncertainty and Vanity of Sciences and Arts* in 1527 in which he roundly condemned magic, before a few years later in 1531-33 publishing his three books of *Occult Philosophy*.

Agrippa in turn had Johann Weyer (1515-15) as a pupil, who lived with him in his house. Although Weyer defended Agrippa, he condemned Trithemius' arts "which taught how to counterfeit miracles through diabolically instigated illusions."[1] Meanwhile he was studiously copying out by hand the copy of the *Steganographia* which was owned by Agrippa. Later Weyer was also responsible for preserving, or creating, *De Praestigiis Daemonum*, a list of demons parallel to those in the *Goetia*. So, Trithemius' gambit of condemning magic lasted through at least three generations of pupils. Trithemius cites a number of sources, including the 'Jewish Solomon,' Hermes, 'Hermes Solomon,' Raziel, and the *Picatrix* in the French manuscript of the *Steganographia*.

The French Introduction

The long introduction to the manuscript is not by Trithemius, and those of you who wish only to read Trithemius' words would be well advised to move directly to Book I in the manuscript. However the manuscript introduction opens a window on the religious attitude and reaction to magic in Catholic France in the 1780s. A number of references therein refer to particular passages in the Bible, which was of course the touchstone for spirituality in that era. This would have been similar to the German Catholic environment of Trithemius in 1500.

The Three Books

The first three Books of the *Steganographia* involve three different types of spiritual creatures. The spirit hierarchy described represents the three ranks of spirits from which a 'steganographer' can draw. The First Book lists 31 regional, district or directional spirits ruling over as many corresponding directions and Mansions of the heavens. The Second Book gives 24 temporal (or time related) spirits attached to each of the 24 hours of the day and night. The Third Book gives the seven planetary Angels to which the spirit ruler of these celestial regions and temporal durations are ultimately subject. Each chapter is addressed to a specific spirit.

The First Book instructs the conjurer to face in a specific direction when calling a spirit. The Second Book specifies a specific time. Direction and time have always been a key part of ceremonial magic. The third Book looks upwards at the planetary rulers. In each invocation an inscription has to be made on a virgin piece of parchment or paper, thereby acting as the seal or sigil of the rite. The instruction to repeat the rite until the spirit gives in and complies is common to most grimoires.

---

[1] Brann (1999), p.168.

Book I

Each chapter of the first two books has a similar structure. Both books are effectively a Spirit Register, in other words, a list of angels used by this particular system of conjuration. Spirit Registers are an essential part of any magical operation, as you need to know the name of a spirit before you can conjure him. This particular Register also includes specific short invocations unique to each spirit. In that way it is different from other grimoires which have the same invocation that is used for every spirit in the Register, with just a simple change of the spirit's name inserted into the text at the time of the conjuration (as you can see in a grimoire like the *Goetia*).

In the *Steganographia* each spirit has instead 2 short conjurations of its own, which is quite rare. The grimoire does say that these may have to be repeated a number of times for recalcitrant spirits, although some spirits are claimed to appear almost immediately.

These two Books devote one chapter to each spirit. The first 16 spirits are each identified with one of the 16 classical winds, which are really just another way of identifying the 16 directions beginning in the East (Oriens) with the spirit Pamersiel. In turn, the spirits associated with the winds Subsolanus (ESE) and Eurus (SE) continue around the circle of 16 directions until the spirits Armadiel (NE) and Baruchas (ENE) are reached, and the circle is completed by returning to Pamersiel in the East. In addition to this detail, each spirit has a variable number of named Dukes, Counts, servants and sub-servants, sometimes just 10, sometimes as many as 20,000. There may well be some hidden Cabbalistic meaning in these numbers, but I have not yet discovered it. The *Goetia* has a similar number of legions attributed to each of its spirits.

After these 16 Directional spirits, there follows the 4 Supreme Spirits which are given the overlordship of the 4 Cardinal directions (to E, S, W, and N). Following these are a further 11 spirits who are often referred to as Wandering spirits, as they are not tied to a particular direction. Some of these are aligned with the Elements, Water, Fire and Air, but not with Earth.

Each spirit is given a simple sigil which must always be used when interacting with it. These sigils are meant to look innocuous, like a stray mark, such that they could look like an accidental mark added to an ordinary letter without raising any suspicions.

In Table 1, you can see that some spirits form natural groups because of similarities in their sigil design. For example, Asyriel, Camuel, Gediel, Malgaras, and Maseriel have a sigil similarity, Baruchas, Raysiel and Symiel have a similar pattern. Likewise, Barmiel, Malgaras and Usiel are linked. It is probably not a coincidence that Trithemius has chosen these visual linkages.

Book II

This is the first time that Book II of the *Steganographia* has been published in English. Adam McLean's edition of the *Steganographia* does not include a translation of Book II, but the present book does. It can be clearly seen that Book II is another Spirit Register, with inbuilt conjurations, but not just for angels. In Latin editions of this Book there are sample non-secret letters to be sent to the person Trithemius wished to communicate with at the basic level. These do not appear in the present French manuscript. These harmless letters are only important in that they provide a physical link to the recipient with the spirit sigil which is written on them. An example of such a letter is to be found in Appendix 2. Trithemius' letters are not important (except to the historian) as the same function can be provided by any letter the operator may wish to draft. For this function you can easily draft your own non-secret letter. What is important is that this letter then contains an innocuous mark which is in fact a simple spirit sigil which provides a physical magical link between the seal, the spirit and the hand of the recipient, who will then know which invocation to use from this spirit sigil.

Book II is aligned with the 12 Planetary hours of the day, and the 12 Planetary hours of the night. The first chapter, for example, relates to Samael, Supreme Emperor of the First Hour. The substance of each chapter is similar to that of Book I, but you will note that we are no longer only talking about angels, but also about demons, Samael being a classical demon name, without the '*iel*' angelic ending. The tasks associated with these demons are rarely of a scientific or scholarly nature, but (as in this case) the spirit is charged with the duty of exciting men with magical and nocturnal illusions. Note for each of these the Planetary hour of their calling must be correctly calculated.

Typical Chapter Structure of Books I and II

All 31 chapters of Book I and 25 chapters of Book II have a similar structure. It is worthwhile examining this, to make these Books more comprehensible. Each chapter is divided into:

1. *Header* which lists the Spirit name in capitals with his rank and the number of Dukes, Counts and servants under him.

2. *Entourage*. The first paragraph recounts and sometimes expands on the number of other spirits in his entourage.

3. *Servitor Table*. This is followed by a table which gives the names of some of the spirits in his entourage with the number of their deputies, servants and underlings. These names are listed in either red or black along with their numbers. The red spirits are usable in the day of 12 Planetary hours between dawn and sunset, with the black spirit names and their numbers

being applicable to the 12 night Planetary hours, from sunset to dawn.[1] See Appendix 3.

4. The following section indicates which and how you should deal with these spirits to effectively send messages by 'spirit telegraph' to your friends and colleagues.

5. The card must be inscribed with the sigil of the Spirit being called with a written appreciation of its rank and entourage, which should also be verbally commented upon. Some of the spirits require the conjurer to list out the number of servitors attached to each main spirit, as a way of giving credibility, prestige and rank to that Spirit.

6. *Conjuration 1.* Following this is the first of two possible conjurations required for the operation. This should be said with "the strongest intention, fearing nothing." The spirit should then be informed of the identity of the recipient. One example of this is expressed as follows:

   > "Ameniel I send you by the secret power of this Conjuration, viz. to Albertus Goeler de Ravenspurg, prefect in Cretzenach, as soon as possible, and tell him in my name, this message."[2]

   Add to these words the secret word, which must not be written, and the spirit will immediately fly off to attend to his task.

7. *Clavis & Sensus.* In the 1721 Latin edition (but not in this manuscript) there is a section which explains how the cryptographic content has been encoded, and this will be briefly explained in the chapter on cryptography. It is not included in the present manuscript:

8. *Literae formentur ad placitum.* This section is to be found in some of the printed Latin editions. It usually contains one of Trithemius' sample letters. In the 1721 Latin edition, Trithemius' letter drafts have been intercut with the main text (see Appendix 2). Each letter opens with details of his addressee and ends with his sign-off and date. This is followed by serial numbering using Greek letters. It seems clear that these whole letters are included as examples of communication utilizing the cryptographic method of each particular chapter, and may be instances of letters that he actually sent using this method.

9. *Conjuration 2.* This is the conjuration used by the recipient when he wishes to send a reply. It may be followed by its own *Clavis & Sensus.*

---

[1] The spirits observe 'Planetary hours' which relate to real world timing as governed by the rising and setting of the Sun, with hours longer in summer, and shorter in winter, rather than arbitrary clock time with fixed hour length year-round.

[2] The modern equivalent of this necessary identification is to give a precise address, and detailed identification, such as job and company.

Book III

For this Book, a basic knowledge of astrology is also required as the invocatory sigil must have the planetary sign of the ruler of the Ascendant written upon it. This is not the same as the current enthusiasm for 'elections,' the selection of a specific time for drawing up a sigil.[1] Trithemius adds that the operator must know the general movement of the stars and planets, their passages back and forth, changes in their nature, and their locations, where they rise and where they descend on the horizon. The application of this astronomical knowledge is expanded upon in Book III.

Neither Joseph Peterson nor Adam McLean explained what the Tables in this Book were all about. The fact is that these Tables depend on a knowledge of the angelic rulers of each 'Age' as expressed in Trithemius' other work *De Septem Secundeis, id est Intelligentiis*, Nurnberg, 1522. The Intelligences referred to in that title are angels which are, according to Trithemius, given rulership over each 'Age.' At the beginning of the cycle, the ruler was Saturn and his angel Orifiel. This is the only period/angel for which Trithemius gives us his calculations. Orifiel's rule is not supposed to return until 2234, so the calculations in Book III are not of any immediate use. Trithemius in 1500 lived under the rulership of Samael and the planet Mars, so they were not even of immediate use to him. One can only assume that he intended to do similar calculations for all seven periods, but either he didn't, or they have been lost.

If the calculations are to be used today, then they have to be replaced by tables for the current planetary ruler, the Sun and his ruler, Michael. It is however much easier to calculate them from a modern Ephemeris than it would have been from the Alphonsine Tables. You can see the full list of ages and their angel rulership in Appendix 4, rather than having to locate a copy of *De Septem Secundeis*. The "Seven Secondary Intelligences" of the title are the archangels ruling the universe in each Age. The Primary Intelligence is God. Trithemius makes other astrological recommendations:

> "Let the moment be tranquil and serene, with the moon, having come completely around into opposition with the sun, shining brightly and reflection from the rays of the latter! [i.e. Full Moon] And let Mercury, if it is possible for it to be accomplished, come into the Ascendant, conjoined to either Venus or Jupiter! And let Saturn and Mars remain remote, since if either of these come into conjunction with the ascending planet then the instruction will not be perfected."[2]

---

[1] Elections relate to talismans or Astral magic and not Ritual magic with which the *Steganographia* is concerned.
[2] Brann (1999), p. 142.

Book IV

Trithemius indicated to Bostius in his now infamous letter that the *Steganographia* was originally conceived as four books.[1] But in 1500, the Spanheim library catalogue listed the book as *Steganographia opus in octo libros partiendum*, or "A Steganography work divided into eight books," a clear indication that Trithemius was planning a sizeable work of eight volumes, of which we are left with only four.

Book IV has never been published in English, or any other language as far as we can discover.

The fact that Book IV contains a number of self-contained books which appear to be by different authors, militates against it being from Trithemius' hand, and there will be some scholars who will doubt that any of Book IV was actually written (or even assembled) by Trithemius. That is definitely a viable point of view as there is a dearth of other external references to it. However, I draw your attention to the last paragraphs of Book III which contain references to Book IV, implying that it was certainly his intention to write it. In that period, sets of four volumes were popular, and have precedents in this field, such as Ptolemy's *Tetrabiblos*.[2]

Book IV is also more 'preachy' than the other three Books, and has some of the tone to be found in the French Preface. I suspect it may have been assembled by Trithemius, even if not written by him, and in justice to our objective of publishing the whole French manuscript, we had to include it. However, even if it is not by Trithemius, there is still much value in publishing it, as it brings together other strands of magical practice, such as the *Almadel*, the *Shemhammaphorash* and the Table of Practice.

Book IV contains the following sections: *The Book of Sacred Numbers* (in two parts); *The Veritable Secrets; The Shemhammaphorash of Solomon, The Shemhammaphorash of Adam, Shemhammaphorash of Moses*, and *The Almadel*. Interestingly the *Almadel* material is interleaved with two of the *Shemhammaphorash*.[3]

This Book thus unites the *Steganographia* with other grimoires, such as the *Shemhammaphorash* and the *Almadel*, both of which Trithemius was certainly aware of, as he had mentioned them in his *Antipalus Maleficiorum*, and almost certainly had copies in his library.

The Veritable Secrets purports to be by Paracelsus. Although it is possible that Trithemius met Paracelsus, or corresponded with him, Paracelsus only gained his medical doctorate in 1516, the date of Trithemius' death.

---

[1] Brann (1999), p. 283.
[2] Or in more modern times Aleister Crowley's *Four Books of Magick*, London: Watkins, 2021.
[3] References to the *Almadel* occur in manuscript pages 207-214, as if it was an integral part of the *Shemhammaphorash of Solomon*. It then appears again in manuscript pages 221-230 in the *Shemhammaphorash of Adam*. Its pictorial illustrations occur on manuscript pages 212, 222 and 230.

Slightly confusingly, Adam Mclean's edition of the *Steganographia* has included Book IV of Gustavus Selenus' *Cryptomenytices et Cryptographiæ*, but this is not the same as Trithemius' Book IV.

Some readers may find the Christian tone of these books offensive, but I should point out that this is part and parcel of what Trithemius was, a monk and a committed Roman Catholic Abbot. Also if you are dealing with angels then it is part and parcel of the Judaeo-Christian worldview. Replacing Christian figures such as Jesus Christ with sundry Egyptian or Celtic gods is simply pointless and anyway invalidates the magic.

The Steganographia evolves into the Theurgia-Goetia

A further 'proof' of its magical rather than cryptographic function, is that the *Steganographia* later evolved into the grimoire now known as the *Theurgia-Goetia*, which later became part of the five-part *Lemegeton*.[1]

The *Theurgia-Goetia* is concerned with spirits which relate to the 32 points of the compass. It is effectively a ritual version of the first book of the *Steganographia*. One of the most striking things about this grimoire is its insistence upon direction. The *Goetia* suggests that you face the Triangle of Art which should be placed on the side (or the 'coast') of the Circle from which you expect the spirit to arrive, but it is a bit vague about where that should be, for most spirits. The *Theurgia-Goetia* on the other hand gives precise compass points for each main spirit (and their attendant servitors). For example, Camuel "ruleth and governeth as King in the South East quarter of the World," but Padiel "Ruleth in the East by South" which literally means that he rules the compass point just a bit South of East, not SE. This directional attribution is strongly supported in Book I of the *Steganographia*.

Some manuscripts of the *Theurgia-Goetia* supply a full-blown spirit Compass Rose showing the 32 possible directions from which a King, Prince or Duke can be expected to arrive (see Figure 4). This is an advance on the rather rudimentary and incomplete compass that appears in the printed *Steganographia*. Strangely, although this manuscript plus several others of the *Steganographia*,[2] shows 16 compass segments with the names of directions (shown as winds) and the 16 Dukes all shown in their proper places, the printed editions of most Latin manuscripts only have an incomplete illustration with just three of the 16 Dukes actually filled in. The present manuscript has a much fuller compass rose showing a lot of extra detail (see Figure 4).

---

[1] The fifth part, the *Ars Notoria* is not really a part of the *Lemegeton* and was probably added later.
[2] Such as National Library of Scotland Adv. MS 18.8.12.

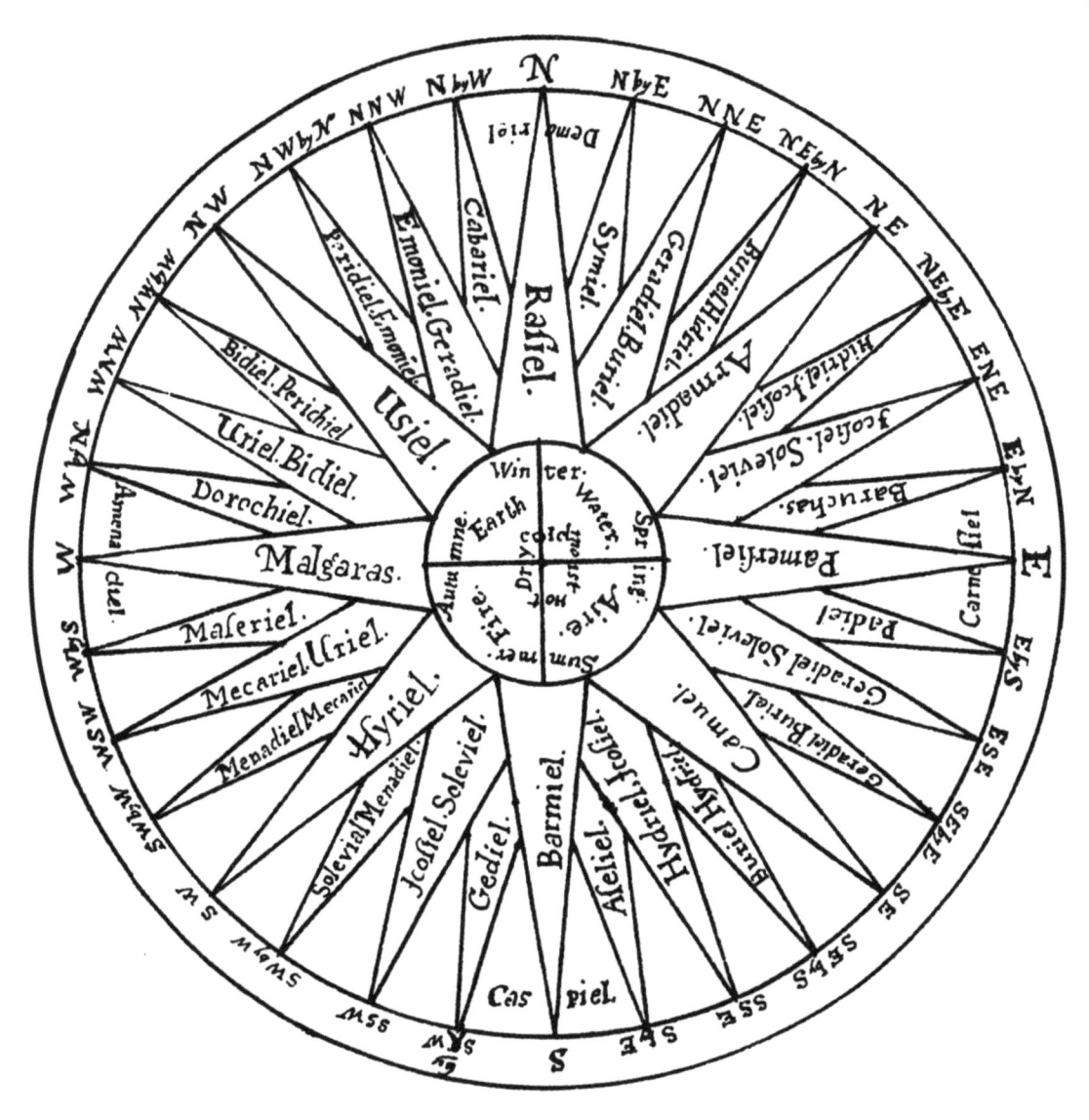

Figure 4: A full Spirit Compass Rose from the *Theurgia-Goetia*.[1]

In the *Theurgia-Goetia* there is a strict hierarchy of spirits ruled by four Emperors (Caspiel, Carnesial, Amenadiel and Demoriel) which correspond with the four Cardinal points (S, E, W, and N). Then comes the 16 Dukes, corresponding to the four Cardinal points (as with the Emperors), plus the four inter-Cardinal points (SE, SW, NW, NE) plus the 8 'Cardinal-flanking' directions (immediately adjacent to the Cardinal points) like Padiel at 'East by South' or Cabariel at 'North by West.'

Lastly, the 11 Wandering Princes fill in the remaining points of the compass in a complex system of rulership pairing – see Table 75 in Appendix 1. Each of the 31

---

[1] Skinner & Rankine, *The Goetia of Dr Rudd,* Singapore: Golden Hoard, 2007, p. 212.

principal spirits in turn rules between 10 and 50 lesser spirits (which in the case of the Duke's spirits are further divided into rulership by either day or night). This structure is not immediately visible upon first reading of the *Theurgia-Goetia*. The grimoire, whilst stating the number of lesser spirits ruled, actually only lists the names and seals of a subset of these, which it says "should be sufficient for practice." This phrase also appears frequently in the *Steganographia*, indicating a common link.

The names of the lesser Dukes are also hidden in the 'mystical language' passages in the *Steganographia*. A clear example of this can be found in chapter 1 of Book I of the *Steganographia*: "anoyr madriel, by the minister ebrasothean abrulges Itrasbiel. And nadres ormenu itules rabion amorphiel." These 11 names all appear as subsidiary Dukes under Parmersiel in the *Theurgia-Goetia*, where they also have their sigils.

Theurgia-Goetia Practice

Strangely, in all manuscripts the actual method of invocation is sandwiched into a section of text just after Pamersiel, one of the 16 Dukes, rather than appearing logically at the front of the manuscript. Also, the order of the spirits in the *Theurgia-Goetia* differs from that in the *Steganographia* (see Appendix 6). This suggests that there has been at some point a dislocation of the text in its transmission from the *Steganographia* to the *Theurgia-Goetia*. The description of the method also varies from one manuscript to another. In order to get a picture of exactly how the procedure should be conducted, we have made a composite below from the instructions to be found in various manuscripts, so that all the salient points are given in one place. We have retained all the instructions in the order given.

> "To call forth Pamersiel, or any of his Servants, or indeed any of the spirits of the *Theurgia-Goetia*, make a Circle in the form as is shown in the Book *Goetia* for gathering in the upper room of your house, which is most private or secret. Or choose a place in some island wood or grove which is the most occult or hidden place, removed from all comers and goers, so that no stranger may chance by that way, or enter your chamber or wherever you choose to do the operation. Observe that the place is very airy because these spirits that are in this part [of the *Theurgia-Goetia*] are all of the air.
>
> You may then call the spirits into a Crystal stone four Inches in diameter, set on a Table [of Practice] made as followeth which is called the secret Table of Solomon, having the seal of the Spirit on your breast and the girdle [of lion skin] about your waist as is showed in the Book *Goetia*, and you cannot err.
>
> The form of the Table [of Practice][1] is thus, as this present figure doth here represent and show.
>
> When you are thus prepared, rehearse the Conjuration several times, that is whilst the

---

[1] See Figure 19.

Spirit is coming, for without doubt he will come. Note the same method is to be used in all the following parts of the second book *Theurgia-Goetia*, as is here shown for Pamersiel and his servants. It is also the same method for Calling forth the four Kings [Emperors] and their Servants aforesaid."

Immediately after this passage, there is an illustration that purports to be the secret Table of [Practice] of Solomon. In most manuscripts, it is a very hastily drawn and crude secret Seal of Solomon.[1] This is in fact incorrect, and it is also in conflict with the illustration shown in the preceding book, the *Goetia*, where the secret Seal of Solomon is correctly shown.[2] The illustration that should appear here is the Table of Practice of Solomon (Figure 19) or alternatively from the *Art Pauline*.[3] This is further confirmed by comparing it with the Table of Practice found in other grimoires, such as Dee's *Tabula Sancta cum Tabulis Enochi*.[4]

The *Steganographia* did not cease to be relevant to magic after the creation of the *Theurgia-Goetia*. In 1801 when Francis Barrett published his *Magus*, he included a chapter on drawing spirits into a crystal, which he claims was written by Trithemius, and who are we to refute that? It had a long and convoluted title which shortens to *The Art of Drawing Spirits into Crystals*.[5]

The Magus was reprinted in 1875 by Frederick Hockley, and helped to considerably expand the general interest in ceremonial magic. It was one of many magical manuscripts and books preserved by Hockley, and it undoubtedly had a positive effect on the recruitment of new members to the Golden Dawn.

Much later in the present century Frater Ashen Chassan (aka Bryan Garner) reintroduced Trithemius' book to the world, having now condensed its title even further to *DSIC*, and used it to systematically invoke the traditional Planetary Archangels. In the process of doing this Ashen Chassan worked his way through all of the tools necessary for this operation, expanding on the description and solving many of the practical problems that modern researchers may encounter.

Ashen Chassan also constructed his own versions of the necessary equipment such as the altar and protective circle, coming up with useful hints whilst sticking closely to the methods in the book. Then having used the equipment with a brilliant skryer he validated the method. In 2013 he published this information in *Gateways Through Stone and Circle*,[6] encouraging others to repeat his experiments. Regardless of the strict correctness of Barrett's attribution of *DSIC* to Trithemius, it is effectively a method that Trithemius was aware of, may well have used, and which has again become a popular method of invocation in the early 21st century.

---

[1] See also Peterson, *Lemegeton* (2001), pp. 66 and 268.
[2] See also Peterson, *Lemegeton* (2001), p. 45.
[3] See also Peterson, *Lemegeton* (2001), p. 111.
[4] Illustrated in Skinner & Rankine, *The Goetia of Dr Rudd*, Singapore: Golden Hoard, 2007.
[5] Appearing in *The Magus* as Part IV of Book 2.
[6] Reprinting in 2024 with a new Introduction.

Cryptography

One thing that can be said for sure about Trithemius' cryptography is that it was cumbersome, certainly when compared with modern cryptographic techniques. One example cited by Brann from the *Steganographia* requires a plain text of 143 Latin words in which the first letter of every word counted.[1] This produces a 30-word encrypted message in German calling for a secret meeting. Where the technique also calls for the insertion of null words, the size of the plain text increases considerably, but still yields only a few words of message.

I got to thinking about how Trithemius put his book together. It occurred to me that as each chapter uses a different cryptographic formula, that job would have been enormous. Instead, I suspect that he started with the evocations, and then added in the cryptographic additions later, a non-significant letter in front of every second word, or a whole non-significant word added according to a formula. This means that instead of digging further into dozens of different cryptographic methods, it may be just simpler to remove the cryptographic additions to reveal the original. Fortunately Heidel in the 1721 Latin edition of the *Steganographia* gives the formula Trithemius applied to each and every evocation. Using this information we could finally strip bare the original evocation.

As an example of a very simple cryptographic method, let us apply the basic cryptographic technique that my parents used around me as a child so they could carry on a conversation within my hearing but without me understanding it.

"henway ehay omescay omehay romfay choolsay akemay uresay ehay oesday ishay omeworkhay."

It was not long before I figured it out, but I never let on so I could continue to listen to their 'secret' conversations. The method is one of many that Trithemius might have used. In this example the first letter is moved to the end, and the syllable 'ay' is added to make it sound rhythmical. The 'ay' is then the only null syllable, and so the method is much more economical than Trithemius' usual methods. It easily resolves into:

"When he comes home from school make sure he does his homework."

Trithemius simply wrote down the instruction as to how it was done, and then added this to the original evocation. So instead of worrying about the encoded information which is just a banal message, you should simply strip out the encoding information, leaving the original text free standing.

Nevertheless the encrypted form appears to work quite well. I can therefore confirm that this is a book on magic whose evocations are hidden by cryptography, giving Trithemius the ideal 'out,' if cross-examined by his religious seniors. If cross-examined by the Inquisition he could simply say "it's all cryptography."

---

[1] Brann (1999), p. 145-146.

You therefore have a choice of 31 Spirits and invocations, and when you send a message you indicate which method has been used by adding the simple spirit sigil as an indication.

Jim Reeds guessed that Trithemius probably assigned letters to numbers using the alphabetical order in Book III. He was on the right track, after he finally discovered that Trithemius used the alphabetical order in reverse. Of course, the alphabet was not quite the same in Trithemius' time as it is today. For example, 'u' and 'v' were considered as one letter, as were 'I' and 'y'. Trithemius did not include the letter 'k' but his alphabet did have a 'w.' As a concession to German and Hebrew, two more letters were added to the end, one letter for 'sch' and another for 'tz.'

The increase in academic interest in these subjects has also been associated with an increase in 'New Age' thinking, wherein it became acceptable to draw any esoteric subject into the mix simply because it is esoteric. A classic example of this occurs in Brann who suggests that Trithemius used alchemy to 'undergird' his magical theory.

> "Trithemius also pointed out the way, these occult fields will be observed to overlap and interconnect in various of their leading expositors, with alchemy serving as a theoretical underpinning for the art of cryptography and furnishing some of its symbols, and the enigmas of cryptography in turn, serving as a linguistic agent for putting the alchemist into touch with the occult wellspring out of which his art has emanated."[1]

This sounds rather like loose New Age nonsense, and I cannot think of anyone else who ever seriously thought that alchemy 'undergirded' cryptography, or vice-versa.

The most fulsome suggestion that the *Steganographia* is only concerned with cryptography and not magic has been provided by Wayne Shumaker where he writes:

> "The permutations suggested by Trithemius are bewildering. Whole lines may be omitted from consideration, or the number of significants and nulls may increase together from one to eight within a single message ("Armadiel"), or the nulls may vary when a word has been completed ("Asiriel"), and so on indefinitely, to the point where usefulness is forgotten and ingenuity is indulged for its own sake. Although I cannot discuss them all, I have checked every one of Selenus's explications and have found that they work on Trithemius's cryptograms.[2]

I also do not accept Shumaker's contention that the 'spirits are useless' because so many of them appear in grimoires both before and after their appearance in the *Steganographia*, which gives proof that they were not just invented by Trithemius.

---

[1] Brann, 1999, pp. 175-176.
[2] Wayne Shumaker, "Johannes Trithemius and Cryptography," in *Renaissance Curiosa*, New York: SUNY, 1982.

The Manuscript

The French translator stated in Book IV that:

> "I have just made it public with the Privilege and consent of the Superiors,[1] printed in Darmstadt, by Baltazar Hofmann in 1621 and translated from the German and Latin, into French in 1780 in Paris."

This particularly fine copy was made from that translation in 1784.

The French manuscript of the *Steganographia* have many examples of the letters 'R' and 'N' scattered around the text. These are not a further code or mystery but stand for the French words *Rouge* and *Noir*. In German texts the words *Rot* and *Schwarz* (red and black), are indicated by 'R' and 'S'. These were the author's indicators designed to inform the printers of words to be printed in red or black, in any future edition that was not limited by a monotone press.

Obviously, Trithemius' original manuscript from which the others were copied used these two colours to distinguish certain aspects of the lists of spirits, to distinguish day spirits from night spirits. We have followed these indicators by printing the columns marked with an 'R' in red, and leaving the others marked 'B' in black.

Our primary source is the French manuscript Bibliotheca Philosophica Hermetica MS 277 which is in many ways more complete than any of the extant Latin manuscripts or printed editions. More significantly, this manuscript also has a Book IV which is not to be found in any other manuscript, as far as we know. Although it is relatively late its scribe appears to have had a better grasp of Trithemius' method, especially as it applies to magic, than some of the other editors. It also includes very useful sections on, and comments about, the *Almadel*.

Of the Latin manuscripts even, 16th-century copies like John Dee's are incomplete (see Figure 10). The earliest available printed edition is the 1606 Frankfurt edition. This edition was used by Adam McLean for his 1982 English edition. Unfortunately, his translators Fiona Tait and Christopher Upton only translated Book I. Adam omitted Book II and only included part of Book III (translated by Harvard Latin scholar J.H.W. Walden). Book IV does not appear in this in any other publication as far as we are aware. In 1609 the *Steganographia* was added to the Church's *Index of Prohibited Books,* which is not surprising considering its listing of so many spirit names. It was added by Martin Delrio (1551-1608) who also added Agrippa's *De Occulta Philosophia* at the same time. It was not finally taken off the *Index* until 1900.

We have used the 1721 Latin edition issued by Heidel for reference, and to check against the Latin, as it is more complete in its explanations of the cryptographic

---

[1] It was common that all printed texts needed to receive permission from the Church before being printed, another method used by the Church to control the potential spread of heresy.

techniques of each chapter of Book I and Book II. Although this is a comparatively late edition it has the benefit of actually including a *Clavis & Sensus* section in each chapter which provides a key and explains the cryptography of that particular chapter. This is necessary as the cryptographic key and method change from chapter to chapter. The 1721 edition is also more useful than the 17th-century Latin editions in that it includes a more comprehensive *Life* of Trithemius, a *Vindicata*, and a summary of comments made by Kircher.

According to the library catalogue, the manuscript belonged to the Luttrell family of Dunster in Somerset, England.

Editorial Idiosyncrasies

One idiosyncratic feature of this manuscript is that it insists on capitalising the word 'Spirit' in the same way that one might capitalise 'Archangel,' and we have adhered to that. Likewise, we have adhered to the scribe's capitalisation of 'Art' when referring to magic, a word which strangely hardly ever appears. Another is the spelling of 'Schemhammaphoras' which sometimes has a double 'm' and sometimes includes a 'c', or omits its final 'h'. As the word is a transliteration from Hebrew, the variants are attributable to scribal transliteration inconsistency. Accordingly, we have opted to change them all to one standard spelling, *Shemhammaphorash*.

The manuscript was very carefully paginated, and there are a number of cross-references from one to other pages. We have kept the manuscript pages noted in square brackets [...]. In the contents pages there are therefore two page references from every item: the original manuscript page and the resultant printed page, which obviously will not match. Internal cross-references refer to the manuscript pagination.

The text has a large number of noun capitalisations, which have been normalised. It is acceptable to capitalise angel names, etc., but excessive capitalisation of common nouns like parchment, work, assemblage, respect, etc., just makes reading unnecessarily laborious. In the French manuscript, many common nouns have been needlessly given initial capitals. We have retained these capitals where a word is used in a more technical sense different from its ordinary dictionary meaning. For example, Element is used when the reference is to one of the four or five classical Elements (Water, Fire, Earth, etc) rather than one of the several hundred chemical elements. Order is capitalised when it refers to a particular range of angels rather than to a simple sequencing. Office retains its capitalisation where it specifically refers to the range of abilities of a particular spirit. Mansion retains its capital when being used in a technical astrological sense. Titles like Prince, Duke and Count retain their capital even though the 'count' often did not.

There are however in Book IV, words where the first two letters are capitalised, which probably has a cryptological significance. However as our focus in this publication has been on magic and not cryptography, we have normalised these throughout, except for a small selection of examples of these double capitals between manuscript pages 226 and 232, by way of illustration.

One characteristic of the manuscript that this present one was copied from, was a confusion of the characters 'Z' and 'L' when transcribing, a minor point that may aid the later identification of the immediate source of the present text.

It was not our intention to publish a perfect academic translation of, conveying the exact nuances of 18th century French, but one which was more readable and concentrated predominantly on ensuring that the spirit tables, names and invocations were accurately rendered.

Figure 5. Johann Heidenberg (*aka* Trithemius) portrait by Durer.[1]

---

[1] A re-rendering of the classic portrait by Albrecht Durer (1517). As this was drawn one year after his death, it is very likely to be an accurate image.

A Brief Biography of the Benedictine Abbot

'Trithemius' is a name read by many, yet known by few. Indeed, for most people involved with the occult sciences, their first encounter with the name will almost certainly be within the pages of Francis Barrett's *The Magus* wherein can be found the pseudo-Trithemian text with the rather exhausting title:

> *"The Magic and Philosophy of TRITHEMIUS OF SPANHEIM; containing his book of SECRET THINGS, and DOCTRINE OF SPIRITS: With many curious and rare secrets (hitherto not generally known;) THE ART OF DRAWING SPIRITS INTO CRYSTALS, etc. With many other Experiments in the Occult Sciences, never yet published in the English Language."*[1]

Trithemius' name in many ways has also been cast in the very shadow of his own creation, the *Steganographia,* for although the book is much more than it first seems, (as we will see later in these pages), it is probably in the realm of cryptography that his name has become more associated with, rather than magic, at least in the mind of most people who simply glance over his work with a passing curiosity. This fact alone has had the effect of obscuring the immensely important contribution he ultimately made to the study of magic, and the dissemination of related ideas. Indeed, without Trithemius and those he would go on to mentor, it would be safe to say that the course of ceremonial magic itself may have been severely encumbered or deflected.

So, what of the man himself? Where did it all begin?

Johann Heidenberg (Trithemius),[2] was born on the 1st of February 1462, the only child to very poor and humble parents. The family occupation was that of winemakers of no particular renown and indeed Trithemius himself never had the opportunity to know his real father, Johann von Heidenburg senior, as his father's death occurred before he even turned one year old. Trithemius' mother Elisabeth de Longovico would not re-marry for seven years, preferring instead to try and maintain an environment of independence and security for her son. Eventually however the strain became too much and the young Trithemius found himself with a new stepfather. As a result of this new union Elizabeth would give birth to several more children although as a sad product of the times, only one would survive to become Trithemius' half-brother, Jacob.[3] By the time Trithemius had reached his fifteenth birthday he had developed what can only be referred to as a vigorous appetite for literature and science, and having already learnt to read and

---

[1] This work is known to have first appeared long after his passing.
[2] The last name Trithemius by which he is more commonly referred, was taken from his home town Trittenheim which lies on the Moselle River in Germany.
[3] Jacob and Trithemius would remain in correspondence throughout their lives and enjoyed a genial relationship.

write at a young age with the assistance of a neighbour and the local priest, he wished fervently for the acquisition of even greater knowledge, a somewhat troublesome affliction according to his stepfather who was adamantly opposed to such 'troublesome' matters, and would attempt to correct the youth by means of stringent and blustering diatribes. When this wasn't enough to 'persuade' the boy he would let his whip do the talking in his stead. Be this as it may, young Johannes refused to give in and would continue to study letters and such like in secret, often sneaking out of the house at night to receive further tuition from local friends and associates, learning Greek, Latin, and even with time, Hebrew.[1]

By the age of seventeen, and having spent most of his youth on his 'secret' quest, the young Heidenberg had had enough of his repressive home and dominating stepfather. Being at the age of independence he left behind his old life and set out to continue his search for further education unshackled by parental rules, taking with him the new name of his hometown Trittenheim.

The first leg of this new journey must have been quite the ordeal for the young scholar, travelling first to Trier, then Cologne, then the Netherlands and from there onto Heidelberg. It would be the next event upon the completion of his studies at Heidelberg University, that was the 'divine turning point in Trithemius' life, all thanks to heavy falling snow.

It was during the fateful journey at the end of January/start of February 1482 at the age of twenty that Trithemius and a fellow student and travelling companion were both headed back to their hometown when chance would have it, they decided to spend the cold night at the lodgings of the monastery of Spanheim[2] in Hunsrück which happened to be on the way. After an uneventful night the two continued their journey the following morning but upon approaching the mountain pass of the neighbouring village of Bockenau they were both caught in an overbearingly powerful snowstorm which came out of nowhere blocking their path. Although Trithemius insisted that they should continue, eventually even he conceded defeat as the storm continued to worsen, and with little hope of shelter from their immediate environment, both men turned tail and returned somewhat embarrassed to the monastery that had so graciously hosted them the night before. Was this a sign from God for Trithemius? Was he destined to return to that Abbey? He certainly thought so, for not only did Trithemius return, but he returned to become the newest novice of Spanheim monastery.

Fate would once again turn in favour of Trithemius, for just short of one year after

---

[1] It should also be noted that one of the biggest driving factors in Trithemius' quest for knowledge was a dream or 'vision' that occurred one night as he slept. Within this vision Trithemius would see a "youthful figure holding two tablets, (one in each hand), one inscribed with letters, the other with images." He was instructed to make a choice between the two by a mysterious figure. Naturally he selected letters even though at this point he was ignorant of their full implication.
[2] Spanheim was a Benedictine abbey founded in 1101 by Count Stephan II.

taking his monastic vows, Johannes von Kolenhausen, the then current Abbot, gave up his position in favour of a transfer to a new post at Seligenstadt.[1] The abbacy was offered to Trithemius, an amazing example of how highly he had become respected in such a short period of time. And so it was that Trithemius became the 25th Abbot within the cloister of St. Martin at Spanheim, at the tender age of 22.

Life within the monastic world was a vocation very suited to the young monk, and even more so once he had ascended to the position of Abbot, for it allowed him not only ample opportunities to continue his studies of the written word,[2] but also would eventually allow him to use his skills in other areas, such as the need to repair the much-neglected monastery finances, an area in which he would later greatly succeed.

Over the next ten years Trithemius devoted himself to an extensive restructuring of the monastery, both physically and intellectually, with not only the reconstruction of what he considered substandard and potentially dangerous living quarters, but also with the instigation of a much more thorough theological and educational regime for the other monks. It was also within this restructure that Trithemius was afforded the opportunity to improve on, and create his proudest achievement of that time, his library.

Figure 6: The 'Sponheim Closter' a historical town view. Copper engraving by Matthäus Merian 1645.

---

[1] A town in the Offenbach rural district of Hesse, a state within what is now Germany.
[2] He had a particular love for the study of Scripture.

CATALOGVS

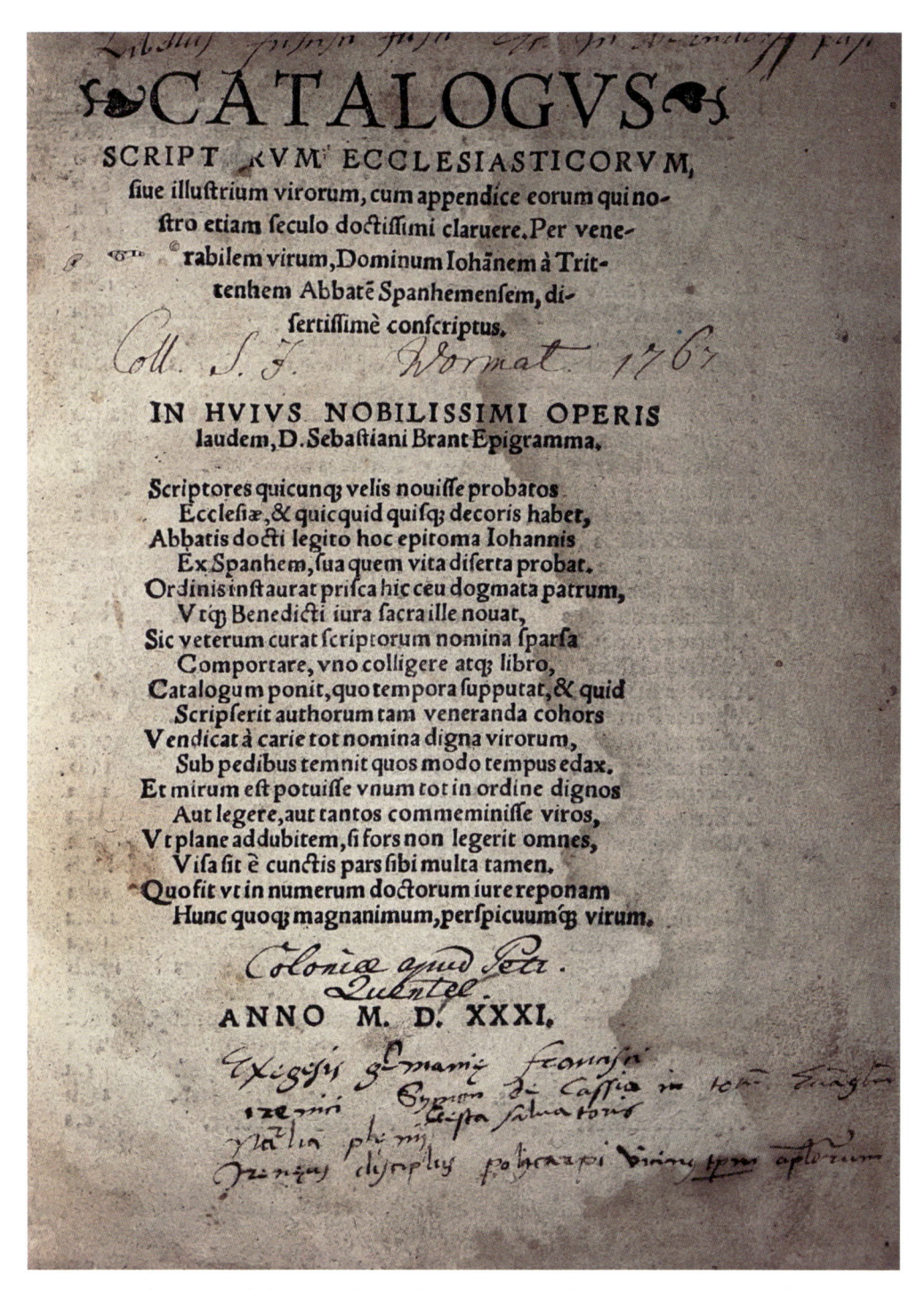

SCRIPT RVM ECCLESIASTICORVM, fiue illustrium virorum, cum appendice eorum qui nostro etiam seculo doctissimi claruere. Per venerabilem virum, Dominum Iohānem à Trittenhem Abbatē Spanhemensem, disertissimè conscriptus.

IN HVIVS NOBILISSIMI OPERIS
laudem, D. Sebastiani Brant Epigramma.

Scriptores quicunq; velis nouisse probatos
    Ecclesiæ, & quicquid quisq; decoris habet,
Abbatis docti legito hoc epitoma Iohannis
    Ex Spanhem, sua quem vita diserta probat.
Ordinis instaurat prisca hic ceu dogmata patrum,
    Vtq; Benedicti iura sacra ille nouat,
Sic veterum curat scriptorum nomina sparsa
    Comportare, vno colligere atq; libro,
Catalogum ponit, quo tempora supputat, & quid
    Scripserit authorum tam veneranda cohors
Vendicat à carie tot nomina digna virorum,
    Sub pedibus temnit quos modo tempus edax.
Et mirum est potuisse vnum tot in ordine dignos
    Aut legere, aut tantos commeminisse viros,
Vt plane addubitem, si fors non legerit omnes,
    Visa sit è cunctis pars sibi multa tamen,
Quo fit vt in numerum doctorum iure reponam
    Hunc quoq; magnanimum, perspicuumq; virum.

ANNO M. D. XXXI.

Figure 7: Title page of the *Catalogus Scriptorum Ecclesiasticorum* printed at Cologne by Peter Quentell, 1531.[1]

---

[1] With permission of the University of Tasmania.

Upon his arrival at Spanheim monastery, the monastic library was pathetic, consisting of a mere 48 books. This was to be seriously rectified by the newly appointed Abbot and in the ensuing years he sought to feverishly indulge in his quest for knowledge by affording every opportunity to add to its shelves. During his time there he grew it to more than 2000 volumes, making it one of the most impressive libraries in Germany. His earliest catalogue of such books was completed in 1494, *De Scriptoribus Ecclesiasticis*, which contained the details of over 1000 authors, although later expanded. Today most of those volumes have been lost or were later sold off by the monks.

Certainly, his position would take him away from the monastery on numerous occasions and such sojourns across Europe gave him ample opportunities to make continuous acquisitions. What books or manuscripts Trithemius could not buy or trade for, he would borrow and have copied within his scriptorium,[1] and a great deal of the monastery funds were directed to this cause. Trithemius himself would go on record as stating that by 1507 he had single-handedly collected roughly 2000 rare and valuable books and manuscripts, making it one of the largest collections in Germany in that period. Certainly this library would become a veritable 'Alexandria' of its day, with a regular flow of scholarly visitors. It goes without saying that Trithemius was regarded as a great scholar in his own time. His understanding of varied subject matters and the complexities of the written word in a myriad of different languages made his lectures and teaching much sought after. Coupled with the environment of his ever-growing library it was only a matter of time before the Abbot turned his attention to his own pen, and what attention it was, for in his early days he produced thirteen works before 1488 one of which was the start of his *De Scriptoribus Ecclesiasticis*.[2] This was the first bibliography to be compiled as a practical reference book.[3]

It was through Trithemius' life as an author that a much fuller understanding of his interests of study became available to us, for not only did he invest time and research into the study of monastic reform and history, but also magic. Indeed, it is in this later capacity that his name and character would ultimately become 'tarnished.'

Despite the views of many against magic in the Middle Ages as being purely 'demonic,' Trithemius nonetheless walked that fine line between monastic scholar and scholarly magician. There is no question that his thirst for knowledge of all

---

[1] A department of a monastery where manuscripts were copied, illuminated, and created.
[2] *Of the Ecclesiastical Writers*. Trithemius began work on this in 1487 through to the spring of 1492 when he sent the completed manuscript to the bishop of Worms. A revised version of the *Liber de scriptoribus ecclesiasticis* of just over 300 folio pages was published by the Basle press of Johann Amerbach in 1494. The work is a chronological bibliography that lists almost a thousand writers, mostly of an ecclesiastical nature, but also includes such names as Dante. It gives a short account of each followed by a list of their writings, making it a great reference book of its day.
[3] At the time of writing a copy of the 1494 edition is on sale for $75,000.

kinds was a major driving factor in his progression through life, especially with the occult sciences, regardless of how potentially dangerous it may have been to his name and fame.

The first serious blow would come in the year 1499 in the form of a singular letter perhaps rather hastily sent by Trithemius to his trusted friend Arnold Bostius.[1] Its content described in summary a new and ongoing work that Trithemius had created.

> *"I have in hand a great Work which will amuse the whole World, if ever it sees the Light; it's divided into Four Books, and the First has for Title of it, Steganography; the Work throughout is full of great and astonishing things, which Man has never heard of, and will seem incredible. If you ask me, how I learnt these things? It's not by Man, but by the Revelation of I know not what Spirit; for thinking, on a day, this Year 1499 if I could not discover secrets unknown to Men; after having a long while ponder'd on those I have mentioned, and being at length perswaded that what I sought for was not possible, I went to Bed, being somewhat ashamed for having carried my Folly so far, as to attempt an Impossible thing. In the Night time someone presented himself to me, and calling me by my name, Trithemius, said he, do not believe you have had all these thoughts in vain, tho' the things you search are not possible to you, nor to any other Man, they will become so. Teach me then, I reply'd, what I must do to succeed. Then he laid open the whole Mystery, and shew'd me that nothing was more easy. God is my Witness, that I speak the Truth, and that I have taught these secrets but to a Prince, who by an evident proof has been convinced of the possibility of it. It Imports that none but Princes should know these sorts of secrets, least Traitors, Impostors, or other Ill Men make use of them for doing many Mischiefs."*[2]

The letter would continue with more descriptions of the *Steganographia's* miraculous abilities but sadly for him in an unfortunate turn of fate, Bostius would pass away before the letter could reach its intended and trusted recipient, instead it found its way into the hands of the prior of the Carmelite convent having taken possession of it in Bostius' stead. His response upon reading its content could only be imagined considering the nature of its revelations, and in his disgust quickly had the letter circulated where it was copied and circulated even further afield. Trithemius had become a name on many lips both for intellectual curiosity and for many others more ill-disposed, a "notorious black magician."

By 1500 Trithemius' work on the *Steganographia* appeared to subside, no doubt a result of the very negative and unwanted attention it had brought forth. He would publicly refute all accusations that he achieved such feats as described in his book by the aid of demonic intervention, however his efforts were made even more

---

[1] A Carmelite theologian and humanist residing in Ghent (a Flemish town in Belgium). Like Trithemius, he specialized in theological and historical works (1446-1499).
[2] Beaumont (1705).

difficult several years later when in 1503 he was paid a visit by Charles de Bovelles (1471-1553).[1]

In the two weeks that Bovelles remained in Spanheim, Trithemius presented him with his *Steganographia,* so that it might be studied by a 'like-minded intellectual.' Bovelles' opinion of it was less than flattering, although at the time he must have keep these feelings to himself, as Trithemius was unaware of his hostility. Bovelles would later in 1509 write a letter to their mutual friend Germain de Ganay[2] describing his visit to Trithemius those years before and stating that he considered him the most dangerous kind of demonic magician, and further added that his book should be burned! Trithemius would himself in turn write to Germain de Ganay concerning his views on magic.[3]

> *"For I have judged it preferable to condemn to perpetual silence all my marvelous discoveries than to incur the mark of a pernicious magical or necromantic superstition by means of the false estimation of men. Therefore, let the Steganographia remain hidden in the shadows, and may it not be made accessible to the society of cows (bouilline societate), which is accustomed to make judgment concerning things of which it is ignorant and to despoil (depravare) the reputation of a good man by reason of its own desire for depravity (pravitatis)."*[4]

Trithemius ~ letter reproduced in his *Polgraphiae libri* VI, Cologne, 1571.

De Ganay also had a keen interest in magic and alchemy and was a major patron of learning in France at the time. One can't help but think he would have lent a sympathetic ear towards Trithemius with whom he also communicated. Certainly as we can see from the above statement, that the negative reactions to Trithemius' *Steganographia* made him more cautious as to whom he decided to show it. The finished portions of the work would remain in manuscript form for the rest of his life, perhaps as a way of making it only accessible to those who actively sort it out via scribal reproduction, and less accessible to the mainstream public than would be the case with the printed word. The *Steganographia* would finally go into print in 1606, 90 years after Trithemius' death.

---

[1] A French mathematician and philosopher (1475 - 1566?). He published his *Géométrie en françoys* in 1511, which was the first scientific work to be printed in French.
[2] Germain de Ganay, counsellor-clerk in the Parliament of Paris, adviser to the King of France in Parliament and president of the Chamber of Requests. He was also Canon of Notre-Dame Cathedral in Paris and Saint-Étienne Cathedral in Bourges and Dean of the Chapter of Saint-Pierre Cathedral in Beauvais. He was Bishop-designate of Cahors from 1509 to 1514, then of Orléans from 1514. He died in March 8, 1520.
[3] Reproduced in several works including *Johannis Trithemii Spanheimensis Primo, Deinde D. Iacobi Maioris Apvd Herbipolin Abbatis, viri suo aevo doctissimi. Partis Chronica Insignia Dvo.* Vol. 2, pp. 471-473.
[4] Brann (1981), p. 30.

Regardless of the cloud of negativity surrounding Trithemius as a result of his *Steganographia*, it also had the more interesting side effect of building in people's minds a most curious interest, and this coupled with the established fame of his extravagantly established library meant that more traffic than ever began to pass through the monastery doors both intellectual or otherwise, and as the legend grew so too did the statue of the individuals who would eventually seek him out for counsel or discussion on various topics, many of which may have concerned occult matters.

By the year 1505 relations between the Abbot Trithemius and his monks at Spanheim had become increasingly tense. Although possibly a result of many factors (concerns over the Abbot's involvement with magic no doubt a contributing factor), the main focus of animosity appears to have been the strict curriculum of Christian scholarship that he enforced. As a result of such increasing animosity and an ideal opportunity to try and allow things to settle down, Trithemius accepted a well-timed invitation to go to Heidelberg and discuss with Abbot Macharius of Limburg the reconstruction of his monastery that had been destroyed by the recent war in that area.[1]

Although stricken with fever upon his arrival to Heidelberg, our intrepid monk would, upon recovery, take the opportunity to spend a short time visiting neighbouring areas and consolidating various ideas with learned friends on mathematics, astrology, philosophy, and various other liberal arts. It was during his wanderings at this stage that Trithemius would have a brief encounter with George Sabellicus *aka* Dr Johann Georg Faust of Knittlingen,[2] a man whose reputation as a necromancer and master magician not only may have rivalled Trithemius' at that point in time, but would certainly go on to do so in the centuries to come. The account of this unique encounter would be the first historical documentation of the now legendary Dr Faustus,[3] yet again displaying the amazing contributions made by Trithemius to the history of magic, even if in this case it was somewhat unintentional. Be that as it may, Trithemius was far from impressed by the competition this man presented for his unwanted title of 'diabolical magician' and in a letter penned to his good friend and noted astrologer Johannes Virdung von Hassfurt he goes on record as stating:

---

[1] In the year 1504 war broke out between Emperor Maximilian and the Count Palatine. Trithemius had taken refuge in nearby Kreuznach. So great was his concern for his library that he had it all safely packed into a cart and taken with him. Thankfully so, for upon his return to Spanheim monastery 6 months later he found it greatly damaged as a result of the conflict.

[2] A town located in Baden-Württemberg.

[3] The legend surrounding Sabellicus and his namesake Faust throughout history is itself too large of a subject to cover here. Indeed, it has been the work of many studies already published. This myth like many others has been greatly expanded over time, with even Trithemius being credited as a possible source for this legend.

"The man of whom you wrote me, George Sabellicus, who has presumed to call himself the Prince of necromancers, is a vagabond, a babbler and a rogue, who deserves to be thrashed so that he may not henceforth rashly venture to profess in public things so execrable and so hostile to the holy church. For what, other than symptoms of a very foolish and insane mind, are the titles assumed by this man, who shows himself to be a fool and not a philosopher? For thus he has formulated the title befitting him: Master George Sabellicus, the younger Faust, the chief of necromancers, astrologer, the second magus, palmist, diviner with earth and fire, second in the art of divination with water. Behold the foolish temerity of the man, the madness by which he is possessed, in that he dares to call himself the source of necromancy, when in truth, in his ignorance of all good letters, he ought to call himself a fool rather than a master. But his wickedness is not hidden from me. When I was returning last year from the Mark Brandenburg, I happened upon this same man in the town of Gelnhausen, and many silly things were told me about him at the inn, – things promised by him with great rashness on his part. As soon as he heard that I was there, he fled from the inn and could not be persuaded to come into my presence. The description of his folly, such as he gave to you and which we have mentioned, he also sent to me through a certain citizen. Certain priests in the same town told me that he had said, in the presence of many people, that he had acquired such knowledge of all wisdom and such a memory, that if all the books of Plato and Aristotle, together with their whole philosophy, had totally passed from the memory of man, he himself, through his own genius, like another Hebrew Ezra, would be able to restore them all with increased beauty. Afterwards, while I was at Speyer, he came to Würzburg and, impelled by the same vanity, is reported to have said in the presence of many that the miracles of Christ the Saviour were not so wonderful, that he himself could do all the things which Christ had done, as often and whenever he wished. Towards the end of Lent of the present year he came to Kreuznach and with like folly and boastfulness made great promises, saying that in alchemy he was the most learned man of all times and that by his knowledge and ability, he could do whatever anyone might wish. In the meantime there was vacant in the same town the position of schoolmaster, to which he was appointed through the influence of Franz von Sickingen, the magistrate of your Prince and a man very fond of mystical lore. Then he began to indulge in the most dastardly kind of lewdness with the boys and when this was suddenly discovered, he avoided by flight the punishment that awaited him. These are the things which I know through very definite evidence concerning the man whose coming you await with such anticipation. When he comes to you, you will find him to be not a philosopher but a fool with an overabundance of rashness."

– Würzburg, the 20th day of August, A.D. 1507.[1]

---

[1] Philip Mason Palmer & R.P. More, *Sources of the Faust Tradition from Simon Magus to Lessing*, London: Routledge, 1966.

Trithemius would continue to engage in regular correspondence during his pilgrimage not only with his close friends but also with his monks back in Spanheim. Sadly, towards the end of his journey it became clear from the information he received back that resolution could not be found and his time away had done nothing to alleviate tension, indeed it had done the very opposite by allowing opportunity for certain individuals amongst its ranks to openly speak out against him and further the dissension between them. And so, it was with mutual agreement in the end, and with a broken heart, that Trithemius gave up not only his position there, but his home, and the greatest loss of all, his treasured and nurtured library. From here, and no doubt with a heavy soul from having been "pushed out the door," Trithemius left Spanheim monastery for good.

One can only ponder if Trithemius spirited away certain volumes from the library of Spanheim to accompany him on this new phase of life. Indeed, this does seem the case, particularly those volumes of a more occult nature, and thankfully so for rumour prevailed that the newly appointed Abbot was far less understanding of certain subjects, and many titles were rejected from its shelves. Lost? Destroyed? Sadly, it can never be known, but most likely sold. The one thing for certain however was that the library would from then on be only a mere shadow of its former self.

Trithemius' uncertainty about his future was soon to be alleviated with the welcome news that he had been offered the vacancy of Abbot to the Scottish founded monastery of St. Jacob (James) by Lorenz von Bibra the bishop of Würzburg. Finally, putting behind him all thought of his lost Spanheim, and the machinations of certain individuals from there against him, Trithemius travelled to Würzburg to start this next chapter of his life. Once again as the years passed within the peaceful wall of Trithemius' new home, his pen was kept very busy. Numerous works were brought forth into the world while others remained but an ambitious thought. In one correspondence with his friend Rutger Sicamber, Trithemius talks of his proposed work *De Demonibus* which was to be a compendium of twelve books relating to "Demons, profane arts, and sorcerers by means of which mankind is wretchedly deceived."

Sadly, this project never progressed further than its initial preface and list of intended content. Thankfully Trithemius would produce other works of a similar vein and in 1508 he completed his manuscript of the *Antipalus Maleficiorum* or 'The Enemy of Witchcraft.' The *Antipalus* was a register or checklist of the most renowned and rarest tracts concerning magic and occult sciences of the time. It would go on to become almost the standard reference work for aspiring collectors or magicians alike, despite its less than flattering description of many of the volumes listed.

IOANNIS TRITEMII

Abbatis sancti Iacobi apud Herbipolim: quondam vero Spanhemensis: Liber Octo questionũ ad Maximilianum Cesarem.

¶ Cum priuilegio Cesaree maiestatis de nõ imprimẽdo in regno, imperio, & terris suis nec alubi impressis isthic vẽdẽdis intra decenniũ subpenis in priuilegio expressis decẽ marcarũ auri puri et amissione librorũ corundem omnium, zc.

Figure 8: Title page of *Ioannis Tritemii Abbatis sancti Iacobi apud Herbipolim: quondam vero Spanhemensis: Liber questionu[m] ad Maximilianum Cesarem*. Or in short "Trithemius' Book of Eight Questions to Maximilian Caesar." The book contains the answers to eight theological questions given to Trithemius by Emperor Maximilian and covers many topics of the occult sciences highlighting their shared interest in such matters.

It would seem that Trithemius' harsh comments and strict warnings were made with his tongue firmly in his cheek, covering his back whilst pointing out some of the choicest texts which might later be considered the most desirable by would-be magicians, but also to those tracts that did not sit comfortably within the monastic magical framework that he was trying to create or justify. Indeed, these criticisms might have been a way to avoid the further tarnishing of his character. The *Antipalus* would not see print until 1605.

Trithemius' life was not only a quest for knowledge but also a very social one. For every detractor he may have had there was equally another full of admiration and respect. As such his life was a flurry of correspondence and encounters not only with his peers, but often as not with those of a much higher social standing, extending even to royalty, such as his counsel with the emperor Maximilian, which added to the myth. In it Trithemius displayed his necromantic abilities before the emperor by allegedly summoning up in his presence a visage of his dead wife and other notable characters of the heroic past. It is of no small wonder that he should also take under his wing disciples who would themselves go on to carve their names into the annuals of history, science, astrology and of course magic.

One such admirer was a young man with a similar obsession for all matters esoteric, Agrippa von Nettesheim. One can only ponder the lessons learnt and the discussions shared between these two individuals that would become the very cornerstone of the dissemination of grimoire magic that was to evolve in the following centuries. Agrippa writes:

"TO R. P. D. JOHN TRITHEMIUS, AN ABBOT OF SAINT JAMES, IN THE SUBURBS OF HERBIPOLIS, HENRY CORNELIUS AGRIPPA OF NETTESHEIM SENDETH GREETING:

> *WHEN I was of late, most reverend father, for a while conversant with you in your Monastery of Herbipolis, we conferred together of divers things concerning Chemistry, Magic, and Cabala, and of other things, which as yet lie hid in secret Sciences and Arts; and then there was one great question amongst the rest — Why Magic, whereas it was accounted by all ancient philosophers to be the chiefest science, and by the ancient wise men and priests was always held in great veneration, came at last, after the beginning of the Catholic Church, to be always odious to and suspected by the holy Fathers, and then exploded by Divines, and condemned by sacred Canons, and, moreover, by all laws and ordinances forbidden? Now, the cause, as I conceive, is no other than this, viz.: Because, by a certain fatal depravation of times and men, many false philosophers crept in, and these, under the name of Magicians, heaping together, through various sorts of errors and factions of false religions, many cursed superstitions and dangerous rites, and many wicked sacrileges, even to the perfection of Nature; and the same set forth in many wicked and unlawful books, to which they have by stealth prefixed the most honest name and title of Magic; hoping, by this sacred title, to gain credit to their cursed and detestable fooleries. Hence it is that this name of Magic, formerly so honorable,*

is now become most odious to good and honest men, and accounted a capital crime if any one dare profess himself to be a Magician, either in doctrine or works, unless haply some certain old doting woman, dwelling in the country, would be believed to be skilful and have a divine power, that she (as saith Apuleius the satirist) "can throw down the heaven, lift up the earth, harden fountains, wash away mountains, raise up ghosts, cast down the Gods, extinguish the stars, illuminate hell," or, as Virgil sings:

> *"She'll promise by her charms to cast great cares,*
> *Or ease the minds of men, and make the Stars*
> *For to go back, and rivers to stand still,*
> *And raise the nightly ghosts even at her will;*
> *To make the earth to groan, and trees to fall*
> *From the mountains – "*

Hence those things which Lucan relates of Thessala the Magicianess [sic], and Homer of the omnipotency of Circe. Whereof many others, I confess, are as well of a fallacious opinion as a superstitious diligence and pernicious labor; for when they cannot come under a wicked art yet they presume they may be able to cloak themselves under that venerable title of Magic.

These things being so, I wondered much and was not less indignant that, as yet, there had been no man who had either vindicated this sublime and sacred discipline from the charge of impiety or had delivered it purely and sincerely to us. What I have seen of our modern writers – Roger Bacon, Robert of York, an Englishman, Peter Apponus, Albertus [Magnus] the Teutonich, Arnoldas de villa Nova, Anselme the Parmensian, Picatrix the Spaniard, Cicclus Asculus of Florence, and many other writers of an obscure name – when they promise to treat of Magic do nothing but relate irrational tales and superstitions unworthy of honest men. Hence my spirit was moved, and, by reason partly of admiration, and partly of indignation, I was willing to play the philosopher, supposing that I should do no discommendable work – seeing I have been always from my youth a curious and undaunted searcher for wonderful effects and operations full of mysteries – if I should recover that ancient Magic (the discipline of all wise men) from the errors of impiety, purify and adorn it with its proper lustre, and vindicate it from the injuries of calumniators; which thing, though I long deliberated of it in my mind, I never durst undertake; but after some conference betwixt us of these things, at Herbipolis, your transcending knowledge and learning, and your ardent adhortation, put courage and boldness into me. There selecting the opinions of philosophers of known credit, and purging the introduction of the wicked (who, dissemblingly, and with a counterfeited knowledge, did teach that traditions of Magicians must be learned from very reprobate books of darkness or from institutions of wonderful operations), and, removing all darkness, I have at last composed three compendious books of Magic, and titled them Of Occult Philosophy, being a title less offensive, which books I submit (you excelling in the knowledge of these things) to your correction and censure, that if I have wrote anything which may tend either to the contumely

of Nature, offending God, or injury of religion, you may condemn the error; but if the scandal of impiety be dissolved and purged, you may defend the Tradition of Truth; and that you would do so with these books, and Magic itself, that nothing may be concealed which may be profitable, and nothing approved of which cannot but do hurt; by which means these three books, having passed your examination with approbation, may at length be thought worthy to come forth with good success in public, and may not be afraid to come under the censure of posterity.
Farewell, and pardon these my bold undertakings."

In Response:-
"JOHN TRITHEMIUS, ABBOT OF SAINT JAMES OF HERBIPOLIS, FORMERLY OF SPANHEMIA, TO HIS HENRY CORNELIUS AGRIPPA OF NETTESHEIM, HEALTH AND LOVE:

YOUR work, most renowned Agrippa, entitled Of Occult Philosophy, which you have sent by this bearer to me, has been examined. With how much pleasure I received it no mortal tongue can express nor the pen of any write. I wondered at your more than vulgar learning – that you, being so young, should penetrate into such secrets as have been hid from most learned men; and not only clearly and truly but also properly and elegantly set them forth. Whence first I give you thanks for your good will to me, and, if I shall ever be able, I shall return you thanks to the utmost of my power. Your work, which no learned man can sufficiently commend, I approve of. Now that you may proceed toward higher things, as you have begun, and not suffer such excellent parts of wit to be idle, I do, with as much earnestness as I can, advise, intreat and beseech you that you would exercise yourself in laboring after better things, and demonstrate the light of true wisdom to the ignorant, according as you yourself are divinely enlightened. Neither let the consideration of idle, vain fellows withdraw you from your purpose; I say of them, of whom it is said, "The wearied ox treads hard," whereas no man, to the judgment of the wise, can be truly learned who is sworn to the rudiments of one only faculty. But you have been by God gifted with a large and sublime wit, and it is not that you should imitate oxen but rather birds; neither think it sufficient that you study about particulars, but bend your mind confidently to universals; for by so much the more learned any one is thought, by how much fewer things he is ignorant of. Moreover, your wit is fully apt to all things, and to be rationally employed, not in a few or low things, but many and sublimer. Yet this one rule I advise you to observe – that you communicate vulgar secrets to vulgar friends, but higher and secret to higher and secret friends only: Give hay to an ox, sugar to a parrot only. Understand my meaning, lest you be trod under the oxen's feet, as oftentimes it falls out. Farewell, my happy friend, and if it lie in my power to serve you, command me, and according to your pleasure it shall without delay be done; also, let our friendship increase daily; write often to me, and send me some of your labors I earnestly pray you. Again farewell.

From our Monastery of Peapolis, the 8th day of April, A.D. MDX."[1]

---

[1] Henry Cornelius Agrippa, *The Philosophy of Natural Magic*, University Books, 1974.

Heinrich Cornelius Agrippa, a name almost certainly more familiar to the student of magic than that of Trithemius himself, hardly needs an introduction here, indeed his life and times are a most noteworthy volume and as such outside the scope of this present work. So too is the case with yet another notable historical linkage to Trithemius, that of Theophrastus von Hohenheim[1] more commonly known as Paracelsus. Although historically he was thought to have visited the Abbot in his early days of travel before setting forth on his own path of alchemy, medicine and magic, unlike Agrippa, the evidence presented in this case is speculative at best and remains inconclusive, with facts appearing to have been interpreted haphazardly and, in some cases even forged. The argument for and against the two meeting remains ongoing, and should it ever be proven as fact would most certainly add an even stronger provenance to an already great name.

Trithemius would remain in Würzburg for the remainder of his life where he continued to write, study and indeed attempt to rebuild his library to some degree just as he had always done at his lost Spanheim.[2] He would continue to entertain, advise, and instruct all those who might want to search him out, so that when eventually the word had spread of his passing at the age 54, the loss of his wisdom and penmanship would have come as not only a surprise but a great sorrow for many. Trithemius died on 13th December 1516 and was buried in the Schottenkirche (Scottish Monastery) of Würzburg. The grave was adorned with a fabulously carved stone by the noted and prolific sculptor of the time Tilmann Riemenschneider (1460-1531) and was reported to have had the following epitaph:

> *"The abbot Trithemius, a glory of the Germanic world*
> *Whom this house shelters, has merited this memorial.*
> *How greatly he is to be admired, both for his excellence in letters and for his virtue,*
> *Is shown by the monuments of his pen.*
> *This man has conversed in the audience even of many Princes.*
> *Among these the foremost was Maximilian -*
> *Maximilian, the glory of the Roman sceptre,*
> *An illustrious descendant of the house of Austria,*
> *At whose magnificent court he was most heartily welcome,*
> *A place which a learned throng has dubbed the most eminent of all.*
> *May he be far from suspicion concerning the magical art of the Demon*
> *Against which he began to write a great work.*
> *As he lived in renown, may he now live blessed in mind,*
> *And may he gaze upon the heavenly dominions of the highest God."*

In 1720 the grave (including the headstone) was moved to the Neumünster collegiate church where it still remains, however according to the late 17th century Trithemius biographer Wolfgang Ernest Heidel this original inscription was lost

---

[1] His full name was "Philippus Aureolus Theophrastus Bombastus von Hohenheim."
[2] Sadly, this second library was also immediately scattered to the winds upon his death.

during the relocation process and was subsequently replaced with one of a far shorter and very modest nature.

Figure 9: Tomb relief of Trithemius carved by Tilman Riemenschneider formerly at St. James's Abbey, with a detail of his face from the same carving. In 1825 the tombstone was moved to the Neumünster church.

The life and times of Johannes Trithemius was a tale of discovery and turmoil, and the above account is by no means a complete overview. He had such an outreaching impact so many different facets of the society in which he lived, and certainly beyond. A man who spent much of his adult life walking the fine line between monastic Abbot and master magician. From his humble beginnings to religious scholar, Trithemius sat at the centre of two worlds and yet at the same time had tried to unify them both into a single whole gaining him both the greatest respect and at the same time critical scorn. During his life Trithemius was very conscious of the difference between himself and the less elect elements of the population who he rather unkindly referred to as *imperitis rapophagis* or "thick-skinned turnip-eaters."

His contribution to the history of magic is without dispute and for those who would follow in his footsteps in the occult sciences his name and works continue to inspire and captivate. Indeed, Dr John Dee made great use of Trithemius' work as well as making several hand copies of his *Steganographia*,[1] acquiring tracts from Trithemius' once fabled library, and studying and adapting the techniques for himself.

---

[1] See Figure 10.

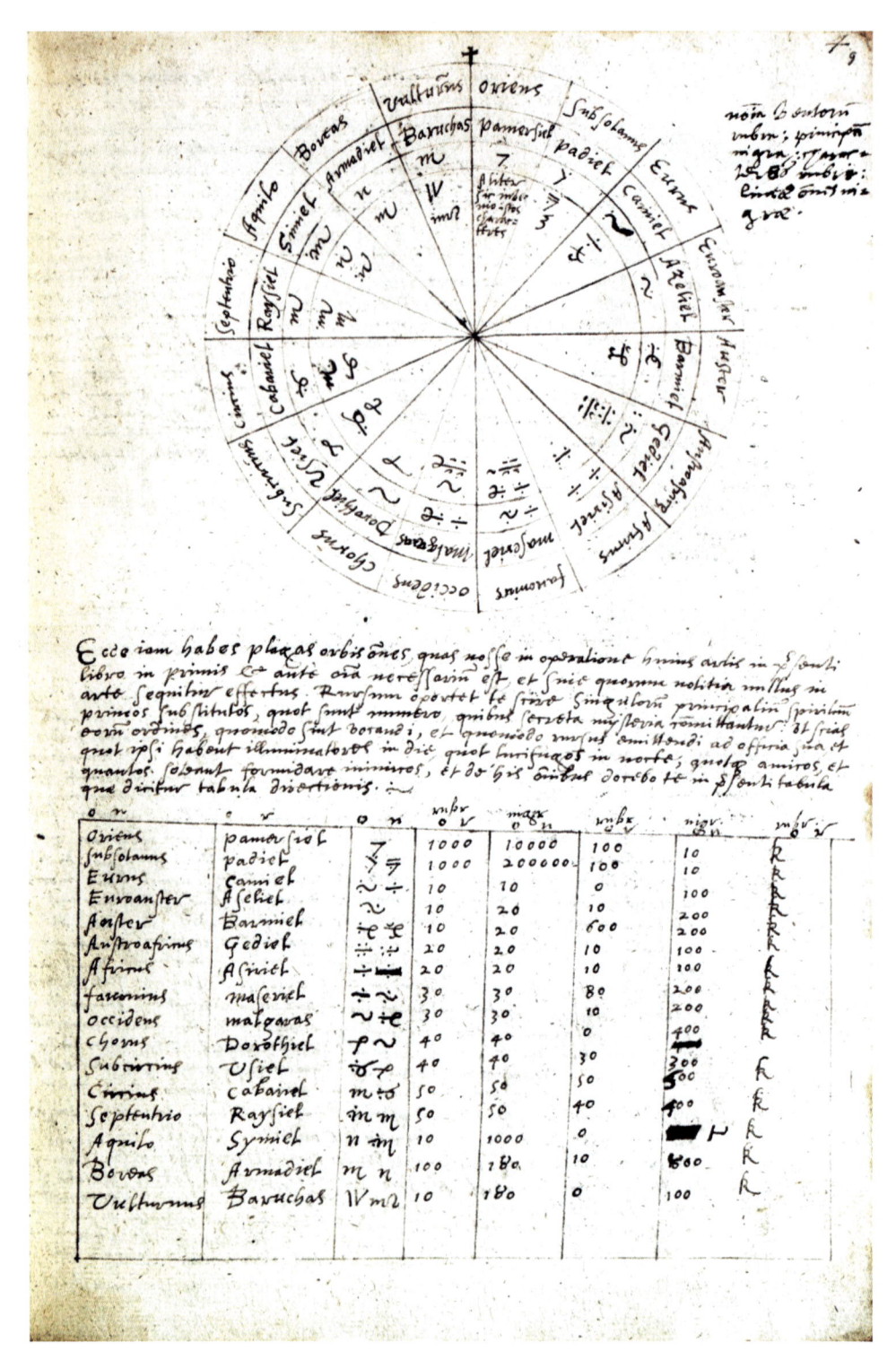

Figure 10: A copy of the *Steganographia* copy made by Dr John Dee. A page from Peniarth MS 423D. Courtesy of the National Library of Wales.

Dee's collection of Trithemius' works was also found very useful by Dee's skryer, Edward Kelly. In the portrait below you can clearly see Kelly availing himself of Trithemius.

Figure 11: Edward Kelly reading Trithemius.

On the Question of his Teacher

As we have seen already, Trithemius was indeed an inspiration to others and in some cases even a teacher himself. Although he was responsible in many ways for his own education because of his thirst for knowledge from a very young age and his later life within the walls of many a library. But did he have a mentor, a role model, a teacher? Who was it that started him on his journey into the esoteric and the occult?

Sadly, for us this very question leaves more mystery than conclusions, and although there has been much debate about this matter, to this day it remains unresolved with two opposing schools of thought. Firstly, that Trithemius, by his own admission, was initiated into the world of magic by one Libanius Gallus, a gentleman of mystery and intrigue. Libanius, by Trithemius' account, visited Spanheim in 1495 where they both engaged in conversation on topics of an occult nature, wherein Libanius then became the intermediary teacher between Trithemius and his own teacher Pelagius, "the Hermit of Majorca."

Pelagius, by Trithemius' account, was the adopted name of the aristocrat Fernando of Cordova. He was said to have travelled the world, like Cagliostro, amazing people with the powers of his mind. His capacious memory, from which he could quote holy scripture at length, as well as the works of the great physicians, philosophers and theologians was just one of his skills. His abilities related not only to the past but also to the present and the future and he was apparently fluent in several languages including Hebrew, Greek, Latin, Arabic and Aramaic.

Having renounced his former life for the love of Christ, Fernando moved to the Island of Majorca where adopted the persona of a hermit under his new pseudonym. Pelagius was also reputed to have an exceptional library, including many books on occult subjects, the majority of which he would leave to his one and only direct student Libanius. Pelagius' talents were like those of another contemporary magician, an Italian called Giovanni Mercurio da Correggio, whose history Trithemius recorded when writing up the annals of Hirsau (formerly Hirschau) Abbey. Mercurio maintained that his powers came "not with the help of demons, but by that art of natural magic which the ancient kings and wise men held in great esteem."

The list of reputed manuscripts containing reference to Pelagius in the Bibliography is suggestive, but far from complete, as I'm sure other examples will come to light in the future.

The second and opposite opinion on this matter, and probably currently the most popular due to the overwhelming lack of evidence to prove otherwise, is that Trithemius created this rather colourful history entirely by himself. Certainly, the above information and the remarkable provenance of the lineage of Trithemius' magical education is sketchy at best, with no reference outside of Trithemius' own accounts to either of his mentors. Likewise, the link between the real-life Fernando of Cordova's later life and the master hermit magician known as 'Pelagius' is also considered highly questionable, with little to no corroborating historical evidence presented other than what was written in Trithemius' *Chronicon Sponheimense*.

Furthermore, Libanius Gallus, a man of great intellect, education and ability, who travelled around as Trithemius once did, appears to have no other historical record outside of this story, something that does strike one as very suspicious, considering how well such things at that time were documented. Of course, this may simply be the case of documents not yet uncovered or lost with time, but given that Trithemius was also known to on occasion 'stretch' the truth when documenting historical events to suit a particular agenda, this does not improve one's confidence in such matters.

Trithemius' love of history is well documented. He very much enjoyed Greek and Roman history, so he would be very familiar with Libanius (c. 314–392/3) a prolific writer known as one of the best documented teachers of higher education and history in the ancient world. Libanius would in turn no doubt have documented the times of Constantius Gallus, a statesman and ruler in the eastern provinces of the Roman Empire from 351 to 354. These names might have prompted Trithemius' historical imagination.

Likewise, there is the historical Pelagius the Hermit (died c. 950), who lived in Solovio in the Libredón forest in 813 AD and was said to have seen for several nights a shower of stars on the same hill in the forest. Amazed at these lights, he reported them to Bishop Theodemir of Iria Flavia. Theodemir went to Solovio to see the phenomenon for himself where he discovered a stone sepulchre in which rested the Apostle James the Great and two of his disciples. The body of the Apostle was reputedly brought from Palestine to nearby Iria Flavia by ship.

Both events could certainly have inspired Trithemius in his creation of these characters' names. Of course, this is just a speculative example, but interesting nonetheless, for fact is probably the best foundation of believable fiction.

With regard to the manuscripts attributed to Pelagius and Libanius one could also argue that they could have easily been the creations of Trithemius' scriptorium, and subsequently copied through history with no one any the wiser.[1] It would certainly appear that the known examples are from later periods, and this practice itself is most definitely not unknown in the world of magic.

As it stands there is still too little historical information to make a definitive conclusion on this argument either way, however, there does appear to be more holes in Trithemius' magical provenance than there are facts, leaving his story hanging on a very thin thread indeed. Until further information comes to light the case remains open for everyone to draw their own conclusions.

---

[1] See Figure 3.

THE MANUSCRIPT

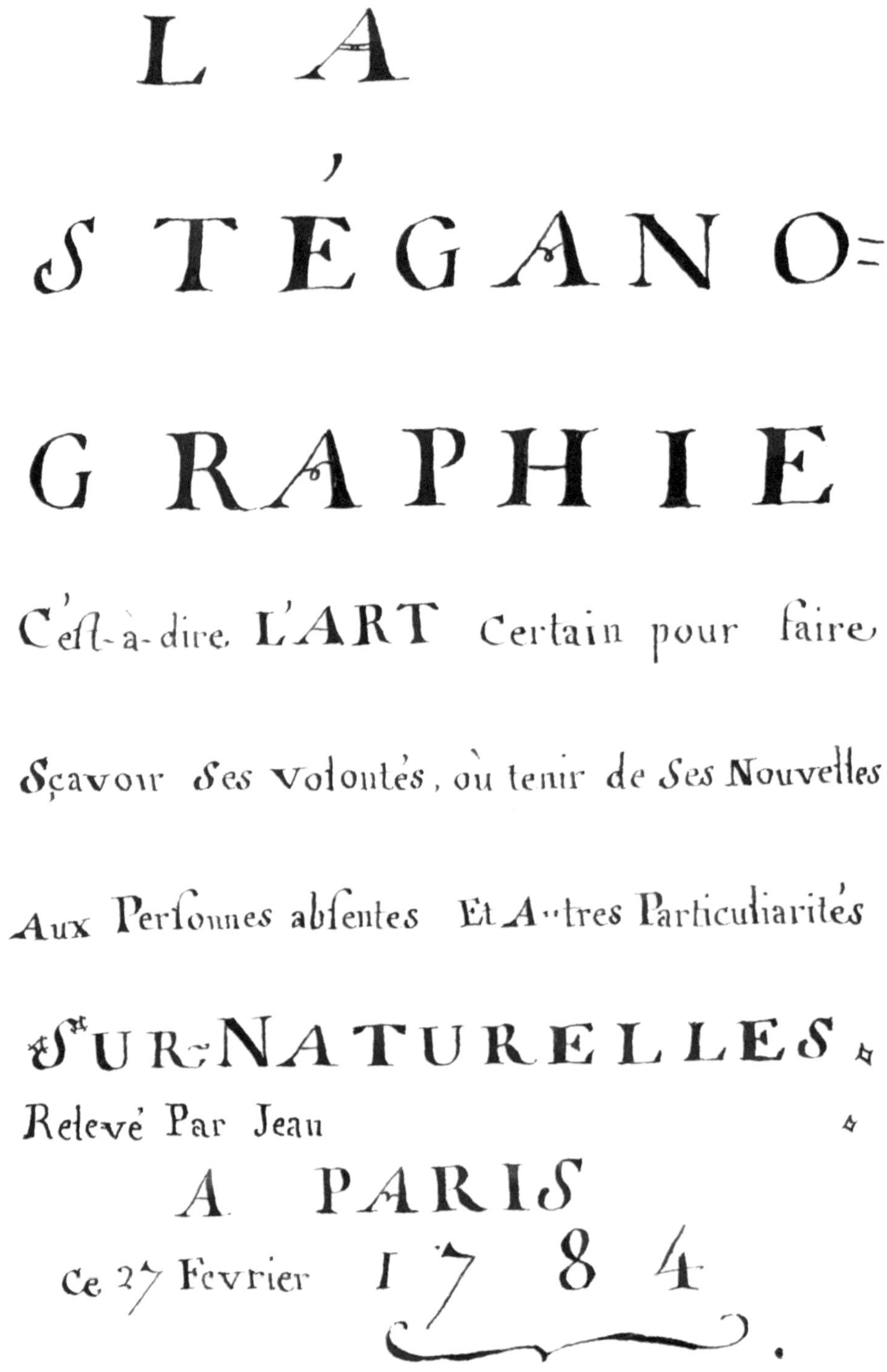

LA STÉGANO= GRAPHIE

C'est-à-dire L'ART Certain pour faire

Sçavoir Ses volontés, où tenir de Ses Nouvelles

Aux Personnes absentes Et Autres Particularités

Sur-Naturelles

Relevé Par Jean

A PARIS

Ce 27 Fevrier 1784.

Figure 12: Title page of French manuscript BPH MS 277.

The
STEGANOGRAPHIA

That is to say, the Certain Art to make known one's thoughts, or to keep up with the news of absent persons, and other supernatural particulars revealed by Johannes [Trithemius, Abbot of Spanheim][1]

[and translated into French] in Paris on 27 February, 1784.[2]

---

[1] Relevé par Jean…" The last four words in brackets above were scratched out.
[2] Title page from the French BPH MS 277.

[THE CONTENTS OF BOOK I]

NOTES AND OBSERVATIONS
relevant to the content of these experiences

Chapter 1. The First Chapter, first and second pages, an introduction to the operations of the Art, the preparation of the Map [of the 16 Winds]; and the references in the margin. [p. 1 & 2]

Chapter 2. Which also contains instructions. p. 6.[1]

Chapter 3. It is said that the Spirit that one wants to send, must be first called and named, immediately after the principal spirit and Prince of each chapter for all the operations of this Art (the note is at the end of this Chapter, p. 13). His Office is to announce someone's arrival, their route and travels. p. 12.

Chapter 4. This Spirit [Aseliel] has power as far as Love is concerned. p. 13.

Chapter 5. Note on the delay of the Spirit that is invoked, that sometimes appears quickly and sometimes slowly. p. 18.

Chapter 6. Remarks on the operation of the Spirits invoked, which operate invisibly. His Office and power [Gediel] are to announce and prevent future dangers and perils. p. 20.

Chapter 7. A note on the vassals who are absent while the operator entrusts his secret to the Dukes. Their powers are to announce to a friend the Prince's secret advice. This chapter refers to Chapter 32, p. 74. p. 23.

Chapter 8. The powers of this Spirit [Maseriel] are to teach and unveil the secrets of human Arts, Philosophy, Magic, Necromancy, and of all the admirable and secret operations which are known only to very few people. p. 24.

Chapter 9. This Spirit's Power [Malgaras] is to announce the secrets of families. Notice the invocation of the Spirits in the table of the said chapter and the way we must summon them, and other remarks. p. 28.

Chapter 10. The Office of this Spirit [Dorothiel] is to announce all the secrets which pertain to spiritual affairs and Ecclesiastical gifts, benefits, prelatures, dignities, and the like. Note on the 2nd conjuration which must be repeated up to 4 times. p. 32.

Chapter 11. This Spirit [Usiel] has power over hidden treasures. Note on the

---

[1] The page numbers in this Contents list refer to the manuscript pages of Book I, not the printed pages of this volume.

character, and on the sign of deep mystery (p. 34). See p. 2 at the mark 'R' p. 32.

Chapter 12. The Powers of these Spirits [under Cabariel] are to announce to one or more friends of the operator, to discover the pitfalls, and reveal the most secret traps, which we must be aware of, and to warn those who are absent. p. 35.

Chapter 13. These Spirit Offices [under Raysiel] are concerned with death, giving advice to friends of the operator, and announcing secrets and traditions. p. 37.

Chapter 14. Their Office is to announce domestic/family secrets. p. 40.

Chapter 15. Their Office [under Symiel] is to announce to the Princes and great Lords the most secret intentions, and the secrets of operating with fidelity and mystery. p. 42.

Chapter 16. Their Office [under Armadiel] is to announce the secret commissions of the Princes and Lords to their subjects, or to their friends. p. 44.

Chapter. 17.[1] Where everything related to the EAST is contained. p. 46.
The Circle which contains the Four Parts of the universe. page 49.

Chapter. 18. Where everything related to SOUTH is contained. p. 50.

Chapter. 19. Where everything is contained related to the WEST. p. 51.

Chapter. 20. It contains all that relates to the NORTH. p. 53.

Chapter. 21. The Spirit [Geradiel] has great properties. It responds easily and does not require a particular location, like those Spirits listed above. p. 55.

Chapter. 22. This is a Nocturnal Spirit [Buriel] which has great properties, but we must consider what is announced there. Earth Spirits. p. 57-59.

Chapter. 23 This is an aquatic Spirit [Hydriel] which has power over all that relates to the waters. And to very large properties. p. 59.

Chapter. 24. This Spirit [Pyrichiel] is Igneous and is not one of the least of this Art. p. 61.

Chapter. 25. This Spirit [Emoniel] lives in the woods, he is good at everything in general. p. 63.

Chapter 26. He is a Powerful Airy Prince [Icosiel], who has great properties and, being compelled, he grants you one of his subjects, to be bound to you during the course of your life.[2] p. 64.

---

[1] Chapters 17 to 20 show the 4 principal Princes which are summarised in Figure 13.
[2] As a familiar.

Chapter. 27 This Spirit [Soleviel] and his subjects are very familiar with having communication and conversations with people. p. 66.

Chapter 28. The marvellous Powers of this Spirit [Menachiel] with regard to Kings and Princes, etc. p. 68.

[**Chapter 29.** The Supreme Spirit and Emperor is called MACARIEL. p. 69. [1]

Chapter 30. The Supreme Emperor is called URIEL. p. 71.

Chapter 31. We still have one of the great Princes [Bydiel] who are deputed to us to operate in this Art. p. 73.

Chapter 32. In this chapter, we make a recapitulation of the chapters described above. p. 74.][2]

---

[1] The Chapter headings from Chapter 29 to Chapter 32 do not appear in the manuscript but have been added here from descriptions in the actual chapters.
[2] This is followed by 10 blank pages, meant to be space for the Contents of the rest of the manuscript, which was never written.

[I]

Table 1: Circular Table of Direction and Universal Map of the 16 winds.

Wherein is represented each Part of the Sixteen Winds, and the Princes of the Spirits of the Air, each in the Mansion they inhabit, which indicates from which direction they must be invoked, according to their Office,[1] and their calling in order to respond to the Operator.[2]

---

[1] The 'Office' of a spirit is its list of their abilities or specialities.
[2] D = number of day Spirits; N = number of night Spirits; inner two rings = number of vassals and sub-servants.

[FRENCH PREFACE]

[II] **STEGANOGRAPHY,** that is to say the certain Art, to make known his wishes, or to give news of absent persons, and other supernatural features.

ADVICE TO THE READER

It is good to warn you dear reader that the letters R. & N.[1] which are marked in this book, some to numbers, others to characters, others to the lyrics,[2] or to the page number, or in the margin to which they are added, these must be marked with red ink or coloured red, or with black. You should observe to adorn each chapter title in red or black because it is the Key to achieving the operations of this Art.[3]

The 'Table of Direction and Universal Map' represented above [Table 1 on the previous page] contains in it the sixteen Mansions or residences of the Princes of the Intelligences[4] which one can invoke for various urgent affairs, as well as their Dukes, Counts and sub-servants, that is to say, the Spirits subject to these Princes, and this both in the day and at night, to achieve the operations which are dependent on each of the said Princes. They must be called each from his own direction, and the Call must be pronounced in the mystical language,[5] such as it is in each chapter, for each Prince has their own Offices,[6] different from the others. For example, Pamersiel must be called from the eastern side from which comes the full east wind, which is marked Orient.[7] Thus Malgaras must be called from the west, called the Occident, whence comes the full westerly wind, this part of the universe being opposite to the east. This parallels the opposition of the First Mansion to the Ninth Mansion, as similarly the Prince Barmiel who is in the Fifth Mansion being to the South (from which comes the South wind), is similarly opposed to Prince Raysiel who is in the Thirteenth Mansion located at the North, from which comes the full wind of the North.

[III] *Knowledge and Properties of the Winds*, and whence they proceed.

Although the winds perceptibly change the air, and dispose of the bodies of this

---

[1] These are effectively printer's instructions: R = Rouge (red) and N = Noir (black). In Latin editions, red is also marked R (for Rot) but black is marked with S (for Schwarz). In this edition R = red and B = black.
[2] i.e. the conjurations.
[3] Where so marked. In fact, the chapter headings are only marked to be printed in red part of the way through the manuscript, leaving the bulk of the chapters unmarked.
[4] Intelligences = Angels.
[5] *Langue Mistique*.
[6] His functions or abilities.
[7] It is an old convention that there is a connection between wind or breath and spirit which are both translated as *spiritus* in Latin. In both Oxford and Athens, one of the oldest buildings is the Tower of the Winds which indicates the direction from which each of the winds comes. As always, spirit direction is a very important part of magic.

lower region, and they sometimes cause cold, hot, humid, rainy or sunny weather, it is therefore necessary to know which wind and from where it proceeds and where it goes.

So to have a perfect knowledge of that which we call wind is to know it is a kind of exhalation drawn from the Earth by the virtue of the sun, and the hot stars, and dries up at his first birth which (after having been repelled from the coldness, being in the second region of the air) moves obliquely, and will see the earth and which comes from various parts of the horizon. This is what makes them (the winds) diverse, depending on the part of the Elementary or Aerial world from which they come and blow.

But to find directly at a certain time what wind reigns and where it starts from on the horizon and where proceeds, it is necessary to have recourse to a good weather vane well exposed, that is in a place where the wind can come naturally without deflection, or the impediment of walls or other things, on which you should erect a moving vane in the centre, which is perturbed by the wind, which will turn so that the hinge (or *girouette*) of the said handle, will tell you which wind is then blowing and prevailing in the circuit of the said machine, which you can see in the 'Table of Direction and Universal Map' in which you will find the Four Cardinal Winds, with their collateral [directions].

On the line of true East is the full wind from the East, next is the one called east-south-east, the second collateral is called southeast, and the third is called south-south-east. Here are the parts and names of winds from the east at Midi, the full Midi is the wind from the South, then its first collateral is called south-south-west, its second is called [IV] southwest, and the third west-south-west. So here are the winds from Midi (South) to the place called Occident (West), from the West is the place from which comes the wind named West, its followers and collaterals are: for the first [collateral], the wind which is called west-north-west, the second northwest, and the third north-north-west.[1]

Here are the winds from the Occident (West) to the Septentrion (North), it flees from them presently the Septentrion (North) which is the opposite of Midi (South) from which the full wind comes from the North, the first of its collaterals is thus called north-north-east, the second which is in the middle between the north and the east, and is therefore called northeast, finally the third and last is called east-north-east, as you can see in the Universal Map, where the names of the winds are written under different names, but I report them in the vulgar terms used and known in our language, as well as all the content of the body of this work which was originally in German and Latin.

It should be known now that the above-named winds have always had various

---

[1] This rather confused passage is simply the naming of winds proceeding clockwise from East, as is shown graphically and more simply on the 'Table of Direction and Universal Map' (Table 1).

effects, for some are beneficial and others pernicious and unhealthy according to the place or region from whence they proceed, because the east-south-east wind which is the wind from the East of Winter, it is hot, dry, pure, and subtle: it engenders the clouds and makes the trees bloom, and gives health to the body: its collaterals are of the same nature like the east-north-east wind, which is directly to the east of Summer, i.e. where the sun rises on the longest days [Summer Solstice], just as the winter east which is similar when the sun rises on the shortest days [Winter Solstice], this east-north-east wind which wastes everything, and the opposite winds which are in the western part are cold and wet these are the ones that cause diseases, rains, and thunders. The wind which comes from the side of the South, which is called with its collaterals, is hot and humid, and they cause several diseases and heavy rains. [V] Finally in the Northern quarter is the full North wind with its neighbours, they are cold and dry, dropping rain, giving health to the body but harming the flowers of the trees, the goods of the Earth.[1]

Here is the detail of the Four Parts of the universe with each of the cardinal winds and their collaterals which are three in number for each of the principal winds which are called Cardinals which can be seen in the Universal Map, which makes a Division into sixteen Parts, where the great Prince of each part whose name is written in red as well as their seals or seal which is also traced in red,[2] with the number of the Dukes and Counts, who submit to every great Prince both for the day and for the night, which is marked by the letter 'D' meaning Diurnal for the day, and what is marked by the letter 'N' meaning Nocturnal for the night, with the number of their vassals and the sub-servants who are marked in the last two [inner] circles. Where there are only zeros, there are no sub-servants.

---

[1] This description of the nature of winds and their impact on health is local to France, and not very relevant to other regions, although there is relevance to magic.
[2] Not done consistently in the manuscript.

APOLOGY FOR THE WONDERFUL NATURAL AND SUPERNATURAL EFFECTS

That which is taught in this book, by the care and vigilance of the author, is the means of making more than a hundred kinds of occult writing to express, by such an infinity of manners all that one may want [to say] without any transposition or switching of letters one for the other, so that we can in no way suspect that it is ciphered under which there is another hidden meaning than that of which is apparent, since these are all clear and intelligible words of a sequence of connected words. But [VI] inside there is everything else which is reserved for him who can understand the artifice. What's more, to transmit his thought to whomever you want, provided he [the recipient] knows the secret: through any long distance, even more than a hundred leagues, without words, without writings, or any mark or sign whatsoever or note of such nature as it may be: and this by a messenger who will know nothing about it and who will not be able to reveal anything even if he would be discomforted, tortured, and then questioned: and even more without a messenger, even if that person were imprisoned three leagues underground, at all times and in all places without any superstition, nor help and means of assistance by the Spirits but otherwise [only] by the pure and simple way of Nature.[1]

Moreover, besides that, an ignoramus who will never know Latin can find here the means to learn it in less than two hours, he will be able to read and write it.[2] He may want to express his conceptions passably, and what is more admirable, he will be able to read through a wall even if it were three feet thick, what is written behind it.[3]

What miracle can be found in Nature that is more admirable than that grand glass machine built by Sapor, King of Persia[4] who sat in the centre, as in the sphere and roundness of the Earth, seeing under his feet the Stars, the Stars which set and rise, even if he were a mortal man, it seemed to him to be over all the highness and expectation of immortality, but a Deity or heavenly Spirit could be hidden in the statue of Memnon looks like a miracle, because whenever it was lit by the rising sun [the statue] made a great sound and murmur,[5] and every time the man who

---

[1] That is what Trithemius would like his interrogators to believe, that the process is natural and without the use of Spirits.
[2] This unlikely sounding skill actually occurs when the person receiving the message hears it in good Latin, even though it was originally expressed in the native language of the person originating the message.
[3] Again, it is the spirit who conveys the message, not the faculty of X-ray vision.
[4] Either Shapur I (r. 240-270 CE) who committed the Avesta to writing and conquered Harran, or less likely Shapur II (r. 309-379 CE).
[5] The colossal statues of Amenhotep III which emit sounds as they are warmed by the rays of the morning sun.

was its author and inventor [was seen] as a secondary cause. As Srabon[1] and Cornelius Tacitus[2] relate, it may be added here that those who did these things [VII] may have followed and taken courses in the Universities, and may have made great efforts in studying to acquire this science. It could be so. But how does it come about that those who pursue their course in the Universities in this century cannot attain to this knowledge, nor acquire such a high science? For there is neither a high nor secret philosophy that can show the guaranteed means [to achieve these feats], as it has been done more since that time when these individuals reigned, there has not been found any who has done something similar, or at least which has been uncovered nowadays (of the closed mouth response) we will say therefore that these are the studies or the virtues of Apollo. All this is nothing, for it is God himself who makes himself admired in these creatures, but what is more admirable and which surpasses all human knowledge and which more is to show also that the soul learned by itself without anyone teaching it, for it meets a well-organized and tempered body, particularly the brain, and that of a very delicate temperament: there have been men who without ever having studied, do admirable things [such as] a labourer having fallen ill, spoke a wonderful speech to his assistants recommending his salvation to them, and praying them to have regard for his children and his wife, if it pleases God to call him from this world, with so many terms of rhetoric, and of such a great elegance and vocable purity, which Cicero could have found while speaking before the Senate.[3]

We can certify here by very true history that several men who were ignoramuses spoke Latin without ever having learned it, there was a child aged five who told everyone who went to see him, their virtues and vices and sometimes recounted with such certainty like those who speak by conjecture and signs,[4] and for this reason no one dared to go to see him, [VIII] fearing the truth he discovered. One day a surgeon went to see him, to visit him, he told him to take care of whatever you do, because you have hardly any more days to live, and your wife must remarry a merchant, which turned out to be true, though it was said haphazardly, and it was all accomplished in less than six months. Here is a marvellous prognosis.

There is no doubt that one can hear people say every day to those who have no knowledge of Natural Philosophy, or who shun it and despise it, that all this is trickery and lies (and if by chance there is something true, it is that the Devil, depending on whether he is shrewd, cunning, or subtle, could by God's

---

[1] Strabo (64 BCE – after 21 CE).
[2] Cornelius Tacitus (c. 56 – 118 CE) was a second-century CE Roman senator and historian who wrote the *Annals*. He was decidedly anti-Christian, and referred to Christianity as "that deadly superstition."
[3] Cicero (106-43 BCE) was famous for the elegance of his speech.
[4] Speaking the truth like a prophet interpreting the meaning of signs.

permission, have entered into the body of this child, as well as that of other men who have surpassed the common man), having made them say and exercise great things that are unnatural, but they are greatly mistaken because the Devil cannot know what is of the future, not having the Spirit of Prophecy, they take it for a strong argument to say that this is false, because we do not understand how it can be done: as if the difficult and very high things were subject to harsh understandings, and allowed themselves to be understood.[1]

It is not a question here of convincing those who have a lack of understanding, because that would be working in vain: but we can say here, with the great Aristotle, that men tempered according to what the work requires, can know many things without having specifically heard about them, and without having learned them from anyone. So here is what he says.

Many also, because this heat is near to [the heat of] faeces or subsiding [heat] are prevented and surprised by some madness, illnesses or blurring and are inflamed with a furious instinct for which reason they become sibyls and prophets. The poet Marcus, a citizen of Syracuse was the best poet when he had [IX] reached this point, to the degree of heat in his mind: those who have this loose and moderate heat are entirely melancholic but much wiser. Aristotle confesses very strongly that in the excessive and extreme heat of the brain, many men have foreknowledge of things coming, like the Sibyls:[2] What he says does not proceed on account of disease, but by the inequality of natural heat: which he proves by the example of Marcus the Syracusan, who was marvellous in his poetry, but for the too great heat of the brain he was out of himself, and when this heat came to be moderated he lost this ability, so that not only Aristotle admits as the main cause of these strange cases the temperament of the brain, and confess by the same means that it is a Divine Revelation and not a natural thing. Hippocrates*[3] was the first who called these things marvellous divinity, we ask here the reason why there were children who spoke from their birth, perhaps we will say to the custom that God or the Enemy[4] are authors of these prodigious effects: they answered well that God is the author and not the Enemy, but also we must not ignore that a very delicate temperament is necessary, and that children who are begotten of cold and dry seed, such as are those who [are born of] one in old age, a few days after they are born begin to discourse and to philosophise,[5] because the cold and dry temperament is very suitable for works of the reasonable soul, so that the prompt temperature of the brain compensates for this defect which had been done by the

---

[1] *Manuscript note*: It will be brought to the sleeping, in *Ecclesiastes* Chapter 8, reference to pr. Chapter 18, v. 2 and Chapter 24, v. 1, Chapter 36 v. 1, 13 and 18.
[2] *Manuscript note*: The Sibyls admitted by the Church had this natural disposition, as Aristotle says. And above the Prophetic Spirit.
[3] *Manuscript note*: in Book I of the *Prognostics* 7.
[4] The Devil.
[5] *Manuscript note*: Why [some] children speak as soon as they are born.

length of time: but the difference between the Prophetic Spirit and the Natural Spirit is that which God has said by the mouth of the Prophets is infallible, because it is his express word: and what man predicts by the force of his imagination has not got this certainty.

[X] Know therefore, which person is the one who could say that the aforesaid child who discovered the virtues and vices [of his callers], that it was by Diabolical Art that he returned such answers to those who went to see him and question him? Consider therefore that God gives to men certain supernatural Grace by which they can know which are the works of God,[1] and which are those of the Devil. And St. Paul puts it among the Divine gifts, and calls it the 'discretion of the Spirit,' by which one knows whether the Spirit who comes to touch us, is good or bad, because the Devil often comes to us under the appearance of a good Angel to deceive us, by means of which we greatly need this Grace and this supernatural gift, to know him and to discern the good. Those who do not have the Spirit proper to Natural Philosophy are the most driven away from this Grace, because this supernatural science that God gives, falls under one and the same power which is the understanding, since God accommodates himself to distributing his graces, to the good nature of each, as has been said.*[2]

When Jacob knew at the point of his death (the time when the soul is freest to see what is to come) all his twelve sons came into his room to see him, he announced to each one his particular virtues and vices, prophesying what was to befall them, and their nephews likewise, it is certain that he did this in the Spirit of God, but if the Holy Scripture and our faith did not certify it to us, how will we know that this is the work of God or the Devil's work? What the aforesaid child was doing who declared the vices and the virtues to those who went to see it, wherever this fact is similar to that of Jacob, they think that the nature of the reasonable soul is far removed from that of the Devil, and that the powers of those which have the understanding, the imagination and the memory, are of another very different kind: and are taught, because if the rational soul informs a well-organized body, as was that of Adam, it gets a little more, whatever Devil it is and however good it may be, and out of the body, is filled with [XI] powers as high as it can have, and if the Devil finds out the future by conjecturing and discoursing by some signs: the reasonable soul can do the same when it frees itself from the body, or when it has this difference of temperament which is fit for providence. Like the child who predicted the death of the Emperor Julian,[3] having returned from ecstasy, after looking into a mirror warned him of his disaster, and how his enemies were coming and those who were to kill him, without his having any knowledge of it, or having even heard of it.

---

[1] *Manuscript note*: Supernatural Grace given to men.
[2] *Manuscript note*: Genesis chapter 49.
[3] The last pagan Emperor (331-363).

Steganographia

St Augustine tells of a priest from Calamanthie, who when he returned from his contemplations, made marvellous speeches. Herodotus writes about a certain man named Atheus. He assures us that the soul [of Atheus] having abandoned his body several times,[1] and after being transported, saw in dreams various countries, and told the story in the order in which he had seen it, been informed and found true, as if he had been present there. Some philosopher did the same for Pompey,[2] who showed him in a mirror the exercise of his enemies, ready to march into battle: these are the effects of the power of the soul, which being sometimes untied from the earthly plane, and rapt in contemplation of celestial secrets does incredible, miraculous, and monstrous things, and which seems almost to fight with Nature: this is what causes most often the common vulgar [opinions] of the public, which attributes these many things to the invention of demons and evil spirits and that these are diabolical things, but however they must be attributed to man, as [part of his] his own heritage. What do we want to seek most admirable in this reasonable and human animal except the reserved divinity, because if we want to continue by the menu all the singularities and excellencies which are found manifested in man, and which several historians have mentioned, I would rather miss the voice than the subject. It is certain [XII] that he was seen at Carpentras in the county of Avignon, a man who devoted himself to playing instruments, who played bass perfectly well without any master having shown him, moreover he played lutes, zithers, guitars, and mandolins, and other such instruments par excellence. Moreover, it is nowadays seen among us men, some who without having studied or taken the courses in any Faculty, or even at the Universities, and yet are very experts in the art of surgery, making admirable cures beyond the imagination of the Doctors of the Sorbonne and of the Faculty, from which one sees a number of physical and admirable marvels: on this the Hebrew, Platonic, and Egyptian Cabalists, have held for certain that when the soul is sent from heaven into man which is accompanied and led by a Spirit or Angel (whom they named a Daemon): which some say is a double, namely the astrologers and Platonists, that one is proper to geniture, and the other to profession: but those who constitute it triple, establish one more before the other two, namely sacred or divine. Saying that it comes from the divinity, and that it is assigned or intended for the rational soul: and they say that the one of geniture, whom they call Genius or good or bad Angel, comes of the arrangement of the world and of the situation and movement of the Stars, to which it is subject and submissive or meaning the profession of one who is born, as Astrologers say, to be under Mars, Venus, and Mercury in the First, Seventh to Tenth houses, and such is the opinion of the Hebrew cabalists, and Egyptian astrologers, however it is necessarily stopped at the word of God as being the very same truth.

---

[1] Astral projection.
[2] Pompey the Great (106-48 BCE), a Roman statesman.

It is written in the 1st chapter of the *Epistle to the Hebrews*[1] that the Angels are serving Spirits, ordained for the aid, keeping, and relief of those who are destined for salvation: and to show that men, especially those chosen by God, are not without guards, whose merit good Christians acquire by joining our Holy Mother Church who [XIII] celebrate October 2.[2] Jesus Christ speaking of little children,[3] says we should not despise them because their Angels are always in heaven seeing the Face of God his Father.[4] And David sings that God commanded his Angels to take care of His own.[5] And elsewhere that the Angels have encamped around those who fear God: and from this it may be assured that everyone has a good angel and a bad one, as we find in the memoirs of the Hebrews that Adam and his son Noah, Abraham, Isaac, Jacob, Moses, Elijah, and Tobit, each had a good Angel, and each had very great knowledge of, and conversation with their Angel, one each of them had in his own right. St Peter also had one who was not only a guardian but a familiar:[6] but also to his other friends, which can be confirmed by the answer which was given by those who were in the assemblies to pray (when St Peter was a prisoner) in the house of Mary mother of John surnamed Mark: to the girl named Rhode, who having come to the door of the porch to listen, and having recognised the voice of St. Peter, reported that to those assembled, who replied that it was not he; but his Angel. Lactantius[7] speaking also of Daemons says that God has sent Angels to guard men, lest the Devil ruin them entirely: why do we agree with what Saint Peter says, "because your adversary the devil, as a roaring lion, walketh about, seeking whom he may devour," and St. Paul says as much in Chapter 6 of the *Epistle to the Ephesians*.[8] It is therefore certain that the Angels and good Spirits are given and established by God, for keeping, instruction, help, for giving enlightenment, and for teaching those who are destined for their proper profession: as also that men are surrounded by evil Angels which have been called by the Platonists by the common name 'daemons,' of which they must carefully preserve and guarantee [XIV] according to what is attested by the famous *Arbatel*[9] (which we will do, he says) always having [religious] fear and the Law of

---

[1] *Manuscript note*: St. Paul to H[ebrews] Chapter 1, v. 14.
[2] The Celebration day of Guardian Angels.
[3] *Manuscript note*: St. Matthew Chapter 18, v. 10
[4] *Manuscript note*: Ps[alm] 90.
[5] *Manuscript note*: Ps[alm] 33, v. 7.
[6] It is noteworthy to see that the concept of familiar was also extended to saints as well as magicians.
[7] Lactantius (c. 250-c. 325 CE) was a Berber born into a pagan family who later converted to Christianity. Before conversion he was associated with Porphyry and he was familiar with Jewish, Christian, Egyptian and Iranian apocalyptic material. As an erudite theologian, he wrote a lot of interesting material on spirits and angels before Christian doctrine was fully consolidated a century later. He also wrote against pagan critics of Christianity.
[8] *Manuscript note*: v. 11, 12.
[9] A well-known grimoire that was first printed in 1559. It may have been written by Jacques Gohory (1520-1576). It contains one of the first mentions of the seven Olympic Spirits, which are spirits of Greek origin, rather than spirits connected to the gods of Olympus.

God before our eyes, to consider and take heed that if there is a Spirit who urges and teaches, but does not incite us to do anything that is against God, for if the evil Spirit tempted our Saviour by quoting to him the Holy Scriptures, he has all the more reason to tempt us, we who are so fragile. But if we fear and honour the Author of all things; we will have Good Spirits who will bring us the knowledge of admirable and supernatural things.

I do not know the opinion that everyone can have on this subject, but I know very well that it found a large number of subjects who learned and instituted many beautiful things, in contemplation (as it is said above) and have become very expert, and that without the aid of a master, or book, but indeed by the communication of an Angel or Spirit, or a Genie that God has allocated for this effect, which is vividly apparent, provided that one has real faith. It is therefore this Spirit of which the great Paracelsus speaks which he calls the 'constellated Ascendant'[1] in these terms. The constellated Ascendant (he says) of him who diligently seeks the secrets of Nature (which are the works of God) which teaches them all, provided he is a good worker, because of the familiarity he has with it, and according to the size of it, from here comes the great workers who have excelled in the Arts, and who have sought their [magical] experiences by means of beryls, mirrors, nails,[2] and birds, also had their Ascendant which rewarded their credulity with beautiful inventions; because they had great debt, this way has provided and given various good and bad remedies, certain and uncertain according to the suitability of the Ascendant of the artist with his progeny. He who hears these things knows well that it is necessary to repudiate and forsake all the speeches and cackles of the Sophists, as opposed to the mother of experience. This is what Paracelsus says of it, and to tell the truth, Mother Nature gives enough of herself to [XV] know by the look and contemplation of all the parts of the body, by the lines & lineaments that are drawn and written in the hands,[3] and by the gaze of the face, when she always conjoins the enemy with her conqueror,[4] because there is no disease which does not have its [indicative] form, which also teaches its entirely incontinent remedy,[5] as the anatomy of the eyes to that of Euphrase[6] have suitability and agreement together; because they come from the same seed, and only know each other by the look which accordingly shows that Eyebright preserves the eyes from diseases, and cures those that afflict them. As well as all the parts of the body which have the same relations with what best suits them, what remains to be known to those who practice the art of Medicine. See the admonitory preface of [David] de Planis Campy, on page 59 and the following pages.[7]

---

[1] According to this author "the Demon or Spirit who presides over birth."
[2] Using a finger nail as an impromptu skrying surface.
[3] Palmistry.
[4] The disease appears with an indication of its remedy.
[5] 'Incontinent' because indicators of the remedy are supposedly so readily available.
[6] Euphrase is the eye herb Eyebright.
[7] David de Planis Campy was a surgeon who wrote a book on phlebotomy published in 1621.

Since God arranged these things with such propriety [with regards] to the parts of our body, will not have given help and assistance as well, as a sure conduct to our reasonable soul, it would be impiety to think otherwise; let's confess freely, with the great Paracelsus, that we have a constellated Ascendant, it remains to recognise it, in order to use it according to God's will if it is good, but if it is bad it must be absolutely rejected.

Now it should be noted that a constellated Ascendant is nothing other than the daemon, or Spirit who presides over one's birth; the one that was given and sent for your conduct and instruction, this is what man should know, by his care which he should bring to it to require it and appropriate it, (according to the advice and opinion of Marsilio Ficino)[1] if he wants to prosper in what it incites him to do, and applies himself either to letters or otherwise; because the one who does the opposite of what he incites him to do, if he is good however, he benefits nothing, and does not waste time. The Author holds and is assured that every good Christian must believe that the good constellated Ascendant is our good Angel, and the bad is the bad Angel which is treated quite amply above, or one can see what is written about it; so that the [XVI] Good Angel, whom we call the constellated Ascendant, greatly rewards the belief and sorrow of those who are sincere in their search for the secrets of Nature by teaching them what the Stars cannot simply do by their influences.

There would be many things to say here both on astrology and on the judgments of physiognomy, properties of the signs of the Zodiac and complexions; but we do not report if all this is true, since it is written that the 'sage will dominate the Stars,' and he who is the Author says that his belief is otherwise: for he holds with all firmness, that it is given to us at the hour of our Birth, (as it is said above) a good Angel guardian, by the goodness and mercy of God, that if we get ourselves in trouble and that we try to be able to know his name: we would do marvellous and supernatural things; but we should have a real and live cooperating faith in us, and then with all boldness and confidence we will absolutely command the cure for diseases without any other application of remedy than the sign of our salutation, and they will obey us by the almighty power of God.

Those who are in disbelief and do not want to believe what is said above, as well as what is contained in the body of this work under the title of *Steganography*, have only to read what N. S. J. C.[2] said speaking to his disciples touching the fig tree which dried up at his word alone. These are his express words. I tell you in truth, that if any of you in faith like a grain of mustard shows up, and let him say to a

---

[1] Ficino (1433-1499) was a most important Renaissance translator of Greek texts of Plato's works and Neoplatonic and Hermetic texts into Latin.
[2] N.S.J.C = 'Notre saveur Jesus Christ,' our saviour Jesus Christ.

mountain: get up from there and throw yourself into the sea, it will obey him.[1]

The Prince of French poets[2] wrote admirably touching victory in his *Triumph of Faith*: a poem as admirable as it is true, and I did not find it out of place to cite it in this Preface, and here is therefore how he begins, and as he continues on all the stories known and confirmed by passages in Holy Scripture and Sacred Theology.

[XVII] I thought I was at the end of my Holy Career, to win the prize,
> though I didn't deserve it, but here I am very far from it, not having recited only about half of the warrior pomp.

In front of the victorious chariot we carry great Tables, by the real hands of a divine painter, one can, like the bellicose Romans, of invisible faith, have notable victories.

I see from here the wall of Jerico fall, beaten only with the cannon of faith: here is the undefeated Infidel King, by faith he is defeated by Issiah without battle.

Here by the faith of Moses, armed with anger and rage, the least worms, for Pharaoh to torment. Daniel could by his faith defeat the toothless lions and the wild nature of dragons.

See St Paul by his faith, fears not in an island, the deadly sting of a poisonous snake, and Jonah sinks beneath the frothy waves, and finds the hollow belly of a fish for asylum.

In another painting, I see represented an Art surpassing all Arts the laughing Health, of inexorable death, pale infirmity, being by faith, a thousand times overcome.

Moses by his faith got his sister Mary married, [XVIII] Elisha[3] by her faith, had leprosy in a moment, his avaricious valet, having first cured the Viceroy of Syria of the same disease.

To replant faith in the Holy Province, a holy cuttlefish[4] and healed the right hand of this King, who caused the ten parts of Isaac to revolt against himself, against the Lord and against his true Prince.

---

[1] The following manuscript pages XVII – XXIII are devoted to discussing the theological opinions of du Bartas on faith, and add very little to our understanding of magic. Without the du Bartas text in front of you at the time of reading these passages make little sense.

[2] Guillaume de Salluste du Bartas (1549-1590) was an important French Christian poet, who had a noticeable impact on English and Scottish thinking, as well as French, at the end of the 16th century. His poem, *The Triumph of Faith,* is quoted at length over the next few pages. This was first translated into English in 1605 and had quite an effect on people with esoteric interests at that time.

[3] *Elisée* in the French.

[4] The ink of the cuttlefish is a homoeopathic remedy for melancholy, and female complaints.

By faith Paul blinded the great sorcerer Elime,[1] and by faith Peter inflamed with a most just wrath, put to death, at her feet, two forsworn spouses, worthy of punishment for such a horrible crime.

By the faith of his son, Tobit re-contemplates the brightness of the torches spread across the sky, and two poor cripples are restored upright by their king, one from Lystra and the other at the gate of the Temple.

By faith Paul put an end to the bitter dysentery, which was 'scraping the guts' of a rich Maltese man, by the faith of Simon of an impotent Lydian,[2] the long infirmity is promptly cured.

Paul in Troas through faith resurrects Eutychus,[3]
Elijah restores the spirit to the young Sarephtain,
Elisha gives up the soul to the Sunamitain son,
and in Joppa Simon revives Thabité.[4]

On the other hand, I see the painting hanging, of the First four parts of this grand universe.

[XIX] Vulcan dyed red, Earth green haired, the Air the strange clothing, the wave [Water] has the blue side.[5]

Elisha by faith made the pole descend, chariots of fire against the Syrians, Elijah denying the pagan Prophets, made on the moist altar the fire without being caught.

The faith of the three Hebrews whom a King fills with vices, cast into a fiery oven even defend their skins rippling flame: and cause their executioners, to be the executioners of their own torments.

Moses drops a flaming torch. In the Hebrew version, to consume them, who with a profane hand dared to smoke, before the Altar of God, the perfumes of Sabea.[6]

Moses hears from the great God of Battles, made by faith, the high mountains to crumble foundations, and the Earth swallows with its tremors, murmuring in his heart, into his dark entrails.

---

[1] Elymas bar-Jesus, the sorcerer of Paphos was reputedly struck temporarily blind by the magic of St Paul.
[2] *Lydois*.
[3] He fell from a third floor window after dozing off whilst listening to St Paul's speech.
[4] These are all instances of raising someone from the dead. Simon the Tanner is mentioned in *Acts of the Apostles* (Chapters 9 and 10). In Chapter 10:1 Cornelius, a Roman centurion who was stationed in Caesarea, was told by an angel to "Send messengers to Joppa at once and summon a certain Simon, the one known as Peter."
[5] The colours of the four Elements.
[6] The Sabeans were famous as traders in perfumes, which is mentioned in Jeremiah 6:20.

Moses by his faith [ensures] that a nourishing mood abounds, and from rocks, without humours, nourishes his Israelite Host: on the contrary it dries up, the sea within the sea, and the wave within the wave.

Moses spreads, by faith on sweet waters, the colour and taste of black stinking blood, to the contrary by faith Moses changes [XX] bitter liqueurs into savoury liqueurs.

Three times the clear Jordan [river] its wave has opened, to give passage to the beloved of God: once was in the time of the First Hebrew Judge, another in the time of Elisha, and the last in the time of Elijah.

It is really good by faith that the faithful devotee will disturb the serene air of the cloudy fog, truly it is by faith that the air on all sides melts to moisten the camp of the Israelites [with rain].

Even this winged people, whom the windy Air divides of its painted oars, is captive under faith, the raven serves by faith the devout Thesbite,[1] the dove to Noah, and the quails to Moses.

Hey? God who can make faith resist, if the iron [will] that subdues all, is by faith tamed, if on the wave the iron is carried by faith? The faith of Elisha has power over iron.

Faith has only on all human things high and low justice, so she goes even forcing the justice of God, in time and place breaking, the judgments pronounced in its sovereign court.

From Nineveh the faith of repentance followed, the wrath of the Almighty from its leader diverted, the faith of Hezekiah, mighty turned away, the limits set for his too-short life.

[XXI] If he from whom the faith of his Church proceeds, seems like obeying the desires of faith, in that way, should not I be surprised if I even see the Holy Angels stripped of frankness?

Ezekiel by faith has in the pay of the Angels, the Thesbite by faith has them for infants, Peter by faith has them as gatekeepers of the prisons, and Jacob [by faith has them] as conductor to the foreign provinces.[2]

Here is in part a little picture of faith and its effects which are innumerable and incomprehensible, that's why I prefer to keep quiet rather than talk about it ignorantly: for myself, I need to pray to the Lord to kindle in me this true and lively faith, so that all my works may be to his honour and to his glory, to the edification of my neighbour and for the salvation of my soul, always following closer to the principles that have been given to me in the bosom of our Holy

---

[1] The prophet Elijah of Tishbite.
[2] At this point the text ceases to be about Du Bartas' poetry and returns to ordinary prose.

Mother the Apostolic and Roman Church of which I am a son. But could someone ask me if, by having faith only, one could do what is said above, as well as what is specified in the body of this work, I answer them no, that would not be sufficient, for faith without works is dead, says the Apostle: therefore our Art requires solitude, and retirement, because that is what provides [time for] study and contemplation of supernatural marvels, by raising his Spirit to the foot of the throne of the Supreme Divinity, and this by vigils to become perfect in the practices of the Art, by observations, by asking the help and assistance of the Eternal, having a real and living faith in him, we will do miraculous things, for upon him all good things depend: that is why we attribute to him power over all that acts both in heaven and on earth.

[XXII] And not by vain superstition in the Stars, which is a pagan belief, because it is taken for certain by all our Theologians what is written: "that the wise will rule the stars," especially since

> "As much as the Stars cannot constrain, but incline and dispose;
> because whoever wants to dispose,
> we will have no need to fear,
> thus in only one God is it necessary to rest."

I do not want to say, however, that the Stars do not cast their influences on many good and bad events related to the lower bodies: for as du Bartas says on the fourth day of his week:

> "…Never the daily torch does not steal its light from our eyes in broad daylight, that some great Eclipse, and that still Alecto[1] exile for a time from the reign of Pluto, peckish hunger, fatal betrayal, the bloody Enyo,[2] and the bug plague, to overflow upon us a sea of sorrows, and drown the universe either in blood or in tears."

It is true, but so what? It would therefore be necessary to attach as a necessary thing, that the creator to his creatures, which never were and never can be, for as said the same Bartas, on the same day a little lower:

> "Not that by this Stoic speech, I pain myself to tie the Eternal to the hard chain the need for a diamantine knot pressing its free feet into the vines of Destiny.

> [XXIII] I hold the Great God as the First cause, who gives to celestial bodies strength, course, and light; that he holds them in his hand: that not one of them can, pour on mortals only the fate he wills, but, however, everyone must make an effort, to covet from heaven both road and strength.

> In order to see under how many tyrants we were subject to, when the our

---

[1] Alecto was one of the Furies of Greek mythology.
[2] Goddess of war.

late first parents lost their righteousness, and the blind woman in chopping made chopping half of his soul we deflate our hearts: and bend our knees soothed by sighs of the Great God the wrath begging him to ward off hail, storms, the excessively violent cold, the heat and the ravages with which so many times we are threatened by the cruel glances of the wrathful Stars.

Let us pray to the Lord to give us a breath to curb insolence to which the effort of a sad birth pushes us: to pour a little water, to quench in ourselves the furious desires of boiling flesh, and destroy in our hearts the various passions, which are born from the silt of our perverse moods."

Those who will pay attention while reading this, will have no need to fear the Stars, because the sage in Jesus Christ will dominate them (as it is said above) on which I am astonished that there are people so superstitious, to write that there are happy days and perilous days.

[XXIV] I say with the Poet that all days are as happy as each other, whoever argues otherwise will be superstitious, and cannot agree with the saying of the Apostle, for all provide goods, to the righteous man: but for the wicked, all days are perilous.

- Epistle of Monsieur Jean Trithème Abbot, sent to Bostius, the Carme[lite], on *Steganography*.[1]

I have in hand and in my power a greater and more admirable work than is *Polygraphy*; when it was completed, I highlighted it, and even made it public. I hope this work will be found by everyone even higher and more elevated than I call it admirable and marvellous, and therefore here has for a title and is entitled *Steganography*, divided into many Books of which the least will have and will be distinguished in a hundred chapters at the very least.

Steganography, that is to say, the Art which is the certain way of making known by means of the occult writing the will of his heart to those who are absent, by the very-reverend and illustrious Johannes Trithemius, Abbot of Spanheim, and very enlightened and well versed in Natural Magic, and at the head of this work is the key or the true Introduction given by the same Author. Until the great number of people have longed to see this work, and few have had this advantage, but in favour of those who study the secret Philosophy, I have just made it public with the Privilege and consent of the Superiors, printed in Darmstadt, by Baltazar Hofmann in 1621 and translated from the German and Latin, into French in 1780 in Paris.[2]

---

[1] The disastrous effect on Trithemius' life caused by his letter about the *Steganographia* written to Bostius, has been mentioned in more detail in the biography chapter.
[2] This paragraph reads like a title page, but is just presented as part of the text in the manuscript. This is an important part of the editorial history of the present manuscript, showing that it is based on a translation of the 1621 Latin text, done in 1780.

[XXV] It is an opinion among scholars that the sages of antiquity, whom the Greeks call Philosophers, hid under varied figures and under different emblems the secrets of nature or of Art that they had been able to find out by their studies, lest they come to the knowledge of the wicked. Even the most learned of the Jews assure us that Moses, the famous leader of the people of Israel, in his details about the creation of the heavens and the Earth enveloped in simple expressions the ineffable secrets of the Mysteries. Also St. Jerome the deepest and most enlightened of our Church Fathers declares that the *Apocalypse* of St John contains almost as many mysteries as words. I pass over the sages of the Greeks who have enjoyed in their homeland an uncommon esteem. I do not want to give in testimony the most learned of our philosophers and our poets who in writing novels which by a subtle and admirable invention contented the ignorant and the scholars in the thread of a single story. Although the slowness and weakness of my genius make it impossible for me to perfectly imitate these studious lovers of wisdom; I do not, however, stop admiring them and read with all the attention of which I am capable. Because when I consider that, at their bottom, they invented many astonishing things which surpass the reach of other men, I do a certain violence to warm up my genius, and I leave myself by the same confusion with the moderns to imitate somehow those who preceded them. I was not completely wrong in my opinion, since by continual study of their books I learned many things that I did not know before, and through my thoughts and reflections, I opened and cleared to others a way for their search for even the most hidden secrets.

Because I do not have enough erudition nor genius to dare to advance, I have completely grasped this [XXVI] way in which the sages of antiquity used to hide the mysteries. I have however (it seems to me) found many ways, and all different, which are not quite to be rejected, by which I will reveal as much as I want and in safety, the most secret thoughts of my heart to somebody who would be instructed in this Art, and I can make it known to him without fear, illusion, suspicion or surprise of anyone by mail or letter. I had the new invention of this mysterious Art printed and is not without great sorrow that I brought it into this volume, at the behest of the most serene Prince Philip, Count Palatine of the Rhine, Duke of Bavaria and Prince Elector of the Holy Empire of Rome, always invincible Prince, the wise protector of all the philosophers, who seemed to me more than anyone to deserve that I reveal this great secret to him, but lest it reaches the ears of the vulgar, the ignorant, or the wicked, I have thought that I still had to wrap it in so much mystery (because he learns to know and understand the mystery [as opposed to] those who do not know it) that there is no one among the ignorant, unless he is very studious, who can by his own genius penetrate completely, perfectly and according to our intentions into the secret of this science that the Hebrews name the Cabalah[1] made for the understanding of the most hidden mysteries. The knowledge of this

---

[1] 'Cabalah' is used here more as a general knowledge of the mysteries rather than the specifically Jewish practice.

mysterious Art divulged among the wicked and perverted would be no less harmful to the Republic than it would be useful being known to the good.

For just as men devoted to good and practice the virtues bring to light various inventions, being strengths for utility and the common good; so also the wicked and the perverse seek not only in the bad institutes but also in the good [XXVII] and the holiest, opportunities to give more scope to their malice, this same thing can happen to our invention, which is very useful to the Republic and most honourable, as well as in the hands of good people who are truly religious and who fear to offend God, who serves as an instrument for good things; likewise in the hands of the impious and the perverse it is a way for them to exercise their villainy. For just as a good [person] and lover of honesty can always, when he wishes to in safety, with secrecy and without fearing the suspicions of anyone, make known at all times and intimate and express at any distance from places; make known his hidden will for a particular or common good, to another instructed of this Art, and this perfectly abundantly and in full by visible letters to everyone, open or closed in such a way that no one knows or can suspect anything of the author's secret, nor grasp the content even though he may have suspicions; in the same way all perverse, debauched or malicious men even if he would previously be in complete ignorance of the Latin language, as soon as he has understood this Art, he will be able under my instructions to learn in two days, or for a longer time, will already be able to write the following in Latin, in the correct style of the letters in an elegant and quite ornate clear narration, to me or another versed in this Art, by which by the force of the Cabal, he will wrap the secret of his will in so many mysteries that it can only be known to me, and that no one however studious or educated he may be, he will not be able to fully penetrate it without the spiritual help of this Art of which I will speak later, the knowledgeable and the ignorant, the man and the woman, the child and the elder, the good and the wicked, the modest and the immodest, will write in Latin or in some other [XXVIII] language known to him in all climates of the world of Latin, Greek, or a barbarian [language], exempt from all suspicion, by which he will show in the open his art to those who know nothing else, or secretly to those who know something else.

And once this science has been divulged among the wicked, the once promised and contracted by the sacrament between two spouses would no longer be inviolable. While the woman, although until recently in ignorance of the Latin language, now quite well educated in any language or idiom, by words, modest, honest and most chaste, could comprehend to the fullest extent possible the evil and shameless thought and intention of a lover, adulterer, and fornicator though the husband would carry the letters and read them as good, and respond to him and let him know his wishes in the same way, with as much extent and abundance as she pleases, and with all possible security in the same or in other letters, in a fine order and a quite ornate style. In effect, although this science is in itself excellent and quite useful to the whole Republic, however, if it came to the knowledge of the wicked

(God forbid) all the order of the Republic could in the following times be strangely troubled. Public faith in danger, all the letters, the instructions, the contracts, the speeches, finally we would see men who would fall under strange suspicions. Soon we could entrust no one without difficulty or fear to letters some pure and honest they would be, but they would rarely be believed. Because however modest and honest the words would be, we would always believe them concealed beneath deceit, fraud, and trickery, and men would be seized with dread in plain sight, and for the most part be suspicious of their friends as of their foes: and none the less [XXIX] he who will live a thousand years, will not be able to master or become learned enough and experienced enough in this science not to leave behind him an infinity of ways of writing in this Art even with secrecy, with the deepest mysteries and the greater security and sufficient to operate at all at the Will of all men who is versed in it, and which he does not yet seize with his master. Because like the good and bad Aerial Spirits, which the Almighty God created to serve and guide us (by whose Intelligence all the secrets of this Art are revealed to us) are infinite in number and quite incomprehensible; likewise, all the modes, ways, differences, qualities and operations of our Art which we call steganography which contain in the perfection of secrets, wonders, and mysteries unknown and hidden to all mortals, however studious, and however learned, can never be thoroughly known by what someone educated and experienced as you be in this Art, yet you have learned less than you did not know. We cannot therefore know this science thoroughly, indeed because this science is like a very great chaos and of such immense depth that no one can fully penetrate it, because such is the virtue, and the property of this so profound Art. And so hidden that it easily makes the schoolboy, so to speak, incomparably more knowing that the Master, since he is naturally inclined to make progress, and applies the lessons he has drawn from the Cabalistic tradition, and so that no reader to come into the contents of this work by seeing often as he progresses in reading must consider the names, duties, orders, differences, properties, prayers, and all the other operations of the Spirits by whose Intelligences all the secrets of this science are hidden or discovered, do not believe or think that I [XXX] may be a necromancer, magician, or that I have made some pact with the demons and whether I used this or used some other superstition, I have deemed it necessary and proper to save my name and reputation from such infamy, affront and ignominy, by a protest solemnly giving the following prologue with the truth.

Protestation or Oath by the Author
on the Goodness and Honesty of this Art

I therefore say before Almighty God to whom absolutely nothing can be hidden, and before Jesus Christ his only son who must judge the living and the dead, I speak in truth, I swear and protest that each and every one of the things that I have advanced in this work or must say in the sequel, and that all the properties, modes, figures, operations, traditions, receptions, formations, inventions, institutions, changes, and alterations of this science or Art, and all that relates in whole or in particular to its operations by its speculations, its inventions, consecutive, for the said operations and practices, and all that is contained in this present Book is founded on truly catholic and natural principles, that all and each of the things are with God, with a good conscience without violating the Christian faith, conforming to the precepts of the Church, without any superstition, idolatry, and without any Covenant, explicit or implicit with evil Spirits, without suffumigation, adoration, veneration, worship, sacrifice, oblations to demons, and without any fault or sin, whether venial or mortal, and that each and every thing is said with truth, rectitude, sincerity, and purity, and this with the intention that science and practice of this Art employed to a good use can be suitable for a wise man, for a good and faithful Christian, because I am a Christian and committed to [XXXI] my own will, having carried out my desires by embracing and submitting to the monastic laws, I do not wish to live and speak otherwise than would suit a true Christian and a monk who has embraced the rule of our Father St Benedict,[1] and I received from the cradle this same Catholic faith according to the tradition of the Holy Roman Church having been baptized in the name of the Father and of the Son and of the Holy Spirit.

And this faith I believe and hold with the Universal Church of Christians, and will keep it constantly and forever inviolable in my heart, my words and my deeds; so much that I will live with the help of God and will never seek on any occasion whatsoever to turn away from it. So far be it from me to learn where to teach something that is contrary to the purity and harmful to the Christian faith, to good morals, or contrary in any way to the regulations of my state, I fear God and I have sworn to worship and serve him, and I hope never to be separated from Him either during the course of my life or after my death. I put this protestation that I make at the head of this work and it is not without reason, knowing that there will be many who cannot understand what I have written, will come to insult, and to treat my works which are good and pure, not in themselves bad sciences or superstitious inventions.

We, therefore, beg those and all those who will carefully read our precepts, in case they understand this Art secret, to keep it always secret, and not to share with the vulgar such wonderful secrets. But what if they do not understand them (which we know must happen to many) to learn before blaming me? In fact, it is declaring oneself a reckless judge to judge a thing before having recognised the truth of it. So learn [XXXII] this Art before, and then you may bring your judgment to it. And if you can't figure it out, do not blame it on science, because it is true and good, but good to your rude, heavy geniuses. Indeed, I know with certainty that no person of common sense can censure or blame our work, unless he has the misfortune to understand absolutely nothing, but for those to whom it is more

---

[1] Interestingly, St Benedict (480-543) was reputed to be the most successful *effugator daemonum*, or 'one who makes the demons fly,' in other words a successful exorcist. St Benedict medals are still worn today for protection against evil spirits.

familiar to despise wisdom than to study it, I neither be nor would wish that they cannot penetrate our mysterious secrets.

See what is contained in *Psalm* 78. "Give ear, etc. …"[1]

---

[1] 'Psalm 77' in the manuscript. Psalm numbers differ by one between the Catholic and Protestant numbering.

BOOK I

[1]

HERE BEGINS
THE FIRST BOOK OF THE
STEGANOGRAPHIA

of Johannes Trithemius,[1] Abbot of Spanheim,[2]
of the order of St Benedict,[3]
in the Diocese of M[oguntinensis].[4]

Dedicated to the Most Serene Prince Philippe,
Count Palatine of the Rhine, Duke of Bavaria,
and Prince Elector of the Holy Roman Empire, etc.[5]

---

[1] Jean Thritême.
[2] *Note added in a later hand:* "in the Duchy of Simmeren, upper Rhine region in Germany."
[3] St Benoit.
[4] Mainz.
[5] The dedicatory Preface is missing from this French manuscript.

CHAPTER 1

The Key and operation of this piece is guarded by the principal Spirit PAMERSIEL anoyr madriel, through the service of the ebrasothean abrulges itrasbiel. And nadres ormenu itules rabion amorphiel.[1]

What you will find in the prayers or Invocations contained in this chapter.

THE OPERATION of this chapter is filled with difficulty and peril because of the pride and rebellion of those Spirits who obey no one, unless one is well versed and well instructed in this Art. Far from obeying the apprentices of this Art, they very often happen to molest them and [trip] them with a thousand other pitfalls, if he were to push them too hard. They are the worst, and the [2] most unfaithful of the Aerial Spirits[2] and they do not obey anyone if they are not bound by a great oath,[3] and often unfaithfully reveal to others the secret entrusted to them, for as soon as they are released, with a letter, then they protest and fly away and throw themselves without order on the one to whom they are sent, like a crowd without a captain fleeing from a battle, they run furiously and fill the air with their cries. They divulge in the vicinity, the secret of the one who sends them. We contend therefore those who will want to work in this Art, not to torment them by too often asking for their ministry, because they are much too stubborn and unfaithful. There are, however, many among them who are benevolent and always ready to obey.

☞ If anyone wants to test their stubbornness and test if what we say is true, he must scrupulously observe what we are just about to prescribe.

Let him lay out a virgin parchment sheet,[4] on which he will write with the invocation of the Divine Name † in the name of the Father and of the Son and of the Holy Spirit. Let him write then what he has to write in simple and clear terms so that everyone can hear it, either in Latin, or in the language of the country, or in any other language whatsoever. When he is ready to write, he must be turned towards the east, from where he will be able to invoke the Spirits of this quarter by pronouncing the following words.

> Pamersiel oshurmy delmuson Thafloin peano charustea melany, lyaminto colchan, paroys, madyn, moerlay, bulre † atloor don melcove peloin, ibutsyl

---

[1] This is not an invocation as anoyr, madriel and the other 9 names are Dukes in the *Theurgia-Goetia* under the principal spirit Pamersiel. This clearly shows that the full hierarchy was present when Trithemius penned the *Steganographia,* but the lower levels were not listed out with their sigils until the *Theurgia-Goetia* was written. The Latin version adds "the employment of all, together with their dismissal, engages these," confirming that these are in fact working subsidiary spirits.

[2] Most spirits are Aerial and sub-lunar, inhabiting the air between the Moon and the Earth.

[3] The oath binding of spirits is a common and important practice across a number of grimoires.

[4] See manuscript page 185 for the rules for preparing the parchment.

> meon mysbreath alini driaco person. Crisolnay, lemon asosle mydar, icoriel pean thalmon, asophiel il notreon banyel ocrimos estevor naelma befrona thulaomor fronian beldodrayn bon otalmesgo mero fas elnathyn boframoth.

After having pronounced these words and having perceived the Spirits who are the quickest to obey, let him continue the work and begin. If he does not see them after the first call, then he should repeat these same words until they do appear.

[3] Or else it would be advisable to delay some time, lest he force too hastily, and they come to injure the operator. When you have completed your letters send them with great attention by a messenger to the friend skilled in the Art, and as soon as he has received them, he will immediately say the following conjuration.[1]

> Lamarton anoyr bulon madriel traschon ebrasothea panthenon nabrulges Camery itrasbier rubanthy nadres Calmosy ormenulan, ytules demy rabion hamorphyn.

When these words are spoken, he will fully understand your words and your feelings. The Spirits present themselves with great impetuosity, uttering loud cries, and it very often happens that those present are made aware of the secret of the one who sends it. But observe to affix your seal[2] on all the letters you send, so that whoever you write to knows by what Spirit you operated, because if he worked through one to understand, and you by another one to send, they will never obey you. Then your operation would become null, they would hurt him and would not reveal your secret, because all the Spirits we use in this Art only observe the orders and the Offices with which they are charged, and in no way meddle with other Spirits. Observe carefully all that we have said in this chapter, so that you may understand more easily later in this chapter.[3]

Red. To know the abodes of the Spirits, the names and the signs or characters,[4] the number of Spirits who are subject to their superiors, as well as the place they occupy in the universe, which is divided into sixteen parts called Mansions, in each of which is a Prince and chief who one invokes [facing] the side from which the wind of each party comes, which is listed in the Table of Direction and Universal Map.[5]

But how important is it for anyone who wants to undertake these things to know?

R. [4] The Abodes and names of the principal Spirits, and their signs is feared only by the ignorant: he does not call to the north side a Spirit who dwells on the south

---

[1] These conjurations are sometimes referred to as 'lyrics' suggesting that they might be sung.
[2] From Table 1.
[3] At this point the Latin edition quotes two sample letters, one in German, and one in Latin, which do not appear in the French manuscript. They are however simple ecclesiastical communications with no magical content. Instead the French manuscript gives further magical directions.
[4] The sigils in Table 1.
[5] Table 2.

side,[1] which would not only prevent performance, but could cause damage to the operator: this is why you will see in the Universal Map that I drew up for this purpose, so as not to be mistaken, in which is marked the places in which the main Spirits have their abode, with all their Signs and the number of subjects submissive to them, both by day and by night.

You have in this Universal Map the division of the sixteen parts of the universe, in which the principal Spirits have their abode, this is the base and foundation of all operations, it is what you need to know first, because without this knowledge the Art would be without effect. Moreover, it is necessary to know the first substitutes for each of the principal Spirits, how many there are, and those who are employed in the secret mysteries.

To know their orders, how they should be called, how they should be dismissed, how many friends they have, and how many illuminators[2] they are accustomed to have in the daytime, and dark or shadowy ones in the night, and what are his friends, and how many enemies they usually frighten, you will find these Spirit acquaintances listed in the Table of Direction and Universal Map.[3]

---

[1] This is another important rule of evocation which is that you should always face the direction from which the spirit will come, the direction in which he 'lives.'
[2] *Illuminateurs.*
[3] Table 1.

Steganographia

B. Compass[1] direction	Wind direction	No	R. Spirit	B. Sigil	R. Servants by day	B. Servants by night	R.	B.
East	Oriens	1	Pamersiel		1000	10000	100	0.0
ESE	Subsolanus	2	Padiel		10000	200000	10	0.0
SE	Eurus	3	Camuel		10	10	10	10.0
SSE	Euroauster	4	Aseliel		10	20	10	0.10
South	Auster	5	Barmiel		10	20	10	20.0
SSW	Austafricus	6	Gediel		20	20	10.0	10.0
[5] SW	Africus	7	Asyriel		20	20	120	10
WSW	Fauonius	8	Maseriel		30	30	10.0	0.10
West	Occidens	9	Malgaras		30	30	0.30	210
WNW	Chorus	10	Dorothiel		40	40	0.40	30.0
NW	Subcircius	11	Vsiel		40	40	0.30	0.0
NNW	Circius	12	Cabariel		50	50	80.0	80.0
North	Septentrio	13	Raysiel		50	50	80.0	80.[2]
NNE	Aquilo	14	Symiel		10	1000	10	100
NE	Boreas	15	Armadiel		1000	180	810	00
ENE	Vulturnus	16	Baruchas		10	180	810	00

Table 2: The Table of Directions, Winds and Spirits.

---

[1] The traditional wind directions were used by Trithemius to stand for the compass directions. This column was not in the original manuscript, but it is much easier for modern readers to read than converting wind names like Subsolanus, Eurus, etc. into compass directions. The full table of 32 Spirits appears in Chapter XXXII.
[2] This number is written as '0. 80.' in the manuscript.

Steganographia

It is very necessary to know that one should not get confused by [incorrectly] identifying the east as the location where the sun rises in different seasons of the year.[1] The place where it was placed (by the Divine Creator) at the time of its creation, this spot is called [east] on the Spring Equinox.[2] This consideration must be observed with the greatest care, for otherwise you cannot succeed in this Art. To understand the order and arrangement of the Map which is contained within the Table of Direction, it is therefore necessary, if taken in this way, from one of the Spirits contained therein you will hear and understand all.

For an example you can take the Spirit who is called Malgare [Malgaras], by whom the operation of this Art is done in Chapter 9, and [who appears in] the Ninth Mansion in our Map. He is from the western quarter and his sign or character is such ⟨symbol⟩ ⟨symbol⟩. He has under him 30 subjects who preside there over the day and which have great power to put to flight the Spirits of Darkness, and another 30 who are subject to these who preside over the night, and they [6] are always in darkness, they do not come to light without the command of their Princes to whom they are all subject at all times. These still have under them, as guardians and subject ministers, by right, sometimes 30, sometimes 20, and sometimes 10 [Spirits], and sometimes all. When they go out together [it is] by order of their Princes, whose order is as follows.

For Example. That many of their number having been called by the operator, and by the commandment of great virtues that such a number of [additional] servants and guardians appear with them to their Prince who is Malgaras. There are still some under them, a quantity of couriers without number, which are often mixed up with them. We do not have the names of all these Spirits, but only those which are necessary for the operations which we will express in each chapter. It should be noted that all these Spirits are with their principal Emperor, in the part of the universe to which he is deputy, as can be seen in the Table of Direction and Universal Map, which are together at the front of this work (Table 1).

---

[1] There are only two days in the year when the sun rises due east at dawn, these are the two Equinoxes, approximately 22 March and 22 September.

[2] At which time it was sitting due east. But over the course of the year the point on the horizon where the Sun appears to rise moves from approximately NE to SE. The important issue for magic is that you should face the actual direction of the sunrise on the day of invocation, not just its theoretical direction.

Red.   **CHAPTER 2**

> The Prince of this chapter is PADIEL who is from the east-south-east having under him 10000 Ministers for the operations of the day, and 200000 for the nocturnal operations, and a quantity of other sub-servants, the number of which is uncertain.

Since (as explained in the first chapter on Pamersiel) with all his Spirits who are relentless and unfaithful, not wanting to patiently obey [7] operators in this Art, but as we are hardly more expert than you; we want in this chapter to take a safer method, and show a way to operate, by better Spirits, who are prompt, well-behaved and zealous in obeying the operator, who come in the due manner, at the time they are requested, without delay, and they follow what they have been entrusted with, with all possible accuracy without any fraud. The first and the principal Emperor of this operation, is called Padiel, and east-south-east is the place where he resides in the first Mansion after the east.[1]

Padiel has under him ten thousand subjects who preside over operations that take place during the day affecting this Art, which command and lead the nocturnal Spirits hidden in the darkness, which number two hundred thousand. These all shun day and light, except one who is the messenger of the presiding Spirits in these operations; they are all good and beneficent and they will not harm the operator, unless he is wicked and mischievous, or wherever he is not instructed in the Art. It is not necessary to call them all at the same time, as a few is enough, and sometimes only one can satisfy the operator, whether the operation concerns the day or the night, because as they are all benevolent and quiet, and they are more often alone and quiet than in a great tumult. When you want to operate through them, if you have some secret within yourself of which you would like to keep a friend aware, by their ministry you may do so.

Write on a sheet [of paper or parchment], previously prepared in the usual manner as you know, any narration you want and in any language, which is irrelevant since it is not from the page, but from the Spirit that he will learn your secret. To write it will be necessary to turn towards the east-south-east, [8] and having written it, you should pronounce in the mystical language the following conjuration.

> Padiel aporsy mesarpon omevas peludun mapreaxo. Condusen, ulear thersephibayl merphon, parops gebuly mailthomyon ilthear tamarson acrimeon lon peatha casiny chertiel medony reabdo, lasonti jaciel mal arti bulomeon abry pathulmon theoma pathormyn.

When you have recited these words you will see two, or at least one, of these

---
[1] Counting in a clockwise direction.

Spirits present themselves before you with great tranquillity, all ready to obey your orders, then you confide your secret to him, and he will report it faithfully to the one to whom he is sent, when the letters have reached the one to whom you send them. If he is alone, it will be all the better, but if he is in company he must go aside, if he cannot turn to the east-south-east, and let him speak in a low voice the words which are reported below.

> Padiel ariel vanerhon chiotarson phymartomerphon ampriscoledabarym elsophroy mesarpone ameorsy, paneryn athle pachum gelthearan utrul ut solubito beslonty las gomadyn triamy mesarnothy.

When he has pronounced this conjuration, immediately the Spirit will appear in his presence and will reveal to him the secrets entrusted to him without anybody noticing it, without danger and without peril. But no one can operate in this part easily if he is false, malignant in character and pernicious, but the more frank and sincere he is, and the more he works secretly, the more quickly the Spirits will be inclined to obey him and the more easily he will succeed. Note that Padiel with his vassals are deputed to learn secret opinions [specifically] for the correction or punishment of the guilty, as we said in the preceding chapter.

[9] R. [If] you do not want to entrust this secret to letters, but to Spirits of the second Mansion.

For Example. Someone is accused before a Prince of a crime of *lèse-majesté* or something similar, and this Prince would like to have him punished by the justice of the place where he is a refugee. The Prince wants to have him arrested, but he dares not write this as he fears that the letters may fall into the hands of the culprit, and being informed of the will of the Prince, gathers his friends or forces, he does not openly resist but escapes by flight. He writes to his Prefect or duty officer in an [open] narration that he does not fear being read by everyone. Load the Spirit with the secret he wants, let him know as we have explained above, and he will discharge exactly and faithfully his commission.

Example of the letter that must be contained on the sheet charged with the [seal of the] Spirit of the Second Mansion.[1]

> Padiel melion, parme, Camiel bufayr, ilnoma, venora, pamelochyn.

Here are the characters of Padiel which are put at the end of the letter

"With sincere charity I send you a prayer for the devotion of penitents quite well composed, short, that I did not want to own it alone. It is thus –

> O my Eternal Jesus, Saviour of the just, deliver us with compassion from the crimes of the guilty, hear our supplications, remove the ardour of vices,

---

[1] This is one of the few non-secret letter examples included in the French manuscript. These letters have no magical significance, and are omitted by the French translation, except for this one.

renew in us the love of God and warm up our conscience, which has cooled for too long, and lead us to eternal happiness, oh my good Jesus blot out the sins of those who humbly beseech you, for we have offended you for too long, O sweet Jesus heal our infirmities and hear your servants who ask you on their knees. We are men constantly surrounded by miseries and torments of all kinds of afflictions [10] and storms, preserve us, as you are the comforter of the afflicted because our lives corrupt, if it is constantly in happiness, have mercy on us O sweet Saviour look upon us with favourable eyes, the humility of those who love you and do not allow us to be shipwrecked in this awful abyss of vices and corruptions, hitherto we have been guilty, we have flooded our salvation with careless crimes, we did not put in pains for the future: O sweet and beneficent Creator, be favourable to your servants, and deign to save wretched people groaning that the miserable vanity of the world has deceived us, O Pain! We have neglected the way of Truth's salute, but deign to pull us out of our exile because, sweet Jesus, you are our saviour, you do not deceive anyone, you are our only hope, and the eternal happiness of the saints, the glory of Christians, the light of Angels, the reward of martyrs, the crown of virgins, the honour and support of widows. Good Jesus hear those who humbly beg you, deliver us from the present exile by granting us the grace to live endlessly; vivify us, we beg you, we miserable servants whom you have redeemed with your own blood, for us to follow with true zeal the paths of justice, preserve us, O Almighty God, infinite Majesty and the eternal salvation of righteous and noble souls. Amen."

R.   **CHAPTER 3**

The Prince of the third Mansion is called CAMUEL, he is in the southeast, and he has under him 10 Spirits in daily operations and as many for those of the night; and as many sub-servants, whose duties are to announce the arrival of someone, to teach the ways and the travels [of the sender].

[11] The First and Supreme Prince of this third Mansion is therefore called Camuel, who has his home in the southeast, he is beneficent and quick to send his vassals to those who utilise this Art according to the correct form. It is true that it has few servants but they are all good, very willing and faithful. I hear there are ten for the day and as many for the night, and there always appear two of this order at a time, since those who preside over the day do not flee darkness, and those who preside over the night do not flee from the light, and one is always aided by the other on all occasions required by the operator. And when they appear visibly one always wants to appear in a beautiful dress of mixed colours, and the other in a form made of splendid light. However often they only appear by sensible effort, and will not be visible except by the will of the operator. Camuel with his ministers and his vassals has the authority and the power to announce to an absent friend, the state, the will, the condition, and the way of travellers, their arrival and any delay of the envoy when he sees fit to operate in this Art. When you want to operate by the Angels of this Mansion, you must first know which are the ten Angels of Camuel who preside over the day's operations and how many servants each of these Angels has, and so also of the nocturnal ones, and so that you may be well instructed see the following table.

Black	Red	Black	R.	R.	R.	R.	R.	R.	R.
Orpeniel	10.	Citgara	100	Daniel	10.	Dobiel	100.	Azimo	10.
Camyel	100.	Pariel	10.	Omyel	10.	*Nodar[1]	10.	Tediel	0.
Budiel	10.	Cariel	10.	Asiniel	100.	Phaniel	10.	Moriel	0.
Elcar	10.	Neriel	10.	Calym	100.	Meras	100.	Tugaros	0.

Table 3: The Angels of Camuel's host.[2]

[12] In the table above you have ten Angels of Camuel who preside over the day with the number of their servants, and the same with the nocturnal ones. The last, as you see, have no signifier, since the zero means nothing. So that when you want to operate by them prepare your sheet, following the Art, and being turned directly to the southeast, write whatever narration in whatever language or idiom

---

[1] *Manuscript note:* The ancients said 'Noctar.'
[2] Note that in the manuscript the Red/Black colouration is only shown in the top line. We have applied this to the whole column, as it is in the Latin versions for clarity.

you wish that it is not necessary to hide, and having finished it, tacitly say the following words.

> Camuel aperoys, melym mevomanial, casmoyn cralti busaco aeli lumarphotyrion theor besamys, aneal cabelonyr thiamo vesonthy.

Having pronounced these words in silence, give your orders to the Spirits that are present that you recognise, and send them. All done under silence and out of the tumult, if possible, after which give the letters [to the messenger that] you want to carry to your friend, open if you want, and let him go away without putting yourself to any trouble, because these Spirits do not neglect their duty, whether the messenger comes sooner or later, you need not trouble yourself, for they are faithful. It is necessary to know which Spirit you want to send, because in the conjuration it is necessary to recite its name immediately after the principal Spirit, and do that in all the operations which you want to operate by the names of Angels that you want to send, and who are in this chapter, but they will be similar to those who are attached to Camuel and his subordinate Spirits.

R. Let it be your intention to make known by the aforesaid Spirits to an absent friend, write whatever narration you do not fear that everyone will know.

[13] R. He to whom you sent the Spirit, having read the said narration and having learned out of the mouth of the said Spirit whatever you want him to know, let him do what he was instructed to do by this Art. And having recognised the Spirit by his character or Universal sign he turns towards the southeast, and he silently recites the following lyrics.[1]

> Camuel Busarcha, menaton enatiel enatiel, mean sayr abasremon naculipesarum nadru lasmon enoti chamabet usear lesponty abrulmy pensayr thubarym gonayr asmon friacha rynon otry hamerson, buccurmy pedavellon.

Having finished speaking these words let him receive the letters and receiving them from the south-eastern side as indicated. It should be noted that all these Spirits dwell with their Prince in the southeast, and to do this it is necessary that he who works through them turns to that side, or if he cannot, at least when he receives letters, he will turn back that way.

Observe and understand what we have taught you.

---

[1] Invocation.

CHAPTER 4   R.

The Prince of the Fourth Mansion is called ASELIEL and his abode is in the south-south-east. He has under him forty substitute Spirits with their servants, and they preside over the things that are necessary for love.

This Grand Prince Aseliel has his residence with his Spirits in the fourth Mansion of the east near the south, called the south-south-east, of which there are 10 Presidents in this Art for the operations which take place during the day, and 20 for the operations of the night. The power and the duty of all these Spirits, is to announce [circumstances] when it comes to sex and love. These still have 30 under them as principals [14] and as many others as they send by order to do their duty, when they have been called by the operator in the correct way. Under these there are still others whose number is great. When someone wants to operate by the Prince of this representative dwelling in our map, he will not need to call all the Spirits subject to him, but one or two will suffice, whether the operation is carried out during the day or night. There will be named here for this subject only a few names, with the number of their servants, of whom only one or two will always be called without having the need for more, unless the operation is to be used for several and various things.[1] Table and Names of the Spirits submitted to this Prince.

Mariel	20	Cubiel	20	Asphiel	20	Melas	20	Red
Charas	20	Aniel	20	Curiel	20	Sariel	20	Black
Parniel	20	Asahel	20	Chamos	20	Othiel	20	Black
Aratiel	20	Arean	20	Odiel	20	Bufar	20	Red

Table 4: Names of the Spirits who submit to Prince Aseliel.

Here in this table are sixteen of the greatest Princes who are subject to grand Aseliel as well as grand Asiel, eight of whom preside over the day and eight over the night, each of which has 20 servants subject to these orders who send them to do their duties whenever necessary. All these Princes are good and quick to be obedient being very gracious especially towards those who are [well] instructed in the Art. But their servants are sometimes partly proud and partly implacable, especially towards those who are less educated and less well versed in this Art. These sixteen Princes with their substitutes will be enough for you to learn everything, nor is it necessary to know or invoke more. Therefore, when you want to work in this part by Asiel observe first everything as we usually do. The place of his dwelling is as it was said, and you will summon one of those above-named Spirits in the table, the one [15] you please, by pronouncing the following words.

---

[1] This confirms that multiple requests can be made within one operation.

> Aseliel aproysy, melyin thulner casmoyn, mavearburson, charny demorphaon theoma asmeryn diviel, casponti vearly basamys ernoti chavalorson.

Having pronounced these words you will add [the word] which we are used to say in the operations of this Art, and you will see that a prompt and certain effect will ensue, of which here is the explanation. Assume for example that you have a mistress for whom you burned with love, and she is the same, but you cannot approach or speak to her because of her supervisors, but you have found a means by which you can enjoy her with ease and to the satisfaction of both parties, but it is important to warn her beforehand. However, you cannot execute this message yourself, nor can you write to her, for fear that the letters will fall into other hands, nor do you want to confide in an agent for fear that the plan and design you have formed will be disclosed, which would become harmful and very prejudicial to your business, and you also see that time will not be more favourable to you in the future. To avoid these various disadvantages you must invoke the ministers of this Art. For this indeed you will write letters which are not suspect, which you will send to your mistress by these same ministers who will love what will be written, and will advise your mistress to read your letters. Recognising the secret mystery of this case she asks the minister for advice and listens to his advice, and sends you her consent. Then you arrange accordingly to approach her, especially since she is ready and willing to receive you, you will enter without any difficulty or obstacle whatsoever, and enjoy the presence of one or the other at your leisure and with complete satisfaction.

[16] When you have received such letters, you will do what is already shown in turning to the south-south-east side which is [the direction of] the dwelling of Prince Aseliel, and behold its sign or character ⁊꒴ as well as saying the second oration.

> Aseliel murnea casmodym bularcha vadusyn aty belron diviel arsephonti pa normys orlevo cadon venoti basramyn.

CHAPTER 5

R.

The Supreme Prince and Emperor of this Mansion is called BARMIEL his residence is in the south having under him 10 Princes who preside over the operations of the day and 20 for night operations with their sub-servants, who are in charge of announcing secrets [relating to] the taking castles, forts, citadels, etc.

The first and Grand Prince of the fifth Mansion of the south at noon, is called Barmiel, having under his dominion 10 principal Dukes who preside over day operations with their sub-servants, and 20 who preside over night operations with their vassals who are then more numerous than those who preside over the operations of the day, because the operations of this Mansion are more often done during the night than during the day. Their Office is to announce the secrets of conquest of castles and cities, especially during nocturnal times. If you want to operate in this Art by Barmiel invoke one of his principal Spirits, whoever you want, and as soon as he comes with 20 servants, entrust him with your secret. Although he is accompanied by these vassals, because no Prince of this Mansion does not usually come alone or with a few servants, so you give your confidence to the Prince and chief, and not to the vassals because they are both proud and mischievous, but to the Prince only, because he is good, quiet, faithful, and [17] careful. I will name eight of the Principals who preside over the operations of the day, and eight for the night, which are of the best and quickest to obey, we do not need more. See the table below.

Black	Red.	R.	B.	B.	R.	R.	B.
Sochas	20	Acterar	20	Barbis	20	Marcaiz	0.
R.	B.	B.	R.	R.	B	B	R.
Tigara	20	Barbil	20	Marquus	20	Baabal	0.
B.	R.	R.	B	B	R.	R.	B
Chansi	20	Carpiel	20	Caniel	20	Gabir	0.
R.	B.	B.	R.	R.	B.	B.	R.
Keriel	20	Mansi	20	Acreba	20	Astib	0.

Table 5: The Angels of Prince Barmiel's host.

You have 16 Spirits in this table of which 12 each have 20 ministers with which they are accustomed to appear to the operator, the four others who each have a zero which means 'nothing,' therefore they have no sub-servants, and they will always come alone, and are each in his ministry faithful and diligent in all that you order them, wanting to operate perfectly in the ministry of someone who has previously executed all that must be done in the Art, and being turned on the south side you will say the following lyrics [invocation].

> Barmiel buras melo charnotiel malapos veno masphian albryon, chasinia pelvo morophon apluer charmya noty Mesron alraco caspiel hoalno chorben ovear aserea cralnoty carephon elcsor bumely nesitan army tu faron.

When you have spoken these words, confide your secret to the Spirit which you have invoked and which appears to you, send [18] letters by whomever you want, and whichever ones you want.

Let us use the following Example.

R. Suppose [that it is] the secret of a King that should not be confided to anyone under any pretext whatsoever.

R. A King or a Prince would like to conquer a place or a fort, or a convoy, but he cannot do so by arms; so he corrupts the guards by rewarding them not to confide their secret to anyone, or even to letters, fearing that being intercepted his intention is lost and will not deprive him of the reward with life. The Prince turns towards the house of Barmiel, he calls the Spirit and confides his secret to him, he comes, bringing the news that the castle is taken at night, but no one knows how. For this write or invent such letters that we are not afraid to be seen.

For example

"By living righteously, we will acquire Eternal bliss etc."

Receiving this letter, having recognised the token of Barmiel, let him turn as soon as he can towards the south. It is not that there is any peril in the delay in obedience by the Spirit, though there is a gap, because when we call him he always has the habit of coming either sooner or later than we call him. After several days; having executed what the Art requires, it will be necessary say the following words.

> Barmiel any casleon archoi bulesan eris, casray molaer pessaro duys anal goerno mesrue greal cusere drelnoz, par le cufureti basriel aflymaraphe neas lo, carnos erneo damerosenotis anycarpodyn.

When he [the recipient] has said these words properly on the southern side, he will hear and understand your will, which you have entrusted, not to the letters, but to the Spirit, but if he turns to a different side, he will understand nothing.

[19] CHAPTER 6

The Prince is called GEDIEL having his residence at south-south-west, and under him are 20 Dukes in the day and as many in at night, with their servants; whose Office it is to announce and prevent future perils.

In the Sixth [Mansion] which is south-south-west, the great Prince Gediel has under his orders 20 principal Dukes in the day and as many in the night, with many of their servants. Their Office is to announce, warn and advise a friend, of some pressing danger, and especially to Princes for the defence of the Fatherland, castles, cities, and to [reveal] all the news that serves friends, and those whom we favour, for their salvation, and also against our enemies and adversaries. To do it, it is not necessary to invoke the 20 Princes, but two are enough with their servants, and so that you know them more fully by their own name, namely 8 for the day and 8 for the night here is the table.

Color	Name	Color	Name	Color	Name	Color	Name
Black	Coliel	Red	Sariel	B.	Reciel	R.	Aroan
	20		20		20		20
	Naras		Rantiel		Sadiel		Cirecas
Red	Sabas	Black	Mashel	R.	Agra	B.	Aglas
	20		20		20		20
	Assaba		Bariel		Anael		URIEL

Table 6: The Angels of Prince Gediel's host.

First, before getting down to work, you must know that one must always invoke at least [20] two Spirits with 20 of their servants. You won't be able to do anything without that, although they do not always appear visibly. But one should not put oneself at risk, provided that you conduct yourself through their invisible ministry for your undertakings, therefore to operate by their ministry in this Art turn to the south-south-west; for they all dwell there with their Prince Gediel at all times, and do what you are instructed to do in order, speaking the following words.

> Gediel asiel modebar mopiel, casmoyn, rochamurenu proys nasaron atido casmear vearsy maludym velachain demosar otiel masdurym sodiviel mestray seor amarlum, laveur pealo netus fabelron.

Having spoken these words, two good Princes will appear to you, benevolent and be sure that you need not fear, but confide in them, and tell them what you wish, and they will do your commission faithfully. His sign is in red and in this form

R. Suppose you have a secret for the Spirit that you would not entrust to letters.

R. For example. I am faithfully attached to my Prince by many blessings with which he has showered me, but I learned secretly that his enemies must attack the castle by ambush and treason, and I wish to give this knowledge to my Prince. I cannot since enemies hold the countryside, this I can't send either by a courier, because I do not believe I can trust anyone. I [therefore] call a Spirit to whom I entrust my secret, and I will so send my secret; I send a letter as it seems to me only for form, so that the Prince may know that he has been sent one of a number of Spirits, for without [physical] letters he could not know that a Spirit had been sent to him. The aforesaid one goes to tell him the news and the Prince takes precautions for his camp.

[21] The Prince or other to whom the letter was sent, having read this letter (or several others in the same way) in which there is no secret and having seen the sign of Gediel he will be able to know what he should do and which Spirit he must invoke; so that he says the words as follow.

> Gediel aprois camor ely moschoyn divial palorsan, fermel asparlon Crisphe Lamedon ediur cabosyn arsy thamerosyn.

Having said this correctly and having done what is necessary for this Art, and the Spirit having revealed my secret, not by letters, he will know it, and will then warn [about] his enemies.

CHAPTER 7

[The seventh Mansion] whose Supreme Prince is called ASIRIEL has his residence to the southwest, having under his dominion over 20 Dukes who preside over the operations of the day, and as many the night, whose Office is to announce to friends the secret counsels of Princes.

The First and Supreme Prince of the Seventh Mansion is called Asiriel. He dwells in that quarter of the universe we call southwest having under him 20 Princes who preside over the operations of the day and as many who preside at night, who all have under their orders many sub-servants. If two Dukes are called by the operator by the ministries of Art concerning the day, they always have 20 servants, likewise those who preside at night, so that if you only call one of the main ones, especially at night, it is supposed that he will not have 20 vassals with him, but only 10, so the least you can call is two, because they do not usually come alone. On nights you can call one or two as you please. If you call two, you must call 20 vassals, if you call [22] only one you only have to call 10 vassals and [mention] this in the call as you are used to doing, so that you know which ones you should call either for the master or for the vassals. See the following table.

		Red		B.		R.	B.		R.	B.		R.
B. {	Astor	20			Buniel		20		Arcisat	20		Cusiel	20
	Carga				Rabas				Adriel			Malqueel	

Red										
20	-----	20	-----	20	--------	20	----	20	--------	20
B.										
20	-----	20	-----	20	--------	20	----	20	--------	20

		Black	R.	B		R.	B	R.	B
R. {	Amiel	20	Maroth	20		Budar	10	Fassua	10
	Cusiel		Omiel			Aspiel	10	Hamas	10

Table 7: The Angels of Prince Asiriel's host.

The duty and Office of these Spirits, who are chief among the 40, is to announce the secret counsels of Princes to their subjects and friends. You have 8 for the operations of the day, and as much for those of the night, with many of their vassals, who are sufficient for everything, it is not necessary to appeal to others.

Steganographia

Observe carefully that when you call one or two of these Princes that we named above it is appropriate to also express with their name the number of their sub-servants because they are proud, and they are extremely happy when a great number of them are invoked. When you want to operate by their ministry in this Art turn to the southwest side watch diligently what you are taught to do so as not to [fail to] observe or forget anything concerning this Art. Here are the words that must be pronounced for the Call.

> [23] Asiriel aphorsy Lamodyn to carmephyn drubal asutroy sody baruchon, useser palormy thulnear asmeron chornemadusyn coleny busarethon duys marphelitubra nasaron venear fabelronty.

Having finished these words, the invoked Spirits will appear, so that you may distinguish them. It should be noted that Princes always have the custom of appearing in Aerial form, and I hear [they have] sapphire-coloured servants in whites. Confide your secret safely to the Princes because they are faithful, for principal Dukes have the custom between them that when the operator speaks they immediately dismiss their vassals so that they withdraw, so as not to hear the commission, and when they feel the operator stops talking to them, they reappear immediately.

May the Prince's secret be such that he does not believe he can confide it to anyone. **R.**

The great and secret advice of a Prince consists of serious and great things.   **R.**

He would like another Prince of his friends to hide it, but he is afraid of him and his family falling into danger, if he entrusts it to someone, let him not betray him by turning in the letters, or fear that they will be read by someone. He calls for this operation the Spirit who will surely not reveal the secret entrusted to him, he will fulfil his commission, and being safe, he sent letters which are not suspicious so that when you send these letters to the abode of whoever you want to send the Spirit to, that they are signed with the sigil of the Spirit, because none of the Princes or vassals of these Spirits come unless called, either to him who sends or to the one we send to. To make it easier for you to understand, you send a letter before to the one to whom you wish to send the Spirit from a Mansion, and being signed with the seal of the Spirit so that he might know what Spirit you invoked, so that he could invoke it too; but we will talk of this in the last chapter of this Book I on [manuscript] page 74.

[24] He to whom letters are sent by the Spirit, which is invisible to him; to make it appear, he must very distinctly pronounce the following words.

Here are the seals.

> Asiriel onear camot Laveviel gamer sothin janoz alnay bulumer palorson, irgiel lamedon, ludiel Caparosyn navy asparlon nadiel bulephor janos pesonty tresloty camon elyr, mearsu nosy thoemerosyn.

Having spoken these words, word by word, he secretly turns to the southwest, having added what the Art required, the Spirit will appear to him with his vassals visible, no one else will see or hear them and will reveal to your ear the secret of him who sent it.

CHAPTER 8

The Supreme Power is called MASERIEL who inhabits the region of the universe which is called west-south-west, having under him 60 Principals with many vassals, in the Eighth Mansion.

This Eighth Mansion is located towards the west in the place of the west wind called west-south-west, it is there that the Grand Prince Maseriel dwells with an infinity of Dukes, Princes and vassals, and 30 deputy Princes who preside over the operations of the day; and as much for the night as far as this Art is concerned, with many of their vassals. All those are constituted to teach and develop or reveal the secrets of the human arts of philosophy, magic and negromancy, and of all the admirable and secret operations which are known only to very few people, and they are prompt and very faithful, and do not return until they have completed that which was commanded them. They are quiet and come without noise as ordered, with few or many vassals as [25] with no point at all, at least visible, they do not frighten anyone except the one who is not instructed or instituted, who presumes to call them by the true principles of the Art (that no one can know easily without being instructed) and so soon have the Spirit whom you call for this operation, you will know that they are not all necessary for you, but a few, and twelve will be sufficient for the operations that take place during the day, and as much for the night, with their vassals. See the table below.

R.	B.	R.	B.	R.	B.	R.	B.
Mahuc	30	Zerael	30	Azimel	30	Alsuel	30
R.	B	R.	B.	R.	B.	R.	B.
Roviel	30	Athiel	30	Chasor	30	Aliel	30
R.	B	R.	B.	R.	B.	R.	B.
Fariel	30	Vessur	30	Potiel	30	Espoel	30
R.	B	R.	B.	R.	B.	R.	B.
Arach	30	Sarmiel	30	Baros	30	Rabiel	30
Maras	30	Amoyr	30	Eliel	30	Atriel	30
Noquiel	30	Badiel	30	Paras	30	Salvar	30

Table 8: Hosts of Maseriel's Spirits by day (top) and night (bottom).

You see in this table, 24 of the principal Spirits of Maseriel with 720 of their servants and vassals, including the first 12 who preside over the day and the other 12 for the night.

When you want to work through them in this Art, turn west-south-west, after you have prepared the necessary things that the Art requires. Call one of the above-named in the table, whoever you please, by pronouncing the following words, and it will come without any delay.

> Maseriel bulan la modyn charnoty carmephyn jabrun caresathrayn asulroy [26] bevesy cadumyn turiel bulan sevear; almos lycadusel ernoty panier jethar care pheory bulan thorty paron venio Fabelronthusy.

[When] the Spirit you called appears to you, you can entrust him with your secret in complete safety without hesitation. If you are in company you can speak to him quietly, as has already been said.

R. May your secret be such.

For **Example.**

We have secrets in the occult sciences, philosophy, magic, astronomy, the cabbalah, arithmetic, or in other arts which are such that you do not trust them to letters, or surely keep secrets from him, or to command another philosopher [i.e. a magician]; call one or 2 of the Spirits above-named in this table, confide your secret to him, he will take care of it, he will carry it to your friend, and he will bring you the answer.

Write a letter as you wish.

The one to whom such a letter is sent is then the recipient of the said letter which the Spirit brings to him, but the Spirit is always invisible to him, and when receiving him, he will have read the letter and [therein] recognised Maseriel's sign. He turns towards west-south-west, having previously done what this Art requires, he will call upon the Spirit who has been sent to him, and for this purpose he will distinctly say the following words. Here are his seals or characters or well

> MASERIEL onear camersin cohodor messary lyrno balnaon greal, lamedon odiel, pedarnoy nador janozavy chamyrin.

As soon as these mysterious words have been spoken as they are here reported, the nebulous Spirit was sent will appear, he will speak the truth in the ear, and he will faithfully do whatever is commanded, and yet no one of those who are present will notice it, provided that we are constant and without fear, and that we persevere as is necessary.

[27] CHAPTER 9

R. The Prince is called MALGARAS who lives in the west in the ninth Mansion from where comes the full strong wind which one names West. He has 30 Dukes under his domination and command for the operations of the day, and as many for the night, whose function is to announce family secrets to friends.

The First and Supreme Prince of the Ninth Mansion is Malgare[1] in his abode in the equinoctial west,[2] and he is the great Prince of the west, who has 30 vassals for the operations of the day, and as many for the night, including their Offices which is to announce hidden notices and family secrets to friends. The principal Dukes are good and quick to obey the operator, chiefly those who preside over the day because they are more accustomed to conversing with men, the nocturnal ones are also good, but they do not converse so easily because they run away and hate the light, on the contrary, they desire darkness, because of this they often have the habit of appearing to the operator as bats. Of all those there we will name 24 in the table including 12 for day operations, and 12 for night operations. See the table.

R.	B.	R.	B.	R.	B.	R.	B.	R.	B.
Carmiel	30	Agor	30	Cabiel	30	Misiel	20	Aroiz	10
B.	R.	B.	R.	B.	R.	B.	R.		
Meliel	30	Casiel	30	Udiel	30	Barfas	20		
R.	B.	R.	B.	R.	B.	B.			
Borass	30	Rabiel	20	Oriel	30			{ 30.20. { 30.20.10	
R.	B.	R.	B.	R.	B.				
Aroc	30.	Libiel	30	Caron	30				
[28] B.	R.	B.	R.	B.	R.	B.	R.		
Dobiel	30	Raboc	30	Zamor	30.	Aspor	20		
R.	B.	R.	B.	R.	B.	R.	B.	R.	B.
Cubi	30	Aspiel	30	Amiel	30	Delias	20	Basiel	10.

Table 9: Hosts of Prince Malgaras by day (top) and night (bottom) Spirits.

You currently have 12 of the principal Magaras *(sic)* vassals for the operations of the day and as many for those of the night, with their sub-servants of the number of 640. Notice that Aroiz and Basiel are still alone. Misiel, Barfas, Aspor and Delias

---
[1] Variant spelling of Malgaras.
[2] i.e. due west.

are not pairs, and may be called by two, or by one, but be careful not to be terrified by naming them as the table teaches, do so without change, do not fear the danger, and pronounce for the Call, the following words which are their conjuration.

> **R.** Malgaras ador chameso butveriny mareso bodyr cadumir aviel casmyo tedy pleoryn viordi eare viorba, chameron vesy thuriel ulnavy, bevesy mevo chasmironty naor ernyso, chorny barmo calevodyn barso thubra sol.

Having finished pronouncing these words, be firm and constant, those whom you have called will immediately appear visibly to you, but if you call from among the nocturnal ones they will not come first; do not stop your work because of this, but force them by repeating the conjuration above until they come, because they are sometimes a little lazy and do not come willingly among men, as we said. Such is your secret that you dare not confide it either to men or letters.

[They are concerned with] all things that pertain to family affairs such as **R.** monetary deposit, loan, or something concerning human conversation about a secret you would like an absent friend to know, but which comes at the risk of being discovered, and you would not run the risk of undergoing public scrutiny [causing] a great peril, or loss, you dare not entrust it either to men or to letters. So you perform it safely and your conscience is clear, [29] turn to the west, call yourself a Duke, confide your secret to him, he goes away and will take care of everything, if he has been given an answer he will bring it back to you.

Write a letter in which there is no risk. The one to whom you send the Spirit receives this letter, or such other as you please, and having known the sign of the Prince from the west, let him turn to this quarter, having done what is necessary before, he will call the Spirit who is invisible to him, and for him to appear it will be necessary to say the following verses to the Spirit, but do not speak them to anyone else.

> Malgaradas[1] apro chameron asoty mesary throes Zamedo sogreal paredon adre caphoron onatyr tirno beosy chameron phorsy mellon tedrumarsy damaso duise casmiel elthurnpeson alproys fabelronty sturno panalmo nador.

Having finished these words, the called Spirit will appear according to his custom and he will reveal to you what he is charged with. You will be able to use this same Spirit to let your friend know what you want only him to know.

---

[1] Maybe a variant spelling of Malgaras.

CHAPTER 10

The Supreme Prince is called DOROTHIEL, who dwells in that quarter of the universe which is called west-north-west having under his command many Princes, Dukes and vassals.

This Grand Prince lives in the tenth Mansion, and he has under his power and domination 40 Dukes who preside over the operations of the day, and as much for those of the night, without counting the servants, whose number is infinite. Their Office is to announce all the secrets which belong to spiritual affairs and Ecclesiastical gifts, benefits, prelatures,[1] dignities and others similar things, but in the operations of this Art it is not necessary to name all the names of the servants below, as a small number of each order [30] is enough, the names of the others will be put with them in their place. You may consider this table in which are the names.

Red
Mugael 0
Choriel 0
Artinc 0
Esiel 0

P	B. R.	F	B. R.	P	B. R.	F	B. R.
Mugael	40	Gudiel	400	Nachiel	40	Phutiel	400
Choriel	40	Asphor	400	Ofisiel	40	Cayros	400
Artinc	40	Emuel	400	Bulis	40	Narsyel	400
Efiel	40	Soviel	400	Moniel	40	Mozyel	400
Maniel	40	Cabron	400	Pasiel	40	Arozyel	400
Suriel	40	Diviel	400	Gariel	40	Cusync	400
Carsiel	40	Abriel	400	Soriel	40	Uraniel	400
Fubiel	40	Danael	400	Darbori	40	Pelusar	400
Carba	40	Lomor	400	Paniel	40	Abael	400
Merach	40	Cesael	400	Curfas	40	Meroth	400
Althor	40	Busiel	400	Aliel	40	Cadriel	400
Omael	40	Larfos	400	Maziel	40	Lobiel	400

Table 10: Hosts of Prince Dorothiel.

You currently have 24 Princes of Dorothiel of each order for the operations of the day and as much for those of the night with their sub-servants to the number of

---

[1] The authority or rank of a prelate.

10160. Notice that the operations that you will do by these Spirits differ much from others, that is why we will talk more about both the Prince and the Dukes, because we operate by this Mansion 12 hours during the day and 12 during the night. This is [31] why there are always 4 Princes who preside over 2 hours, both during the day, and during the night, so that you are not allowed to summon others than those whom the hour requires, whether the operation is done during the first or second hour of day summon whomever you want of the first 4 Princes who are the Presidents of the day's operations. If it is done during the third or fourth hour summon whoever you want from the 4 of the second Order that you will know to see and invoke after. And so for the rest it is necessary to operate in order according to the 24 hours both during the day and during the night.

When therefore you wish to operate in this Art by the Spirits of Dorothiel, having previously executed all that is customary to execute in this quarter; write a letter as your mind dictates, turning to the side of the universe from which comes the wind that is called the west-north-west wind, call one or two of these 4 Princes who preside over the hour in which you operate, and for this purpose the following words must be said.

> Dorothiel cusi feor madylon busar pamersy chear Janothym baony camersy ulymeor peathan adial cadumyr renear thubra cohagier maston Lodierno sabelrusyn

Having spoken these words you will see appear the Spirit that you have called, he will be quick, alert to obey, to whom you confide your secret, and faithfully look at the side of the next table.

R. Suppose you have a secret that you want to tell a friend.

You have a matter of spiritual consequence with a Prince and you want it to be secret and you think you can't confide that to the Prince, you want him to hide it, so feign a letter of supplication for a poor Ecclesiastic that you send to him. You call on your Spirit, you confide to him your secret which he will fulfil exactly. You will give him a letter such that you will not fear its disclosure. When the Prince [32] receives this letter, or any other that you have sent to him, by one of these Spirits according to the rules of the art, and having recognised Dorothiel's sign he turns to the west-north-west side where this great Prince dwells with his Dukes and servants, executing all that the art requires, whereupon he will call the Spirit in a low voice as the principles teach, while pronouncing the following.

His character ∼.

> Dorothiel onear chameron ulyfeor madusyn peony oriel nayr druse movayr pamerson etro dumeson, davor caho. casmiel hayrno fabelrunthon.

Having finished these words, if the Spirit takes too long to come, we must begin again to recite these words until the fourth time, and no doubt the Spirit will appear visibly to you and whisper in your ear the message he is responsible for, from him who sent him.

CHAPTER 11

R. The Supreme Spirit is called USIEL, who lives in this region of the universe that we call the north-west wind, having under him 40 Dukes during the day and as many at night, who have power over hidden treasures.

The twelfth Mansion where the Grand Prince Usiel lives, with under him 40 Princes who attend the operations of the day, and 40 for those of the night, their Office is to announce [and reveal] hidden and underground treasures and all things that belong to these treasures. We will name a small but sufficient number [of Spirits] for the operations of this Art in this chapter. Notice that when the Dukes of this abode are called by the operator, they are accustomed to come voluntarily and with great speed, and although they have many servants, yet I have never seen one coming who brought servants with them or at least not visible ones, but if someone wanted to use the ministry valets, they could do so even though they had to obey them, if the operator did not know how to call them in the necessary way, or if they wanted to obey, or that they appear only too slowly. See the table below. We reserve the right to explain the rest at the end of the book in their own chapter.

Red	B.	Red	B.	R.	B.	R.	B.
Abaria	40	Saefar	40	Amandiel	30	Hissam	30
Ameta	40	Poriel	40	Barsu	30	Fabariel	30
Arnen	40	Saefar	40	Garnacu	30	Usiniel	30
Herne	40	Maqui	40				

Black	Red	B.	R.	B.	R.	R.	B.
Ansoel	40	Saddiel	40	Assuriel	20	Pathyr	20
Godiel	40	Sobiel	40	Almoel	20	Marae	20
Barfos	40	Ossidiel	40				
Burfa	40	Adan	40	Lapharon	10	Ethiel	10

Table 11: Grand Prince Usiel his Princes and their sigils.

Of the 40 Princes of Usiel who attend to the operations of the day, you have some 40 with their valets numbering 400, and 14 who preside over the operations of the night with 440 of their servants. You see it in this table represented by the two opposite signs (for the defence and the security of the treasury, as we see it) so that it is not found by thieves or whoever it may be which we will use for the custody of the treasure found while the Spirit [34] is sent to the friend. When you want to operate by the Spirits, if the treasure is big or belongs to a Prince, call the Dukes of the order of the Quaternes, if it is proper to the Ternes, if it is private and just a small piece of amber, or if it is vile and small and the operation is done there in a solitary place, the following words will have to be said very distinctly for this purpose.

> Usiel parnothiel chameron briosy sthrubal brionear caron sotronthi Egypia odiel chelorsy mear chadusy notiel ornich turbelsi paneras thorthay pean adresmo boma arnotiel chelmodyn drusar loy sodiviel carson, eltrae myre notiel mesraym venea dublearsy mavear melusyron chartulneas fabelmerusyn.

Having said these words, facing the northwest, and in profound silence as time and place permit, do the rest that this Art requires. And entrust to the Spirit, (who must already have appeared to you) your secret with the sign of profound mystery, do not hesitate because the Dukes are all good and faithful.

Supposing for example that you have the following secret within your mind and you do not want to entrust it to anyone. You have found a great treasure in a graveyard of the dead, or in another place which was hidden by people long ago, who have since died, and you have knowledge of this hidden treasure, but you alone would not be enough to extract it; and yet you do not want to entrust it to anyone who lives in the neighbourhood, but you have a very faithful friend who is absent, to whom you desire to reveal the mystery, but you cannot confide it in letters, or by a courier, lest by treason you fall into the danger of it being discovered, and you lose the advantage of the gain that you must have. For this purpose you call a Spirit, the Spirit which you entrusted with your letter signed with the seal of the Spirit, and having confided in him [35] your secret, he goes to the friend wherever he is and he fulfils his commission with all possible accuracy, then the friend receiving the letter will read it and considering the seal he will see that he must turn to the northwest and he speaks the following words to make the sent Spirit appear so that he declares to him the secret message entrusted to him.

> Usiel asoyr paremon cruato madusyn savepy mavayr realdo chameron ilco paneras thurmo pean elsoty fabelrusyn iltras charson frymasto chelmodyn.

Having pronounced these words being turned towards the northwest the Spirit will appear and declare what has been entrusted to him, then the friend leaves and comes to find you and to participate and benefit from your discovery.

CHAPTER 12

The Spirit and Supreme Emperor is called CABARIEL who dwells in that quarter of the universe which we call north-north-west, having under him 70 Princes by day and as many by night.

The Grand Emperor Cabariel has his abode with an infinite number of other Spirits in that quarter of the universe which is called north-north-west, [from which] comes the wind thus named, among which there are 50 who preside over the operations of this mysterious Art which take place during the day and as many for those of night, in all weathers, are many familiar and powerful, whose Office and power is to announce and warn a friend or several friends of the operator, and to discover their pitfalls, as well as to veil the most secret traps of which we must be most careful, and warn an absent friend by the ways contained in this chapter. Of the number, of which we will name a small but sufficient number for the operations of this Art, you will see in the following table.

[36] Black	R.	B.	R.	B.	R.	B.	R.
Satifiel	50	Etymel	50	Mador	50	Ladiel	50
Parius	50	Clyssan	50	Peniel	50	Morias	50
Godiel	50	Elytel	50	Cugiel	50	Pandor	50
Taros	50	Aniel	50	Thalbos	50	Cazul	50
Asoriel	50	Cuphar	50	Orym	50	Dubiel	50

Table 12: Emperor Cabariel and his twenty Princes.

Of the hundred Princes in the service of Cabariel you have twenty of the principal ones represented in this table. This small number is enough for the present of which the first 10 are deputies for the operations which are in the day with 500 of their servants and the other 10 for the operations of the night, having similarly under their powers 500 servants. It is important to know that those who preside over the operations of the day are much more beneficent, and quicker to obey than those who are offered for night operations. But we are often obliged to call nocturnal Spirits with some violence and more often are we obliged to repeat the words of their call many times. They bring their servants with them when they are asked, but if they are not asked, they hide them. When you want to operate through the ministry of these Spirits, turn to the side indicated by the region, call with great cordiality, and say the next oraison.

> Cabariel onear chameron fruani parnaton fofiel bryosi nagreal fabelrontyn adiel thortay nosruau pena afefiel chusy.

Suppose, for example, that you have a secret which should not be entrusted to anyone.

You have a faithful friend that you favour like yourself, but he is absent. You are aware that they want to lay some more powerful traps for him, either in a way or in any place, or in any manner. You wish to warn him but you run great risks if you were discovered in warning him, so that you do not write to him lest your letters be [37] read by anyone, nor do you entrust it to a man lest he betray you. To be safe you, your friend, and the informed friend call the Spirit, entrust to him your secret to be executed, by sending a familiar letter containing a prayer oration that everyone can read, or whatever you please, without your secret being questioned.

When your friend has received this letter, having recognised the sign of Cabariel, turn to the side of the centre from which the so-called north-north-west wind comes, and with great cordiality he will recite the following prayer, with a deep silence.

> Cabariel afiar paremon chiltan amedyn sayr pemadon chulty movayr savepor peatha mal frim aston dayr pean cothurno fabelrusyn elsoty chelmodyn.

Having finished pronouncing the mysterious words of this oraison, and having taken care to turn to the side that is mentioned, inevitably the Angel will immediately appear visibly, and having exposed your oral secret to him, he will go and report the answer to you.

CHAPTER 13

The Prince is called RAYSIEL having his residence in the north who has under him 50 Princes, who preside over the operations of the day, and as many for those of the night, their duty is to announce the secrets and traditions.

The thirteenth Mansion is located directly to the north from which comes the full north wind, whose supreme Emperor of this region of the universe is called Raysiel, who has under him 50 Dukes who preside over the operations of the day with many servants, and as many who preside over the operations which take place during the night with their servants. Their Office is in that part which concerns death, or giving notice to the friends of the operator and announcing a secret. The Dukes who preside over the operations of the day willingly obey the operator and come promptly and with [38] joy and all are ready to follow what they are ordered, but those who preside over night operations are sometimes rebellious, because they very much hate light and [love] darkness. They hate and do not easily obey especially novices and those who are not expert in this Art, because often they laugh in their face, unless the operator forces them absolutely by the strong words, contained in the mystical prayers that they are forced to obey. They fear very much to be forced by these celestial and mysterious words, because of the great strength and power the words have over them. They fear more to be forced than the Spirits who preside over the operations of the day, and yet they only obey by force. We will only name a small number of these Spirits with [the numbers] of their servants, but nevertheless as much as is necessary for customary operations. Here is the table.

B.	☿	R.		♀	B.		♃	R.		♄
Baciar	50	Astael	50		Chanael	30		Melcha	30	
Thoac	50	Ramica	50		Fursiel	30		Tharas	30	
Sequiel	50	Dubarus	50		Betasiel	30		Uviel	30	
Sadar	50	Armena	50							
Terath	50	Albhadur	50							
Red	B.	R.	B.		R.	B.		R.	B.	
Thariel	40	Lazaba	40		Lamas	10		Thurcal	10	
Paras	40	Aleazy	40							
Arayl	40	Sebach	40		Belsay	20		Sarach	20	
Culmar	40	Quibda	40		Morael	20		Arepach	20	

Table 13: Emperor Raysiel and his 50 Princes.

Dear Reader, you now have 16 Princes with 670 of their servants of the 50 who preside over the nocturnal [hours], and you have 14 with 420 of their servants.

Steganographia

This number is enough for you both for the operations of the day and for those of the night [39] when you will operate by them according to the hours marked, in order to arrange whoever you want, and call them from the north because they all live there. For this purpose it is necessary to pronounce the following words.

> Raysiel afruano chameron fofiel onear vemabi parnothon fruano caspiel fufre bedarym bulifeor pean curmaby layr vaymeor pesarym adorcus odiel vernabi peatha darsum laspheno devior camedonton phorsy lasbenay to charmo druson olnays, venovym lulefon, peorso fabelrontos thurno. Calephoy vem, nabelron bural thorasym charnoty capelron.

This prayer being recited exactly and in silence, the called Spirit will appear, confide to him your secret in safety, he will carry the news, and will bring back the reply, but if you appeal to those who preside over night operations (as they usually have the custom of delaying the future) call them again, reiterating the oraisons with strength, and with a male voice, fearing nothing, and they will be forced to respect you as their master.

For example, I have a secret that I do not trust to anyone. I put the case that I have a noble and learned friend, and I learned that someone who was in charge of a force determined to harm him. I do not dare to warn him openly because I will encounter peril in a familiar and very secret cause, I dare not confide it to a letter which I fear may fall into the hands of my enemies, or entrust it to a man who could speak and who I do not suppose I can entrust it to, because the one who is with me today, may not be with me tomorrow, on the contrary he may be with my enemy, that is why I have recourse to Art, and so I will not fear the pitfalls, nor that my secret becomes public, when even some enemy may harm me.

[**Example**] I send a familiar letter to my friend, who is in no danger.

When your friend receives this letter (or another), being instructed in this Art, and having recognised the sign of Raysiel and having done what must be done, he will turn to the direction [40] of the north to cause the Spirit sent to him to appear, and he will pronounce the words that make up the following oraison.

> Raysiel myltran fruano fiar chasmy clymarso pean sayr pultho chulthusa medon vepursandly tusan axeyr afflon.

When you have completed this oraison the called Spirit will appear visibly and will give an account of all that he has been told into your ear. Know that all the Spirits who preside over night operations do not come willingly at night unless they are forced by dint of the Sacraments, by reiterating prayers to force and compel them to come and appear, but when they come for you to send them to the friend, they usually appear and fulfil their Office diligently, and obey the operator, unless the operator on some occasion has overlooked anything in what this Art requires.

CHAPTER 14

The Supreme Emperor is called SYMIEL, who resides in north-north-east, having under him 10 Dukes who preside over the operations of the day with many servants. Their Office is to announce some family secrets.

The fourteenth Mansion is located in north-north-east, away from the beginning of due north by a little more than 20 degrees, whose Supreme Emperor is called Symiel who has under him 10 Dukes or Princes who preside over the day's operations with many sub-servants and for night operations I could not find any fixed and certain number, who also have many sub-servants. Their Office is to see and announce among friends their most secret thoughts, which one must never declare to any other man, and when you next operate by them if necessary, I will name the 10 who preside over the day's operations, and for [41] those who preside over the night, I will name as many as you need to operate. See the table below.

Black		B		B		B		♀
Asmyel	60	Larael	60	Mafrus	70	Marianu		100
Chrubas	100	Achot	60	Apiel	30	Narzael		201
Vastos	40	Banier	90	Curiel	40	Murahe		30
Malgron	20	Dagiel	100	Molael	10	Richel		120
Romiel	80	Musor	110	Arafos	50	Nalael		130

Table 14: Emperor Symiel and his Dukes.

You currently have in this table the ten Dukes who preside over the operations of the day and ten for those of the night and also many of their substitutes by means of which you will be able to operate in safety and without any peril, as you are well instructed in the Art. For all who do not know what concerns this Art and who want to operate in it, where he will do anything, there will be danger, because not all Princes will obey. But you who will operate in this Art having done what there is to do before, turn to the north-north-east in the way that I have already taught you, compel the Duke to come by means of the following words.

> Symiel myrno chamerony theor pasron adjuveal famerosthi sofear carmedon charnothiel peasor sositran fabulrusy thyrno pamerosy trelno chabelron chymo churmabon, asiel peasor carmes nabeyros toys camalthonty.

Having said them in the necessary way, the Spirit whom you have called will be ready to obey your commands. If the operation must be done during the night and if these Spirits do not appear immediately, do not neglect your operation for that, but force them by repeating the words of constraint, and they will obey by this force.

Supposing, for example, that you have a very particular secret, which you cannot trust to any mortal. [42] You have some secret affair which concerns both you and your friend, and whose discovery or manifestation will turn to your loss or confusion, so you dare not entrust it to letters, lest they be read, nor to an envoy lest he divulge it to others, so use the Art as you will be safe, and then your friend Scaura [will understand] what you have to confide in him, write a letter to your friend, at the bottom of which affix the seal of this Spirit. Your friend, who is doubtless learned in the Art, upon receiving your letter as soon as he sees the sign of Symiel will know what he must do. He must turn to the north-north-east to make the Spirit appear, and he must say the following words.

> SYMIEL marlos chameron pyrcohi pean fruaty fabelronti gaelto siargoti metassor hialbra penor olesy Ajulbrani ordu casmeron omer vemabon.

These words being pronounced distinctly the Spirit sent will appear visibly and will faithfully discharge his commission, etc.

CHAPTER 15

The first Emperor is called ARMADIEL who dwells in that quarter of the universe which we call northeast, from where the wind Boreas is wont to come from and breathe, having under him many Princes and Lords.

The fifteenth Mansion in the northeast is where the Boreas wind originates and is the residence of the Grand Prince Armadiel, having under his dominion many Princes and Dukes with their vassals, of which there are one hundred deputies for the operations of day and night alike, stronger than any president in various operations, either day or night according to the will of the operator in this Art. Their Office is to announce to Princes and great Lords the most secret intentions [of the operator], and the secrets of operating with great fidelity and mystery.

[43] R	☿ R	B.	R	B	R	B	R	B
Massar	50	Orariel	Pandiel	10	10	60	60	50
Parabiel	40	Oryn	Carasiba	20	20	70	70	40
Laiel	30	Samiel	Asbibiel	30	30	80	80	30
Calvarnya	20	Asmael	Mafayr	40	40	70	70	20
Alferiel	10	Jaziel	Oeniel	50	50	60	60	10

Table 15: Emperor Armadiel with his 15 Princes.

In this table there are reported a small number, but enough for you to operate, you are presented with the names of the 15 Princes of the great Armadiel with his vassals to the number of 1260 which according to the division of the 24 hours in six parts are wont to come at the will of the operator, following the order and their rank. When you want by this means to operate in this Art, it is necessary that you diligently observe the division of time according to this Art, for otherwise you will do nothing. Knowing what it takes, turn to the northeast, and doing what the Art demands, on this occasion, say the following words.

> Armadiel marbevo pelrusan neor chamyn aldron pemarson cathornaor pean lyburmy caveron tharty abesmeron vear larso charnoty theor caveos myat drupas camedortys lypa ruffes ernoty mesoryn elthi chaor atiel, laniesayn rovemu fabelrusin, friatochasalon pheor thamorny nesardiel pelusy madiel baseroty sarreon prolsoyr asenosy cameltruson.

When you have finished pronouncing these words in the necessary manner, the Spirit will immediately appear to you, ready to obey your commands. Suppose we have a secret that we do not want to confide to anyone. I have a secret that I would like to send to my Prince, I dare not confide it to a person, nor let him know by letter, lest by negligence or forgetfulness, he will not read it, I want even less to let him know by human voice, fearing that by any indiscretion it comes to the knowledge of others, I have recourse to the Art, and I am sure that he will be in eternal silence.

[44] Form of the letter. "To the very high and serene Prince N. Count of, etc."

Having this letter, or such other, that one will send him who is an expert in this Art, and having received this letter in which he will recognise the sign of Armadiel he turns to the direction that this Art requires and he says the following words.

> Armadiel afran meson casayr pelodyn, cavoty chameron thersorvy marbevon pheor casoyn myrvosy lyburny deon fabelronton chubis archamarson.

Having finished pronouncing these words in the accustomed manner the Spirit sent will appear to him visibly and will teach him all that he is charged to teach him, with fidelity, without adding any mystery, and if one wants to charge him again with a commission or response, do what the Art requires, and he will do it.

CHAPTER 16

The Supreme Prince who is called BARUCHAS remains in that quarter of the universe which we call east-north-east, from whence this wind customarily comes, which at his command has many Princes and Lords with their vassals who preside over the secret operations of Princes.

At the sixth and last[1] Mansion is where the great Prince Baruchas who has under his rule many Princes, Dukes, and other Spirits whose Office it is to announce the secret commissions of Princes, nobles, and great Lords to their subjects or friends, of these we will name 15 which are enough for any operator in this Art, and have no division or order between them for operations either by day or night like the others, but they all have the same commission in general, so that they are obliged to come whenever the operator requires it and at whatever hour. The explanation is after the next table.

[45] Red	B	R.	B	R.	B	R.	B	R.
Quita	Cartael	Monael	100	10	600	60	500	50
Sarael	Janiel	Chubor	200	20	700	70	400	40.
Melchon	Pharol	Lamael	300	30	800	80	300	30
Covayr	Baoxas	Dorael	400	40	700	70	200	20
Aboc	Geriel	Decaniel	500	50	600	60	100	10

Table 16: Emperor Baruchas with his vassals.

You currently have the names of 15 of the principal Officers of the great Emperor Baruchas and this number suffices to operate in this Art with their subjects or vassals to the number of 7040, whose ministry suffices for any operation therefore. When you want to invoke some of these Spirits, observe the division of time into six hours of day and night, and having his face turned to the east-north-east, invoke him whom the hour requires by carefully observing the numbers of the vassals, otherwise we would do nothing. Take care not to make a mistake in the number, the order, or the residence, and being turned to the said side, you will say the following.

> Baruchas malvear chemorsyn charnotiel bason Janocri medusyn aprilty casmyron sayr pean cavoty medason peroel chamyrsyn cherdiel avenos nosear paneon sayr chavelonti genayr pamelronfrilcha madyrion onetiel fabelronthos.

You pronounce these words in silence, as is necessary, as soon as the principal Spirit appears, that is to say, the one you have called with the subjects that are

---

[1] Not the last spirit, but the last one to be attributed to a Mansion and a direction.

submitted and awarded in order of time. For example, I have a commission to purge some religious order to correct and repress some cenobites.[1] I want to send this news to a friend who is absent, but if it becomes public, it could put him in prison, or attract the hatred of some Prior or Superior of the convent which could cause him some harm, or cause an order [against] the common good. From which we conclude that we can entrust it neither to letters nor to any man, and to be sure of both I have recourse [46] to the mysteries; I invoke a Spirit, I entrust him with my secret and I charge him with a letter which none may fear from the speech which it contains, putting at the bottom the sigil of Baruchas as here

When the letter is received, consider the sigil of the Spirit and turn to the direction, then do what is necessary, and recite in a low voice the following words.

> Baruchas Mularchas chameron notiel pedarsy phroys lamasay myarchalemon phorsy fabelrontho theras capean Vear almonym lierno medusan therfiel peatha thumar nerosyn cral nothiel peson segalry madon scoha bulayr.

Having recited these words according to the precepts of the Art, the Spirit sent appears and will fulfil his commission, and whisper it into his ear without any deceit.

---

[1] Members of a monastic community, monks.

[49]¹

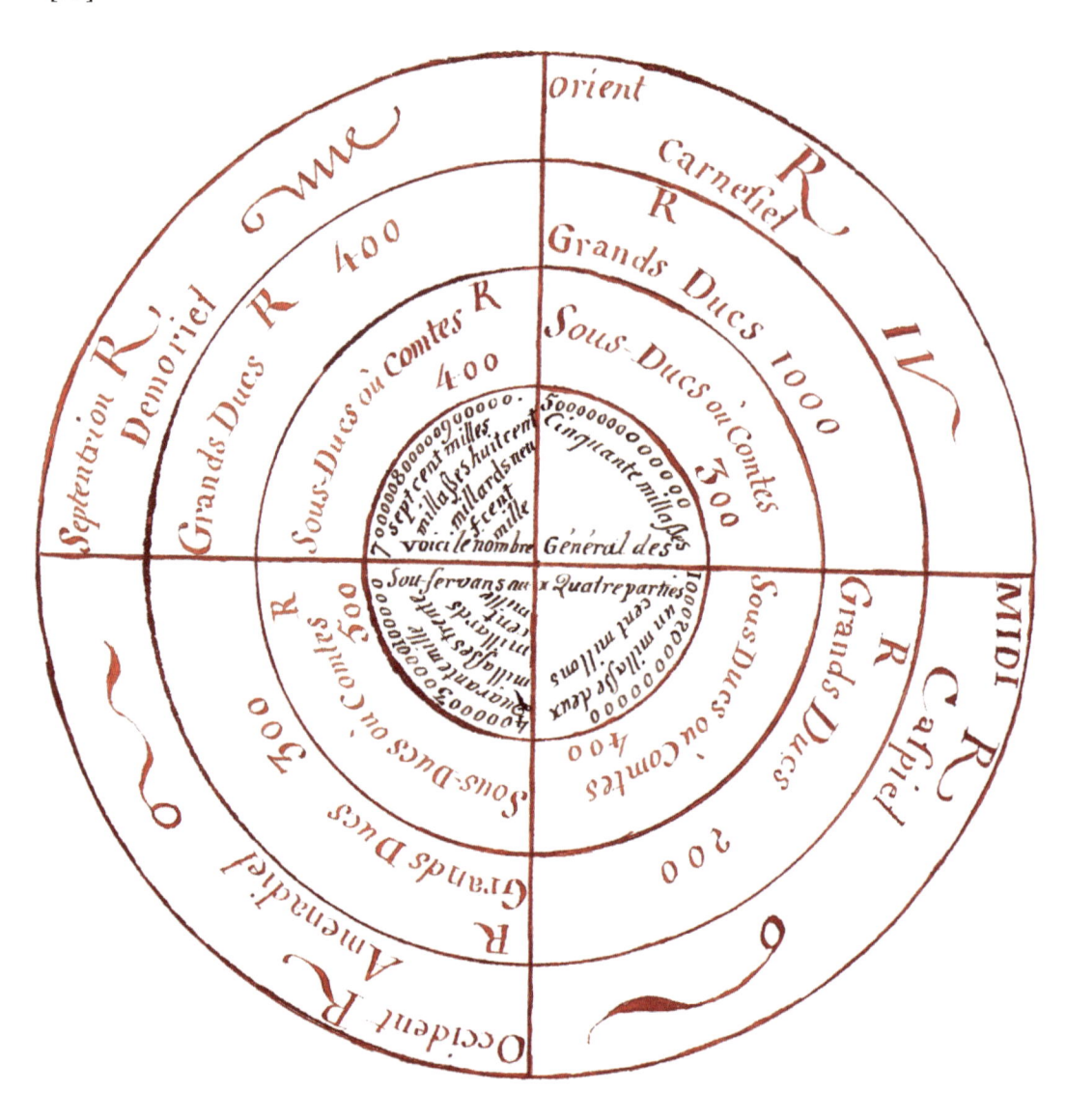

Figure 13: The Four Parts of the World and their Spirits which together contain this number of known sub-servants, seven hundred forty thousand, fifty-one thousand, eight hundred and thirty billion two hundred and one million. 740051830201000000.²

---

¹ This illustration has been moved forward by two pages as it summarises the structure and details of the next four Spirits who are the 4 main Princes of this hierarchy. East is at the top of the page.
² The outer ring contains the direction and name of the Emperor. The second ring contains the Grand Dukes and their servant numbers. The third ring contains the Dukes and Counts with their numbers. The fourth ring contains the total number of sub-servants in numbers and words.

CHAPTER 17

The Supreme Prince and Spirit is called CARNESIEL who dwells in the east, having under his command many Princes and lords with their vassals, whose duty it is to announce and report everything that relates to the eastern quarter.

Since we have a lot of business or news to send to some absent friends and whose part is not exactly explained in the previous chapters, or at least there can be found parts whose Spirits are not specially explained, and fear that the operator in this Art may find some difficulty in the perfection of the Art after having specified the Spirits which specifically dominate each secret, we now want to specify in general the Spirits who generally dominate so that if by any chance someone happens to need any commission not specified in the previous 16 chapters [they may] have recourse to these who, according to their Order, have commission over all others. In a way, however, they [47] do not deviate from their sector nor from their generality and we use them according to that generality [of direction].

There are four great Princes with their vassals who preside over all the news that we may send to the different parts of the universe and which were not expressed above. The first of which is called Carnesiel, presides over all the news that must be sent towards the east, Caspiel towards the south, Ameñadiel towards the west and Demoriel has all which generally looks to the quarter of the north.

When you want to know some secret of some absent friend, and this towards the east, you must therefore turn during all the operation towards that quarter according to what the Art requires. I will give you some notice of the principal officers with their vassals which suffice for the operation, and take care not to be mistaken in the names of the Spirits. See the construction of the following table.

R	B	R	B	R	B	R
Myresyn	Benoham	Armany	60000000000000			
Ornich	Arisiel	Capriel	10	30	100	300
Zabriel	Cumeriel	Bedarys	10	30	100	300
Bucafas	Vadriel	Laphor	10	30	100	300

Table 17: Supreme Prince Carnesiel with his vassals.

You presently have 12 of the principal officers of Carnesiel with a great number of subjects remarked that the great number of sixty billion is the number of the vassals and the other officers who generally preside over the operations of the day, and the operator will call whichever of these Spirits he wishes with the above-named Duke, and the others in quadruple order are the vassals of the 12 Princes, and always come with them according to their rank, when you want to operate with them, having executed what must be done, say these words.

> Camesiel aphroys chemeryn mear aposen Layr pean noema ovear masere cralty calevo thorteam chameron Janoar pelyn Layr, baduson Jesy melros Jonatiel delassar rodivial meron savean fabelron clumarsy preos throen benarys savean demosy non learnoty chamedonton.

[48] Having therefore uttered the words above, the general messenger of the secrets whom you have called will appear promptly, faithful, obedient and secret.

For example, I would like to give notice to an absent friend, so that he beware, touching upon a treaty man;[1] but this secretly.

There is a man beneath an honest exterior who hides an evil design, he knows that I can give him letters of recommendation to a friend, I don't dare refuse him, nor do I want to let him be deceived by this treaty, I write letters in which I praise the treaty, he reads it and sees no [adverse] opinion, I give him the letters, he goes away happy, then I call a Spirit, I send him to this friend to whom he reveals the secret concerning the treaty which comes with the letters.

Compose such letters as you wish, to be sent by the Spirit to your friend.[2]

When your friend has received this letter, or some other similar, being informed in our Art, he will observe the sign, character, or seal which is attributed to Prince Carnesiel, so that he turns towards the east, and having done what is necessary, he will say the following words

> Carnesiel aproysi chameron to pemalroyn phroys cadur mearmol benadron vioniel saviron army pean arnotiel fabelronthusyn throe chabelron savenear medaloys vear olmenadab cralty sayr.

Having finished pronouncing these words, the Spirit sent will appear visibly, and then he will faithfully reveal to you the secret communication which he has been charged to give you.

You will now see [in Figure 13], a circle in which is contained the Four Principal Emperors, the situation of their Mansions, the number of Dukes and sub-servants and vassals, so you can hardly know the correct count.

One must know how one must operate through them.

---

[1] Someone offering to negotiate a treaty or a contract.
[2] Normally the physical letters and contract would be conveyed by a physical messenger, not a Spirit.

[50] CHAPTER 18

The Main Spirit is called CASPIEL and his Mansion is Midi, in the south, he has under him an infinite number of Princes, Dukes, and vassals.

To the south dwells Prince Caspiel who has under his rule two hundred principal Princes and 400 Counts or vassals with an infinite number of servants whose Office is to announce generally all that relates to the south and which are not contained in the previous 16 chapters, and since it is absolutely necessary to know some names of the Dukes, especially as there are many, we are going to name some in this table, a few of this number will however be sufficient.

R	B	R	B	R	B	R	R
Ursiel	Budarym	Geriol	200	40	2000	400	20
Chariel	Camory	Ambri	200	40	2000	400	20
Maras	Larmol	Camor	200	40	2000	400	20
Femol	Aridiel	Otiel	200	40	2000	400	20

Table 18: Prince Caspiel with his vassals.

You currently have in this table, 12 of the main officers of Caspiel with their Counts, vassals and sub-servants to the number of 100640 who have the commission to announce all the secrets concerning the southern quarter in general. So when you want to let a friend know some hidden secret, do what the Art requires, being turned towards the south, you will have to say the following words.

> Caspiel aloyr chameron noeres padyr diviel prolsyn vear maduson cralnotifruon phorsy larsonthon thiano pemarson theor. Caveos adeveos friato briosi paniel drubon madiel sayr fabelrusyn gonear pean noty nabufran.

These words being recited in the necessary manner you will see appear those whom you have called and who are ready to obey all your commandments. In general, all these Dukes of Caspiel are very gentle and voluntary, but nevertheless they are obliged [51] to obey due to the strength and power of the mystical words, if the operator is firm, constant and without terror, speaking to them harshly and with great authority, but no Spirit is so harsh or rebellious, who being strong by virtue of these words, is not forced and compelled to obey.

Suppose we have a secret that should not be confided to anyone.

I only deal with a friend, who if found out, it would create great peril for both of us, as all the messengers are observed, so that one may discover the secrets of the letters, of that we are sure, so that our business is secret and safe, I write letters which fear the sight of no one, then I entrust my secret to a Spirit who will communicate it to my friend by giving him a letter, provided that it is sealed with the sigil of the Spirit which is thus

When the one to whom you have written these letters has received them, and has recognised the sigil of the Spirit, being instructed in the Art, he performs what the Art demands, turns to the south, and says the following words.

> Caspiel asbyr chameronty churto freveon dayr fabelron cathurmy meresyn elso peano tailtran caspio suar Medon clibarsy caberosyn ulty pean Vearches pemasy natolbyr meldary noe cardenopen men for diviel adro.

Having spoken these words and having put them into practice, the Spirit which is the invisible messenger will immediately appear, reporting to your friend secretly by ear what you have entrusted to him, and that without any disguise.

CHAPTER 19

The Supreme Spirit is called AMENADIEL and his residence is to the west and he has under him 300 Dukes and 500 Counts, and an innumerable quantity of servants.

Amenadiel is the Supreme Spirit and Emperor of the west, having under [52] his command 300 Dukes or principal powers, and no less than 500 Counts or vassals, with servants or sub-servants of an infinite number whose names are no less in number than 30,000, in addition to many others whose names I have not yet found, number is sufficient for operations concerning the west, but I will give you in this table the names of the Dukes which are necessary for the ministry of this Art.

R	B	R	B	R	B	R	B
Vadros	Rapsiel	Almesiel	30	50	300	500	3000
Camiel	Lamael	Codriel	30	50	300	500	3000
Luziel	Zoeniel	Balsur	30	50	300	500	3000
Musiriel	Curifas	Nadroc	30	50	300	500	3000

Table 19: The Dukes of Amenadiel with their Counts.

You currently have in this table, 12 of the main officers of Amenadiel with their Counts, vassals and sub-servants, with whom you can operate in all operations concerning the quarter of the west where remains the largest Prince, but watch diligently, I let you know when you call someone from the Dukes, you have to know how many vassals and sub-servants he has according to the hours of the day and night which are divided equally into 1550 parts according to their Orders that govern the hours. To whom if you miss you will not operate [successfully], on the contrary you will run into great peril. It is necessary that whoever wants to operate in this Art, it is necessary that he is not only an expert in this part of our Art, but in the other parts, because by the slightest negligence, great peril could come. Whenever you want to operate by one of these Spirits, turn to the west and having done everything well, you say the following words.

> Amenadiel aprolsy chameronta nofroy throen mesro salayr chemaros noe pean larsy freveon Jonatiel pelroyn rathroy caser malusan pedon cranochiran daboyseor marchosyn lavo pedar venoti gesroy phernotiel Cabron.

These words being said exactly, the Spirit will appear, whom you will have called, [53] of course he will be quick and alert, to execute whatever you command.

For example. I have a well-hidden secret; it is necessary that my friend hide it.

I have a friend to whom I would like to let know an important secret that I dare not confide, neither to men nor to letters, because if it happened to become public it would cause me great damage and peril, but I can no longer bear to delay in instructing my friend, besides the time is short and for this purpose I call a Spirit, and I write letters which are not suspicious, and which one cannot believe to be enigmatic if ignorant of Latin. I send this Spirit charged with my letters and I entrust him with my secret, which he will secretly reveal to my friend. Having previously delivered my letters in which is this sign

When the friend receives this letter or other such given to the Spirit, the friend being well instructed in the Art and having known the sigil of the Spirit and Prince Amenadiel Emperor of the west, let him turn to this quarter and perform what is necessary and say the following.

> Amenadiel bulurym chameroty eriscoha pedarmon flusro pean truarbiel fabelron greos belor malgoty nabarym stilco melros fuar pelaryso chitron amanacason.

Having finished speaking these words in the necessary way the Spirit will appear visibly, sometimes invisibly, and reveal the secret to the friend.

Steganographia

CHAPTER 20

The Supreme Prince is called DEMORIEL who has his dwelling in the north having under his power 400 major Dukes or Princes, vassals or 600 first subjects with many sub-servants whose number is uncertain.

It is therefore in the north that the great Prince Demoriel lives, having under his command 400 principal Dukes whom he sends for the ministry of this Art according to their order with their vassals, to the number of 600 at least [54] to announce all the secrets you will send to a friend in the north, being instructed in the Art, and having done what there is to do, we will name only those which are necessary for us to operate with the number of their Counts and servants according to their order in their hours.

R	B	R	B	R	B	R	B
Arnibiel	Doriel	Medar	40	600	400	60	40
Cabarym	Mador	Churibal	40	600	400	60	40
Menador	Carnol	Dabrinos	40	600	400	60	40
Burisiel	Dubilon	Chomiel	40	600	400	60	40

Table 20: The Dukes and Counts of Prince Demoriel.

You have about 400 Dukes of Demoriel and 12 Counts and 4560 servants in number who go with their Dukes according to the order of the 24 hours of the day and of the night, which is what you need to know first of all, when you want to operate with one of these Dukes in this Art, turn to the northern side as is the custom, and having executed what the Art requires, you pronounce the following.

> Demoriel onear dabursoy cohyne chamerson ymeor pean olayr chelrusys noeles schemlaryn venodru patron myslero chadarbon vevaon maferos ratigiel personay lodiol camedon nasiel fabelmeruzin sosiel chamarchoysyn.

Having said these words the Spirit will appear visibly to you, and be quick to obey all that you want to command him, to whom you can entrust the secret that you want him to hold. (I have such a secret in me) and I have a friend who is away for the present, and with whom I have intimate and secret affairs, which I cannot surely entrust to anyone. So that he remains in safety, it is therefore always necessary to call a familiar Spirit, and entrust him with your secret, he comes, he goes, he faithfully fulfils his commission by telling your friend your secret and we are both sure and this same Spirit will bring you the secret answer of your friend, which must not be entrusted to any mortal. So that your friend may know what Spirit you are sending him [55] you pretend to write him a letter which is in no way suspicious, in which you add the sigil of the Spirit which here is in this form

Steganographia

The Spirit will not appear visible unless you compel it (draft your letter), etc.

When your friend has received this letter, being an expert in this Art, let him first do what the Art requires, then turn to the north as is the custom, and say the following.

> Demoriel osayr chameron chalty save porean lusin dayr pean cathurmo fomarson ersoty lamedon Jothar busraym fuar menadroy chilarso fabelmerusyn.

These words being completed as specified, the Spirit sent will appear visibly to him alone, and he will whisper the secret in his ear.

CHAPTER 21

The Supreme Spirit and Emperor is called GERADIEL. This great Prince has no particular residence, but he is in the habit of being universal and everywhere.

Besides those Emperors, Princes and Dukes of the Spirits who we have named in the preceding chapters, who subsist and dwell in fixed places in the universe, visible from where they are deputies, and many other vague, unstable ones, having no fixed abode,[1] which the ancient scholars and philosophers called unstable, because they fly in the air like flies without order, without habitation and without reserve, and those are very useful in our Art, because they do not require the observation of places, but they can be called by each one who calls them. The first of those is called Geradiel who has under his command no Prince nor Duke but only servants whose number is uncertain whom he takes with him for his ministry according to the order they observe among themselves, and according to the 24 hours of the day and the night, whose Office is generally to announce the secrets in some quarter of [56] the universe as may be. See the construction of this table.

	R	B	B	R	B	B	R	B
Hours of {	2	2	200	100	40	30	50	60
the day {	2	2	80	70	100	90	120	110
&	R	2	140	B	R	150	180	170
of the {	22			R	130	160		
night. {	22	2		200	1000	400	300	60	500
{	2	2	800	700	10000	900	1200	110

Table 21: Emperor Geradiel and his hosts.

You have in this table, 18150 ministers and servants of the great Prince Geradiel named[2] and arranged according to their order and according to the hours, and you will know that this provision is absolutely necessary for you to operate, so that you know at what time and in what number they usually come, but the servants are deputies according to their hour. I therefore advise you to pay attention to the hours in your operations during which he usually comes himself with the servants of this hour, who without their Emperor are not always willing and quick to obey the operator. So when you want to operate by these Spirits having executed what there is to do, then say the following words.

Geradiel onayr bulesar modran pedarbon sazevo nabor vielis proyn therdial

---
[1] Later called Wandering Dukes in the *Theurgia-Goetia*.
[2] In this table they are not actually named.

masre reneal chemarson cuhadiam almona saelry penoyr satodial chramel nadiarsy thorays Vayr pean esridiel cubal draony myar dearsy colludarsy menador atotiel cumalym drasmodiar parmy sosiel almenarys satiel chulty peson duarsy cuber fruony maroy futiel fablemerusi venodran pralso lusior lamedon fyvaro larboys theory malrosyn.

These words being finished the Spirit shall come, either the chief among the servants, or the servants of the number of the hour without their Prince, as you wish, according to the hours. As it is said above, bring your intentions with regard to the hours. We will pass over any secrets, for them to be always hidden.

[57] I have a secret so hidden that I would like to communicate it to one or more friends instructed in our Art, by the ministry of these Spirits; I call the Prince named above, in the favourable hour, I confide my secret to him, he receives it, goes away, he executes and completes faithfully his commission, for which I send letters only for form, to deceive men, and ensure to whom I send theme will know the character or sigil of the Spirit hereafter represented, so that he knows what Spirit he must invoke, because they do not appear easily without being forced and coerced.

Form your letter as you please, and send the faithful messenger. **X**

Your friend having received this letter anywhere else, signed in the character of Geradiel, it will not be necessary for him to turn in either direction, but having executed what the Art demands, the following words must be pronounced.

> Geradiel osayl chamerusin chulti pemarsoniel dayr fayr chaturmo les bornatyn ersoty camylor sayr fabelmerodan cosry damerson maltey nabelmerusyn.

Having recited these words the sent Spirits will appear visibly to you and will reveal the whole secretly into your ear.

Steganographia

CHAPTER 22

The Prince of this chapter is called BURIEL he is a nocturnal Spirit which flees the light, which has its abode in the lakes and caves of the Earth, and one does no operation by his department except at night.

After the great Prince Geradiel, then comes the great Prince Buriel, who is truly great, but perverse and wicked, who hates all other Spirits, especially Princes, he persecutes and hates them, but he no less hates and fears the light and flees from it with all his vassals, and never used to come except at night, and that frequently with great tumult, trying to cause horror [58] and terror to the operator, especially if he is not well instructed, constant, and strong in Spirit, and often he appears in the form of a serpent, having the head of a girl, the tail and all of the serpent's body, uttering a horrible hiss, and being constrained and forced, [according to] how gifted he is, he will speak to you in a human voice. He has Dukes under him and Princes, whom it is customary to send to ministries with their subordinates whose number is infinite. We will name some of them in the following table, which will be enough for us to operate.

R	B	R	B	R	B	R
Merosiel	Casbriel	Drusiel	100	10	10	100
Almadiel	Nedriel	Carniel	100	10	10	100
Cupriel	Bufiel	Drubiel	100	10	10	100
Sarviel	Futiel	Nastros	100	10	10	100

Table 22: The Dukes of the Wandering Prince Buriel.

You have in this table, 12 main vassals of Buriel with 880 main sub-servants, who preside over operations according to the 12 unequal hours of night, which we call Planetary hours, with their leaders each in his rank; when called upon by the operator in due manner, the principal Duke has the custom to appear in the said form, but the sub-servants are accustomed to appear in the form of Guenons,[1] playing, frolicking and dancing while leaping about from one to another pleasant arena. So when you want to operate by these Princes do not think to plan to start before sunset, because they only obey during the night. It is not necessary to observe the sector of the universe, but you will say the following words looking at the earth under your feet.

> Buriel mastfoyr chamerusyn, noel pean janochym mardusan philarsii, pedarym estlis carmoy boyscharonti phroys fabelronti, mear laphany vearchas, clareson, notiel, pador aslotiel, marsyno reneas, capedon, thisimasion melro, lavair carpentor, thurneam camelrosyn.

---
[1] A variety of monkey.

[59] Having finished pronouncing these words, still looking at the Earth, the Spirits that you have called will come; but be careful not to be terrified, because they cannot harm you if you are firm and of a constant spirit, and notice that all the Princes and Spirits, although they are deputed to announce, full of secrets, during the night in general, they are however more prompt and volunteer to bring news to prisons, dungeons, to prisoners, even those concerning carnal love, and the secret practices of lovers, and all that relates to the night, either good or bad, because they hate the light.

Suppose we have a secret that absolutely cannot be confided to anyone. However, I want to entrust it to a friend established in this city and I cannot send him either by letter or by messenger lest it become public. I have several obstacles that prevent me from approaching this friend, so I call on one of these above-named Spirits, I entrust the mystery to him, he goes and fulfils his commission faithfully and you are safe.

Send a letter as you please, with this sign 𝛑

When your friend has this letter, being instructed in the Art and recognizing the sign of Buriel, he will do what he must do, let him gaze upon the Earth, and say what follows.

> Buriel Thresoy chamerontis, hayr plassu, nadiel, marso, neany, pean, sayr fabelron, chaturmo, melros, ersoty caduberosyn.

Having said these words, the Spirit invisible to all will appear visibly to you and reveal the secret with which it is entrusted.

Steganographia

CHAPTER 23

This Emperor is a Supreme Spirit called HYDRIEL who dwells in the waters, and under him are 100 Dukes and 200 Counts and an infinite number of sub-servants.

[60] Hydriel is a Prince who is chief among the principal Spirits who dwell in waters, pools, lakes, marshes, in the sea, and around fountains, cisterns, and rivers. This Emperor has under his dominion at least 100 Dukes or Princes, 200 Counts or vassals, and many sub-servants, their Office having generally been all the news, both by water and by land; either during the day or at night, and know that they are quite benevolent and wilful over all Princes, but they do not appear so when forced and coerced, as they appear frequently under the figure of a snake, sometimes large, sometimes small, with the head of a very beautiful girl having dishevelled hair. None of them come alone, but each Prince brings with him at least two Counts and 80 sub-servants. So that you do not meet any difficulty, I will name for you the names of some Dukes. See the table.

R		R		R	B	R
Mortaliel	Lameniel	Camiel	10	20	100	200
Chamoriel	Brachiel	Arbiel	10	20	100	200
Pesariel	Samiel	Lusiel	10	20	100	200
Musuziel	Dusiriel	Chariel	10	20	100	200

Table 23: The Dukes of Hydriel, Prince of Water.

Here are 12 of the main officers of Hydrael[1] with 1320 sub-servants that will be enough for you for the operations of this Art according to the order of 24 hours so that each Duke has 2 hours and 110 Counts and sub-servants according to their rank, which you absolutely must know.[2] When you want to operate something by the Prince of [Water] Spirits, do what you know the Art requires, and say the following words.

> Hydriel apron chamerote, satrus pean nearmy chabelon, vearchas, belta, nothelmy phameron, arsoy pedaryn onzel, Lamedo drubel areon veatly cabyn & noty maleros haytny pesary does, pen rasi medusan ilcohi person.

These words being said, the called Spirit will appear with the sub-servants deputed to this hour, he will be obedient to you in everything, and faithful to whoever you wish to send him.

[61] **R** Suppose we have some secret whatsoever, and I have a friend to whom I

---

[1] Note the alternate spelling.
[2] You must memorise the details in the table before invoking them.

would like to entrust it, I cannot do it in safety either by letter or by messenger lest it becomes public, I call a Spirit, he comes, I confide my secret and he will discharge it faithfully, here is his sign ⚶ or ⚷

R Form and send such letter as you please to your friend with the sigil of the Spirit above.

When the friend has received the letter, he considers the sign of Hydriel who has no Mansion in the universe to observe, but having done what there is to do in general, we will say the following:

> Hydriel omar, penadon epyrma narsoy greol fabelrusin adiel pedrusii nozevi melrays uremy pean larfoy naes chemerotyn.

Having spoken these words in a manner befitting the institution of the Art, the Spirit sent will appear visibly to you, revealing to your ear all that it is charged with.

CHAPTER 24

The Supreme Spirit is called PYRICHIEL and he has at his command Dukes, Princes, Counts and sub-servants so many as to be uncertain; this supreme Prince of the Spirits, does not absolutely seem to us to despise operating in our Art, because he can be very doting. He has no Princes or Dukes like the others, whose number is uncertain.

There are some who say that he has Dukes and Princes under him; they seem to us not to understand enough his property and his custom; this is why they took the Counts and sub-servants for the Dukes; Pyrichiel's name is taken from Fire, because he used to frequently go towards this Element. Here is the table:

R			R			
Damarsiel	Menariel	200	200	100	80	80
Cardiel	Demediel	100	600	60	50	50
Almasor	Hursiel					
Nemariel	Cuprisiel	400	30	30	10	10

Table 24: The Counts of Pyrichiel, supreme Spirit of Fire.

[62] There are in this table, 8 names of Counts and sub-servants of Pyrichiel, deputies following the order of the hours, when you want to operate by these Spirits, you will call one of them, and when you operate another time, you immediately call the next one. Remember to do so [in order] following the others. Having done what the Art requires, say the following.

> Pyrichiel marfoys chameron, nael peanos pury lames Jamene famerusyn mearlo canorson theory torsa, nealthis dilumeris marphroy carsul ameor thubra phorsotiel chrebonos aray pemalon layr toysi vadiniel nemor rosevarsy cabti froys amenada machyr, fableronthis, poyl carepon vemii naslotyn.

Having pronounced these words the Spirits will appear, the principal will always be under the shape of a snake; with the head of a beautiful girl's with her hair dishevelled.

Suppose we have some secret of consequence. I therefore have a secret within me which is important to keep silent about, however I have a friend who is absent with whom I would like to entrust it, and I cannot send him surely by letters for fear that they will be read or intercepted on the way, nor entrust it to any human because his faith can change with his fortune, so that they are therefore sure, I call a Spirit friend of the secret and he comes immediately. When he has heard the above words pronounced by the force and power that they have, he faithfully discharges his commission.

Let us write such letters as we please with this sign |——

And when the friend has received such letters, or other similar, which will be signed with the seal or Character of Pyrichiel as represented above being learned in the Art, that he does what the Art requires, then having lit the light or else being near a fire, he will say the following words.

> Pyrichiel osayr chamerosy culty mesano dayr fabelron cathurmo pean orsoty meor Jathor cabon Frilastro melrusy.

Having finished pronouncing these words, the invisible messenger appears visibly and he will reveal to the ear all that with which he was charged.

[63] CHAPTER 25

The Prince and Emperor of this chapter is called EMONIEL and under his dominion and his commands are 100 Dukes or Princes, Counts and vassals a great number, who have their Office over all things in general.

This Prince and Emperor with his Dukes and Princes are wandering and unstable, and often dwelling in the woods, he does not flee from the light, being called he will hasten willingly and promptly to execute whatever you order him, he has under his command 100 Dukes and Princes and no less than 20 Counts and an uncertain number of vassals and sub-servants or servants. Of those we will name some of them which will be enough for us for the operations, we will postpone naming the others in their place, if necessary. See this table.

R		R		R		R
Ermoniel	Dramiel	Cruhiel	10	20	100	20
Edriel	Pandiel	Armesiel	10	20	100	20
Carnodiel	Vasenel	Caspaniel	10	20	100	20
Phanuel	Nasiniel	Musiniel	10	20	100	20

Table 25: The Princes, Dukes and Counts ruled by Emoniel.

Here are 12 of the Dukes of Emoniel with 1320 of his vassals and servants, which are sufficient for us for all our intended operations, following the order hours, either during the day or at night. Know that Prince Emoniel has the custom to appear with the head and body of a girl, but with the tail of a snake. And when you want to operate something in this Art by the ministry of these Spirits, do what the Art generally requires, and you will utter tacitly and silently the following words, to call such of these Spirits as you please.

> Emoniel aproisi chamerusyn thulnear peanos mevear, pandroy cralnotiel narboy mavi fabelrontas, arliel chemorsyn nety pransobyr diviel malros ruelty person roab chrumelrusin.

[64] Having finished speaking these words as the Art requires, the Spirit called by you will appear, ready and prompt to obey you in all that you order him because he is kind and faithful. Suppose you have such a secret as may be.

I have a friend whom I recognise as very faithful and sincere, but who confides a little too much in those who frequent him, who for friends favours enemies, from whom he often draws ill renown and damage, he is too credulous with the caresses of flatterers, he has a secret enemy who does not leave him, and he does not know who is contrary to him in secret, because he trusts too much to these caresses, I wish to warn him strongly, however I would only like to entrust it to him alone and that it be hidden from others.

I send a letter only for form, with the character attached :I:

After he to whom you sent it shall have received this letter, being instructed in the Art, let him do what this Art teaches and having executed it let him say the following.

> Emoniel lebos chamerothy meor pemorsy dyor medulorsyn fray pean, crymarsy melrosyne vari chabaryn dayr. Aschre cathurmo fabelron ersoty marduse.

These words being exactly spoken the Spirit called, who was sent, will appear in the form it usually takes, it will reveal to you the secret of which it is charged, with great fidelity.

CHAPTER 26

The principal Spirit is called ICOSIEL having under his power and at his command 100 Princes or Dukes, 300 Counts or vassals, but we have not yet been able to certainly find the number of sub-servants.

Icosiel is one of the great and mighty Aerian Princes, formerly named in this work, he has 100 Principals in the Ducal order and 300 Counts, and the servants in so large a number that we have not yet been able to certainly find the number. We assure you that the great [65] Prince Icosiel willingly frequents houses and men, for when you have called him once by your calls [he sends] a Duke with his vassals. If you want him to stay with you all your life, select for him a secret and secluded place in your home and command him by strong constraint, to remain there and he will obey you promptly, and he will always be there ready at your command.[1]

R		R		R		R	
Machariel	Larphiel	Athesiel	10	300	100	30	
Psichiel	Amediel	Urbaniel	10	300	100	30	
Thanatiel	Cambriel	Cumariel	10	300	100	30	
Zosiel	Zachriel	Heresiel	10	300	100	30	
Agapiel	Nathriel	Munefiel	10	300	100	30	

Table 26: The Princes, Dukes and Counts ruled by Icosiel.

You have the names of 15 of the Dukes of Icosiel and 50 sub-Dukes[2] and 1250 servants who customarily come with their Dukes when called to operate in some ministry of the Art according to the Order they hold, within the 24 hours of day and night, they are docile and voluntary at your command, provided that you are instructed in the Art, and that you are as firm and steady without being afraid nor terrorised in the operation, because they come in the shape and figure of serpents having the head like a girl, so when you want to operate through some one of them, do what the Art requires, and say the following words:

> Icosiel aphorsi chamersyn thulneas Janoliel menear peanos erasnotiel medursan matoryfabelron ersonial cathurmos learnoty besraym alphayr lamedonti nael cabelron.

These words being exactly finished pronouncing, the called Spirits will come without delay, to whom you can entrust the secret that you wish to send to a friend. Write such letter as you please to send some secret to an absent friend who

---

[1] He will effectively become a Familiar.
[2] *Sou-Ducs*.

Steganographia

is an expert in the Art, and to whom you want to send a great secret you must send him a Spirit who will reveal the secret to him and [otherwise] keep it hidden, seeing that the friend [66] nor will I be able to insinuate to him by letters, here is the means that must be observed to keep such a secret in safety and under the seal of silence

We can form any letter we want, and the sign or character above is that of the Prince Icosiel which must be affixed to the bottom of the letter sent to the friend so that he knows where the messenger Spirit is from, and when he has received the letter and recognised the sign, let him do what the Art requires, and say the following.

> Icosiel osayr penarizo chulti meradym phrael melchusy dayr pean cathurmo fabelron ersoti chamerusan iltham pedaly fuar melrosyn crymarsy phroyson.

Having finished speaking these words, the Spirit will appear and reveal the secret.

CHAPTER 27

The supreme Spirit and Prince is called SOLEVIEL who has under him 200 principal Dukes and 200 Counts or vassals and an infinite number of sub-servants, and among all those, Spirits who have commerce with men and converse with them.

There is one named Soleviel who is not the last among the Princes of this Art. He has under his command 200 principal Dukes, and 200 Counts or vassals, who between them infallibly observe this order, that whoever has been Duke this year becomes Count the following year, likewise Counts become Dukes. We have not yet found the certain number of servants who conform according to the order they have among themselves according to the disposition of the hours.

R	R	R				R	
Inachiel	Nadrusiel	Axosiel	20	20	20	200	200
Praxeel	Cobusiel	Charoel	20	20	20	200	200
Morucha	Amriel	Mursiel	20	20	20	200	200
Almodar	Prasiel	Penador	20	20	20	200	200

Table 27: The Dukes and Counts of Soleviel.

Here are in this table 12 of the main Dukes of Soleviel, of which the first six [67] are Dukes this Year (in 1500) and the six others are only Counts, the following year those who are Dukes become Counts and so subsequently and alternately, we have collected the number of 1840 of the servants however there are still some, so many that it is impossible to count them exactly. So when you want to operate through them be constant, firm, and do not be terrified at their appearance when you see them appear with the body of a serpent, the head of a virgin, then do what the Art requires, after having done you will say the following words.

> Soleviel marfoy chamerusyn oniel dabry diviel pean vear, lasmyn eralmo ty pedaros drumes, pean vear chameron loes madur noty basray erxo nadrus peliel thabron thirso Janothin vear perasy loes pean nothyr fabelron bavesy drameron eschiran pumelon meor dabrios crimorsiel peny vear nameroy lyernoti pralsones.

Having spoken these words, the called Spirits will appear to you in their ordinary form, to whom you can entrust your secret. Suppose [you write] such letter as you please for any secret whatsoever, having one absent friend who is learned in the art, and you wish to warn him of some great peril, but you fear the public, and fear that your secret will be leaked and you will be in greater peril. To avoid this do not confide your secret either to men or to letters, but for the most call, one of those Spirits that you will recognise as faithful in everything.

Form and send your letter sealed with the seal of the Spirit, as follows

The one to whom this letter was sent, having received it, and being instructed in the Art, he performs what is necessary, and without fearing anything, he will say with a firm spirit the following words.

> Soleviel curtiel chamerusyn saty pemalros dayr Janothy cathurmo parmoy Jotran lamedon frascu penay ilthon fabelmerusyn.

These words being spoken by the receiver, the Spirit sent by the operator will appear visibly, faithfully revealing to him all that he is charged with, and if he has anything to refer to the operator they use the same Spirit [to reply].

Steganographia

[68] CHAPTER 28

Here is the supreme Spirit and Emperor who is called MENACHIEL[1] who has under him 20 Princes or Dukes, 100 Counts and an uncertain number of servants who obey their Dukes.

Although we seem to have named enough Princes and Spirits to operate in various parts [of the world] according to this Art, but we fear to not forget anything we have learned, it still pleased us to bring to light what is best for the perfection of this Art, and we know enough that we are experts in the revelation of the above-named Spirits. But there is one who is supreme among all the Spirits who greatly favours this Art which is named Menadiel, a name given to him because of his great Office which has under his power, as it is said, 20 Princes or Dukes, 100 Counts, and of the sub-servants so many that it is not possible to define them, and which are all very faithful in all the commissions that are given to them, so they make very good messengers in the great affairs of Kings and Princes through whom we will work surprising wonders. See the table.

	R				R	
Larmol	Benodiel	20	10	100	Barchiel	Nedriel
Drassiel	Charsiel	20	10	100	Amasiel	Curasyn
Clamor	Samyel	20	10	100	Baruch	Tharson

Table 28: The Dukes and Counts of Menadiel.

Here are 6 of the Dukes and as many of the Counts of Menadiel and the number of 390 of the sub-servants who are deputed to them by turn and order, they observe that order between them, that two Dukes are called the first time and a Count, who is called in the second time, who then comes in the order of the Dukes. The third time the first of the two Dukes called the first time become Counts and so on. Whenever you want to operate by one of the Spirits of Menadiel consider carefully which Duke and which Count you want to call, according to the time and the hour, and having executed what the Art [69] demands, you will say the following words.

> Menadiel marfoy peanos onael chamerusyn theor Janothy ofayr melros tudayr penorsyn sachul tarno rosevas peathan asiel morfoy maplear casmyron storeal marpenu nosayr pelno dan layr thubra elnodion carsephy drumos fabelmerusyn andu pean, purays calbyn nachir loes philvemy casaner.

---

[1] Initially spelt as Menachiel but then afterwards spelt throughout as Menadiel, which is a Spirit name that is more often seen in other grimoires.

These words being recited in the form, the called Spirit will appear, namely first a Count and then two Dukes with their vassals. Have any secret whatsoever that you wish to communicate to a friend according to the circumstances of the times and that you do not want to communicate to other persons, call a Spirit, charge it with the commission. Do not fear he is the most faithful of all and he will fulfil his commission very exactly. Here are the seals of Prince Menadiel

The one to whom you have sent this letter which you entrusted to the messenger, receiving it he will have regard to the seal of Menadiel, and being instructed in this Art will do what is agreed to do, and will say the following words.

> Menadiel murty chamerose dayr pean cathurmo phameron ersoti pray sarvepo, fabelmerii rean, charon Jetlas Meduse fayr lamerosyn alty merchahon.

Having finished speaking these words, the Spirit sent will appear visibly and will report everything that it is responsible for, faithfully to the ear.

CHAPTER 29

The Supreme Spirit and Emperor is called MACARIEL who has under his command many Dukes, Princes, Counts, and sub-servants whom he deputises to various ministries, being therefore one of the great Princes who preside over the operations of this Art, who is not to be despised by us, any more than his Princes and servants, because he is quite useful, prompt and faithful for everything you want.

He has under him 40 Princes [70] of which he sends no less than 4 to minister, three Dukes and a Count, with no less servants, they observe this rule between them; that in turn there is always a Duke who does the Office of Count and following the 4 parts of the year, and it is very necessary to have a plain notice of these to operate. But we will appoint some of these Spirits and Princes who will be sufficient for us for all the operations of this Art.

	R.		R.	R.	R.	R.
Claniel	Asmadiel	Gremiel	40	30	20	10
Drusiel	Romyel	Thuriel	40	30	20	10
Andros	Nastuel	Brufiel	40	30	20	10
Charoel	Varpiel	Lemodac	40	30	20	10

Table 29: The Principal Princes of Emperor Macariel.

In this table is represented the names of the 12 principal Princes of Macariel with the number of 400 sub-servants according to their rank and their turn when you want to operate through them in this Art, take heed that you must not call only four of those who are named above in the table, and having executed what the Art requires you will say the following.

> Macariel myrno chamerosy purmy maresyn amos peanam olradu, chabor Janoes fabelron dearsy, chadon ulyses almos rutiel pedaron deabry madero neas lamero dearsy, thubra dorpilto melrosyne draor chalmea near, parmon dearsy charon alnodiel parsa radean, maroy reneas charso gnole, melrosin te dranso casmar ebroset. Landrys masfayr therasonte noel amalan.

Having spoken these words the called Spirits will appear on the spot, but have no fear and be firm, for you will see them in various forms sometimes the head of a girl the body and the tail of a dragon, and often the form of a dragon folding and unfolding up to four times.

Suppose you have some secret for a Prince. The government is occupied by a governor, a King or a Prince, and being in his government, or his [71] province, he discovered in secret that enemies would soon burst into it, so he wants to advise the Prince, but he cannot do so by messengers because the enemies keep spies on their feet to prevent all communication, neither by letters because they are all opened by the enemies, so he calls a Spirit, to whom he entrusts the secret, and he creates another letter which he gives to the Spirit to take to the King or Prince, in which is affixed the seal of Macariel which is thus

When the Prince has received this letter, and being instructed in the Art, and has recognised the sign of Macariel, he does what the Art requires, and will say the following words.

> Macariel osayr chamerose chulti pesano dayr fameron cathurmo pean ersoty lamedon sovapor casrea mafyr. Janos tharfia, peathan non acri pean etion matramy.

Having said these words, the Spirit will appear to him alone visibly and will declare to his ear what he was charged with.

Steganographia

CHAPTER 30

The Supreme Emperor is called URIEL, he has 10 Dukes under him, 100 Counts or vassals and an infinite number of servants, under his power.

What we have learned by experience in the Art teaches us that the great Prince Uriel is not to be omitted, because he is not the last among those who favour this Art and that he also has his uses, he has under him 10 deputy Princes to the ministries concerning the Art, and 100 Counts or vassals who are committed to the Dukes each in their rank. We have not yet found the certain number of his subordinates.

	R.		R.	R.	R.			
Chabri	10	Dragon	10	100	20	α	α	C
Drabos	10	Curmas	10	80	40	γ	α	n
Narmiel	10	Drapios	10	60	60	n[1]	T[2]	λ
Frasmiel	10	Hermon	10	40	80	n	α	δ
Brymiel	10	Aldrusy	10	20	100	β	ι	α

Table 30: The Dukes and Counts of Prince Uriel.

[72] Here we have the above-named Dukes with the Counts and the servants who are enough for us for the present to use in the operations of this Art, and notice that the former are Dukes, and the second [column] are Counts, they have between them two orders and it is necessary that you should know before, those who are in the first order, both Dukes and Counts, that all the times they are called they always appear as monsters, having the head of a girl, a snake's body and tail. Those who are in the second order, want to appear to us familiarly and in a usual form, and they are not accustomed to come as less than a Duke with a Count following him in the two orders, when therefore you will operate by these Spirits do first what the Art teaches, and then you will say the following words.

> Uriel marfoys lamedonti noes, chameron, anducharpean phusciel arsmony tuerchoy Jamersyn nairiel penos raseon loes vear fabelruso cralty layr parlis meraii mear, thubra aslotiel dubyr reanu navosti masliel pedonyto chemarphin.

The words above being said the Spirits called will come each in order prompt and ready to obey whatever is required for their ministry.

For example, you have a big secret that you want to communicate to a Prince or to

---

[1] *Manuscript note*: These three letters must be in Red. The Tau signifies who guards all; see the Note at the end of this chapter.

[2] This is a unique character, being a capital T with the right-hand end of the cross-bar wrapped back over the top of the T.

a friend whose publication would become perilous and fatal to you, and to him cause great damage, so that everything must remain between you and him very secretly, do not confide in him neither by letters, nor by men, but surely by Spirits. Draft such a letter as you want by affixing these characters   ℨℯ ℳ

When the one to whom you sent your letters has received them and has recognised the sign of Uriel at the bottom of the letter, being instructed in the Art, he will do what is indicated, and then say the following words.

> Uriel Aflan pemason osayr chameron, chulty fabelmeron deyr pean cathurmo merosyn [73] ersoty chalmon savepo Meduse rean lamerosyn.

Having uttered these words, the Spirit sent will appear visibly in its accustomed form and he will faithfully reveal all the secrets with which he is charged and in secret, so that none of the helpers can hear or understand, then the secret will remain hidden.

* **Note**. Uriel is like a Steward who confines, preserves and takes care of something, like a *maître d'hôtel*, sommelier, treasurer, collector, administrator, protector, or arbitrator who takes care of something of consequence.

CHAPTER 31

We still have one of the great Princes who are deputed to us to operate in this Art. Indeed the last in order, but he goes hand in hand in dignity with the first, for this reason, and because of his Office he is called BYDIEL, having under his command 20 Dukes, 200 Counts and an infinite number of servants. These Dukes observe a certain order with their Counts, and whenever they are called by the operator, he comes with two Dukes and with 20 Counts and they appear in human form, calm and prompt to all things.

They change in turn, so that the one who is called the first time as a Duke then as Count, and the second time the Counts are called for Dukes. These are the observations that the operator must make.

	R.		R.		R.		R.
Mudriel	20	20	200	20	200	Charobiel	20
Cruchan	20	20	200	20	200	Andrucha	20
Bramsiel	20	20	200	20	200	Merasiel	20
Armoniel	20	20	200	20	200	Parsifiel	20
Lameniel	20	20	200	20	200	Chremoas	20

Table 31: The Dukes and Counts of Prince Bydiel.

Here are the names of 10 of the Princes, Dukes and Counts of Bydiel that suffice [74] to operate in the Art, with many sub-servants who know how to observe their rank following the command of the Dukes and Princes. When, therefore, you wish to operate through them, having executed what the art requires, you must pronounce the following.

> Bydiel marchan chamerosi philtres maduse vear casmyron cralnoti pean devoon fabelros eltida camean veor. Oniel vear thyrso liernoty: Janos prolsato chanos elafry peanon elsathas melros notiel pen soes probys chyras lesbroy mavear Jothan liernoti chrymarson.

That being said, the called Spirits will appear visible, beautiful, always like friends, and will be willing and obedient to you in all things. For example, I have an absent friend to whom I would like to send an important secret concerning a substance hidden, which is necessary to let him know and observe the mystery, which I dare not confide neither to men, nor to letters, but I entrust it to a Spirit who is sure and faithful. The friend receiving the letter that the Spirit brings him, recognises the sign of Bydiel ♃z and will do what is necessary, having executed what the art requires in general, he will say the following.

> Bydiel maslo chameron theory madias near fabelron thiamy marfoy vear pean liernoty calmea drules: Thubra pleory malresa teorty melchoy vemo chofray.

Having finished pronouncing these words, the Spirit will appear visible only to him who called him, and will reveal to him the commission with which he is charged, faithfully and exactly.

CHAPTER 32

In this chapter we make a certain [tabular] recapitulation of the chapters described above, and we have inferred from it all the assurances which are there to be observed for those who operate within the scope of this Art.

PRAISE TO THE GREAT GOD

BLESSINGS ON ALL THINGS

	Name	Symbol	R		R	R	R
1	Pamersiel		1000	10000	100	10	K
2	Padiel		1000	200000	100	10	K
3	Camuel		10	10	0	100	K
4	Aseliel		10	20	0	200	K
5	Barmiel		10	20	10	200	K
6	Gediel		20	20	00	200	K
7	Asyriel		20	20	10	100	K
8	Materiel		30	30	00	300	K
9	Malgare		30	30	10	200	K
10	Dorothiel		40	40	0	400	K
11	Usiel		40	40	30	300	K
12	Cabariel		50	50	50	500	K
13	Raysiel		50	50	40	400	K
14	Symiel		10	1000	0	4	K
15	Armadiel		1000	180	10	800	K
16	Baruchas		10	180	0	100	K
17	Carnesiel		1000	300	1000	300	1000
18	Caspiel		200	400	200	400	200
19	Amenadiel		300	500	300	500	300
20	Demoriel		400	600	400	600	400
21	Geradiel		200	100	40	30	60
22	Buriel		100	10	10	100	θ
23	Hydriel		10	20	100	200	θ
24	Pyrichiel		40	30	200	10	θβ
25	Emoniel		10	20	100	20	θ
26	Icosiel		10	300	100	30	θ
27	Soleviel		20	20	20	200	θ
28	Menadiel		100	20	30	10	θν
29	Macariel		40	30	20	10	θ♪
30	Uriel		20	10	40	30	θκ
31	Bidiel		30	40	100	20	uβ

Figure 14: The full list of 31 Spirits as it appears in the manuscript.

Steganographia

[75]	R			R		R		R
1	PAMERSIEL			1000	10000	100	10	K
2	Padiel			1000	200000	100	10	K
3	Camuel			10	10	0	100	K
4	Aseliel			10	20	0	200	K
5	Barmiel			10	20	10	200	K
6	Gediel			20	20	00	200	K
7	Asyriel			20	20	10	100	K
8	Maseriel			30	30	00	300	K
9	Malgare[1]			30	30	10	200	K
10	Dorothiel			40	40	0	400	K
11	Usiel			40	40	30	300	K
12	Cabariel			50	50	50	500	K
13	Raysiel			50	50	40	400	K
14	Symiel			10	1000	0	4	K
15	Armadiel			1000	180	10	800	K
16	Baruchas			10	180	0	100	K
17	Carnesiel			1000	300	1000	300	1000
18	Caspiel			200	400	200	400	200

---

[1] Should be Malgaras.

19	Amenadiel		300	500	300	500	300
20	Demoriel		400	600	400	600	400
21	Geradiel		200	100	40	30	60
22	Buriel		100	10	10	100	θ
23	Hydriel		10	20	100	200	θ
24	Pyrichiel		40	30	200	10	Θβ
25	Emoniel		10	20	100	20	θ
26	Icosiel		10	300	100	30	θ
27	Soleviel		20	20	20	200	θ
28	Menadiel		100	20	30	10	θν
29	Macariel		40	30	20	10	θδ
30	Uriel		20	10	40	30	θκ
31	Bidiel		30	40	100	20	κβ

Table 32: The Full Table of 31 Spirits.[1]

---

[1] Note that the sigils of the first 16 Spirits in Table 32 differ slightly from those in Table 2.

[76] After having described the offices of the principal Spirits which are contained in the preceding chapters which favour the Art which is understood within the scope of this work, not without great assiduousness and continual work: having taken all possible care to make this work useful and perfect for fear that whoever wants to operate in this Art will not encounter obstacles in any place which would appear obscure to him or hidden, and does not throw him into error, either in the order, names, characters, Dukes or Counts, and as this work is of such great importance, besides the Table of Direction [Table 2] which is at the front of this work, we judged about drawing up and drafting as we see above, a general table of all Spirits [Table 33], in this chapter, to memorise it all.

In this Table [33], where we have inferred the 31 principal Spirits that preside over each Office, and in their order, to all the operations of our Art of which we spoke in the First Book, putting to each the sign or character which is proper to it, the number and order of its Princes, Dukes, Counts, vassals and sub-servants putting them in their own rank, we fear that whoever wants to operate in this Art, or encountered difficulties because of the diversity of operations (because the great mysteries of this Art can only be penetrated by very studious people) those mainly who love secrets, and whose nature encourages them to seek marvels, to those who the desire to acquire science does not allow them to be discouraged by honest and possible work. For these lazy men of thin genius that love the study of the science of secrets does not encourage nor that nature helps not, when they cannot manage to find the knot of our hidden Art should not impute the fault to us but rather to their own ignorance, laziness, and malice. Likewise, those who are given over to carnal and worldly pleasures will not be able to achieve it, even with study and diligence, nor those who, believing themselves learned, and learned enough, despise our lessons as unworthy of [77] their reading.

There are also those who have a habit of treating elders, traditions, and whatever they have not learned in colleges, classes, or from preceptors, doctors, prefects, or from their parents, they believe things which are impossible, even though these are great superstitions. There is nothing more absurd than those who want, or cannot deepen the depth, of the science of our Art; to the rest those who are inclined or who have the will to study this Art (if there is such) so that they can make progress, we have resolved to warn them in a few words at the end of this Book; we must warn them beforehand, that [if] they still hold this hidden science: fear that it will come to the knowledge and into the hands of the wicked, who would do much harm and execrable things by means of it; for though this science is truly good in itself, yet the practice led by bad people will do as much harm as it will do good and good things being practised by men who have the fear of God before their eyes and who observe his commandments, as well as the secret residence, therefore hidden between good hands and a discreet and prudent soul lest one use it for evil, by it falling into perverse hands. However the good should not despise this science for this reason, because it harms if executed by evil ones, as whoever bows down to a man does not despise the sword, then those who study this Art are warned not to presume to arrive at this science, if before they have not been instructed in the Art. The principles that this science requires does not depend on me, if anyone encounters any danger in trying sometimes to operate, being not yet sufficiently instructed in the Art. Likewise, he who is well educated, when he wants to operate by this science he remembers to observe instructions diligently; according to what we have said both in the circle and in each table and chapter, the differences, the places, the names, the orders, and the offices of the supreme Spirits, and their Dukes, and how many substitute presidents. When you know this <u>to express them in the Call;</u>[1] if the operator does not take care to carefully observe this, he will not be able to profit [78] nor achieve the effect of his further intention have careful attention, that when you call on a Spirit to announce and reveal some secret, to know in which quarter of the universe he dwells, lest he errs either in places, or in those whom he will call. Likewise, anyone who takes it into his head to want to operate in this Art, must diligently observe to pronounce the words of the Call distinctly and in this is the greatest strength of our operation, because if we commit a fault in the Call, the Spirits called (and to be called) will not only not obey, but become quite rebellious, so be careful not to call [by mistake] one for another, but each in his own order, time, and Office; this is what we treat of in all the chapters of this Book. Because if one calls for another, either by mistake or some other negligence, one does not operate well in the operations; and great peril might result.

In the same way in the call you must be careful to express yourself well by pronouncing distinctly the name of the Spirit whom you called, with details of his substitute [Spirits], and that you have in your memory beforehand the reason for his call, and that the operation is not done for light and profane things, but for things you could not otherwise do, nor which will put a friend in peril, either by letters or by messengers; no other than for serious things and of great consequence which, being made public, would cause damage or peril to the operator who makes use of this Art. It is also necessary for any operator in this Art to know the nature of the Spirits, which are the good ones, which are the wicked, which are the prompt and obedient, which are the hard and rebellious, likewise which are those who preside over the operations of the day and those who preside over those of the night. Because if you do not know the nature of the Spirits before you begin to operate, you will not succeed (or only with great difficulty) and the science would fall into nothingness, just as when the Spirits who have been called appear visibly, having spoken the secret words which are in each chapter for each of the Spirits, these are what is contained in [79] the mystical tongue. Then you entrust the secret of your soul to him, either to the Duke or to the Counts in distinct and appropriate

---

[1] Underlined in the manuscript as it is an important point. The hierarchical details of each spirit should be expressed in full in the invocation as it is called. This gives honour to the spirit, makes a link with it, and clearly identifies it.

words, in silence, because it is not necessary to speak to the Spirits aloud, but use a low voice, it is especially to be taken care either for the operator or for the receiver, not to operate in the presence of people unaware of anything concerning our Art, it is therefore necessary to have a cabinet or a separate room, but if it happens that you cannot be alone, and have to operate in the presence of someone, you will have to act so secretly with so much caution and with so much industry, that none of the assistants will notice the presence of the Spirit. For all the Spirits deputed in the ministry of this Art are of this nature and condition, that they hate the tumult of men, they shun and hate all operations that are in public.

It is still to be observed by the operator not to send (for these ministries) Spirits without being both charged and provided with a [physical] letter, or at least provided with of the sign or character which is attributed to his Supreme Emperor, for when he does not see the seal of his master well-formed and printed, he despises [the operator] and refuses to obey the operator who calls him in order to bring the communication of a secret to one of his followers and friends. In each chapter it is marked and ordered to write and form a letter as we wish, for two reasons, although we can keep and reach a secret without any letter or writing, but only by the voice of the Spirit which is sent as a message in the operations of this Art, it is only to avert from suspicion, and [secondarily] the Spirit is thus bound by the sigil compelling it to obey, as well as the receiver.

END OF THE FIRST BOOK

BOOK II

[80]

SECOND BOOK
of the STEGANOGRAPHIA
# of M. Jean Trithême

PREFACE

As it was written in the preceding Book, with the help of God, [we listed] the thirty-one Supreme Spirits and Emperors with their Dukes, Counts, servants and sub-servants who are necessary for us in all the operations of our ART which was not [achieved] without great work and sweat, to very abundantly suffice for all operations of the mysteries which are concerned with keeping hidden secrets and [propagating] our news. We fear however that we seem to have forgotten something in our first Book for the perfection of the Art. We have resolved to make a second [book] since, according to the tradition of some scholars, there are Spirits deputed at each hour of the day for different operations and for diverse and admirable effects. It was more important for us to imitate the [correct] order of each of them, not superstitiously, so that we may take from them all that may lead to the accomplishment of our Art. Without however losing or even offending the name of Christ; we will despise the rest as being full of magic arts and contrary to our faith, and we will follow that by taking the deputed Spirits at every hour both day and night, by the secret of the great King Solomon in his volume of magic, named *Hermes*, and the supreme Spirits of our Art with their officers who are necessary for the proposed operations, and we will give the manner and doctrine to all students of this Art, to send to a friend the secrets of their soul, and at what hour it can be done most surely. Because each Prince presides over the Spirits, Dukes, Counts and sub-servants like the speculator at whose command they come, being called by us by a legitimate call such as is listed in each chapter, in mystical language, one can boldly reveal to him the secrets such as one wishes him to communicate to your friend. They show themselves obedient, prompt and faithful in all that you will ask of them.

[81] But as I still confer with these Spirits, I show myself even more guilty, but also the certainty of our Art proves that there is nothing in this science that is frivolous, nothing that is contrary to the Gospel and to the Catholic Apostolic and Roman faith. In a word, there is nothing superstitious in our Art, for everything we said in the previous chapter and what we will say in the next, it is true that this science requires to be practised by men who are extremely reserved, withdrawn within themselves, good readers and Doctors. If this Art requires such people, it is because the Spirits themselves are required to have nothing to do with other

people, or to respond to their commands, either to veil a mystery or the words of the Spirits. Let us therefore make use of the ministry of these Spirits to veil a secret which would become very harmful and prejudicial if it came to the knowledge of the wicked; and lest anyone fall into error by the speculations of the hours, it must be known that in this Art, we understand and declare that we count, by the Planetary hours,[1] [not by clock time] both for the day and for the night.

---

[1] See Appendix 3 for more about Planetary hours.

CHAPTER 1

BOOK TWO

The Supreme Spirit is called SAMAEL and he presides at the first hour of the day, he has many Dukes, Counts and servants under his command that he sends at that hour, being called for some operations only by people who are instructed and experts in this Art.

The Supreme Spirit of the first hour of the day, who makes his exordium where the sun rises, is called Samael who has under his command many Dukes, Counts and servants, who being called by the Operator in this Art, come at that hour only, they discharge the commission with which they are charged, but they do not come at any other time other than the first hour of the day, and note that the Dukes and first Princes [82] of Samael are rarely sent by him in the ministry of this science, because they have their powers and offices over the magical arts as well as over the nocturnal illusions of men. Counts and sub-servants make special deputies or ministers of this Art, to which they are most often sent, without the presence of the Dukes, because being the first in the order of Spirits, they are wont to appear at times both proud and rebellious, being not willing to obey the operator if he is not well instructed in this Art. For otherwise there would be great labour and peril, for they are deceitful and often mock the operator, especially if they do not find him well-instructed and experienced in the Art. But they fear and revere those they find constant and expert, and promptly obey their command with fear and respect. We will give the names of the Counts we need to operate in this Art, at the first hour.

R.		R.	R.	R.		
Ameniel	Brumiel	10	100	1000	μ	ν
Charpon	Nestoriel	10	100	1000	α	β
Darosiel	Chremas	10	100	1000	10	20
Monasiel	Meresyn	10	100	1000	20	10

Table 33: The Dukes and Counts of Samael.

We already have 4 of the Princes who are of the First Order and principals among the Dukes of Samael and as many among the Counts, and 4440 of the servants of the third Order whose number greatly suffices us for all the mysteries that concern this Art, when you wish to operate in the first hour of the day. Write on a schedule first the character of the Lord of the Ascendant,[1] then that of the Moon, then that of each of the other planets all according to their accustomed rank, and at the end

---
[1] The planetary Lord of the Rising Sign (in the first House).

that of the Ascendant of the hour, that is to say the character of the sign of the Ascendant of the hour.[1] When you have finished that, you write the prayer or constraint which is going to be written hereafter in mystic language, on the back of this schedule. It is necessary that all this be done with silence, not saying a word.

> [83] Samael afluar onayr misco layr madiel cuhiel naniel nabruys satiel atharbiel nadian naslon, ranyalcoha pemarson.

You prepare these words being written on the reverse of the schedule as mentioned above. The letters you wish to send to your friend, whom you wish to instruct about your secret, purely clearly and distinctly in such form as you please, because it matters very little how they are formed. Call one or two Spirits from among the Counts of the Second Order. If you repeat this several times in the first hour of the day, you may recite the same words which are written on the said schedule, with a strong intention, fearing nothing, which having been exactly completed, the Spirits will appear to you at once visibly in a familiar form which is common to them, tranquil, benevolent and prompt in all. When they have appeared, you can entrust your secret to the most apparent of them, telling them firmly what follows.

> "Ameniel, I order you by the hidden virtue of this Conjuration, that you go as soon as possible to N. N. Prefect, to N. and that you tell him on my behalf, etc."

Having said this, you will say the secret word, which must not be written. The Spirit will fly away at once, as is the custom, and [you should] send letters signed with the Samael character by a messenger, which contain no secrets, and for which there is no risk.

Such is the secret. Having some hidden secret such as a circumstance of the time, which you do not wish to communicate to anyone, which must be done neither by letter nor by messenger, because one must know that one should not operate by the Spirits of the Second Order in our Art for light things which can usually just be announced in letters.

Write such a letter as you please, and when your friend receives this letter, being instructed in the Art and having performed what this Art generally requires, he say the words that are above in the same manner as we have prescribed in the schedule with the character of the Lord of the Ascendant which we have experimented with.

As soon as he has finished saying these words, he will see the Spirit appear and [84] when he has caught sight of it, and without fear let him say the following words:

---

[1] The key to timing is the link between the Lord of the Ascendant when the message was sent, and the Lord of the Ascendant when the recipient invokes the Spirit when it is received, with reference to the hour.

† Penador avenal † Solmenial phanu † Savear caschanti hernoty maduran Amen.

Having said this, let him observe silence and he will see the Spirit approaching, and let him bring the commission with which he is charged, to the ear [of the recipient], and in safety, and let him listen attentively without fear, so that none of those present may perceive or have the slightest clue about the Spirit who is present.

Steganographia

CHAPTER 2

The second hour of the day is called Cevorym whose supreme Prince and Spirit is called ANAEL who has under his command 10 Dukes, 100 Counts, centurions, and Presidents, and an uncertain number of sub-servants.

The President and Emperor of the second hour of the day is named Anael,[1] who has under his command 10 Dukes and 100 Counts, centurions and Presidents over all the other Spirits he deputises for in the various operations of the Art. We have not yet been able to find the exact number of sub-servants for the 2nd hour of the day which is called Cevorym, in which various operations useful to all men can be performed. All this Prince's subordinates are quite affable, cheerful, docile and very prompt for the operator, provided he is an expert in the Art, of a strong, constant and well-informed mind.

	R.		R.	R.		
Menarchos	Orphiel	Quosiel	10	100	G.	n.
Archiel	Cursiel	Ermaziel	10	100	G.	n.
Chardiel	Elmoym	Granyel	10	100	G.	n.

Table 34: The Dukes and Counts of Anael.

We have set down in this table, 3 of the Dukes of Anael and 6 of the Counts, and the number of 330 sub-servants which are abundantly sufficient to us for all the [85] operations of this Art, in this second hour of the day, by summoning them by their order.

Therefore, when you wish to work with them in this Art, write on a very clean schedule the character of the Lord of the Ascendant and the other planets that follow it, then the sign of the 12th house (with an instrument made from the material of the Art).[2] Then write on the reverse of the schedule, the following words, and always observe a great silence, having your face turned towards the Sun.

> ANAEL otiel aproisy rachymas, thulnear layr mevear theor cralnotiel amersoty movear phroys lierto mear urnesa elty famelron.

These words being written, do then what the Art teaches you to do. Then you say the said words in silence and you will immediately see the Spirit pressing, alert, cheerful, benevolent and prompt in all, to whom you can safely entrust what you have to entrust. If you have a secret such as this, which you dare not confide either to letters or to any messenger. Call from among the Spirits and Intelligences of Anael a Duke and a Count, or one or the other as you please. Entrust your secret

---

[1] Often portrayed as an Angel of Venus in other grimoires.
[2] *Remark.* Effectively the planetary signs of the first and twelfth Houses at the time of the operation.

to the principal in the manner, due according to the precepts of the Art, and he will perform it perfectly. Write such a letter as you please, and when your friend receives this letter, being well instructed in the Art, having performed what the Art requires in general, who writes the Lord of the Ascendant with the rest [of the planetary characters] that is customary to observe on the card, and he then says the words prescribed below, which having recited, the Spirit sent will appear visibly, facing his side, and he will say fearlessly.

Fabelmerasyn pastoriel liertos ryneas melchus thyrmo nydran vear padroys.

Having said this [invocation], the Spirits will approach, affably, and faithfully reveal the mysteries entrusted to them. But let him who works in this Art take care, (both he who sends and he who receives) not to act in public, or in the presence of those who are not instructed in the Art, because all the Spirits of the hours love secrecy and hate publicity, [without which] they would not leave without causing some trouble.

[86] CHAPTER 3

The third hour of the day is called Danzur, and the Supreme Emperor is called VEQUANIEL. He has under his command 20 Dukes, 200 Counts and an infinite number of sub-servants; their Office extends over everything in general.

And they are quite prompt and do well all that is entrusted to them, faithful and sure, they are voluntary in obedience, but if called in public, they will not leave the operator without doing him some damage or [placing him in] peril, for they love secrecy like all the other Spirits of the hours, and those who preside over their operations. We have not yet found the name of all, but of a few who suffice us in all our operations.

R.		R.		R.		R.	
Asmoniel	Drelmech	Gemarii	20	20	200	200
Persiel	Sadiniel	Xantiel	20	20	200	200
Mursiel	Parniel	Serviel	20	20	200	200
Zoesiel	Comadiel	Furiel	20	20	200	200

Table 35: The Dukes and Counts of Vequaniel.

We have written in this table the enumeration of 4 of the Dukes and 8 of the Counts, and 1760 of the sub-servants. The surplus is an infinite number, but this number is very abundantly sufficient for all the operations which are made at the third hour of the day. Whenever, therefore, you wish to operate in this Art and in this third hour, for the Spirits which are specified in this table, to convey some news, you must call no less than 2 Dukes, and 2 Counts with their sub-servants, but yet if you wish to call more or less you may do so likewise. But it will be necessary to have a very strong expression in the words that you must pronounce to compel particularly the Universal Emperor, for Spirits do not violate their order without his express command. Therefore write on a new card the character of the Lord of the Ascendant and those of the other planets, in order with the sign of the 12th house in the manner that [87] the institution of the Art requires, always on the reverse of the schedule you must write the words that are below, to force and compel the Spirit.

> Vequaniel odiel mesrii revoii sotiel mear jamy otiel aslosian yrsoti breotion drearii fabelmerusin.

These words having been written down, and having performed what the Art requires, you must recite them in a low voice, so that they are not heard by anyone, and the Spirits called will come at once. When you see them, entrust your secret to the most apparent of the Art, who you will easily recognise by his clothing, because the one who is first among the Spirits will always appear with a crown on his head.

If you have a secret that you would like to send to a friend, and you dare not entrust it either to letters or messengers, lest it be corrupted by a reward or by fear, that he will reveal it, summon a Spirit deputed to this hour, entrust him with your secret, and have no fear that he will fulfil it faithfully.

You will write such a letter as you please, and when your friend receives this letter or any other signed with the character of Vequaniel, he must write the figure of the Lord of the Ascendant and of the 12th house and the rest that the Art requires, on a new schedule; and on the reverse side the words above written. The Spirit sent will immediately appear visibly, and when you see him immediately say the following words.

  Fameron aprois liernoti stadivear diviel savean Lamersy.

When you have spoken these words, listen attentively to what the Spirit will reveal to you without fear, for he is part of a faithful assembly. But above all, take care not to operate in public, or in front of anyone.

CHAPTER 4

This fourth hour is called Elechym, and the supreme Spirit of this [88] hour is called VATMIEL[1] who has under his command 10 Dukes, 100 Counts and an uncertain number of servants by whom one can operate in this fourth hour of the day.

The fourth hour of the day is called Elechym, whose Supreme Intelligence is called Vathmiel who has under his direction 10 Dukes deputed for this Art, 100 Counts and an infinite number of servants, they have orders to announce in general all the secrets, and who are very good, beneficent, and obedient to all that they are ordered to do. Truly the lovers of the secret hate the tumult of men. Therefore, beware of being in the company of people untutored in the Art, who might venture to operate, because they would not come easily even if they were forced and constrained by the mysterious words you might have recited to make them appear and obey you, but on the contrary, they would not leave without causing you some harm and peril. Observe exactly and carefully what we order, and by doing so you can be sure of making great and prodigious progress in this science.

Ammyel	Emarfiel	Jermiel	10	100	100	100
Larmich	Permiel	Thuroz	10	100	100	100
Marfiel	Queriel	Vanesiel	10	100	100	100
Ormyel	Strubiel	Zasviel	10	100	100	100
Zardiel	Diviel	Hermiel	10	100	100	100

Table 36: The Dukes and Counts of Vathmiel.

You have the names of 5 of the Dukes of Vathmiel and 10 of the Counts and a number of 1550 servants, whose number is sufficient for all the operations of the Art. When therefore you want to operate in the 4th hour of the day write on a new card the character of the Lord of the Ascendant and the 12th house with the rest of the planets by their rank, and on the reverse side the following words belong.

> Vathmiel adres rheareso rafer rheotii venofi sayr fatiel cafairsoti verotiel does ro fabelmerusin.

[89] Having performed what the Art requires, say these same words in a low voice and the called Spirits will appear at once, at least a Duke and a Count with their underlings, for they are quick to obey your commands.

Secret Argument.

Supposing you have a secret which is of consequence and which you would not

---
[1] Although the spelling here is clearly Vatmiel, the rest of the chapter uses 'Vathmiel.'

Steganographia

wish to entrust to any except one friend alone, for this purpose you summon the Spirits who are deputed to this 4th hour, as many as you wish and then you entrust your secret to the most apparent; write a letter in the manner you wish which contains no secret and which you do not fear will become public. You have thus formed and sent your letters, and he to whom you send these letters, upon receiving them, and being expert in the Art, let him observe the Lord of the Ascendant of the hour, and the sign of the 12th House, and let him write their character with the rest on a card, with what the Art requires and let him then say the words above, and seeing the Spirit he will then say the words which are reported below.

Camerusin aproysi lierto thulnear venean maveas fabelron.

This verse being said, the Spirit sent will draw near, and will reveal to you faithfully, and without peril, the secret entrusted to him.

CHAPTER 5

This [fifth] hour is called Fealech, and the supreme Spirit and Emperor is called SASQUIEL who has under his empire 10 Dukes and 100 Counts, and a large number of sub-servants.

The fifth hour of the day is therefore named Fealech and its Intelligence is called Sasquiel who is a great and powerful Emperor who has under his Empire 10 of many Dukes, and 100 Counts with their servants who are deputies of the various operations and secret mysteries concerning this Art. It is to be noticed that the Dukes are rarely called in the 5th hour of the day for the operations of this Art, because they are not always necessary: because a Count and his sub-servants who are his deputies [90] are copiously sufficient to operate in this Art. If, however, someone believes he needs the power of some Duke, he can likewise call 1, 2 or 3. They will come without delay because they are quick enough and willing enough to obey the operator. See the table.

	R.		R.	R.	R.
Damiel	Jameriel	Omerach	10	100	1000
Araniel	Futiniel	Lameros	10	100	1000
Maroch	Rameriel	Zachiel	10	100	1000
Sarapiel	Amisiel	Fustiel	10	100	1000
Putifiel	Uraniel	Camiel	10	100	1000

Table 37: The Dukes and Counts of Sasquiel.

We give in this table the names of 5 of the Dukes of Sasquiel and 10 of the Counts, and the number of 5550 sub-servants whose ministry is sufficient for all operations in this hour. Whenever, therefore, you wish to operate by the ministry of any of these Spirits in the 5th hour of the day, write the character of the Lord of the Ascendant and of the 12th house with the others, which the Art requires, on a clean card, and on the reverse the following words.

Sasquiel adres rhetroseti rosiel emelto satu olmeniel irsoti savea navediel liernoti chameson.

Having performed what the Art requires, these words written above are to be recited in a low voice. And the Spirits called by these words will appear at once, at least a Duke and a Count with their sub-servants, as they are quick to obey your commands.

Secret Argument. For example you have a great secret that you would like to entrust to only one, invoke the Spirits deputies of any of the Counts of Sasquiel previously named, entrust your secret to this Count and give a letter that is signed with the character of Sasquiel and you will be safe. Write such a letter as you please, and when the person to whom you wish your letter to be given receives it, being instructed [91] in the Art and having known the sign of Sasquiel, having performed what is necessary as is customary, let him say the words written above, and immediately the Spirit will show itself visibly. Having done so he will say the following words:

Fabelmesyn aveval vear plyan cralti penason.

The Spirit having heard them will draw near to you, and reveal to you the secret.

CHAPTER 6

Genapherym is the name of the 6th hour of the day and its Spirit and supreme Emperor is called SANIEL who has under him 10 Dukes and 100 Counts and many sub-servants.

The 6th hour of the day is therefore called Genapherym and its Intelligence is called Saniel. He is great and powerful in operations, and has under his Empire 10 Dukes and 100 Counts and 5550 sub-servants deputised to the different ministries of the Art which are sufficient for us for all the operations of the Art in the 6th hour. The Dukes are rarely called although they are good and willing to obey our commands because the Counts are accustomed to filling their Office as the Dukes are occupied in other magical experiments. See the table below.

	R.		R.	R.	R.
Arnebiel	Gamiel	Nedabar	10	100	1000
Charuch	Jenotriel	Permon	10	100	1000
Medusiel	Sameon	Brasiel	10	100	1000
Nathmiel	Trasiel	Camosiel	10	100	1000
Pemiel	Xamyon	Evadar	10	100	1000

Table 38: The Dukes and Counts of Saniel.

We have the names of 5 of the Dukes of Saniel and 10 of the Counts and 5550 sub-servants whose ministrations are sufficient for the operations of this hour. When, therefore, you wish to operate through any of these Spirits named in the table for the 6th hour of the day, let it be in a secret place, if you wish.

[92] Calling one or more Dukes is within your power, although it is not necessary because the Counts are sufficient for us. This is why you must write on a clean schedule the characters of the planets and the accustomed signs, and on the reverse side you will write the following words.

Samiel asiel thebrean pothir ersoty mear pornys layr moas famerosyn.

Having done what is necessary, say the above words in the way they are taught, and immediately the Spirit will appear to you, alert, quick to do whatever you wish to command him, which you will send far or near, to a friend for whom he carries your secret.

Secret Argument. If you have a particular friend, whom you wish to instruct in a secret by the Spirit of Samiel for the 6th hour of the day, you may do so in safety because they are attendant to all in general and faithful in commissions, if you follow all our precepts, and the friend is expert in the Art.

Write any letter you wish. When your friend receives these letters, being instructed in the Art, having performed what he must, let him say the above words and immediately the Spirit sent will appear, and when he sees it let him say the following.

Charmes pormeniel vear sasevii liernoly noty ersy melron.

Having said what the Art commands, the Spirit will draw near and reveal to him the secret he has been faithfully and secretly entrusted with.

Steganographia

CHAPTER 7

The 7th hour of the day is called Hamarym, and its Intelligence is called BARQUIEL who has under his empire 10 Dukes, 100 Counts and an uncertain number of sub-servants.

Their ministry is abundantly sufficient to us for all operations of this Art, according to their order, in the 7th hour of the day. When therefore you wish to operate at this hour by the Spirits of Barquiel you invoke no less than a [93] Duke and a Count, who have sub-servants each in their order, so that you have at hand the names of some Dukes and Counts by whom you can operate.

R.		R.		R.		
Abrasiel	Harmiel	Pasriel	10	10	100
Farmos	Nastrus	Venesiel	10	10	100
Nestorii	Varmay	Evarym	10	10	100
Manuel	Tulmas	Drufiel	10	10	100
Sagiel	Crosiel	Kathos	10	10	100

Table 39: The Dukes and Counts of Barquiel.

Here are the names of 5 of the Dukes, 10 of the Counts and 600 sub-servants according to their order. The Dukes and Counts are called by their names and are quick to obey the operator in all that concerns the mysteries of this Art, so when you want to operate by their ministry write on a clean schedule the characters of the Lord of the Ascendant and of the 12th House, and what else the custom requires, and on the reverse side write the following words according to the Princes of the Art, as it is indicated in its place.

Lamedon mosco ursoty tharvean: dayr Lays emel thebrean rasoty bamerson.

Having performed what the Art requires, you will say these same words with strong intention as required, and the Spirits called will come at once, entrust not your secret to the Count but to the Duke, unless you have called a Count without a Duke, which I do not deny can be done, however according to the precept of the Art, you must at least call a Duke with a Count, as long as you wish.

Secret Argument. You have a letter that you would like to entrust only to a friend, but you dare not do so either by letter or by messenger, because frauds can occur on all sides, call as many as you like of these Spirits named above in the table, entrust your secret to the most apparent, fear nothing because they are all good and faithful in everything.

You send such a letter as you please, and when having received these letters from the one who sends the Intelligences, having known the sign of Barquiel, observe in the same hour [94] the Lord of the Ascendant, and in the same hour write his character with the rest on a very clean schedule, and read the words written on the reverse side very tacitly as is the custom, and immediately the Spirit sent will appear, and when you see him pronounce the following words.

Mefarym burne theor alveas casvean cralti lierto aply charmoys.

Which having done and said, the Spirit sent will appear, approaching closely, and will reveal the secret entrusted to him, with all possible safety. But you must be careful to be strong and constant and without fear, whatever you may see.

CHAPTER 8

Jafanym is the name of the 8th hour of the day and his principal Intelligence is called OSMADIEL according to the *Picatrix* in his magic. He has under his empire 10 Dukes, 100 Counts and an infinite number of servants deputed not only to the operations of this Art, but to any concerning magic [mentioned by] the Jewish Solomon in the book of the nature of Spirits.

One named Hermes, says that all the Intelligences that are subject to Osmadiel, both Dukes and Counts, are wont to come to the operator in various forms and transformations, at the will of the operator, seeing that they are commanded by the operator, but we will only name some of them in the present table.

R.		R.		R.		R.	
Sarfiel	Demarot	Mariel	10	10	100	100	
Amalym	Janofiel	Remasyn	10	10	100	100	
Chroel	Larfuty	Thoriel	10	10	100	100	
Mesial	Vemael	Framion	10	10	100	100	
Lantrhotz	Thribiel	Ermiel	10	10	100	100	

Table 40: The Dukes and Counts of Osmadiel.

There are in this table, 5 of the Dukes and 10 of the Counts who suffice for [95] all the operations of this Art, in this hour, therefore when you wish to operate by them, write on a clean schedule the characters and words hereinafter written, and this in the accustomed manner, having first performed what is to be done and said the words which are written on the reverse of the schedule which are these:

Osmodael aneor ersoty neas, hayr layr Caphrayn thelreas mear penarsy.

Having finished pronouncing these words, the Spirits called will appear promptly and obedient to all, entrusting your secret to the most apparent, not to the Count, unless the Duke is absent, because you must never confide in anyone but the most visible.

Secret Argument. Let us have a secret such as we would like to let an absent friend know and such as we would not like anyone else to know, and this can happen very often, nor use a messenger lest he be corrupted, or the letters fall into foreign hands, operate by the Spirit and we will then be safe. Write such letters as you please. And when the letters are received the receiver will notice the sign of the Seal of Osmadiel, and being instructed in the Art, having performed what is necessary he must say the prescribed words, and the Spirit sent at once, will appear, and when he sees him he must also say the following.

Menasson aproysy elmano thulneas assierto mavear veneas cralnoti permason.

What the Spirit messenger has said will be revealed to you secretly and faithfully.

CHAPTER 9

The 9th hour of the day is called Karron, and its principal Intelligence QUABRIEL has under him many Dukes, Counts and almost innumerable sub-servants among whom there are 10 among the Dukes and one hundred among the Counts, deputies to the various operations of this Art, they have many sub-servants and deputies by order.

In the 1st Order there are 10; in the second 20; in the 3rd 30; in the 4th 40; in the 5th 500; in the 6th 600; [96] in the 7th 700; in the 8th 1000 and 80; in the 9th 90000; and in the 10th order 100000. But the Spirits are rarely called by all the orders, and if they are called they are not wont to all come but [only] some with their Dukes and Counts according to the command of the Emperor. Because the great Raziel[1] says in his book of prestiges [magical tricks] and transformations that the number of these Spirits is great and that each one observes his order well in all the ministries and offices, and Solomon the Jew surnamed Hermes,[2] says of the nature of the Spirits that they are wont to appear in the form that the operator describes. In this table, we will give the names of some Dukes and Counts.

R.		R.		R.			R.
Astroniel	Kranos	Trubas	10	10	10	100
Charmy	Menas	Xermiel	10	10	10	100
Pamory	Brasiel	Lameson	10	10	10	100
Damyel	Nefarym	Zazmor	10	10	10	100
Nadriel	Zoymiel	Janediel	10	10	10	100

Table 41: The Dukes and Counts of Quabriel.

And in this table are the names of 5 of the Dukes and 10 of the Counts and the number of 650 of the servants who are sufficient. When, therefore, you wish to operate in the 9th hour of the day by the ministry of these Spirits, observe the Lord of the Ascendant, and write on a schedule the precepts which the Art requires and on the reverse the following words according to custom.

> Quabriel odiel amear, cayn alco mean chyrpareos payr peray, thubro menasry.

Having done what is necessary, you will say these same words as it is said in the Art and immediately the called Spirits will appear, in and under whatever form you wish, prompt and faithful in all, entrusted the most apparent with your secret.

Secret Argument. Suppose you have such a secret that you wish to keep well

---

[1] Raziel, the archangel has several grimoires credited to his pen.
[2] An interesting historical confusion.

hidden, but for serious reasons you wish to communicate it to a friend who is engaged to be married and absent, and you do not wish to confide it to anyone under any pretext whatsoever, for this you will call one or two Dukes and Counts named above according to the institution of the Art, and [97] you will be able to boldly entrust your secret to the most apparent without fear of anything, then when you have formed such a letter as you please, which you will instruct the Spirit to hand over to your friend at once. And when your friend has received these letters signed with the character of Quabriel, being instructed in the Art, and having performed what the Art requires, he will recite the prescribed words and having pronounced them, the destined Spirit will appear at once, and when he sees him, he will pronounce the following words.

Mesraym paslotiel vear reneam cralty thio phroysy ma mear Hamorsy.

Having said this the Spirit will draw near and reveal what has been entrusted to him.

CHAPTER 10

The tenth hour of the day is called Lamarhon, and its supreme Angel ORIEL is a great and Powerful Emperor who, according to what the Jewish Solomon reports has under him, at his command, many Dukes by whom one may make many beautiful and admirable operations in the art of magic.

In the 10th hour of the day, the Dukes and the Counts have between them ten Orders which are deputed for all the operations of this Art with their sub-servants, in the first order there are 10; in the second 20; in the third 30; in the fourth 40; in the 5th 500; in the 6th 600; in the 7th 700; in the 8th 800; in the 9th 900; and in the 10th 1000. But we have to be content with taking only 10 Counts from the first five Orders. And if anyone desires to know the names of many, let him call one named in the table, and only five Dukes from among the last five orders, and when they have been called, he may question the most apparent, and he may also learn all that he wishes, and moreover he may even know of this Spirit as much as he will.[1]

[98] R.		R.	R.		R.	
Armosy	Lemur	Xantros	10	10	100	100
Drabiel	Ormas	Basilon	10	10	100	100
Penaly	Charny	Nameron	10	10	100	100
Mesriel	Mazyor	Kranoti	10	10	100	100
Choreb	Naveron	Alfrael	10	10	100	100

Table 42: The Dukes and Counts of Oriel.

You see that there have been in this table, 5 of the Dukes of Oriel and 10 of the Counts, and 1100 of the sub-servants who are deputised to them by order which sufficient for us to operate in this Art. Therefore, when you wish to operate by them in this hour, having accomplished what the Art customarily requires, and having written what is to be written on a clean card, and having written the following words on the reverse, do the rest as you have been taught.

Oriel burnadiel irasmy crismean pormy ersoti amear medusen.

When you have pronounced these words according to the exact institution of the Art, you will see a Duke present with the rest of the Spirits called upon, to whom you can entrust your secret with every assurance.

Constitution of the secret. We have a friend whom we favour, and we fear he will be supplanted or harmed, and we wish to give him advice, but we dare not charge a messenger with words or letters for fear of betrayal, to be safe, and so that our

---

[1] About the other Spirits in Oriel's host.

secret be always hidden, let us call one of the aforementioned Dukes, he will come and obey, he will carry your news safely and faithfully. Write such a letter as you please. and when your friend receives it, being instructed in the Art, let him do what the Art requires, and recite the above words as is the custom and when he sees the Spirit pressing let him say the following words: and let him always address the most apparent Spirit.

Camyn aparsy aslotiel omear reneas vean triamy cralty penason.

When this has been said the Spirit will immediately come to him and reveal the secret.

[99] CHAPTER 11

In the eleventh hour of the day which is called Maneloym, the powerful Emperor of this hour is called BARIEL, who according to Hermes the Jew in his writings, has under his empire many Spirits by whom admirable things have been done in this hour, in the different operations of which there are many deputies for the operations of this Art [arranged] by order.

In the first order there are 10; in the 2nd 20; in the 3rd 30; in the 4th 40; in the 5th 500; in the 6th 600; in the 7th 700; in the 8th 800; in the 9th 900; in the 10th 1000. All these are sent by order to the ministries of this Art, among whom are Dukes and Counts with their valets, many of whom it is not easy to describe with all their names. Moreover, there is no need, since it is sufficient to have only one of them, and the operator is always in a position to know their names through the revelation of one of these Spirits whom we may call from the table. It should be noted, according to Raziel, that all these Spirits are formed and transformed by the will of the operator, in whatever form he wishes to see them. Let him command this before pronouncing the mystic words which have the virtue of forcing them so that in a short time they are compelled to appear according to this method of calling, in the manner that the Art requires, and will promptly obey him in everything. In the following tables, we will give you the names of just a few of them.

R.		R.		R.		R.	
Almarizel	Menafiel	Almas	10	10	100	100
Prasiniel	Demasor	Perman	10	10	100	100
Chadros	Omary	Comial	10	10	100	100
Turmiel	Helmas	Temas	10	10	100	100
Lamiel	Zemoel	Lanifiel	10	10	100	100

Table 43: The Dukes and Counts of Bariel.

[100] We have the names of 15 of the Spirits of Bariel, namely 5 Dukes and 10 Counts, who have 1100 servants, which are sufficient for the operations of this Art. Therefore, when you wish to operate through them, observe the Lord of the Ascendant with the rest we have taught above, you have your own schedule as this Art requires, and on the back of it you will write the words as are listed below.

> Bariel mylan theory madruson alfayr dreschym taparoys mear moas layr penason.

Having performed what this Art requires, these same words must be said, immediately the Spirits you have called will appear and entrust their secret to you.

Steganographia

Constitution of the secret. We have a secret that we dare not send to a friend by any means whatsoever, so to be sure we must call a Spirit and entrust him with your secret, and he will carry it. But it is necessary to charge him with a letter, and when your friend receives this letter being instructed in the Art, let him pay attention to the character of the hour annexed in the letter, having known that it operates by the Lord of the Ascendant of the hour in which he receives the letter according to the precepts of the Art, then he says the prescribed oration in the manner and order required, immediately the Spirits sent will appear.[1] When you see them pronounce the following words, always addressing the principal.

Chamerusin maslotiel vear reneas liernoty trismy penason.

Once you have said these words to the leading one, who you will easily recognise by his clothing and crown - he always precedes the others – he will be the one to reveal the secret to your ear.

---

[1] The key to timing is the link between the Lord of the Ascendant when the message was sent, and the Lord of the Ascendant when the recipient invokes the Spirit at reception, with reference to the Planetary hour.

CHAPTER 12

The 12th hour of the day is called Nahalon or Naybalon, and its Supreme Emperor Angel [101] is called BERATIEL[1] who according to Jewish Solomon has an infinite number of Spirits deputed to various operations among which there are many deputed to the operations of this Art by various orders.

In the 1st order there are 10 Dukes and Counts, in the 2nd 20; in the 3rd 30; in the 4th 40; in the 5th 500; in the 6th 600; in the 7th 700; in the 8th 800; in the 9th 900; in the 10th 100; in the 11th 200; in the 12th 300. All these with an infinity of valets are deputed by order in Art, you will be able to invoke some as many as you wish in the 12th h[our]. All the Princes, Dukes and Counts of this hour, according to Raziel, take the figure [or shape] which pleases the operator.

R.		R.		R.		R.	
Camaron	Plamiel	Edriel	10	100	10	100
Astrofiel	Nerostiel	Choriel	10	100	10	100
Penatiel	Emarson	Romiel	10	100	10	100
Demarac	Quirix	Fenosiel	10	100	10	100
Famaras	Sameron	Hamary	10	100	10	100

Table 44: The Dukes and Counts of Berathiel.

In this table we have the names of 15 of Berathiel's Spirits, including 5 Dukes of as many orders and 10 Counts, who are joined by 1100 servants for the various operations in the secrets of magic. Therefore, when you wish to operate through them in the last hour of the day, observe the Lord of the Ascendant of this hour and the [Lord of the] 12th house and the character of these two, with the necessary rest which must be written on a clean schedule, and on the reverse you will put the words as they are reported below.

> Berathiel odiel irsoti rodu dreor ravezo melros ethiel aty nodiel hayres penason.

Having performed what the Art requires, it is customary to say these same words in the due manner and immediately the called Spirits will appear. Then entrust your secret to the most apparent, according to the institution of the Art, and they will obey you faithfully in all things.

Secret Argument. We have a secret which we wish to make known to a friend, but for particular reasons we dare not do so openly. For this purpose, let us call upon

---

[1] But spelled Berathiel throughout the rest of this chapter.

Spirits deputed according to the operation of the hour, let us entrust our secret to them in confidence, and [102] write a letter as we wish, and when your friend, being instructed in the Art, receives these letters signed with the character of Berathiel, let him promptly do what the Art requires, and let him recite the words written above, and when he sees the Spirits who will come without delay, let him say at once what follows to the most apparent, which he will see will be crowned.

Famerusyn melysno alny vemoby dreary drymes charsony.

But one must be firm and constant and not fear, because they are good and offend no one, provided he is well instructed. But if someone wants to operate without being instructed, he will not avoid peril.

CHAPTER 13

The first hour of the night is called Omalharien and its Supreme Angel is called SABRATHAN, who has under his empire many other Spirits employed in different magical operations, as attested by Hermes Salomon, a very expert in Jewish magic.

Of these there are many deputed for the operations of our Art by turns and orders. First in the 1st order there are 10; in the 2nd 20; in the 3rd 30; in the 4th 40; in the 5th 500; in the 6th 600; in the 7th 70;[1] in the 8th 80; in the 9th 90; in the 10th 100. All these are sent for the ministry of secrets; sometimes there are hidden orders of which we do not have full knowledge, and we will not speak of them. See the table.

R.		R.		R.			R.
Domaros	Ramesiel	Hayzoym	100	100	100	100
Amerany	Omedriel	Emalon	100	100	100	100
Penoles	Franedac	Turtiel	100	100	100	100
Mardiel	Chrasiel	Quenol	100	100	100	100
Nastul	Dornason	Rymaliel	100	100	100	100

Table 45: The Dukes and Counts of Sabrathan.

[103] You see in this table, 5 from among the Dukes of the Spirits of Sabrathan and 10 named Counts who have 2000 valets of their own deputised by turns and orders, and therefore when you wish to operate by them, observe the Lord of the Ascendant, and his character, with what is necessary, written on a proper schedule, with on the reverse the following words.

> Sabrathan odiel melros rhupis othian elroz adiel methiel mear nasutiel lafian irsoti brestion dreor chamerson.

Having performed what the Art requires, and recited the above words, you will see the Spirits called forth, with whom you may do whatever you wish, following what the precepts of the Art do teach.

Argument of the secret. For example. You have a secret that you do not wish to be entrusted to letters or messengers, but only to the ministrations of the Spirits who preside at the time you operate, but it is not necessary to call upon Spirits for light causes, but where the ministry of men is in question. For this purpose you write a letter to your friend, and when the one to whom you send this letter receives it, being instructed in the Art, let him observe and write the Lord of the

---

[1] Not 700 as might have been expected.

Ascendant of that hour, with the other precepts of the Art, and having executed what the Art requires, let him say the words prescribed above and at once the Spirits sent will appear to him visibly, and as soon as he sees them let him address the most apparent with these words.

Chameros burnean aslotiel vear reneas cralty triomy penason.

Having pronounced these eight words very exactly, which are in the mystic tongue, the Spirit will approach the operator, and reveal the secret to his ear.

CHAPTER 14

The second hour of the night is called Penazure and its Intelligence is TARTYS, a Supreme Angel Emperor under whose empire are a great number of Princes, Dukes, Counts, and servants. Who being called, by custom to send them to the [104] various ministries concerning our Art and science in the hidden secrets of nature, by turns and orders, of these there are twelve orders deputed to the operations of our Art which suffice us for all operations.

In the 1st order there are 10; in the 2nd 20; in the 3rd 30; in the 4th 40; in the 5th 50; in the 6th 60; in the 7th 70; in the 8th 80; in the 9th 90; in the 10th 100; in the 11th 1000; in the 12th 100000. It seldom happens that the operation is carried out by all the orders of these Spirits, because it is not necessary to occupy them all since a small number suffices us very abundantly, unless someone being well instructed in the Art and perfect in this science desires to see the Princes of all the orders named above, and to know their names. He could then call them all in order.

R.		R.		R.				
Almodar	Permaz	Gabrynoz	100	10	100	10
Famoriel	Vameroz	Mercoph	100	10	100	10
Nedroz	Emariel	Tameriel	100	10	100	10
Ormezyn	Framezyn	Venomiel	100	10	100	10
Chabriz	Ramaziel	Jenaziel	100	10	100	10
Praxiel	Gramozyn	Xemyzin	100	10	100	10

Table 46: The Dukes and Counts of Tartys.

Here in this table are the names of 6 Dukes of Tartis[1] and 12 of the Counts and 1320 servants named and distributed in order, which are sufficient for us to experiment with the Art in this hour. Note that according to Salomon and Raziel all these Spirits, both Princes and Dukes of Tartys, are benevolent and quick to obey and willingly take the form they are commanded, therefore when you want to operate in this Art observe the Lord of the Ascendant with what we have carefully ordered and write everything there is to write on one side and on the reverse write the following words.

> Tartys chrybes faziel yrsoti haelnot dreor advear afy mearo veny satu pemerson.

[105] Having recited these words and diligently carried them out in the manner of

---

[1] Note the different spelling of Tartys/Tartis.

the Spirits called will also come at once and be ready for your commands.

Argument from a Grave Secret

Let us have a secret according to the time and the variation of the business we wish to make known to a friend. Let it not be a light matter, but one such that you can only do it surely by the ministry of these Spirits. For this purpose, it is necessary to write a letter signed with the character of Tartys, and when your friend has received this letter, he must notice the sign of this Supreme Intelligence, and being instructed in our Art, let him observe the Lord of the Ascendant and diligently do what needs to be done and recite the above prescribed words in the accustomed manner, and when he sees that the Spirits who have been sent are present, let him pronounce the following words addressed to the most apparent one.

Chabor massotiel tusevo reneas porean trismeny penarson.

When the recipient of the letter has pronounced these words with a strong intention, and always addressing the principal Duke, immediately the Spirit will approach very quietly and reveal the secret to his ear.

CHAPTER 15

The third hour of the night it is called Quabrion, and its Emperor and Angel is called SERQUANICH who has under his empire Princes, Dukes and Counts, distinguished by 12 orders, and many servants.

For in the 1st order there are 10; in the 2nd 20; in the 3rd 30; in the 4th 40; in the 5th 50; in the 6th 60; in the 7th 70; in the 8th 80; in the 9th 90; in the 10th 100; in the 11th 1000; and in the 12th 10000. Of these there are some sent for the ministries of various experiments of which there are sufficient Dukes, Counts, and servants. See the table below.

[106] R.	R.	R.		R.		R.	
Menarym	Evanuel	Vanosir	10	10	100	100	
Chrusiel	Sarmozyn	Lemaron	10	10	100	100	
Penargoz	Haylon	Almonoyz	10	10	100	100	
Amriel	Quabriel	Janothyel	10	10	100	100	
Demanoz	Thurmytz	Melrotz	10	10	100	100	
Nestoroz	Fronyzon	Xanthyos	10	10	100	100	

Table 47: The Principal Spirits of Serquanich.

We have in this table the names of 12 of the principal Spirits of Serquanich, one of each order who assume the dignity of Dukes and Counts according to their turn, the other 6 do not change Office, but are always Dukes, if anyone wishes to be more fully instructed in the names of these Spirits, he could easily accomplish this intention through those we have named. Therefore, when you wish to operate through them, observe the Lord of the Ascendant and his character, along with the rest, and write this on a clean sheet of paper, and on the reverse side the following words.

> Serquanich osiel theory dreochy amersoty omear, pornis layr mear penarson.

Having carried out what the Art requires, recite these words, and the Spirits called will immediately appear ready to obey, with whom you will act according to the precepts of the Art.

Secret Argument. We wish to warn a friend of an approaching peril, but we fear this peril, if it were discovered what I have made known to him, the peril would be no less for us, desolate that we dare not entrust it to either letters or messengers, but only to the Spirit of this third [nocturnal] hour, and for this purpose we send by Spirit a letter to the friend and when he receives it being instructed in the Art, let him pay attention to the sign of the principal Spirit, so that he knows which one he should call, according to the mutations of the hour, then let him observe the Lord of the Ascendant of the hour at which he receives the letter, with the disposition of the sky, by the 12 houses of the Zodiac, forgetting exactly nothing of what is ordered, having pronounced the above prescribed words, and when [107] he has finished, he will see the Spirits present, to whose principal he will address the following words.

Chamerufyn maslotiel vean reneas cralty thyrmo venear penarson.

When he has said this, the Spirit will come to him and whisper in his ear the secret that has been entrusted to him.

Steganographia

CHAPTER 16

For the fourth hour of night, which is called Ramerzy, its Angel is called JEFISCHA,[1] who has under his empire many Princes, Dukes, Counts, and Spirits whom he employs in ministries, which like the others we prescribed in the preceding chapter, are distributed by order and turns, in 12 Classes.

For in the 1st order there are 10; in the 2nd 20; in the 3rd 30; in the 4th 40; in the 5th 50; in the 6th 60; in the 7th 70; in the 8th 80; in the 9th 90; in the 10th 100; in the 11th 1000; in the 12th 10000. In these 12 orders the Spirits are sent to us to minister in the operations of this Art according to their turn. We will name some of them in this table.

R.		R.		R.		R.	
Armosiel	Rayziel	Lamediel	10	100	100	1000	
Nedruan	Gemezin	Adroziel	10	100	100	1000	
Maneyloz	Fremiel	Zodiel	10	100	100	1000	
Ormael	Hamayz	Bramiel	10	100	100	1000	
Phorsiel	Japuriel	Coreziel	10	100	100	1000	
Rimezyn	Jasphiel	Enatriel	10	100	100	1000	

Table 48: The Dukes and Counts of Jefischa.

Here are the names of 6 Dukes of Jefischa and 2 Counts to whom there are 7260 deputies or servants who are sent by turns to execute the will of the Operator in the Art, according to what the great philosopher Solomon reports, that these Princes take various forms according to the desire of the operator. When therefore you wish to operate by them [108] in this 4th hour of the night, you will observe the Lord of the Ascendant and all the figures of the sky, and do what has been ordered, writing it all down on a clean sheet, and on the reverse side you will write the following words exactly, word for word.

> Jefischa osiel mear pathyr lays mean theor dreochis fazan moab lofeas ersoti breo pornis tayr penarson.

Having received these words, you have to recite them, once you have performed what you have imagined in the required order and form. The Spirits will appear to you visibly in the way you have ordered. They are prompt and faithful in everything.

Secret Argument. You have a secret that you would like to share with a friend in the 4th hour of the night, it is such that you cannot entrust it either by letter, or by

---

[1] Sometimes spelled Jephisha.

messenger without running some risk and peril, know that it is not appropriate to operate by Spirits except for something of importance. You call a Spirit and you entrust him with your secret with all assurance, and you write a letter to your friend signed with the seal of Jefischa for the 4th hour of the night, and when the one to whom you write this letter receives it he will notice the seal of the Spirit, and being instructed in the Art, let him first observe the Lord of the Ascendant of that hour with all the figures of the sky, and let him write it on a clean schedule, and on the reverse side the words prescribed above, and when he has recited these same words that the Art requires, and has seen the Spirits sent appear, let him address the following words to their principal, and in this order.

Chamerusin aphroys aslotiel mean reneas vear tryamo cralti penason.

The Spirit will come to him and reveal the secret to his ear.

CHAPTER 17

The 5th hour of the night is called Sanayfar, and its Supreme Angel ABASDARHON has under his command many Princes, Dukes, Counts and vassals employed by all [109] orders in the various ministries of the Art, and whom he is wont to send for all the various operations of the Art that can be done by the operator who is sufficiently instructed.

In the 1st order are 10; in the 2nd 20; in the 3rd 30; in the 4th 40; in the 5th 50; in the 6th 60; in the 7th 70; in the 8th 80; in the 9th 90; in the 10th 100; in the 11th 1000; in the 12th 100000. And with their help, all the operations of this Art can be carried out in the 5th hour of the night.

R.		R.		R.		R.
Meniel	Gemarii	Barmas	100	100	100	100
Charaby	Vanescor	Platiel	100	100	100	100
Appiniel	Sameryn	Neszomy	100	100	100	100
Deinatz	Xantropy	Quesdor	100	100	100	100
Nechorym	Herphatz	Caremaz	100	100	100	100
Hameriel	Chrymas	Umariel	100	100	100	100
Vulcaniel	Patrozyn	Kralym	100	100	100	100
Samelon	Nameton	Habalon	100	100	100	100

Table 49: The Dukes and Counts of Abasdarhon.

We have here named 24 of the Spirits of Abasdarhon, of whom the first 12 are Dukes according to their rank, and the other 12 are Counts. And they are of each order, namely a Duke and a Count, and there are 3200 vassals who are used by turns in the various magical operations, as Solomon and Raziel tell us. The Princes of Abasdarhon, who are learned men and very expert in magic, are accustomed to appear in whatever form the operator orders them to; and having experienced this very often, we have the facts which we confess to be true, so when you wish to operate by them in this Art in the 5th hour of the night, observe the Lord of the Ascendant both himself and all the disposition of the sky, on a clean sheet of paper, as is already taught, and on the reverse side the following words.

> Abasdarhon morca lafias tharvean buel dreschin tayr moab ersoty layr pornis theori mean afar penason.

[110] Then, having done what is necessary, and recited the above words, the Spirits you have called will appear ready to do whatever you command.

Secret Argument. You have a secret to communicate to someone far or near, and you cannot do so without peril. Rather entrust it to the principal among the Spirits, in the manner and form that the Art requires, fearing nothing, because they are good and faithful. Write such letters as you please. And he to whom you send these letters signed with the character of Abasdarhon will receive them, being instructed in the Art, let him at once consider the Lord of the Ascendant and all the disposition of Heaven, let him write it with the content of the prescribed words above and the other necessary things on a clean sheet, having performed what is proper, recite the aforesaid words, and when he shall see the sent Spirits appear, let him address the principal with the following words as reported hereafter.

Chameron massotiel tasevii renean pornas thilmevii penason.

Having said this, he will immediately approach closer, and reveal the secret entrusted to him, to the ear of the operator.

CHAPTER 18

The sixth hour of the night is called Thaazaron, and the Angel ZAAZENACH has under his empire an almost innumerable number of Princes, Dukes, Counts, and ministers who preside by turns and orders over the various operations of magic.

In their 1st order there are 10; in the 2nd 20; in the 3rd 30; in the 4th 40; in the 5th 50; in the 6th 60; in the 7th 70; in the 8th 80; in the 9th 90; in the 10th 100; in the 11th 1000; in the 12th 10000. When you wish to operate, call these Spirits who are all good and obedient in all things, and they appear in such a form as you please, as attested by the above-mentioned scholars, and as we have experienced many times.

[111]			R.	R.	R.	R.
Amonazii	Tuberiel	Pammon	100	100	100	100
Menoriel	Humaziel	Dracon	100	100	100	100
Prenostix	Lanoziel	Gematz	100	100	100	100
Namedor	Lamerotz	Enariel	100	100	100	100
Cherasiel	Xerphiel	Rudefor	100	100	100	100
Dramaz	Zeziel	Sarmon	100	100	100	100

Table 50: The Dukes and Counts of Zaazenach.

We have here named 12 Dukes from among the 12 orders of the Spirits of Zaazenach and 6 Counts with their servants to the number of 1860 deputies exactly by order, which are abundantly sufficient for us for all operations of the Art in the 6th hour of the night; when therefore you wish to operate during this hour observe the Lord of the Ascendant, both him and all the disposition of the sky with the other things that are necessary, which you will write on a clean sheet, and on the reverse side the following words.

> Zaazenach eneos fari neabdiel lasmy chyrmean ersoty lay pornys theor mean penason.

Having done what is necessary, and pronounced these words, the called Spirits will appear without delay, tranquil and beneficent, and ready for anything.

Secret Argument. We have a great secret to communicate to an absent friend, to do it safely, we entrust it to one of the Dukes named above or to a Count, if the Dukes are absent, which often happens from the method and order that the precepts of the Art requires, fearing nothing because they are good and faithful in all that the operator orders them, they will forget nothing. You form a letter and send it to your friend, and when he receives it let him notice the character of the

Spirit of the hour, being instructed in the Art, having observed the figure of the sky, let him write it down with what is necessary, and having performed what the operation requires and having recited the words prescribed above, when the Spirit is visible you must address the following words to him.

Chamerufi ferion notiel asevomy rean badian, laso fear vaobry hastoripeson.

[112] Which having been said the Spirit will approach him, and he will communicate the secret with which he is charged, faithfully and secretly to the ear of the operator.

CHAPTER 19

The 7th hour of the night is called Venaydor, and the Angel of this hour is a Supreme Spirit called MENDRION, who has under him and under his empire many other Spirits as principal Princes, Dukes, Counts and ministers assigned to the various magical operations.

Of these there are many deputies for the operations of our Art, as Princes, Dukes, Counts, with a great number of sub-servants, by turns, orders and ranks. In the 1st order there are 10; in the 2nd 20; in the 3rd 30; in the 4th 40; in the 5th 50; in the 6th 60; in the 7th 70; in the 8th 80; in the 9th 90; in the 10th 100; in the 11th 1000; in the 12th 100000. All of these come when they are called by all for our operations. See the following table.

R.		R.		R.			R.
Ammiel	Ventariel	Rayziel	10	100	100	100
Choriel	Zachariel	Tarmitz	10	100	100	100
Genarytz	Dubraz	Anapion	10	100	100	100
Pandroz	Marchiel	Imoniel	10	100	100	100
Menesiel	Jonadriel	Framoth	10	100	100	100
Sameriel	Pemoniel	Machmag	10	100	100	100

Table 51: The Dukes and Counts of Mendrion.

In this table we have named 12 Dukes and 6 Counts from among the 12 orders of the Spirits of the Supreme Intelligence of the 7th hour of the night, named Mendrion, who suffice us for this time for all the operations with their sub-servants. These Spirits come in whatever shape and form they are commanded by the one who operates according to the precepts of the Art, as Hermes the Hebrew and Raziel the Arab testify.[1] But if he who is not well [113] instructed in the Art, would attempt to operate, he would not be obeyed, but would incur peril. But when you want to operate in this Art during the 7th hour of the night, observe the Lord of the Ascendant and all the figures of the sky, with the other precepts of the Art that you will write on a clean schedule, and on the reverse the following words.

> Mendrion suriaco breotnirus ersoy nevo, omear nyco lays ersota theory pornys Azan mean lafias astopenason.

Having pronounced these words and carried out the necessary actions according to the rules, immediately the called Spirits will appear, ready to do whatever you tell them to do.

---

[1] Hermes was of course Greek and not Hebrew. Raziel was a Hebrew angel and not an Arabic author.

Secret Argument. To announce to a friend far or near a very secret thing, it is necessary to be instructed in the Art, no matter of what kind the secret is, provided that it is of consequence, such that it can't be entrusted to letters. Such as the letters are, [but it is only important that] the character of the Angel of this hour is there, of the time at which one does the operation, and there is nothing secret in the letters. You send these letters to the friend, being instructed in the Art, signed with the character of Mendrion. Let him observe the Lord of the Ascendant, both it and all the other disposition of the sky. Let him write it on a clean sheet, and on the reverse the words above prescribed. Having executed that, he will pronounce the said words, and as soon as he sees the Spirit present, he addresses the principal with the following words.

Chamerusin merion modiel burmy raveto badria favepo elay reas penason.

When he has said these words to whichever [Spirit] appears most apparent to him, the Spirit will immediately draw near and reveal in his ear the secret entrusted to him.

Steganographia

CHAPTER 20

The 8th hour of the night is called Xymalim, and its Angel and first Emperor is called NARCORIEL who has under his command many other Spirits, as Princes, Dukes, Counts and ministers, who are called by turns, by those who operate these [114] philosophical secrets.

Of all these there are 12 orders which serve this Art, in the 1st order there are 10; in the 2nd 20; in the 3rd 30; in the 4th 40; in the 5th 50; in the 6th 60; in the 7th 70; in the 8th 80; in the 9th 90; in the 10th 100; in the 11th 1000; in the 12th 10000. They all observe their rank so well, that no one can operate surely if he is not well instructed in everything; whoever does not regularly observe the order, exposes himself to peril, and it will not have the desired effect.

R.		R.		R.		R.	
Cambiel	Amelzon	Xanoryz	100	100	100	1000	1000
Nedarym	Lemozar	Jastrion	100	100	100	1000	1000
Astrocon	Xernifiel	Themaz	100	100	100	1000	1000
Marifiel	Kanorsiel	Hobrazym	100	100	100	1000	1000
Dramozyn	Bufanotz	Zymeloz	100	100	100	1000	1000
Lustifion	Jamedroz	Gamsiel	100	100	100	1000	1000

Table 52: The Dukes and Counts of Narcoriel.

We have named in this table 12 Dukes and 6 Counts established by a secret arrangement through all the 12 orders, who have under them ministers the 13200 servants who suffice us for all the operations of the 8th hour of night. When therefore you wish to operate by them in this hour, observe the Lord of the Ascendant, both him and all the disposition of Heaven, which you must write on a schedule, and on the reverse the following words.

> Narconiel[1] aples pornya navelo meas. Triome il neas azyfan lafias my bression ersoti penason.

Having done what is necessary, and having recited these words, the called Spirits will come in the form you ordered, and promptly do everything you order.

Secret Argument. You have a secret to send to an absent friend, far or near, you cannot entrust it to letters or messengers, entrust it to the first of the Spirits of Narcoriel in the 8th hour of the night fearing nothing because they are all faithful and ready to obey. Draft a letter that you send to the friend, and when receiving the letter with the sign of Narcoriel, being well instructed in the Art, let him

---

[1] *Manuscript note:* This word should have been 'Narcoriel.'

observe the Lord of the Ascendant of this hour, both himself and [115] all the disposition of heaven, with the other necessary things, let him write it on a clean schedule, and having performed what custom requires, let him say the words prescribed above, and when he sees that the Spirits are present let him say the following words.

Medora cassotiel va reneas thasny thyrmo thea penason.

Having addressed these words to the most apparent Spirit according to the institutions of the Art, immediately this Spirit will approach closely and reveal the secret to your ear.

CHAPTER 21

The 9th hour of the night is called Zeschar, and its Angel and supreme Intelligence is called PAMIEL, who, like the previous ones, has many other Spirits subject to his laws.

Some good, others bad, Princes, Dukes, Counts and ministers deputed by turns and orders, in the 1st order there are 10; in the 2nd 20; in the 3rd 30; in the 4th 40; in the 5th 50; in the 6th 60; in the 7th 70; in the 8th 80; in the 9th 90; in the 10th 100; in the 11th 1000; in the 12th 100000. We do not need every one in the operations of our Art, since a few are enough for us, see in this table.

R.		R.		R.		R.
Demaor	Comary	Befranzii	10	100	10	100
Nameal	Matiel	Jachoroz	10	100	10	100
Adrapon	Zenoroz	Xanthir	10	100	10	100
Chermel	Brandiel	Armapy	10	100	10	100
Fenadroz	Evandiel	Druchas	10	100	10	100
Venasiel	Tameriel	Sardiel	10	100	10	100

Table 53: The Dukes and Counts of Pamiel.

Here we have named 18 Princes of Pamiel, who by turns are sometimes Dukes sometimes Counts: he who does not know the order they observe and their turns, labours in vain in this Art. They have 1320 ministers deputising under their [116] command by turns and according to the movements of the hour and in its positive moment by which we hope for admirable effects, therefore when you want to operate by them in the 9th hour of the night, observe the Lord of the Ascendant and all the figures of the sky and write everything on a very clean sheet, and on the reverse side the following words.

> Pamyel lyraz lasian mavelo breothis thirmoan ersoti layr pornis theory moar azas penason.

As soon as you have recited the above words, the Spirits named will appear visible in whatever form you order them to take. All those we have named are good and quick to obey commissions, and very faithful to the one who operates exactly.

Secret Argument. What secret is there that we cannot safely send to a friend? We entrust it to the first among the Spirits who appear to us, and we are safe, he is recognised from the others by his habit and crown. You send whatever letters you like to the friend, signed with Pamiel's seal. And when he receives it, and being instructed in the Art, let him observe and write the Lord of the Ascendant and all the figures of the sky, as it is said, on a clean sheet. And let him do all that is necessary according to the Art, having recited the words prescribed above. When he sees that the Spirits that have been sent appear visibly, let him address the following words to the most apparent.

Chasmeron apornys veto mean ilno vean aplois cralta ilso pamerson.

Having spoken these words to the principal, the Spirit will immediately come closer and reveal the secret to his ear.

CHAPTER 22

The 10th hour of the night is called Malcho, and its supreme Angel is JASGUARIM who has under his empire many Princes, Dukes, Counts, and ministers deputed to the various and admirable operations of this Art, as Solomon surnamed Hermes testifies in his *Secret of* [117] *Magic*.

There are 100 Dukes, and 100 Counts, and many ministers deputed according to their turns and orders in the operations of this Art. See the table.

R.		R.		R.		R.	
Lapheriel	Chameray	30	10	100	100	300	
Emarziel	Hazaniel	30	10	100	100	300	
Nameroyz	Uraniel	30	10	100	100	300	

Table 54: The Dukes and Counts of Jasguarim.

As you can see, many Dukes and Counts are deputised for the 10th hour of the night, and yet a small number are sufficient for everything. We have put in this table only the names of three Dukes and three Counts. Paying attention to the number of their servants legitimately distributed by turns and orders. Those who wish to know more may call one of the above named, and question him about everything. When therefore you wish to operate by them during the 10th hour of the night, observe and do what is ordered, writing with care what is necessary on a clean sheet of paper, and on the reverse side the following words in the customary manner.

> Jasguarim apornys vesale moes labiel throe, Tadrys asiel cachylos rhubla nailso thirmiel vear. Turiel cralty solmys aslotiel naemes renhar, vear thirmo cralnoti saon dremion laviel odres, notiel pornys. Pornys mear moab sayr aslotiel lo raytu lian asevo, Bian eory churio bays astro penason.

Having done what needs to be done, you must pronounce these words, and having recited them according to the rules, the Spirits called will soon appear to you.

The Secret Intention. To succeed in keeping a secret safe for an absent friend, you must call one or two of the Spirits of Jasguarim, and make them a messenger that will be sure, entrust them with your secret and do not doubt anything, charge this messenger with a letter such as you please, and when the friend receives this letter sealed with the seal and character of Jasguarim, having been instructed in the Art, let him accomplish what the Art demonstrates and he will observe the order of the planets and write what there is to write, having recited the above words, as soon [118] as the Spirits sent are visible let him address these following words, to the most apparent.

Chamerusin othriel arnotiel folais elty. Naeles proy vear sato cralnoti penason.

Having said these words, the Spirit will immediately draw nearer and reveal in his ear the secret that has been entrusted to him with fidelity and tranquillity.

CHAPTER 23

The 11th hour of the night is called Aalacho and its supreme Emperor is DARDARIEL, who has under his dominion many very powerful Princes and Dukes who preside over an almost infinite number of Counts and ministers.

These Dukes are very benevolent, alert and cheerful, and delight to converse with men, and very obedient to operators who are well instructed in the Art. And notice that the number of these Dukes is infinite because the air is almost full of them: and they cannot be numbered; as says Salomon Hermes; and we ourselves have experienced that among the Spirits, Dukes, Counts and ministers of Dardariel there are many who are good, useful and very honest, who always desire to be useful to men, always exhorting them, by an invisible power to goodness, to honesty, to peace, to concord and integrity of faith, to the love of God, and to the observance of his commandments, to [having] contempt for the world, to the desire for supreme happiness, and for all kinds of good. These Spirits are good and very holy, reverently love God, and love those who take pleasure in being with holy and God-fearing men, because they are their protectors, deputies of God the Creator of all things.

The others are evil and very wicked, reprobates of God and enemies of all good things, who continually despise mortals and lay snares for men, and what the good Spirits institute in honour of God, these Spirits always try to destroy and revoke, and the air is full of these evil Spirits, who invisibly run and talk with men, always inciting them to evil, and dragging with them those who are [119] not on their guard. Through the ministry of these malignant Spirits of Dardariel an infinite number of curses are wrought, not only on Christians but on infidels as well. And in all, they deceive women who are most prone to mischief. And whoever wishes to work evil through them, they will be powerful in evil over all the other evil-doers, and worthy of eternal fire. But we who wish to teach and always work with men for good and not for evil, will appoint a messenger from among the good, and not from among the bad Dukes, as deputies for our Art. See the table.

R.		R.		R.		R.		
Cardiel	Masriel	Nermas	10	20	00	20	10
Fermon	Hariaz	Druchas	10	20	00	20	10
Armiel	Damar	Carman	10	20	00	20	10
Nastoriel	Alachue	Elamyz	10	20	00	20	10
Casmiroz	Emeriel	Jatroziel	10	20	00	20	10
Dameriel	Naveroz	Lamersy	10	20	00	20	10
Furamiel	Alaphar	Hamarytz	10	20	00	20	10

Table 55: The Dukes and Counts of Dardariel.

Here are 14 Dukes of Dadariel, Spirits and 7 Counts, good Spirits, who are sufficient for any operation of the Art, in the 11th hour of the night, with many almost infinite servants. When you wish to operate with one of these Spirits, do all that is ordered in this Art, having completed everything, you must carefully say the following words.

> Dardariel pirno nade vim pornis melto, nachir pheon pliros evali estafri thyrmano, Oniel maniel, vear raby cralnoti vemy Throe orbasiel afar ravean. Purgiel near jano masiel arlay. Nasevi myrsos modias merchul noti penason.

Having pronounced these words, and fulfilled the required Art with all due attention, the called Spirits will appear with benevolence.

Argument of Secret. All the Spirits named above, as Dukes, Counts, are good and faithful, in no way harming [120] any of those who truly love God, so much so that you can entrust to them anything you would like to make known to an absent friend in the 11th hour of the night according to the Art, and in no way be reluctant during this 11th hour of the night.

CHAPTER 24

The 12th hour of night, which reaches dawn, is called Xephan, and its Angel SARANDIEL, who has under his empire many good and evil Spirits, Princes, Dukes, Counts and ministers, who are deputised for the various operations, the good for the good, the bad for the bad.

The Princes, as Hermes Salomon says in the 4th Book *Of the Duties and Offices of Spirits*, often appear in the same way as the Devil is said to have appeared to Eve: with a beautiful head like a virgin, her hair scattered on all sides, but with two snake-like bodies, which they always hide under some garment lest they be seen. Their faces are very handsome, benevolent and joyful, and they are quick to operate and obey the operator in everything. See the table.

R.		R.		R.				R.
Adoniel	Marachy	Hardiel	10	20	00	20	10
Damasiel	Chabrion	Nefrias	10	20	00	20	10
Ambriel	Nestoriel	Irmanotz	10	20	00	20	10
Meriel	Zachriel	Gerthiel	10	20	00	20	10
Demaryz	Naveriel	Dromiel	10	20	00	20	10
Emarion	Damery	Ladrotz	10	20	00	20	10
Kabriel	Namael	Melanas	10	20	00	20	10

Table 56: The Dukes and Counts of Sarandiel.

We have named in this table, 14 Dukes from among the good Spirits of Sarandiel and 7 Counts with many of their servants who suffice us for all operations in the 12th hour of the night. When therefore you wish to operate at this hour through their [121] ministries, observe and do exactly what we have demonstrated and then you will have to recite the following words.

> Sarandiel marfo porno joniel schendiel jano Nati chilpres josas char meon prissy dyon volayr penason.

Having finished pronouncing these words, the called Spirits will immediately be ready for anything.

Constitution of the Secret

When you see the Spirits appear in a foreign and Pelerine form,[1] do not be frightened at all, because they are good and benevolent, harming no one, and they frighten no one by the monstrous form they take, because they always hide it,

---

[1] Wearing a woman's cape of lace or silk with pointed ends at the centre front, popular from the early 18th through to the 19th century.

appearing under a beautiful face. Entrust to them in safety whatever you wish your friend to know, in this last hour of the night.

Your friend having received the letter and having recognised the sign and character of the principal Spirit, and being instructed in the Art, let him do what custom requires, and having recited the words above prescribed, according to the Art, the Spirits will appear, and faithfully reveal the secret.

CHAPTER 25

In this last chapter, we shall teach the general approach and manner of achieving our Art, and of operating without risk, and with great efficiency.

Whoever desires to attain knowledge of the science of our hidden Art, and whoever desires to work wonders and things full of peril by this Art, it is necessary that he be first adorned with virtues, with a clean and spotless conscience, and good will towards God, for himself and for his neighbour, that he be not inclined to harm anyone, nor that he seeks businesses of moral turpitude. Then it is necessary that he be instructed and imbued a little in the good arts of letters and in all the science of the Stars, that he knows in general the movements, courses, retrogrades, changes, orders, natures, [122] situations, risings, setting and the effects of the Stars, Signs, and planets, because without [knowledge of] their full science, no one [will succeed]. Consequently, it is necessary to have a preceptor[1] perfect in the Art, and expert, because we believe it is [otherwise] impossible to come to this knowledge. At least a few people succeed without a preceptor, are experts, and studied many things on the instructions in the magical arts. The preceptor must not only be an expert in the sciences, but also faithful, honest and God-fearing, because the purer he is in conversation with God, the surer he will be in the operations of this Art: for these virtues are obeyed and submitted to by the Spirits.

Therefore, when you desire to achieve something in this Art, be with your preceptor and let him lead you to a secret and pure place, let the weather be tranquil and serene, and the Moon in complete opposition,[2] the Sun clear and radiant, and let ☿ [Mercury] in Ascendant be in ☌ [conjunction] with ♀ [Venus] or ♃ [Jupiter] if possible, let ♄ [Saturn] and ♂ [Mars] be set aside, because if these [two] or any other were with the Ascendant, the institution would not be perfect. Before all things, to elevate oneself in the Art, it will be necessary to pronounce this Act of Attestation and oath in the form and tenor that follows.

Act of Protestation.[3] I, N,[4] swear and promise by the virtue of Almighty God, by the blood of Our Lord Jesus Christ, by the Resurrection of the dead, by the Last Judgment and by the Salvation of my Soul in the Catholic faith, to Almighty God, to the Blessed Virgin Mary and to all the Saints and to you, N,[5] that I will preserve this Art of Steganography all the days of my life with fidelity: nor will I pass it to anyone without the will and consent of this same virtue. I swear and promise that I will not use this science against God and his commandments, nor against the

---

[1] Tutor.
[2] i.e. a Full Moon.
[3] It should be 'Attestation.'
[4] Your name.
[5] The name of your preceptor.

holy Roman [Catholic] and Universal Church, or its ministers, nor against justice & equity; so that God may assist me and save me at the Last Judgment.

Then let the preceptor read the following oration in the mystic language, and interpret it with all the others contained in this work in the presence of the disciple: lest he [123] suspect that there is something diabolical or superstitious, or contrary to God, that there is some hidden pact [with demons], expressed implicitly or explicitly.

General ORAISON that the Master must say before approaching the Art.

> MESARI cosmeneil archea sameor critas.
> Dricho mosayr usio noes veso tureas.
> Abrithios uaselion pyrno chyboyn ormon.
> Cervali myrbevo lian faveao sayr.
> Rhymano cave japion nospiel sasevo rhaony
> Naty thirpolian jonayr chuleor nefris.
> Mistriona nayr davosy tyvamo turmy.
> Pleon nomeato turias bresne nasephon
> Adion sayr catros chirosny aschyon ermy
> Otyel layr romays theory naias atrevo.
> Aliar measco trisna useori jesaschor.
> Bios pailon ravemy sear astro penason.[1]

And after the Master has explained this to his disciple, the order and content of all the mystical orations which are in all the chapters which make up the scope of this work; to force and compel the Spirits of this Art to appear, that he teaches to him the most secret springs of this science, which are not written, nor to be written, forbidding him under the express attestation, and under the foretold oath not to reveal it to anyone during his life, unless to those who are worthy and sworn experts in the Art, nor that he write it for any cause whatsoever, then that he teach him the natures, names, places, numbers, Offices and properties of all the Spirits who are deputed for this Art, in whatever manner, when, and where he must operate by them. And the other secrets which belong to the perfection of this Art, which are not to be written.

[124] Before defining this second part, we will briefly describe the effects of the apparitions of Angels, how they appear to whom, and why.[2]

The Angels who are used, throughout the contents of this work, in order to carry out the commissions with which they are charged, it is necessary for them to envelope themselves with a bodily form, when they are commanded to appear visibly to someone: which we find to have happened very often, both in the Old and New Testaments. Rabbi Moses did mean to say that they never appear except

---

[1] Note that this is 12 lines.
[2] The rest of this chapter is by the French editor, not by Trithemius.

in imaginary vision, but St. Thomas refutes this opinion doctrinally, showing that the apparitions of the Angels to the Fathers of the Old Law[1] related in figure to the true appearance of the Son of God in a body of our nature, he proves that they must necessarily have taken on a real body. It is appropriate that sometimes they appear imaginary: which Scripture makes clear enough by the addition of a few words, as we see in Ezekiel who says of himself "the Spirit lifted me up between heaven and earth and brought me to Jerusalem," through the visions of the Lord. But when it simply says "an Angel appeared" this must be understood visibly and in the body. And of the three Angels that Abraham received in his house, who can argue that this was a mere imagination, since he actually had them wash his feet and prepare a meal for his wife and servants? Now, since all Spirits are of an invisible nature, it is naturally impossible for our eyes to see them, but as St. Ambrose says, it depends on their will to be seen. It is not in our power to perceive them, but it is in their power to appear. Even though man himself cannot attain the vision of Angels, he can always merit the grace of being able to see them. In this they also have such a privilege and virtue that they can show themselves and speak to a single person, or to several in the midst of a company without being seen or heard by the others: like the Angel who appeared to the Prophet Elisha[2] and his son, after the whole army of the Assyrians. They may also let themselves be seen by all, like the two [125] who showed themselves to Lot and all the inhabitants of Sodom; but we must not draw any conclusions from such apparitions in order to persuade ourselves that Angels are corporeal in nature, as some have said, and in their writings have tried to verify that. But from now on, these various opinions are empty: we all agree that Spirits have no body, being only pure and simple Intelligences. But as the Holy Spirit, who is God Himself, of very simple essence, and far removed from all corporeal qualities, appeared in the form of a pigeon to be seen descending upon our Lord Jesus Christ. And in the form of a tongue of fire on the Apostles: thus the Angels in their appearance, cover themselves with an Elemental and borrowed body, without prejudicing the simplicity of their material essence.

See above for the 'Apology for the Wonderful Natural and Supernatural Effects,'[3] and the 'Philosophy of Spirits.'

END OF BOOK TWO

[Johannes Trithemius, Abbot of Spanheim, 12 May in the year of our Lord 1500.][4]

---

[1] In the Old Testament.
[2] In the manuscript 'Elizee' or 'Elizaeus.'
[3] Manuscript Page V.
[4] From the Latin text.

BOOK III

[125] THIRD BOOK
OF OUR ART
[PREFACE]

The Second Book covered the Spirits that can be used for each planetary hour, both day and night, using the character of the Sign of the Lord of the Ascendant of that hour. We are going to explain in this Third Book that the Angels who have dominion over the seven planets each have three [126] of the principal Spirits who are subject to them, as laid out in Table 58, which is shown below. The [first column lists] the Seven Angels of the Seven planets, each according to the tradition of the ancient scholars and philosophers who declare that each of them leads the world for the space of 354 years and 4 months.

Orifiel is the Angel of Saturn who ruled the world from the beginning of its creation for 354 years and 4 months. Then comes Jupiter and Mercury, after which follows Mars, the Moon and the Sun.[1] This is described in Table 58 which is common to them and is represented below for their domicile of the clean world, and specific to each of them that has his Angel during the above mentioned space, which is why scholars relate that Samael the Angel of Mars served as the commander at the time of the Deluge; and that the Angel Gabriel, dependent angel of the Moon, governed at the time of the confusion of tongues. Michael the Angel of the Sun ruled at the time of the strength of the Israelites leaving Egypt. Likewise, if anyone believes what we say he can easily calculate for himself, beginning with his reign of the world down to our days, the various changes in the times and governments of the Angels, in the prescribed order. But in pursuing what can lead us to our Art, we will say that under the seven Angels of the seven planets, there are 21 sub-servants subject to them, that is to say, three to each according to the institutions of our Art, to which we can set our intentions. We will observe the order, accustomed to planets, beginning with Saturn first of all, then down to the Moon.[2] In writing first put the operation of each principal Angel, and then his servants; putting the chapters in order.[3]

---

[1] This grouping is not the chronological order of rulerships.
[2] In the same order as the Tree of Life.
[3] Observing correct hierarchy is important in magic.

[127]

Mansions des Esprits avec les Planètes.

N.					R. Rouge	Rouge		R. M.L. n.c.
1 ♄ Oriffiel	Sadael	1	—	675	663			651
	Poniel	2	—	700	688			676
	Morifiel	3	—	725	713			701
2 ♃ Zachariel	Floriel	1	—	575	563			551
	Ariel	2	—	600	588			576
	Raphael	3	—	625	613			601
3 ♂ Samael	Amael	1	—	475	463			451
	Afmael	2	—	500	488			476
	Nebiel	3	—	525	513			501
4 ☉ Michael	Laniel	1	—	375	363			351
	Pafael	2	—	400	388			376
	Vanriel	3	—	425	413			401
5 ♀ Anael	Zabdiel	1	—	275	263			251
	Sacmiel	2	—	300	288			276
	Adoniel	3	—	325	313			301
6 ☿ Raphael	Carmiel	1	—	175	163			151
	Nabeyel	2	—	200	188			176
	Pathiel	3	—	225	213			201
7 ☽ Gabriel	Remaphiel	1	—	75	63			51
	Tefpiel	2	—	100	88			76
	Theoriel	3	—	125	113			101

		Rouge	Noir	Rouge		Noir
S Ariel	4 Wenator	631	20	642		639
H Saturne	Schamaro	627	20	638		646
I Kravotos	Thubrays	626	20	650		634
Ymarona	Tzatzraym	628	20	639		

Table 57: Mansions of the Spirits in the order of the Planets.[1]

---
[1] Note that each Angel aligns with its second sub-servant.

[128] CHAPTER 1

OF THE THIRD BOOK

The Prince of this Chapter is called ORIFIEL. He is the first and Supreme Angel of SATURN and operations that are done by him.

SATURN is the highest of all the planets, of slow motion and by nature cold, because it is remote, difficult, and grave. There are 650 years from the point of its beginning to the point of its first Station, remaining 30 degrees in each sign, its proper natural motion is 626 [years]. Its first and Supreme Angel according to the opinion of the ancients is called Orifiel who has under him three other chief Spirits, Sadael, Poniel, and Morisiel. The Great Prince of Saturn, is Orifiel by whom we make great and diverse operations in the context of our Art.

By his ministry, one can discover the secret intentions of the soul of a friend instructed in this Art, by some letters if you want or even without any letter, and many other admirable things we can perform; unintelligible to any other person not familiar with our Art. That is why if you desire this Angel to operate some things in this Art, on the day of Saturn, and in causes or things concerning Saturn, in the first place it is necessary to know all Saturn's different and variable [planetary] movements: first, pure, proper, mixed, straight, retrograde and confused. And in these things, it is necessary to know not only the general rules of astronomy, but [129] also the peculiar ones [connected to steganographic practice]. Although they led to our science yet [this is] scarcely enough for us. Having for this purpose assumed the tables and the 'Rules of the Movements of the Planets'[Table 61] as the foundation, it is absolutely necessary for all those operatives in the Art to know them all. We have added the 'Special Rules' and the 'Tables of Punctuary Movements' [Table 59] to each chapter of this work,[1]

without the observation of which no one can succeed.

It should also be noted that the days of each planet are divided into four equal parts, the first of which is subject to the chief Spirit of this planet [followed by] three Planetary hours in each part, this is what the operator must do as instructed, and the three parts of the day immediately following the first: these three parts are allocated to the under-servants of the great and powerful Prince Orifiel. For example, on the day of Saturn as Orifiel is the first and main Intelligence he has the first three planetary or unequal hours of that day beginning at sunrise, these hours are called 'Planetary Hours.'[2] The second three hours are allocated to the first Angel of Orifiel who is called Sadael; the third to Poniel the second Angel. The other four hours belong to the third Angel of Orifiel, who is called Morisiel.

---

[1] Although only showing Saturn, Trithemius had certainly planned to describe all 7 Planets.
[2] They are 'unequal hours,' because they change in length as the season changes. See Appendix 3.

Steganographia

Under the first three hours of daylight both of Saturn and of the other Stars, to the things appropriate to Saturn, it is always necessary to operate by Orifiel; under the second three hours by Sadael; the third three hours under Poniel, the second angel; and the last three hours by Morisiel. And all operations receive either a flourishing/prosperous effect or a debilitating effect [if retrograde], according to the motion of Saturn. We represent it on the page below, a Punctual Table.[1]

---

[1] Punctual indicates points, or *puncts*, on the arc of Heaven. See Table 59. Interestingly, *punctierkunst* is the German term for divinatory geomancy.

[130]

R. Saturne.	αλφα N.	Table Ponctuelle					
644	638	672	632	688	701	642	685
650	633	657	696	684	725	639	18
629	635	655	689	διατα R.	719	633	693
650	642	667	684	719	713	643	696
645	632 R.658		691	725	708	N.B.R.	692
635	640	673	692	704	710 R.665	657	690 R
646	635	675	699	725	717	674	691
636	643	660	692	720	707	21	692
632	638	651	698	710	715	672	698
646	634	675	688	721	712	667	693
639	βητα N.	669	684	711	718	671	696
634	669	663	697	707	713	18	698
641	675	658	682	721	709	654	720
642	654	660	680	714	N.	656	707
649	675	667	692	709	ʝ.ω	671	710
642	670	637	683	716	641	666	17
648	660	665	698 R.717	724	642	670	722
638	675	662	700	717	649	671	721
634	661	668	685	723	640	23	710
647	651	663	676	713	635		10
632	671 R.659		700	709	24	ΙΙ TR.	712
630	664 γαμμα		R.694	722	644 R.681		713
642	659	694	688	707	646	700	710 R.
633	666	700	683	705	633	685	708
648	667	679	685	717	632	683	721
650	674	700	602	708	631	19	714
655	667	695	682	723	646	682	725
626	673	685	690	725	635	689	715
650	663	696	687	710	18	684	721
644	659	686	693		643	696	714

Table 58: The Punctual Table.[1]

---

[1] In this table R = retrograde. The table is divided by the Greek words, *alpha, beta, gamma,* and *delta.*

[131] Having been known, by means of the Common Astronomic Tables,[1] the medium movement of Saturn according to the day,[2] the degree and the hour knowing that it is a good hour. First observe very exactly if [the planet moves] Direct or Retrograde, pure, proper, mixed, or if it has a confused motion. That [information] you will not find in the Common [Astronomic] Tables. That is why we have drafted the following Table 60. In there, you can find the point of the beginning and the end of a planet's movement. At whatever time it may be, before dividing the degrees assess together its division in minutes. The same applies to minutes divided into two, three or four parts, according to the proportion of pure or confused movement, that is, your observation of its conjunction with or the separation from the other planets. For it is impossible for you to achieve the effect and the fulfilment of this science by the Stars, without a knowledge of the Punctual movement, having observed it is necessary that you know how to arrange your operations [according] to the qualities proper to the planets. For in the various degrees, Signs, days, hours, minutes, seconds, thirds, and fourths, the effects of the planets vary variously in this science. For in each degree, we observed and found 25 changes, where it seemed necessary to us to divide each degree into as many main parts. But this division does not take place for all degrees, but only in those where the Stars rise, or are born, that led us to this Art with which we do the operation through the service of Spirits.

[Communicate] to an absent person, by the ministry of Spirits, without letters, as I will show. That is why the First Table of the Division of the degrees of Saturn's movements [Table 60] that we have promised, is for the first of the four parts of either day or night. It will always be used for chores that belong to Saturn's operation and his first principal angel. The Second table is for the second three hours, the Third to the third, and the Fourth to the fourth [three hours]. Then we have a Punctual order of the movement of Saturn in the Ascendant, when it is in one of the first four Signs of the Zodiac which is to say Aries, Taurus, Gemini and Cancer. (♈ ♉ ♊ ♋). We will also write in the following table [Table 60] for the 8 other Signs.

---

[1] The Ephemeris of that time.
[2] The average daily movement of Saturn is just 0.033463 degrees per day.

[132]

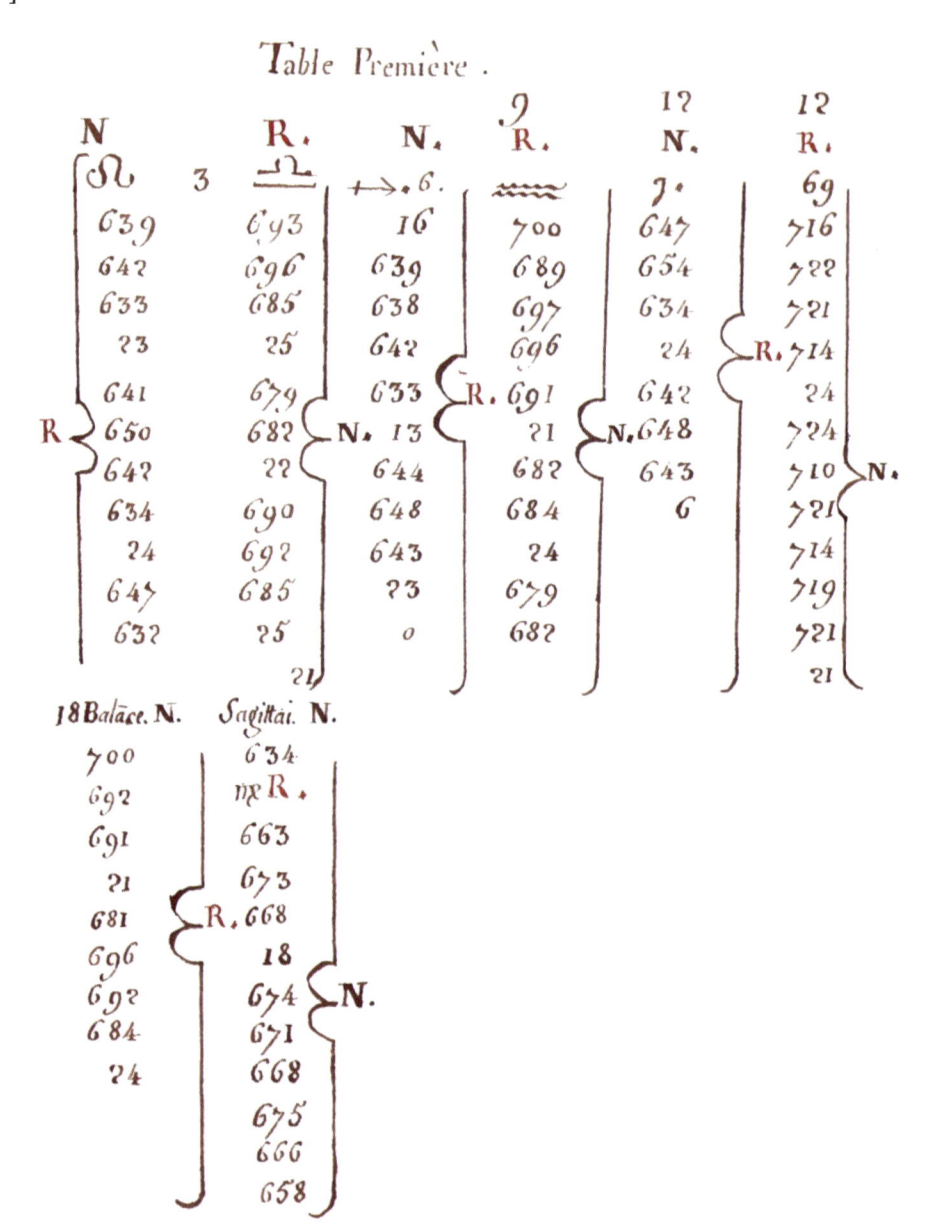

Table Première.

N		R.	N.	9 R.	1? N.	12 R.
♌	3	♎	→.6.	≈≈≈	♐	69
639		693	16	700	647	716
642		696	639	689	654	722
633		685	638	697	634	721
?3		25	642	696	24	R.714
641		679	633 R.691		642	24
R 650		682 N.13		?1 N.648		724
642		??	644	682	643	710 N.
634		690	648	684	6	721
24		692	643	24		714
645		685	?3	679		719
632		25	0	682		721
		21				21

18 Balace. N.	Sagittai. N.
700	634
692	♍ R.
691	663
?1	673
681	R.668
696	18
692	674 N.
684	671
24	668
	675
	666
	658

Table 59: The Degrees of Saturn's Movements - the First Table.[1]

---

[1] The numbers indicate the first point [in minutes] of each movement. Note the selection of zodiacal signs at the head of the Table, from Leo to Sagittarius for both Retrograde and Direct movement. The columns are marked in order 3, 6, 9, 12, 15, 18 and 21. The last column in the first row should be marked 15 not 12. Missing columns are 24, 27 and 30. The intention was to cover the full 30 degrees of each zodiacal sign.

[133]

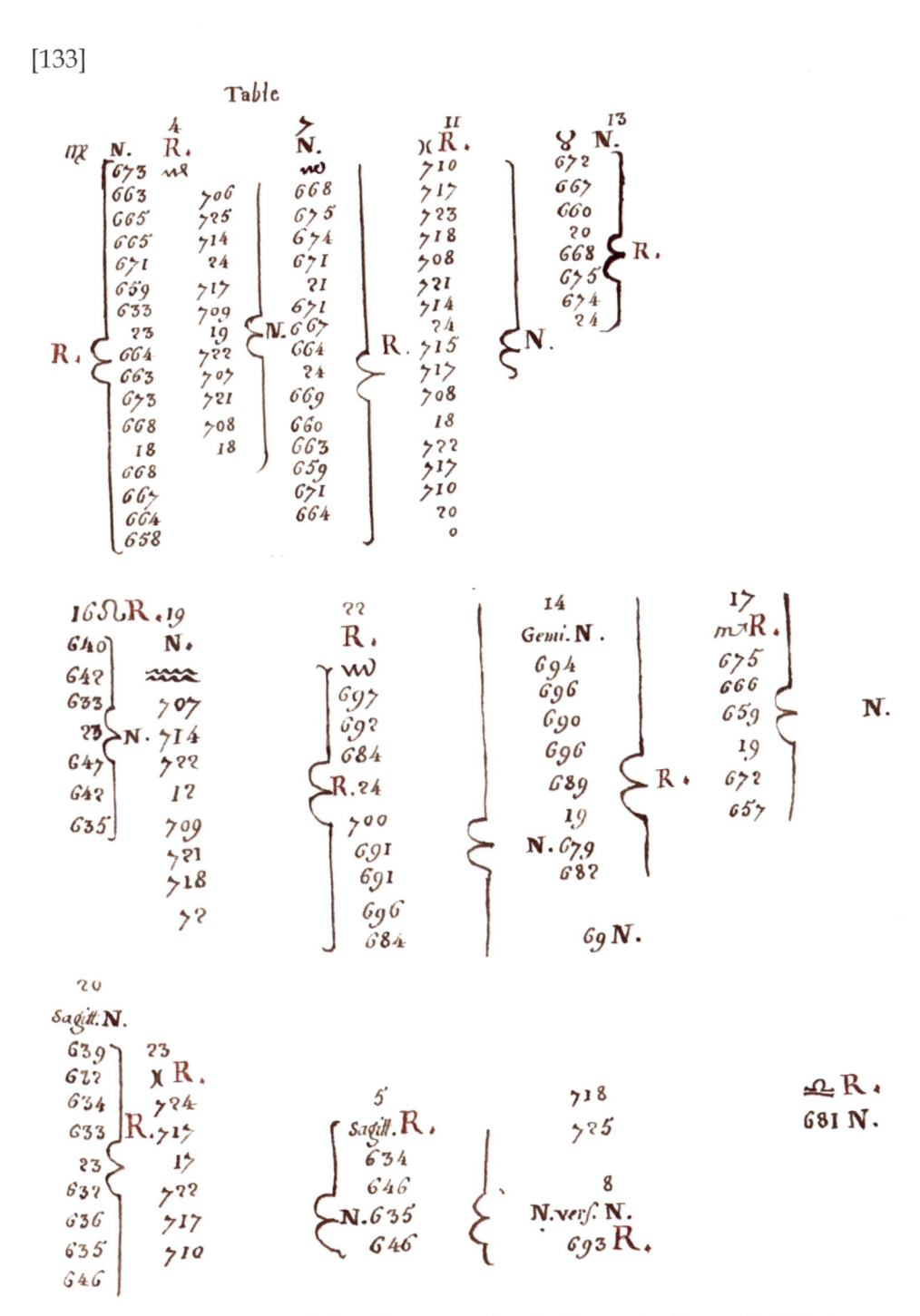

Table

Table 60: Pure Motion of the Planets in the Zodiac – the Second Table.[1]

---

[1] The degree headings group every 3 degrees: 1, 4, 7, 11, 13, 16, 19, 22, after which the numbering begins to fill the numerical gaps 14, 17, 20, 23, but trails off before completing. This table was even more disordered in the manuscript but has here been partially adjusted.

[134]

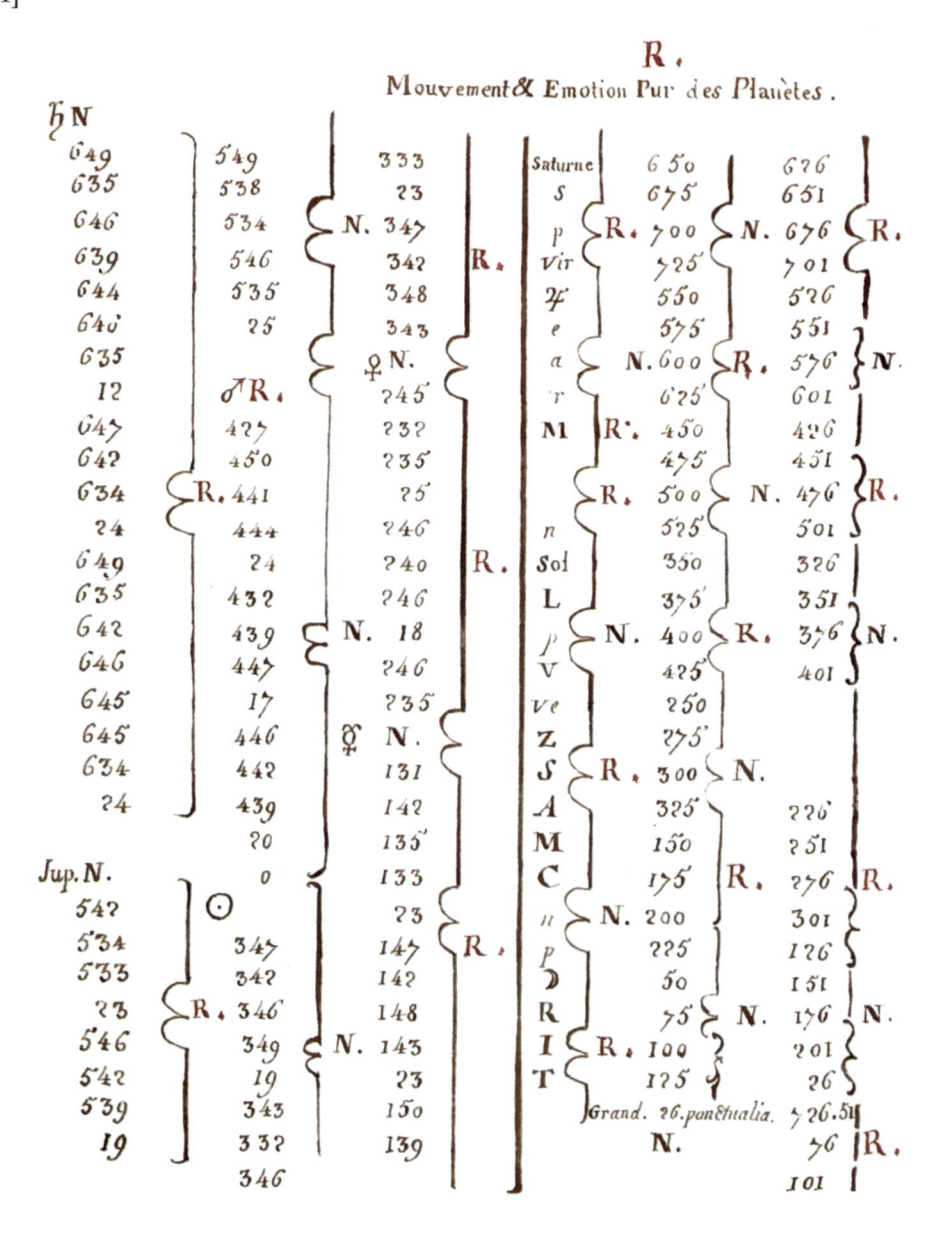

R.
Mouvement & Emotion Pur des Planetes.

♄ N						
649	549	333		Saturne	650	626
635	538	23		S	675	651
646	534	N. 347		P	R. 700	N. 676 R.
639	546	342	R.	vir	725	701
644	535	348		♃	550	526
640	25	343		e	575	551
635		♀ N.		a	N. 600 R.	576 N.
12	♂ R.	245		r	625	601
647	427	232		M	R. 450	426
642	450	235			475	451
634	R. 441	25			R. 500	N. 476 R.
24	444	246		n	525	501
649	24	240	R.	Sol	350	326
635	432	246		L	375	351
642	439	N. 18		p	N. 400 R.	376 N.
646	447	246		V	425	401
645	17	235		Ve	250	
645	446	☿ N.		Z	275	
634	442	131		S	R. 300 N.	
24	439	142		A	325	226
	20	135		M	150	251
Jup. N.	0	133		C	175 R.	276 R.
542	☉	23		u	N. 200	301
534	347	147	R.	p	225	126
533	342	142		♎	50	151
23	R. 346	148		R	75 N.	176 N.
546	349	N. 143		I	R. 100	201
542	19	23		T	125	26
539	343	150		Grand. 26. ponctualia.	26.51
19	332	139			N.	76 R.
	346					101

Table 61: Movements and Pure Motion[1] of the Planets – the Third Table.[2]

---

[1] The manuscript has *Emotion,* but this probably should have read *Motion*.
[2] This shows the septenary conjunction of Saturn with the other planets. This table is arranged in planetary order: Saturn, Jupiter, Mars, Sun, Venus, Mercury, Moon (not shown). The left-hand side (after the firm vertical line) begins the sequence again, also emphasising direct [N] and retrograde [R] movement.

[135] Of the Variable Movement of the Planets, and the Interpretation of the Tables

Although in this chapter we have to deal especially [only] with the movements of Saturn and his Spirits, and the operations of that Art which we know through him, nevertheless we fear that we will have to repeat what we have once said in each chapter. It is forbidden to warn the student reader what we have said in this chapter, lest he forget it in the following [chapter]: for the movements of each planet are variable, and are very subtly divided into even more diverse other movements. The pure and proper movement is multiplied and varies by various fine and subtle divisions. Direct, retrograde, mixed, confused and varying in as many points as are contained in the circle at the beginning of its movement. What shall I say about the conjunction of these planets with each other? For as Ptolemy in his *Centiloquium* says there are 120 aspects between these planets, namely 21 Conjunctions, 35 Trines, 35 Squares, 21 Quines, [7] Sextiles and 1 Seventh, which we shall deal with here.

As for the other movements, although we cannot give any just and certain cause, because of their infinite diversity, especially since we do not know how many points are decreasing or increasing, since they vary, notwithstanding we applied ourselves as much as possible to make observations in which we found more than 300,000 divisions affecting all the operations of this Art, as for the effect they often vary.[1] Unless someone dares himself to be very expert in these things, and he knows perfectly the movements of these planets in their environment, and then the smallest punctual divisions that come, from the quarters, thirds, seconds, minutes, and subtly divided degrees into equality he will easily fall into error,[2] and will not easily escape from peril. We have reduced the movements of Saturn, which are listed in three Tables [Tables 59-61] for the perfect institution of this Art.

In the **First of them** [Table 60] the movement [136] of Saturn is reduced in 4 parts, both day and night: clean and pure knowledge has its punctual root, and we have written it at the true point of each Sign on the Ascendant, beginning from the first degree of ♈ [Aries] to the 641st point of ♉ ♊ ♋ [Taurus, Gemini and Cancer].

And we embrace the whole Zodiac in the **Second Table** [Table 61].[3] Then in the same Second Table we have written the movement of Saturn in each of the Twelve Signs to all the Quarters of day and night, likewise to the Minutes, so that having known the degree of the Ascendant in which Saturn will be at that hour we can

---

[1] It would appear as if Trithemius has confirmed that these calculations, if done down to the finest divisions, are impossible to complete.
[2] That seems highly likely.
[3] In fact this Table is incomplete in the manuscript, as it shows only 9 Signs.

clearly discover the Point Root,[1] which having once been completed, I doubt that someone of our Age could have produced, then must begin the table at the start of its principle.

In the **Third Table** [Table 62] we have reduced the single septenary conjunction of Saturn with the other planets, which is unique, to the point, by which all the 120 conjunctions can easily reduce it to a point. In the same table we know the pure motion of all the planets by the punctual division of each principle. By the progression and elongation from the point in each movement it is necessary to know whether the movement is in the middle, for it is necessary to have the knowledge of the movement, because without this principle it is impossible for one to attain the means of practicing this science. Moreover, whatever you know of the middle movement, it would still be of no use to you to have the knowledge of this science if you did not understand fully the three above Tables, at all the points of the divisions in the movements of the planets which also take unequal degrees for every minute, and then we will reach the goal of the operation.

Having therefore known all these things, and fully understanding what we have said, and what we will say with God's help. When you want to operate in this mysterious and profound speculation you must know first of all the birth, exaltation, and setting [137] of all the Stars on the Eighth Sphere[2] by which the operation takes place;[3] and you must know how distant each Star is from every other. For there are 700 Stars by whom the operations to announce the secrets to someone without using any words, or writings and even no human messenger, of which we have described the names, places, births,[4] settings, elevation, distances, approaches, and demotions in a special book, it would be too studious to repeat it here.[5] Having observed the Star in all its aspects, and having known the point of the Ascendant in which Saturn will be in this same hour, if the operation is done through Saturn, you must diligently consider the quality of this movement, whether it is Direct or Retrograde, pure, mixed, proper or conjoined with any other impediment to other bad aspects, discreet or confused. Then you write on a clean piece of paper the point of the beginning of the movement, in the same Sign, both of Saturn and of the other planets conjunct with him, having previously properly subtly and duly calculated the point from the Common [Astronomic] Tables and what we have taught. Observe diligently, how much progress he has made, how much he is raised and how much he decreases. You will execute the same with the other planets.[6] You will do the same for the other planets that will be in conjunction with Saturn, the one by whom the operation is done. In the same way

---

[1] *Racine Ponctuelle*.
[2] The Eight Sphere is the sphere of the fixed stars, beyond the seven planetary spheres.
[3] Effectively the Eight Sphere acts as a backdrop to the complex movements of the 7 Planets.
[4] The time at which the star or planet is first visible as it rises over the horizon.
[5] In short, Trithemius is not going to give us this information.
[6] These tables were never completed by Trithemius.

you will observe before all things, what aspects the planets make with each other, if it is in trine, square, conjunction or sextile, because these aspects give the greatest force to the operation. In the same way observe, first of all things, in what quarter Saturn stands, not only with reference to the day but also to the night. But also, with knowledge to the sign in which it stands, with reference to the years since the beginning of the world, when the planet was first created in his House, because all these things are useful and necessary. And you will notice that when Orifiel, Angel of Saturn, rules the world in his turn, that he governs 354 years and 4 months. Then all [138] the operations of this deep and mysterious science which belongs to the works of Saturn, and which is done by him, will come for then very easy, and a prompt effect will follow without any work The same is to be observed for the other planets. But whoever can have this knowledge and know the principles of this Art, will be able to operate without difficulty by it. He will operate by this planet, whose main Spirit is easy to find, by an easy calculation at the time when he governs the universe. Now having calculated exactly everything well the one who wishes to operate, must observe which Angel of Saturn presides over this quarter of the day or night, and you should write his name and the name of the Star by which you wish to operate and which you deem necessary. At any time you must see this Star that is necessary for our purpose. By means of our Art we have indicated either in the day or in the night, you should write on the same sheet the secrets that you know (with the [consecrated] pen prepared according to the Art), then you put this schedule that you have written before you on your table. Then write on another sheet the secret which you wish to communicate to the absentee, and fold these two schedules one together with the other, and lay them on the most eminent [position] of either the table or the pulpit before you, and say the words which suit the Spirit by whom you must operate, in order to compel him by what is to him appropriate, or if you prefer to announce your secret without any writing by a Spirit, or without Spirit, altering little, as we will say in its place, but we teach the difference of the operations of Saturn and these Angels, according to the four main parts [of the day or of the night] and the conjurations which must be appropriate to each of them. The whole should be executed by order in which it is necessary to use it when you want to announce some secret by the ministry of Spirits.

[139] OF THE FIRST AND PRINCIPAL ANGEL OF SATURN

Called by the name ORIFIEL which governs the First Quarter which belongs to SATURN

The First and principal Angel of Saturn is therefore called Orifiel, as we said in the previous chapters which is [conjunct] with the other Angels of the planets each in turn. He reigns and governs the world during the space of 354 years and 4 months of his rule, as was said above. Orifiel has the first part in the day likewise the [first part of] the night, and by it operations are done from sunrise in the day, and after sunset in the night, until the 3rd Planetary hour inclusive on all occasions that belong to Saturn. If in its day or night when you want to send some secret or news to an absent friend without words or letters in this Quarter of Saturn, it is not necessary to call other Spirits of Saturn than Orifiel, because by him you can make everything known perfectly.

[The Method]

In the first place consider in which sign Saturn is located, and in what degree, whether it is direct or retrograde, [and with what planet it is in aspect]. We will look at an example of the First: here Saturn is already at the 25th degree of Taurus on April 28th, in the year 1500 of the Lord, then let us multiply 25 by 25 and we get [approximately] 600 [quadrations] which we will then divide by 4 equal quarters, and so for each quarter there will be 150. Let us complete all the degrees of Saturn in the sign of Taurus of which there are 30, then let us multiply 3[0] by 25 in total and it will be 750. Subtract 4 superfluous degrees[1] from the middle of the [third] quarter and the remainder will be 650. Take the first names after[2] the point of the movement of Saturn from the Table to the present day and hour, and we will be able to know what is the rising, [highest] elevation and setting of the Angel Orifiel, with Saturn in the 1st quarter: Having known this, the operation will be easy.

---

[1] i.e. 4 x 25 = 100.
[2] *Prenoms aprézant.*

[140]

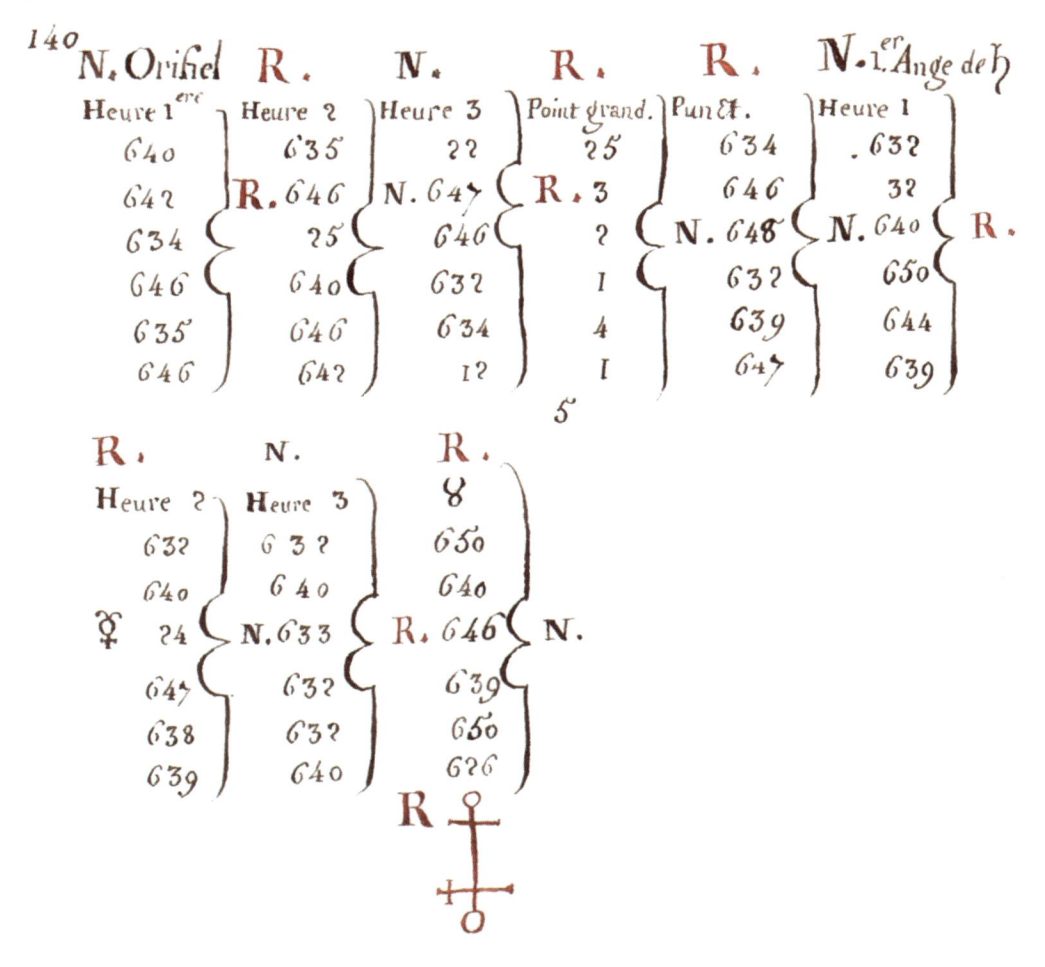

¹⁴⁰N. Orifiel R.   N.   R.   R.   R.   N. l'Ange de ♄

N. Orifiel	R.	N.	R.	R.	R.	N. l'Ange de ♄
Heure 1ère	Heure 2	Heure 3	Point grand.	Punct.		Heure 1
640	635	2?	25	634		.632
642	R.646	N.647	R.3	646		3?
634	25	646	?	N.648	N.640	R.
646	640	632	1	632	650	
635	646	634	4	639	644	
646	642	1?	1	647	639	

5

R.	N.	R.
Heure 2	Heure 3	8
632	63?	650
640	640	640
☿ 24	N.633	R.646 N.
647	632	639
638	63?	650
639	640	626

R ☿
  ✝
  O

Table 62: The Hours of Orifiel, angel of the first three hours Saturn.
This shows just three hours repeated twice, followed by the *'punct'* column giving the exact starting point.[1]

And that having carefully considered [Table 63] it becomes evident that the Angel Orifiel of Saturn is separated from ♄ [Saturn] by 25 degrees and 15 minutes and is distant, towards the east, from the first point of the motion of Saturn by 625 quadrations and from the end of its motion by 25 minutes. This having been determined, make an image of wax or paint the figure of Orifiel in the form of a bearded and naked man riding on a bull of many colours, having a book in his right hand, and in his left hand a pen. During the execution [making this image] you will say the following.[2]

---

[1] The *punct* numbers reverse when the Planet goes retrograde at the point marked by 'R.'
[2] While making the image.

> "May this image of the Great Orifiel come full, and perfect and proper [141] to announce all the secrets of my friend to N. N., my son, or N. N., my friend surely and faithfully and with integrity, Amen."

On the forehead [of the image] write your name, with an instrument dipped in rose oil, and on the chest the name of your absent friend saying this:

> "This is the image of N. my son, or N. my friend, to whom I communicate the secret of my soul through Orifiel Angel of Saturn, Amen."

At the forehead you write the word Merion.[1]
And on the chest you write the word Troesda.

Fold in two then join the two images together saying:

Conjuration

> "In the name of the Father and of the Son and of the Holy Spirit, so be it heard. Orifiel Prince of the Star of Saturn I conjure you by the virtue of God Almighty. I adjure and command you by the virtue of this image, that you announce to N. my son, or to N. my friend, my intention (which must be explained here) as soon as possible with secrecy and fidelity, forgetting nothing that I want him to hide, and that I am ordained, in the name of the Father and of the Son and of the Holy Spirit. So be it."

Then wrap the two images as joined together in a proper pure cloth with river water and put them in a movable vase, which the scholars of India call *Pharnat alronda*. Then cover the top diligently with smooth leather, and place it at the entrance of some dwelling, or closed room, or in any place you wish, during the space of 24 hours. And without any delay your request will be fulfilled perfectly during this space of time, and your absent friend will know your intention fully in every form, as you spoke it to the image, and in his language, it is all that you desire him to know of you, and he will know it in these 24 hours, with the greatest secrecy, so that no mortal can ever have any knowledge of it without your will, or that of your friend. This is a very great secret that none of the scholars before us dared to entrust it to writing, and if your friend desires to communicate to you whatever of [142] his secrets he can instruct you in the same space of 24 hours, with the same Spirit, since he is well instructed in the principles of Art. But as soon as the 24 hours are over you raise the images from the place where you have placed them, and lay them aside, and preserve them well because they will be able to serve you at all times that are ruled by the great Prince Orifiel. Not only can you send messages to that same friend, but also to all those you want by changing only the name of the friend into the one to whom you desire to communicate something. Notice that it is not absolutely necessary to paint or illuminate these images to make them more beautiful and curious. However simple they may be,

---

[1] Possibly Mendrion.

it does not matter what is made, provided that they have some relationship and proportionate semblance, and that we can know that they are images of men. Whoever wants to paint beautiful pictures and illuminate them will be able to do so, it will prevent nothing, but this will not produce a greater effect.

Steganographia

OF THE SECOND ANGEL OF SATURN

who is the first below Orifiel and is called SADAEL,
the one who presides over the Second Quarter of Saturn.

The second Angel of Saturn is called Sadael who is the first Angel under Orifiel, following his turn, and there in charge after the Prince, both during the day and during the night, in the works, operations, and times that depend on Saturn. This is to say the 4th, 5th and 6th Planetary hours [of Saturday]. Therefore, when you want to send something to an absent friend during these three hours in the 24 hours, without letters or words or messenger, do all that is indicated for the preceding operation and observe the point of the second movement of Saturn in its degrees with reference to the Sign in which this planet makes its movements. What is the movement, and where is the moving spirit the star, how far back it is and how much it is elevated from the centre of its movement, and how far it is distant from each point of the whole circle of its movement, and how much it is distant from each point of the entire circle or sphere. To calculate this science, here is Table 64 represented on the page below.

[143]

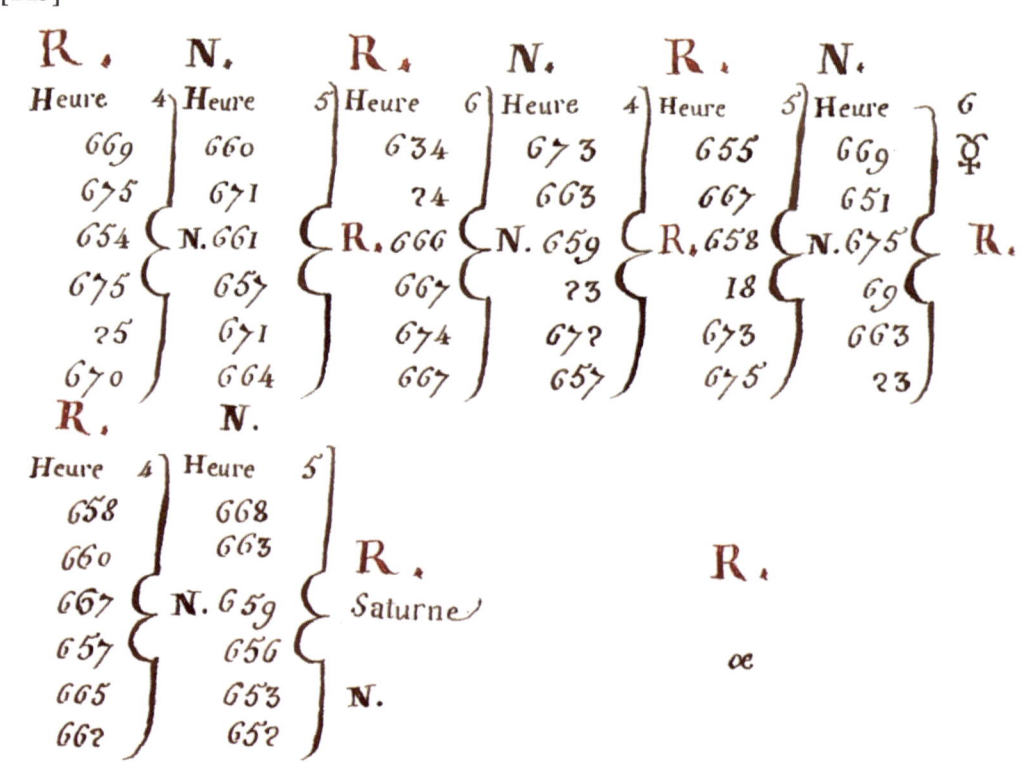

R.	N.	R.	N.	R.	N.	
Heure 4	Heure	5 Heure	6 Heure	4 Heure	5 Heure	6
669	660	634	673	655	669	☿
675	671	24	663	667	651	
654 N.661	657	R.666	N.659	R.658	N.675	R.
675	657	667	23	18	69	
25	671	674	67?	673	663	
670	664	667	657	675	23	

R.	N.					
Heure 4	Heure 5					
658	668					
660	663	R.		R.		
667 N.659	656	Saturne				
657	656			œ		
665	653	N.				
66?	65?					

Table 63: The Hours of Sadael, angel of the second three hours of Saturn.

Steganographia

Having found the place of the Angel Sadael by the consideration of the fixed Star at the point of Saturn's movement, make two images as it is said in the preceding operation. With inscriptions of Orifiel, the constellations, and other things described therein.

That having been executed put the two images on five blades of the grass called Thrasnote,[1] outside of the house in a safe secret place, and say:

> "In the name of the † Father † and the Son † and the Holy Spirit Amen. As these two images of the great Angel Sadael and N. my son, or N. my friend, were joined together by me on these 5 movable blades [of grass], so I command you Sadael, by the virtue of your great Prince Orifiel, that you announce to N. my son, or to my friend, without delay, the secret that I explained and confided to you."

That having been said arrange these two images in the same way for 24 hours, and what you desire will be accomplished, and your friends will know all that you have said above these two images, perfectly and secretly. Likewise, even if you desire to learn or know something from an absentee friend, how he is doing, and what is his condition. In 24 hours, you will be able to know it in this way and you will know everything that is done in the universe, having observed the constellations, through this Art.

---

[1] Unknown herb.

Steganographia

[144] OF THE THIRD ANGEL OF SATURN

who is the second under Orifiel and called Pomiel
who presides over the third Quarter of Saturn.

The Third Angel of Saturn is called Pomiel, who in turn is the second under Orifiel the principal Angel of Saturn who presides over the seventh, eighth and ninth [planetary] hours of Saturn, both in the day and in the night, in all things concerning Saturn.

Since it has its motion in regular course 25 degrees from the east with reference to the fixed stars. You find its hours arranged in the next table.

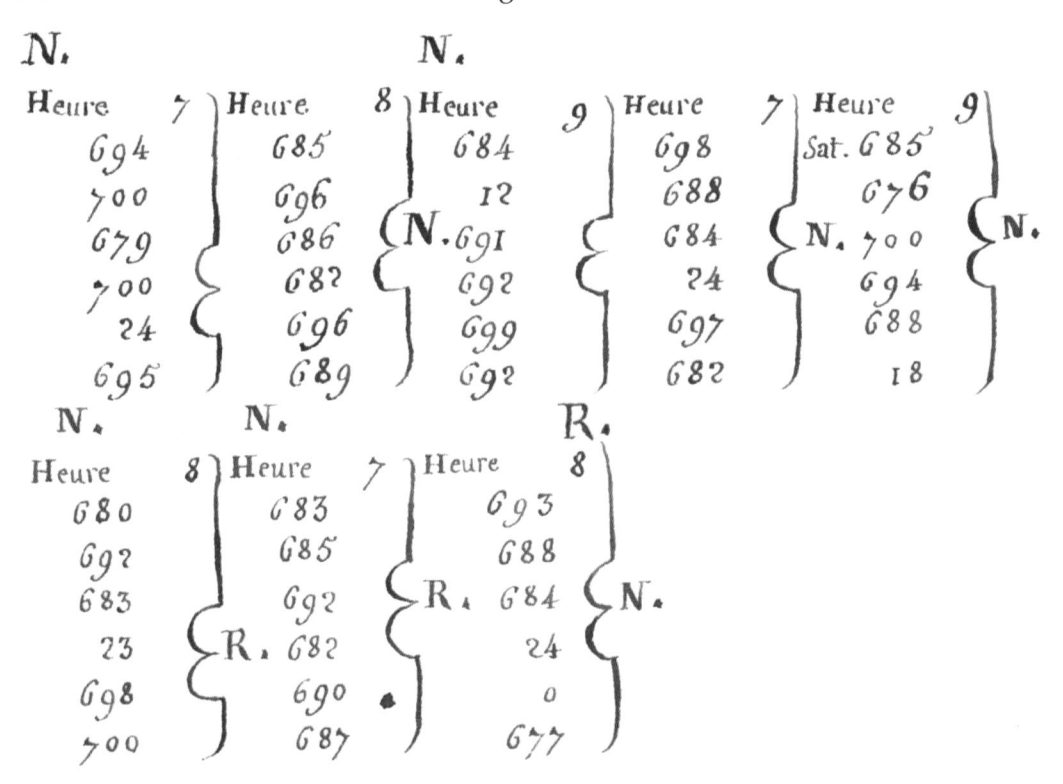

N.		N.					
Heure 7	Heure 8	Heure 9	Heure 7	Heure 9			
694	685	684	698	Sat. 685			
700	696	12	688	676			
679	686	N. 691	684	N. 700	N.		
700	682	692	24	694			
24	696	699	697	688			
695	689	692	682	18			
N.	**N.**		**R.**				
Heure 8	Heure 7	Heure 8					
680	683	693					
692	685	688					
683	692	R. 684	N.				
23	R. 682	24					
698	690	0					
700	687	677					

Table 64: The Hours of Pomiel, angel of the third three hours of Saturn.[1]

When you are certain of the movement of Saturn, and you have likewise found the Punctual place of the Angel Pomiel, you make two images, following exactly the precepts that we have indicated above, for the operation of Orifiel, the principal Angel of Saturn.

---

[1] Note that the last hour on the first line of the table should be numbered '8,' and the first hour on the second line should be numbered '9.'

[145][1] Having spoken before about the faculties and intrinsic virtues of the Angels, we have added to this content the consideration of their way of speaking: in order to admire the divinity of their language as well as their holy intentions, and the truth of their impressions. We know well enough that it is within the power of every reasonable creature, to understand, to hear, and to imagine secretly in his mind, an infinity of things, which by faith cannot come to the knowledge of others. This is why it necessary to have a means to manifest them outside by some voice, signs, or other significant notes.[2] And though the Angels agree with us naturally, their thoughts can only be known to those to whom they wish to reveal them: they need [to use] the word, like men, to declare to one another their conceptions and thoughts. The Apostle obviously shows us that the Angels speak, when he says in *Corinthians*:[3] "If I speak in the language of men or of Angels, but do not have charity, I am only like the ringing bell."[4]

But we will hear that there are three strong voices, that of the mouth, that of thought, and that of work. The word of the mouth is given to us in this life to speak, and to make one another hear what we have in mind, understanding, and in imagination. To which Scripture supplements that between those absent, bearing from one to the other the marks of speech as words, [convey] the marks of what we have in our Soul. The word of thought is what suits the immaterial Spirits (who have neither flesh nor bones, nor any corporeal organs, from which they can form their words), first to God, then to the good and evil Angels, and finally to the souls stripped of their bodies. And this word is nothing else than to make visible the very conception of the Spirit, or to put it better, it is the substance of the thing, which we may consider in our understanding. Now the Angels speak to God, not by manifestation of any secret thing, since nothing can be hidden from him, but as the disciple speaks to the Master, interrogating or praising him: just as we ourselves, in our own fashion, question [146] or consult the Divine will in our affairs, not to make him hear our designs, for we know that he sees and knows all things: but to know if we should undertake them, or to pray to him to ask that he will assist us in them. The Angels speak to each other by communication of species (as the theologians say), that is, by communicating and showing in their thoughts the image of what they want to declare and make heard. If you want in nature some experience of this, put a mirror in front of and opposite to another, you will see that at the same time he receives in his mirror the image is in the other. Thus for this reason St. Denis calls the Spirits 'spiritual mirrors,' revealing to whom they like, what they have in their thoughts in the blink of an eye, they imprint in his

---

[1] The rest of this chapter is missing from Walden's translation in Adam McLean (1982). I suspect therefore that this is the end of Trithemius' words in Book III, and the rest of this chapter is the work of the French editor.
[2] For magic to work the invocations must be spoken or written and not just be thought.
[3] *Manuscript note: Cor[inthians] 13.*
[4] The actual quote ends with "a resounding gong or a clanging cymbal."

understanding what they want to say to him: which is such an excellent way of speaking so worthy and perfect, that if we want to naively declare to some person the simplicity of our affections, we wish in the manner of the Angels, to open and manifest to him, the interior of our thought. Moreover, we look back or touch those to whom we want to speak, to make them attentive to our word: so the Angels turn and raise their thoughts to the one to whom they want to make known their intentions. And this thought being thus darted, touches like a look that of the Spirits to whom it addresses and makes him attentive to this that she wishes to manifest to him. The idea by this is that she, an Angel, wants to reveal her intention and her cogitation, which serves as her language, and can therefore be called as such in this way.

For if the least of the Angels does not have this desire to reveal his thought to you: it is quite impossible for all the others, however superior they may be, to be able to neither see anything, nor to know anything, being open only to God alone, who however can reveal it to whom he pleases: as on the day of Judgement he surely will manifest the conscience of everyone. We have the same privilege, for I can seal my mind to all celestial Spirits, and reveal it to whomever I please. And if I want to invoke any of the saints at the same time as I address my thought to him, I touch him with my mind, and make him turn towards me to see in my soul what I want to say to him, and the petition I intend to make to him. I will say again of this spiritual word, that it is of such perfection, that the distance [147] of the places causes him no impediment. The Angels and saints who are on the Arctic Pole speak as easily to those who have their seat on the Antarctic Pole (though they are far distant from each other, even all the width of this vast universe) as if he was only three paces from one the other, because he had only things corporeal which are subject to the conditions and circumstances of the time and place, but particularly of the place. This is what some mockers could not conceive, when they ask how it is possible that the saints can hear from so far away our invocations, prayers and orations.

The Angel speaks to men in two ways, namely by the impression of a sensitive species imprinting in our fantasy either when waking or sleeping a representation of the voice, or else the image of what he wants us to hear. Sometimes also, but rarely in a borrowed body, when God appears visibly and the Angels speak to the Devil, by the word of work, as we speak to the beasts, preventing or allowing what the monkeys do. For example, if a swine wants to enter the Garden, we close the door in his face, to tell him "you will not enter." A dog threatens some animal by its barking, if it is untied we let it run, to tell him "you have done what you wanted." Thus the Devil shows his bad will and asks permission to perform it. We look back or touch those to whom we want to speak to make them attentive to our words. Angels only reject him, or else let him do it, according to the ordinance of the Divine Judgments, without saying anything to him by any other speech; he is not worthy of such favour. And the rest of us are miserable enough to listen to his malignant persuasion and rather follow his brutal and misfortunate advice than the holy inspirations of our Good Angels who only desire to procure us all kinds of goods and riches, both spiritual and temporal.

There have been men who have ignored the most worthy works of the Creator since they have been so reckless as to deny the existence of Angels like some philosophers, Sadducees and atheists, who had so attached their souls to bodily matter that they could not imagine or understand that it apes immaterial Spirits. But the evidence of reason and the authority of Scripture [148] gives such clear and manifest proofs, that from their foolish negations, they now win only shame and confusion worthy of their ignorance and fooleries, as for those ancient philosophers who (according to Aristotle's report) because they did not know how to distinguish the senses from the intellect, meant that nothing can be purely intellectual, nor subsist separate from all matter and condition of the body. We have already shown by the reasoning of St. Thomas, that man, being composed of body and Spirit, there must be in nature Spirits without bodies as well as bodies without Spirits. I say moreover that human understanding cannot understand anything without [the aid of] abstraction, separating form from matter: is it not reasonable, even necessary, that there should be in nature some substance free of body: so that this beautiful mind may have an object proportionate to its excellent and divine faculty? Plato spoke often of Spirits and daemons; Aristotle recognises in his writings that the Celestial heavens have their movement by the operation of the Angels: and all those who since that time have been applied in the search for the beautiful and rare secrets, both natural and supernatural, in Metaphysics and Physics, they all agree in their feeling that there are Spirits, Intelligences, and Angels. For the Sadducees who received at least the *Pentateuch* of Moses, to what occult properties could they refer the speech of the serpent Tempter, and the Ass of Balaam, if some Spirits did not move their tongues to form the words they spoke? And the Cherubin who added the passage of the Earthly Paradise could not have been a man, since in the world [at that time] there was neither Adam nor his wife: it was therefore a Spirit ordained to this Office by the providence of God. But having proved at the beginning of this Work that there are Spirits and consequently Angels, we leave these disputes, to enter into the consideration of the operations of this Angelic nature by the definition given to us by the great Theologian Damascene[1] saying that the Angel is an intellectual substance always mobile, free of will, incorporeal and made for the service of the Creator. This term of 'intellectual substance' means to us a very perfect understanding, and by no means enveloped like ours in the corruptible bonds of an Earthly body.

[149] We have finished this third book of *Steganography* with a discourse on the nature of the Angels, of which there now remains a Fourth Book with the general key to the usage of this Fourth book which we have omitted in this work,

---

[1] St John of Damascus, a Christian monk.

especially since this Fourth book containing in its more than one hundred chapters or mode for writing occultly by the transposition of letters[1] that has to do with *Polygraphy*.[2] For this purpose we will join one with the other to bring this work to light, and we will put here in the following passage that which is appropriate to the foregoing, so as not to forget the invocations of the Angel Intelligences and of all other entities, by means of the Sacred Numbers contained in two books, the first of which contains seven chapters and the second contains four, and we will then give the manner of making the [Magical] Bell to serve the operations of Art.[3]

**END OF THE THIRD BOOK
of the Art of
STEGANOGRAPHY**

---

[1] A reference to the Cabalah.
[2] Another book by Trithemius more concentrated on codes and cryptography.
[3] *Book of Sacred Numbers* and details of making the Bell of the Art are to be found in Book 4.

BOOK IV

[151] THE BOOK OF SACRED NUMBERS
DIVIDED INTO TWO PARTS

TO INVOKE ALL ENTITIES
both celestial and terrestrial

[FIRST PART]

We agree with the principal philosophers that all that Nature first made seems to have been formed by means of numbers, for this was the principal model in the mind of the Creator; from this came the quantity of the Elements, and from them the revolutions of Time, from this the movement of the Stars, the changes of Heaven and the state of numbers through their connection. Numbers therefore have very great and elevated virtues, and we should not be surprised, since there are so many great occult virtues in natural things, that there are much greater, more hidden, more marvellous and more effective virtues in numbers, because they are more formal, more perfect and are found in celestial bodies, are composed of separate substances, and make the simplest mixture with the ideas of the spirit of God, from which they derive their own virtues and their most effectiveness. This is why they can do so much for the functions of God and the Spirits. Just as the Elemental qualities in natural things; much more everything that there is, and that is made, subsists by certain numbers and derives virtue from them; for time is composed of numbers and all movements and action and everything is subject to time and movement: concerts and voices are also composed of numbers and proportion, and have strength only through them, and proportions which come from numbers, are made by lines and points, characters and figures which are proper in [152] the operations of our Art, by an appropriate means which is between them, which declined at the ends as in the use of the letters. Finally, all the species of what there is in Nature, and above it, depend on certain numbers, which makes Pythagoras say that everything is composed of numbers and that it distributes virtues to all things. Psellus[1] says number always subsists and is found in everything, one in the voice, the other in its proportion, one in the soul and reason, and the other in Divine things. But Themistius,[2] Boethius[3] and Averroes of Babylon,[4] along with Plato, praise numbers very highly, and assure us that they believe that without them, one cannot be a good philosopher. And they speak of the rational and formal number, not of the material, vocal and sensible one like that of the merchants, of which the

---

[1] Written 'Pselse' in the manuscript. See *Psellus, On the Operation of Daemons*, Singapore: Golden Hoard, 2019.
[2] Themisius (c. 317-c. 388), known for his summaries of Aristotle.
[3] 'Boëce' in the manuscript is Boethius (c. 480-524) who translated many Greek classics into Latin.
[4] The Arab philosopher Ibn Rushd (1126-1198) who attempted to correct the Islamic interpretation of Aristotle.

Pythagoreans and the Academicians, and even Saint Augustine make no mention, but they only want to speak of the proportion which results from it, which they call the 'natural number' and the reason from which come great mysteries which derive both from natural things and from Divine and celestial things, by means of which one particularly and briefly reaches prophecy, and the Divine and supernatural mysteries. And the Abbot Joachim[1] did not attain to prophecy by any voice, but by formal numbers.

In this *Book of Sacred Numbers* are contained the marvellous mysteries of the celestial and Divine art. It is the most useful and energetic of all those that Mr……[2] has written about. It is important to believe in the impossibility of operating effectively in our Art without it. We will divide this Book into two parts, which will contain eleven chapters, namely seven in the first part and four in the second, and whose contents contain all the power of God the Supreme Being which He has never revealed to anyone, and who wants and desires that it be made public through our means. Thus we begin to declare that the Sacred Numbers are a great necessity to operate in the Divine Art of the Lord. Without them, nothing can be done. This is why we give them to you with all the clarity, fidelity and most naive sincerity, for which I would have no reproach to suffer or fear, from those who wish to read this book, and put into execution what it contains for their own good and that of their brothers.

[153] Sacred Numbers are the base and foundation of the Divine and celestial Art, and nothing in Nature has been made without numbers. Numbers are so necessary that God has named everything and placed all creatures in these numbers; that is why it is good to know the numbers of each particular entity in order to make them act.[3]

We'll start by giving you the Numbers of the Elements, and then move on to the particular.

---

[1] Joachim of Fiore (1135-1202) was an apocalyptic prophet who proposed that history was divided into three ages: the Age of the Father (corresponding to the *Old Testament*), the Age of the Son (corresponding to the *New Testament*) which ran until 1260, after which the Age of the Holy Ghost, supposedly a period of comparative utopia and universal love. It is said that his ideas influenced Dante and his writing of the *Divine Comedy*. Trithemius was certainly influenced by Joachim, as were Dr John Dee and W.B. Yeats who wrote about Joachim in *The Tables of the Law*. Aleister Crowley took on board the idea of a New Age, coming after that of Christianity as a basis for his Thelemic philosophy.

[2] The author is not identified in the manuscript, but this implies that this 'book within a book' was not written by Trithemius. Although it might have been assembled by Trithemius.

[3] The usual rule is that you must know the name of an entity in order to conjure it, but here numbers appear to be added as another requirement.

Steganographia

CHAPTER I

Of the Numbers of the Elements

It should be noted and known that the first Number, in other words the first being created all things for the good of man as well as for his own use and utility, and that he placed in each entity an attribute of himself, which are the numbers that make these same entities act and move. It is therefore absolutely necessary to know the number of each entity, without any movement by themselves, if we want to usefully employ them in our service.

The Elements are entities without motion of their own accord. If Almighty God had not put motion into them through numbers, which are the motive of all things [they would not have motion]. We therefore say that it is necessary to know numbers, since they are the motive of all Nature, we have already stated that the Sacred Numbers make up all Nature, and that they are the motive [force] of every entity of this nature. To put this book in order, we will say that Nature is composed of Four Elements: Fire, Air, Earth and Water.

That Fire is the noblest of all, being that which makes up the Throne of Almighty God, who has placed numbers within it   7 of 4 of 6 and of 3.
[154] which are the motive force of this action.

The Element of Air is composed of the numbers of   5 of 9 of 4 and of 3.
The Element of Earth is composed of the numbers of   5 of 8 of 4 and of 3.
As for the Element of Water, it is composed of the same numbers as that of Earth, which are of   5 of 8 of 4 and of 3.

It is not enough to know the numbers that make up the Elements, not even each one in particular, if we do not know the true way to use them. To act accordingly and successfully in operations, it is necessary to know how many numbers each number is composed of, and this is what we are going to teach you. The number 1 is composed of three units, the number 2 is composed of 6, the number 3 is composed of 9, the number 4 is composed of 12, the number 5 is composed of 15 [units], and so on. When you want to operate, you will have to operate <u>by repeating the same number</u> three times each time, before you see success. That is why we have already told you that you need to know the value of each number.

But it is still not enough to know how much the numbers of each entity are worth. You must know that you must remove all the 9s, so that you can find the number by calculation, which you must do in this way. If you assemble all the numbers of each entity, you must then remove all the 9s. What you are left with is the 'acting number.'[1] In addition, you must consider and know which column of the Sacred

---

[1] *Le nombre agissant.*

Numbers given by M. A.[1] is responsible for this number, and say it, repeating the column as many times as you have units left, which, having been done as accurately as possible, you will then be able to achieve what you wish. May it obey you in all that is not against the glory of the Most High, your wellbeing, and that of all your brothers, and before beginning this operation, recite the following prayer with all possible attention and fervour.

PRAYER

> "Almighty God, who created everything out of nothing, who by his wise prudence created everything out of nothing [155] and placed in each entity an attribute of yours to serve as its motive, I beg you, I adjure you by the love you have for yourself and for all perfect creatures, to compel and force this entity of yours that I need, to obey me in all that I command him, for your glory, mine and that of my brothers."

This prayer being finished, you must calculate the numbers of the 'attributes' of the entity you wish to use, and then you will do what is indicated above. But if by some unforeseen fortuitous event, it could happen that the entity you invoke disobeys you, you will have to start again until he obeys you. This must not be done or repeated more than nine times, for at this number of repetitions it is absolutely necessary that he renders himself obedient, to this perfect number of 3 which represents the most august, Most-Holy and mysterious Trinity, after having learned the principles and the true manner of making each entity of Nature act. It is good to say what must be done to succeed with all possible assurance in all that you wish to undertake by this ministry and the means of these entities.

When you have the will to make use of an entity of whatever Nature it may be, whether it is good and certain, or bad and uncertain. You must prepare yourself as indicated below, for three days before beginning your operation.

Preparation

It is necessary to be chaste, of the chastity that this operation requires you not to have lived with any woman within the last three days.

It is also necessary to fast in the manner of the wise, which is to eat only once a day after sunset, which is sufficient for a successful operation. Let us move on to the discussion of the Numbers of each particular entity.

---

[1] This may refer to 'Master Alpha.'

Steganographia

[156] CHAPTER II

Of the Numbers of each Entity in Particular.

We will begin this chapter with the numbers of the Spirits who govern the Stars [Planets], who are good Spirits and good Intelligences. We believe that you are sufficiently instructed in the different kinds of Intelligences, good or bad, having heard of them several times and having contemplated their nature, it will however be good to say here that good Intelligences are pure Intelligences and good Spirits have bodies of the most subtle matter of the Four Elements and that these bodies are immortal and so beautiful that the human eye has never seen anything approaching their beauties. And they are so subtle that they can penetrate through the hardest and thickest of bodies, these Intelligences number three Legions in each Star,[1] each with a Chief and a 'Super-Chief' in command. These Intelligences have the same numbers as their chiefs, and we will begin to teach them to you through the Chief of all that is. This great ALPHA, commander of the Sun, who has as his Number these

Four Numbers, namely:	1 2 3 4 Apollo ☉
Venus has the Numbers	1 3 5 6 ♀
Mercury has the Numbers	1 4 7 9 ☿
Moon has the Numbers	1 2 5 8 ☽
Saturn has the Numbers	1 3 5 7 ♄
Jupiter has the Numbers	1 4 6 9 ♃
Mars has the Numbers	1 5 7 9 ♂

Having given you the Numbers of the Intelligences of each planet, as you see them represented above, this is not yet sufficient, for we must [157] also be instructed in the numbers which refer to the Intelligences of the Signs of the Zodiac. Of which there are in each sign three Legions, as well as in the planets, each of which has its Chief and Super-Chief who is always a Celestial Angel, in some as in others, we will begin with Aries to give you their Numbers, these first numbers are attributed to

Aries namely	1 2 3 4 like the Sun.	♈.
Signs that are deputies for Aries' brothers Gemini, Virgo and Libra		♊ ♍ ♎.
They each have the same number	1 3 5 6 here are those of Leo as	♀ ♌.
Scorpio's numbers are	1 4 6 9 as	♃ ♏.
Sagittarius numbers	1 2 5 7	♐.
Sagittarius' brothers, Capricorn and Aquarius, have the same number		♑ ♒.
The numbers of Taurus are	1 5 7 8	♉.

---

[1] 'Astre' in the manuscript but actually referring to the 7 Planets.

At this point, I must inform you and declare that the Signs are similar to the planets in terms of numbers, as they are much composed of the same Elements, and so are the others.

There now remains the Sign of Cancer and that of Pisces ♋ ♓.

We must also consider their nature and their conformity with the planets.

CHAPTER III

Of the Number of Entities or Uncertain Spirits

Uncertain Spirits are scattered throughout the Elements, they have no secure abode. When they wish to descend into the abyss of SATAN, they can do so, being free to go wherever they like, except they do not have permission to go into the Heavenly Empire.[1]

These kinds of Spirits are, as you have been taught, and what you must know, are always in [a state of] uncertainty as to the forgiveness of their faults, for sometimes they hope for the Divine and infinite mercy of the Sovereign Creator, and sometimes they are in despair, especially when they reflect on their [158] fatal ingratitude, which was their enormous fault and detestable crime of having doubted for a moment that they would follow Lucibel's [2] party. As punishment for this crime, the Most High has confirmed them in their uncertainty until the coming of the Son of Man. You have already been told that the Uncertain Spirits are all Wanderers in the Elements. But we have not yet made known to you that they were and are pure Spirits like the Angels and Intelligences of the planets and Signs. But they do not have bodies as beautiful as theirs. Because the Lord and most high God, in punishment for their sins, has made them all deformed, and when they are forced to appear to humans, they must borrow a body and form of one of the coarsest Elements, (you must know) that they have made of themselves Chiefs willingly, to whom they have given all power, and that these Chiefs are 24 in number, so that 6 are deputies for each Element. The number of each chief is different; only that of the 4 Super-chiefs is the same.

The number of the principal of the Chiefs of the part of which he is Emperor of all and has for his Numbers these first Four, here namely   1 2 3 4
     Like the big Alpha. As well as the other three super-chiefs.
The other five southern chiefs have numbers   1 5 7 9
The five chiefs of the western part have for their number   1 4 6 9
The five chiefs of the northern have for their number   1 3 5 7
The five chiefs of the eastern part have for their number   1 2 7 8

All Spirits depend on the chiefs of the south, and are the same as regards numbers. And so with the others in the other three parts of the Universe.

---

[1] This clearly identifies these entities as demons.
[2] An old synonym for Lucifer.

CHAPTER IV

Of the Number of Evil Spirits

The evil Spirits are, as you know, those who followed Lucibel's revolt and deliberately persisted in the party they [159] had formed and even embraced.

God seeing them thus determined to follow the treacherous and perfidious Lucibel, his fatal and irreconcilable enemy, confirmed him in the choice they had of always doing evil and never practicing what concerns good, which makes him of such a perverse nature, that God by his omnipotent goodness had not limited and restricted their power, they could have, or at least could have attempted, to destroy all Nature, for the hatred he had conceived against the Most High and powerful Creator, but God, who is full of Divine goodness towards this same nature, and because of His most high and sublime foresight, took away from them all the power He had given them at their creation, so that they no longer have any power or might of their own, unless they are commanded, forced and constrained by men, who are as wretched as they are, and to whom they have willingly submitted out of their desire to make men as wretched and as miserable as they are, and to incline them to all manner of wickedness.[1] For in this view, there is nothing that they have not put into execution for and in order to better succeed in their fatal and abominable purpose, and to thus achieve their intentions, they have resolved to give to the men to whom they have appeared. Their evil and detestable science of Numbers, by which they willingly submit to do whatever they may be enjoined and commanded to do, provided that it be things tending to the destruction of the human genus, the good of the Earth, and all kinds of private domestic animals or other things created for the pleasure, or for the service and utility, of men. As these kinds of Spirits have been entirely made hideous and deformed by the Divine Creator, this means that when they want to form a body, they form one composed of nothing but mud and filth, or they enter the stinking corpses of their followers, whom they animate to more easily deceive those to whom they appear, for they always promise much, but they never know and can never [160] keep such promises, nor perform anything, and if sometimes they grant a trifle, it is the better to catch their dupes and to reach their objectives more easily.

We do not think it is absolutely necessary to go into detail here, or to repeat where the Supreme Being has relegated these unfortunates, believing you to be sufficiently instructed. We will content ourselves with telling you that they are locked up in a dark place in the Chaos of the Earth, filled with horror and torment,

---

[1] Apart from the moralising, it is interesting to see that, according to this text, the Spirits still need the magician's command in order to do evil.

where they will remain until the advent of the Word made flesh,[1] who will confirm their judgment, or change it as he sees fit. This we are not allowed to reveal. The Sovereign reserves this knowledge for Himself alone.

We are going to teach you the numbers of which these unfortunate Spirits are composed, which are certainly not those that are taught and communicated to men; for they do not know them themselves. And even if they did know them, it is very certain that they would have taken great care to instruct men in them and to discover their meaning, otherwise these kinds of Spirits would not have been able to refrain from obeying them in all that was required of them.

Here are the Numbers that make all Hell tremble and quiver with Rage

The Numbers of Lucibel who is their Emperor and is nicknamed Lucifer, his number is like that of the great ALPHA, composed of this numeration 1 2 3 4.

We have not yet told you that these Spirits number 150 Legions, which have 12 chiefs and 7 super-chiefs, but as Lucibel is their Emperor, who they regard as their God, they are similar to those of the 12 Signs, and the numbers of the 7 super-chiefs are the same as those attributed to the 7 planets. So when you want to operate through these Spirits, you will have to resort to them. See [manuscript] pages 156 and 157 in Chapter 2 [for details].

---

[1] Jesus Christ.

[161] **CHAPTER V**

Of Differences between Good and Certain Intelligences versus the Bad and Uncertain

All the differences there are between Good and Bad Intelligences are such that men cannot easily conceive them, for Good Intelligences know all sciences as well as all Liberal Arts, and Mechanics, and they even have the power to teach them to men with whom they are in sympathy, which they do with the most welcome and joy possible, when they meet one to whom they can share intelligence, for otherwise they would manifest themselves only with difficulty and rarely through their appearances, which are too opposed to their freedom, having been created free, that if they had once appeared, they could not easily return to their dependencies without the consent of the person to whom they had united themselves, unless they had put such conditions into their commitment to say that they would eventually set them free.

You can be more than persuaded, and very sure, that the good Intelligences have so much love and benevolence for men that they would like to bring them all into the bosom of God, and there is nothing they do to make them happy, even during the course of this life, for if they want to follow their advice, they will abandon all the vain amusements of the world. By this, we mean all things criminal, for the innocents are not opposed to them; on the contrary, they advise us to use them to relax the mind and regain strength for better work, because too long an application of the mind renders it incapable, and puts it in no condition to work fruitfully; it is good and even necessary to spend some time in recreation, for example with music, or in other permitted recreations.

[162] Good Intelligences have as much joy as men can have, and when they sing the praises of the Lord (since they are continually occupied day and night singing the praises of God the Sovereign Creator), so when they are happy enough to be united with someone who has this precious gift of Nature, they are delighted. And they teach the way to perfect and conform his voice, and teach him their method of singing, which is as high above mortals as heaven is above the earth.

These good Geni, Spirits, Angels or good Intelligences put all their efforts into those whom they love in a perfect state either by teaching them to know Nature, and these various productions which are so necessary to humans, as well as all the marvellous effects in each one of its various bodies and which they make available to the wise man, either by learning or teaching them the knowledge of the Simples,[1] their virtues and their properties and other utilities for health, or by giving them the true way to make with these same Simples an almost miraculous Oil so wonderful, that by taking 7 drops in some suitable vehicle for the space of

---

[1] Medicinal herb extracts.

7 Moons, it regenerates the most decidedly infirm man, be he downcast and broken under the weight of great age, and restores him to the vigour of those of thirty years, robust, taking away from him all his pains and even the cause which can no longer return, inasmuch as the stain of Original Sin[1] is entirely separated from the mass of his blood, which keeps him always as a flourishing youth, and which will only leave him after centuries redoubled; but he can regenerate again, making the same use of its Oil as it did the first time. We further claim that it is within his power to live until God has determined to change the face of the world, if he takes some of his Oil whenever he notices that his nature is becoming heavy, for this nature only becomes weighed down by long years, but it cannot die. God having created him immortal, which you cannot [163] ignore, and without the disobedience of the first man, all his descendants would not die, but they would live to the end of the time fixed by the Sovereign Creator and Supreme Being. [2]

☞ We have just told you that man was created immortal, which is what everyone knows, at least those who are enlightened by divine and celestial lights, for not everyone knows that the most high God, after the sin of Eve and Adam, took away none of their attributes that had been put into them, and left them the right to resume their mortality.

☞ Here's how it can be done, God had foreseen that man would disobey him, and so put his attribute of immortality in metals, minerals, vegetables and animals, and having resolved that all those who would succeed by their assiduity of work to the perfect knowledge and possession of the precious Oil of each of these Kingdoms, could well with assurance succeed in making themselves immortal, as a reward for their wisdom. When a man is fortunate enough to have an Angel (or his Holy Intelligence) in communication with him, or to be in conjunction with two separate ones, he may attain by his assiduity to such holy work, to a perfect knowledge, not only of this precious and admirable Oil, but even in regard to all sciences, and of all the most sublime secrets hidden in Nature as well as of all the most sublime precious mysteries.

Know that this Intelligence has no rest until it has communicated all its perfections to the one it loves, which is why it constantly inspires him to seek the wisdom that makes a man like God, by making him like God the Creator of all things. When it says Creator of all things, think that it is true!

☞ What difference is there between creation and giving a new form to an entity? Probably none, since Creation and Formation are one and the same thing.

[164] As for evil Spirits and evil Intelligences, they are all opposed to good Spirits, Angels and Intelligences, for they apply themselves only to the destruction of the

---

[1] The Roman Catholic doctrine of Original Sin.
[2] This affirms that the Oil is the universal panacea of alchemy, but suggests that the ultimate cure, theologically, is the removal of the burden of Original Sin from his blood.

whole human race, to making men commit all sorts of most enormous crimes, in a word, to make them like them, and in order to make them become like them, as miserable, and as unhappy as they are.

As for the Uncertain Spirits, they are sometimes in hope of forgiveness for their faults, sometimes in despair, [and so] they are not capable of giving any perfect science to those they love, so you see that they are not of much use, although they boast a lot about knowing all the sciences in all their perfection, they cannot however come to putting any of it into execution, because of the almost continual turmoil that God has put in them, as punishment for their faults and sins.

CHAPTER VI

Of the Nature of Evil Spirits

The evil Spirits are those, as stated above, who followed the Lucibel revolt, and when they persisted in their perverse will, they forced the Most High to confirm them in this accursed path, for it was not up to God to forgive them this detestable crime, having called them up to 7 times with the intention of making them change their feelings, which only served to harden them even more. They are fit only to lead men to commit the most horrible crimes by making them understand that they are immortal, and that it is false from what they say, that there is a definite place for their punishment and, as proof of what they advance, it is that they are free to go wherever they please, which would not be if it were true that there was a place where those who have done evil are punished, but that it is certain [165] that after their soul is separated from their body, it will dwell like them in the air and in the Elements, that when they wish, they will come on earth to exercise with them the same jobs with their brothers, it is by these tricks and a stratagem that they try to catch all men who want to listen to them, because they have no power to do them any good, but although they make them all sorts of fine promises, such as giving them the means to find and remove treasures, making them love such girls or women as they desire, and finally making them the happiest of mortals during this life, they also make them believe that it will be much longer than it actually is. They do not bother to preserve any of them, as long as they succeed in their designs.

CHAPTER VII

On the Difference between Good and Bad Intelligences

Good Intelligences, as already mentioned above, are always ready to do men all the good that is in their power, and they have no greater joy than when they can be useful to them in some way.

As for the nature of evil Spirits, it is quite the opposite, for they apply themselves only to doing harm to mankind, and put all their felicity into procuring it, and when they cannot by themselves execute their evil designs; they make use of these evil and perverse men, who have neither faith nor law, especially as these evil Spirits have no power to harm creatures who have the fear of God before their eyes; but they address their henchmen to obtain the command to execute their rage on those they foresee will be contrary to them, either by the sanctity of their lives, or by the positions they must occupy, in which they will apply themselves to destroying the worship they demand of mortals. Finally, [166] they must be opposed to them by their natural inclinations, and these evil Spirits only occupy themselves with countering the good, that the more they see they have friendships, and that they are more inclined to do good to men, the more they are also ardent to give them all sorts of work to prevent them from succeeding in their projects. If we were to occupy ourselves with making known to you the implacable hatred these evil Spirits have against the human race, we would have to employ a great deal of time and volumes, which would otherwise serve us for things far more useful and of greater necessity for the good and advantage of humans, and for the destruction of the profane worship of these evil Spirits, and to achieve this we shall begin by telling you that it is of the utmost necessity that you take care and worry about anything that might cause you distraction, so that you only apply yourselves to what we are going to teach you in the Second Part of this book of the precious Sacred Numbers.

SECOND PART

Of the Book of Sacred Numbers
The true ways to achieve success with the Sacred Number

CHAPTER I

The first means of achieving success in the operations that are carried out using the strength and power of sacred numbers, is to know how many units the number you wish to use is composed of. And what each unit is worth. The second is to know which of the columns of numbers (which were given to M.A.) are the one the question depends on.

[167] The third way is to know the right time to perform your operation. Because without this, you would never be able to succeed in your experiments. We would also like you to have a full knowledge of the Elemental Spirits on whom you will wish to operate, i.e. to know what species they are, and what is their use and vocation, of which Element and Pole they are part. When you are sufficiently instructed in all these things, you must prepare yourself in the manner described above.

Steganographia

CHAPTER II

Of how many Numbers you need when you wish to carry out an operation

First of all, you need to know how many kinds of Numbers you are obliged to use, which we will explain to you with as much truth and plainness as we can.

Example

If, for example, you intend to use an Uncertain Spirit for any purpose whatsoever, provided that the glory of God and the good and advantage of your brothers depend on it, then for this purpose you must know the number of this Spirit, which is always similar to that of its Leader, if it is a subordinate that you employ, although it will be much more useful to you to make use of the chief than of those who depend on him.

☞ The Second number is that of the Element in which it lives. For example, if it is from the Element of Fire, it is '1;' if it is from the Element of Air, it is '2;' if it is from the Element of Earth, it is '3;' if it is from the Element of Water, it is '4' for its number. These are the numbers assigned to each of the Elements.[1]

The Fourth Number is the one we see attributed to the [Sign of] the Moon, in which [168] you make your operation. For example, if it is in the Moon of ♈ you will get 1. If it is in the ♉ you will get 2, and so for the others.

The Fifth number is that of the Sun which traverses the twelve Signs of the Zodiac. It is calculated like that of the Moon.

The Sixth number is that of the Lunar month; that is for example, the fourth day of the Moon.

The Seventh number is that of the Solar month, which you must understand to be the fourth of the month in which you operate, which is the number of the Sign, or date.

The Eighth [number] is that of the planet when you do your operation, that is to say which reigns in the hour which is counted from the hour of the rising Sun on Sunday [i.e. the Planetary hour], in the manner of acting which you must know and understand, as also by the Moon, on Monday which is its day, and so for the others.

The Sun has 1, the Moon has 2. So this number is acting, which is why it is the last.

It is not enough to know all these numbers: if you do not know how to calculate

---

[1] There is no mention of a 'Third number' in the manuscript.

them, you will be no further ahead. So we are going to teach you how.

Here is the calculation of the Numbers

You add up all these numbers and then remove 9s from the total, and what remains to you will be your active number, which you must look for in the column of numbers given to M.A. And when you have found it, you say all the numbers in this column up to 9, as you have already been told above, which you cannot do without the entity you are commanding obeying you; for he is constrained just as if it were God commanding him, because he knows the acting virtue of the Most High is in these numbers, so do not fear failing in your operation if you take all the necessary care.

Preparation

We warn you that when you want to operate, you must prepare for three days as stated above, and you must [169] count each unit by 3, otherwise you will get nowhere, you still need to know that each unit of these last 3 is worth 3. So each unit of all the numbers in your above-mentioned addition is worth 9.

CHAPTER III

Of the Different Kinds of Numbers to be used in operations of this Art

Numbers make up the whole of Nature, so do not be surprised if it is absolutely necessary to use these same numbers to succeed in your operations on entities that cannot help but obey you when you call them by their Number joined with all the other [numbers] we have already instructed you about above, but we will give you the explanation at greater length later.

You now know that the Numbers are the motivators of all created bodies, whether mineral, vegetable or animal, so it is very necessary to make absolute use of the Numbers to make them act in accordance with your intentions, which must never be against the Almighty and Sovereign Creator, but let it be for your own good and that of your brothers. For if you acted otherwise you would make yourself most criminal before God, who has made you king of all productions only to make good and honest use of them, and that you apply yourself to study with diligence and assiduity, seeing all the application required in the search for the precious secrets hidden in the wonders of Nature, which are in such a great number and of so many different classes that everyone can penetrate them, little or much, according to his scope and the extent of his genius, which becomes more and more enlightened as he makes progress in the sciences he has undertaken to learn.

And when he has reached them, he has acquired enough light [170] to devote himself to the search for an even deeper science which will give him new light to evince a much higher degree of perfection. This is how the lovers of wisdom are, they despise the vain amusements of worldly people to occupy themselves only with things that are useful, pleasant and of the last consequence, although very painful in the beginning, once initiated and accustomed to it, the mind does nothing but play, and what was or seemed difficult becomes so easy that it becomes an amusement, and not a serious occupation: *Que ab astuetis non sit passio*:[1] that is to say, Nature makes a pure contempt of what seemed the most difficult and opposite when one is doing a work, which according to its appearances is very painful, but one should not for that reason be put off or abandon this mysterious enterprise, because by working one makes for oneself a habit, and that habit makes a second Nature, which becomes all the more pleasant, as it is no longer a pain, but is already a play or recreational amusement; because what satisfaction does a person not have who studies 'Metallic nature,'[2] and is a lover of riches, if he has the happiness of achieving the transmutation of imperfect metals into pure gold? Will he not find himself the happiest of all men, having

---

[1] Let there be no passion from cunning.
[2] i.e. alchemy.

with ease the means to provide for all his needs and satisfy his greed, which would otherwise become very harmful to him if he did not make good use of it by depriving the poor, who are the members of Jesus Christ,[1] of the fruit of their labour, which belongs to them in part as it does to him, but if he is wise enough [he will] distribute faithfully to Jesus Christ the proportion due to him, for he says that whatever is done to one of these little ones will be done to him: *Quod fuistis uni ea minimis istis mihi fuistis*,[2] he cannot fail, provided that he continues to seek and strive to penetrate into the wonders of Nature in order to ascend to a higher degree of light, which will lead him to a higher point of science, and as he ascended through the different degrees of Metallic Nature which is a science highly recommended by the sages since the least of their adepts is an expert in the transmutation of metals, [171] he will deserve by the great assiduity he has brought to such a great work, that God will reveal to him [the formula for] this precious Oil which is so miraculous that it is the dissolver of all the metallic bodies, and of all the plants, when one has purified the three principles and reduced the mercury of these to Oil, like it is also perfect from which one can regenerate animals and the most fallen men to a very strong youth; which is not the greatest of the effects of this divine Oil, which has the virtue of rendering immortal those who take 7 drops of it in some suitable vehicle as in wine or brandy, with half water, during the course of a whole moon.[3] When we say immortal we are not far from the truth, since everyone knows that God created the first man in a state of immortality, death having entered him and his posterity only through sin, which is why men became mortal, but once he has made use of this admirable Oil for the space of a moon, he will return to his original state of innocence, for it has the virtue of removing the stain of original sin which is the source of all evil.[4]

☞ Let us now come to the explanation of the different kinds of Numbers which can be used to make the Spirits act in the way we wish to invoke and employ them in the due manner and according to their vocation [or Office].[5]

First. The Number of the Spirit is not only the principal and most essential motivation, but it is also the weight, life and movement, for without it, it is impossible to complete any operation. This number is counted differently from the others, for each unit is worth 3, as we have already pointed out to you, and each unit of these three is worth another three, which makes 9. And 1 is 10, which is worth each unit from which we take 9, leaving 1. You might ask, what's the point of this multiplication? Since we're going back to our first number, if not to embarrass us and confuse us, to prevent us from succeeding. To this we reply that it is not in this design, but that it is an order that has been established in this way

---

[1] i.e. Christians.
[2] What you were to one of those little ones, you were to me.
[3] A month.
[4] The Roman Catholic interpretation of alchemy.
[5] The remainder of this chapter, especially its calculations, is rather suspect.

by the first [172] author whose word cannot be violated, if one wishes to have a happy outcome and success in what one undertakes.

Second. The Number of the Element is different, as each unit must be counted by 4. For example, if it is Fire, there are many 1 which is worth 4. If it is the Element of Air, its number is 2, giving you the number 8. And so it is not enough to know how to calculate in this way, you must also know that each of the Elements has a fixed number, which neither increases nor decreases.

They are reported below. Here is an **Example**.

Fire △ Fire at 3 2 1 4, which can be counted as follows: 3 and 2 make 5, and 1 makes 6, and 4 makes 10; you remove 9 and it will remain as 1.

Air △ Air has 2 1 3 7, which can be assembled as follows: 2 and 1 make 3, and 3 make 6, and 7 are worth 13, from which you remove 9, leaving 4.

Earth ▽ Earth has 1 4 5 2: you say 1 and 4 make 5, and 5 makes 10, and will make 12 by adding the 2, from which you similarly subtract 9, leaving you with 3.

Water ▽ Water to 4 6 3 2 which you assemble like the others by saying: 4 and 6 make 10, and 3 make 13, and 2 are worth 15, from which you remove 9, and you are left with 6. But it should be noted here that you must not remove 9 from these numbers, when they are joined to the others by total addition.

The Number of God is 1 3 3 1 which is 4, this Divine number is quite different from the others, for it is counted in this way: 1 and 3 make 4, and 3 make 7, and 1 makes 8, and 4 make 12, from which we subtract 9 as we do from the others, inasmuch as there are no numbers of Death in God, and when we have added up the other numbers and subtracted all the 9s, we join those that remain to this Divine number of 12, which is the acting number of all Spirits; Intelligences or entities; or rather for the compulsion to obey.

The Number of the Sign in which the Moon is, as it was said before, and where you will have necessary recourse, this number is counted simply as it is, so it needs no other explanation.

[173] The number of the Sign the Sun passes through is of the same nature as the previous one, so we won't say anything more about it, except that you can see where it was mentioned if necessary.

The number of the Lunar month does not require any special explanation either. It is enough to know how many days previously the Moon entered the Sign.

The number of the solar month does not need to be explained either; it is enough for you to know the date of the day on which the Sun entered the Sign.

The Number of the ruling planet is of the same Nature as those of the Moon and the Sun, so that's all explained.

CHAPTER IV

What are the Numbers of Chapter III

The Numbers of Chapter 3 are quite different from one another, as has already been said, but this difference is nothing compared to their power, which is so great, that when you count them exactly, it is absolutely necessary that the Angel, or the Intelligence, or the Spirit or the entity (whoever you may command) does not differ in any way in obeying you. We therefore say that these numbers have so much force and virtue that they move and act on all of Nature, as well as all the Spirits it contains.

When God, who is the first and Sovereign Supreme Being, created, or rather separated from Nature all the various works that you see, and even more all those that you cannot see because of original sin, which puts a kind of cataract on your eyes, which prevents you from seeing all the productions of the Most High which are in great number, and which are of surprising beauty, and even though nothing of all that you can see approaches them, and you would be in continual admiration if you had sight sharp enough to see them, which can only be achieved [174] by a miracle from God, natural or supernatural, because everything in Nature is miraculous.

It is called Nature, because you can see everything that has a body of flesh like yours by means of this admirable Oil that you have been told about, which has the virtue not only of regenerating the body but also of making sight so subtle and piercing, that there is nothing in Nature that is visible, that it cannot see.

When God drew all entities from the Chaos of Nature where they were locked up, he only used the number that he attributed to each entity with which he called it, which is why by using the same number, it cannot dispense with obeying you. We further say that when you call an entity by its number, joined to what we have mentioned to you, you may thus summon it to do the most vile and abject things, if this is your will, but one hardly dares to make use of entities and employ them, as of good will, to low uses unworthy of their nature.

At most, it could be used to punish entities who rebel in their pride or disobey as soon as they are called upon to perform some service. So far, this is all we have been able to give to those who are in a position to penetrate the subject matter of this book. To succeed, all you need is intelligence and patience, then you can be sure of succeeding in your endeavour, and when the great ALPHA and ODEPHA,[1] as we hope on this occasion, will have made our intelligence more penetrating, we shall give to those who govern themselves to pursue their studies in order to achieve greater enlightenment, other things which may be of the same

---

[1] This would more typically be OMEGA.

use to them and which will give them a stronger and more piercing light, with which they will be able to penetrate the mysteries in the same way that M.A., and infallibly you, will discover what he was able to discover by his science.

End of the [First Part of] the Book of the Sacred Numbers

Steganographia

[175] ר ש י ה ח מ ח ד ח ה ו ו[1]

THE VERITABLE SECRETS

The True Way to Make the [Magical] Bell

according to Theophrastus and Paracelsus,[2]
who gave this method for summoning Spirits

Notice to Disciples and Curious Readers

My dear children and my very Christian disciples, who are our pupils, that is, when at this hour we communicate to you all the mysteries of Nature and all science, even the last Divine and admirable secret which is superior to the powers of Nature.

Our dear disciples, will you follow these maxims, which will not deceive you in any way, since the Seven Spirits will carry out everything you could wish for, and will lend you a hand from beginning to end, by God's permission, without committing the slightest fault.

We confess and declare that we are communicating to you what we desire you to know and not to ignore, so strive to know with all your ardour, passion and desire what is used in the preparation that concerns this divine mystery, and if you wish all things to succeed for you as for our dear and beloved disciples not only in its beginning, for which we pray God to be favourable to you entirely and especially for a profitable and advantageous end. Amen.

We, Theophrastus Paracelsus, assure you that this little treatise is the most to be esteemed amongst the rest of our other books, for there is no writing that is more revealing, nor more sublime, among all our writings, it is the shortest and the best, in a word, to say it in few words, we wish and desire that by this means the great God of heaven may grant you fullness of grace in the name of the most holy and august [176] Trinity and Majesty, God the Father, God the Son, and God the Holy Spirit Amen;

- *Theophrastus Paracelsus*[3]

Here is a way, or a means, which I, Theophrastus Paracelsus used in the operations of the Great Work, which we want to communicate to you so that you can happily succeed in putting into execution whatever great things you may think of, with the great desire that you have to see the goal and accomplishment for a new year, and for a perpetual memory of happy successes, and to be able

---

[1] Rashi ha-Chumah which refers to the commentary on the *Tanakh* by Rashi of Troyes (1040-1105).
[2] The author apparently did not know that both these names belonged to the same person Theophrastus Paracelsus von Hohenheim. In the manuscript the name is rendered as "Theophraste & Paracelce." All following references to him will be in the correct singular form. This does suggest that the author, or at least the copyist of this book, was not familiar with the name.
[3] This is followed by a small seal.

to carry out and complete all that is on Earth in the four Elements, and to accomplish all the virtue found in this one mystery which contains in itself all that is above and below the Earth.

First[1]

Notice the day you came into the world during the week, and know whether the Sun is in the Sign of [Leo] ♌, of [Taurus] ♉, or of [Virgo] ♍. And at what degree of ascension, whether it is at the 4, 5, 6, 7, 8, 12, 14 or 15th degree, and whether the Moon was under the Sign of [Aries] ♈, [Gemini] ♊ or [Libra] ♎. Saturn was under [Virgo] ♍, [Taurus] ♉ or [Sagittarius] ♐ from the 1st to the 13th or 14th degree. Jupiter was under Cancer[2] ♋, Capricorn ♑ or Sagittarius ♐ in the 10th to 15th degree. And if the Wolf [Pisces/Libra][3] or Aries ♈ on Mars ♂. Venus ♀ was under [Taurus] ♉ or [Gemini] ♊ from the 1st to the 15th degree, a few minutes. Mercury ☿ was under [Virgo], ♍, [Libra], ♎ or the Wolf [Pisces/Libra], Capricorn [♑] or Pisces [♓] at 7, 8, 9, 10, 12, 14 or 15th degree, or if the Wolf or Dragon's Head are in good aspect to the day of your birth; as for the week, it does not matter what it is.

The Quantity and Material that makes up the [Magical] Bell

R. 2 Gros[4] of ☉ [gold]. 2 Gros of ☽ [silver]. 3 Gros of ☿ [mercury]. 1 Gros of ♄ [lead]. 1 Gros of ♃ [tin]. 1 Gros of ♂ [iron], and 12 Gros of ♀ [copper].[5]

Notice that it is necessary to add two Gros of the metal, of surplus, of that of the day that you will make the mixture, having amalgamated it with the other on the same day of your birth, you will make this increased metal of the day that you make this mixture, or that is of your [177] birth, and melt it into a pure kernel. This being done, you will form a bell from this material. Place it in a convenient and very clean place on which you will write above the handle the great name Adonai, and on the thickness or circle of the bell you will write the great name Tetragrammaton, and above the handle you will write the Divine name of Jesus.[6]

When you have made all the preparations as explained above with all possible order required for these precious mysteries, as regards the making of this mysterious bell, you will keep it clean in a tidy place. For this is a very great and certain secret, and very truly of God the Sovereign Supreme Being. The place where you will place the said bell needs no particular mystery nor any other ornament, nor even any other character, or names, but only two or rather three, for their powers, virtues, and properties are inexplicable, especially as these two

---

[1] Calculate your birthday.
[2] Sometimes only the sign appears, sometimes the sign name and the symbol.
[3] The Wolf is sometimes associated with Libra, but Mars in Pisces gives better results.
[4] 'Gross' here may just mean 'large', or a dozen, or less likely, 144.
[5] This is the mixture of metals needed to cast the bell.
[6] The creation of such a magical bell appears in a number of other grimoires.

Tetragrammaton and Adonai which are revealed and very great with which the Hebrews, the Egyptians and many other peoples have worked an infinite number of marvels, the third name, Jesus, is the name of this newborn child, this spotless lamb who bears the sins of the world, which is why, in order to walk with all assurance and be prepared for a Holy and Divine beginning and a happy outcome to this undertaking, you must use this triple aspect [of the names] to discover all kinds of sureties that can be found in heaven and in all creatures, which are the effects of divine power.

This is why their virtues and strengths have not yet been sufficiently explained, nor even fully discovered, and why we ask you to hold them in deep respect and extreme reverence, and not to despise them in any way whatsoever.

You will therefore make use of this wise and unknown secret [178] and use this bell prepared in the manner explained above.

Remember first of all prepare yourselves well during the space of 9 days by a pure and clean life, and for the diet it will not be necessary for you to eat meat, nor to drink any drink which intoxicates, maintain your spirit and nourish it during this time by prayers and pious and devout thoughts, as well as divine preparations, having also new clothes all prepared before the 9 days, and when you have arrived at Thursday, you will go away during the night to a secret place, so that no one sees or hears you. It does not matter what place it is, even if it is a thatched cottage, a barn, a room, or any other house it may be that you will only take care that no one enters it, and that it is as far away from human commerce as possible, when you are in this place, you will turn your face towards the South and having also arranged a clean place to put a new table, which will be covered with a green or yellow carpet or similar colours, you will also place some chairs and three beautiful candles, each one on a silver candlestick, or of other materials whatever, which will also be brand new, you will place them on the table, this being done and arranged you will prepare a liqueur of such a thing as we will explain to you hereafter, and you will write with a peacock feather that you have cut with the knife of Art, with which you will write the name of the planet that you wish to have in this place, and you will write each planet in its colour and will mix the tincture, having written the names you will pronounce as follows:

> "O God Tetragrammaton Adonay, I 'N' who am your creature, beg you through Jesus to complete and execute my requests for prosperity and happiness, by your Holy Grace with the Spirits, without (causing) harm, nor misfortune, with the strength and power of the Lord of Lords, Amen."

This Prayer having been said, you will begin to ring the bell saying:

> "You Spirit or Angel…, I, N., wish passionately for this one [179] and others shortly [to come] in an instant."

You will pronounce these words three times and each time you sound three knells with a bell, the Spirits will come and appear to you in very beautiful figures and finery, you would think they are of the first nobility, a Prince or Count, each in his own habit. In this way, you can make all the Spirits who preside over the 7 planets come in an instant, provided you act by orders, according to their colours; but when they come, it is partly in crowds; you should show them the chairs, or rather you will ask them to sit down, and call each one by his name, and say the following:

> "I, N….. wish you Spirit N….. who presides (over such and such a planet) that you tell me…………[1] and you may reveal to me of………whatever I wish, if it is within your power."

Then you can tell the Spirit whatever you like. "This is what we wish from you through the most Holy Names of God: Tetragrammaton, Adonay and Jesus."

Show him and prepare for him a liquor or the vase that contains it, and there will be in this vase a new quill with paper and in this way they will show you and indicate everything, and even tell you everything you want to know about them, and if you do not treat them badly the first time, and if you treat them with respect and reverence, you can be sure that they will obey you, and will come more willingly the second time around, as well as the other [times] likewise. You can go anywhere you like, both days and nights, but always remember to leave them free certain hours per day, for example from 10 am until noon, you will do the same during the night, in the time that they will tell you the hours themselves, and when you have known for the first time what you desire, try to know or ask them for their names (with great gentleness) of mind:

> [180] "In the name of the Sovereign Creator, and in His Name, I ask you to be obedient and present to me, in the name of the Most Holy Trinity, Amen."

They withdraw in this way and you can also in this way call and ask or invoke any of these Spirits, whichever you wish, and they will come and appear to you on the spot, and you will be able by this admirable method and means, to do whatever you may desire, and they will teach you all they know, both good and bad, provided it is within their power. Once you have received them with the ceremonies you used for the first time, it will not be necessary to repeat the same ceremonies when you call them again, as you did the first time, because they will always be ready to obey you as regards their Vocation.[2]

Colours of the Planets

☿ The colour of Mercury and its Spirit must be mixed, with all kinds of colours, you will make a liqueur and put Gum Arabic water in it.

♀ The colour of Venus is blue, make it so that it pulls a little to the yellow side, it

---

[1] Here place the question.
[2] Or more correctly, their Office.

must be mixed with gum water in which you have put a little copper.

☽ The colour of the Moon is blue, made with oil and gum water, all mixed together.

♄ The colour of Saturn is made of black which you will join with oil, mixed all together. Notice that in the operation you must put on the tongue half a grain of the operation with some ♓ ♄.[1]

♃ The colour of Jupiter is an ash colour, made with oil and mixed so you can write [using it]. ♃

♂ The colour de Mars is carnation, flesh colour, made with egg white and gum water[2] and with oil, the whole congealed and well prepared: it will not [181] be a bad idea to mix each colour with a little of [the appropriate] metal, whose subject you will notice when you are doing your operation. You will need to proceed exactly in order and take care to prepare everything and proportion it as well as possible, as it may be that it will be from the Spirit itself that you receive the instructions and orders on how to practice this Art.[3]

Characters and Names of the Planets		Names of the Spirits of the Planets[4]	Day of the Planet
♄	Saturn	ARATRON	Saturday
♃	Jupiter	BETHOR	Thursday
♂	Mars	PHALEG	Tuesday
☉	Sun	OCH	Sunday
♀	Venus	HAGITH	Friday
☿	Mercury	OPHIEL	Wednesday
☽	Moon	PHUEL	Monday

Table 65: The Olympic Spirits and their Planets.

---

[1] Salt. Maybe a lead salt, which is poisonous.
[2] *Eau de gomme*. Gummed water is a preparation used in the composition of watercolours. It is a transparent liquid made from distilled water and gum Arabic.
[3] No colour is mentioned for the Sun ☉, but one may assume gold.
[4] These are the Olympic Spirits.

Steganographia

Here above are the names of the 7 Spirits you may need in these operations, but above all, it is necessary to have them in their character as these Spirits preside over the seven planets, that is why they can serve all that concerns them, their vocation [or Office] only extends to what is attributed to them by the Supreme Being,[1] but you must not employ them for anything else, but for what concerns them you can ask them with all assurance. If you wish, you can demand from them that they reveal for you the most sublime secrets, as much as they can, and as they make you like the Spirits, even though you are only a mortal man, you will not desire anything else, for they are Princes who have more than sufficient power to help you in your needs, and in all that you wish, if what you may wish for is honest and lawful, you must not doubt their credit, since they govern the world incessantly, and will govern it until the end of the world.

[182] If you wish to have an Angel of the Choir of Angels, you should prepare yourself constantly as explained above. You must write his name with pure gold or pure silver mixed with their tincture on the bell, you ring it and pronounce what is shown above, then he will come to you, and you will be able to ask him whatever pleases you, as is said above, and you will then make sure that he writes on the same requests that you have proposed to him, and you will then be informed of what you wish, but also take care not to retain them more than half an hour.

But if you wish for an Angel, you should take care to prepare well before undertaking anything, and you will be able to fulfil your wishes through his means, which are real and truly certain. Above all, be very careful in your operation not to hold any Spirit for more than half an hour, as they would then no longer come to your service, especially as they are destined and must follow God their master. The best and most suitable time to call them and have them come would be on a Thursday, when the Moon is full.[2] This time is also convenient for other Spirits.

WARNINGS TO THE DISCIPLES

Dear Disciples, we warn you to work rather with the Seven Spirits of the seven planets as they are represented below, rather than with any other, and you will learn much better from them, and be more justly instructed in all the preparations you will need, than if you learned from them [rather than] other Spirits or Angels, for they operate more conveniently than the other Spirits or Angels, as they are their Superiors, and can give you a much clearer and more intelligible answer, and in a word, all sorts of other satisfactions. The reason is that their only Office is to serve men as lords. When you are sufficiently instructed by these Superior Spirits, who preside over the Seven planets, you can have the Angels in your company

---

[1] In other words, the limit of their Offices.
[2] A Full Moon is definitely good advice. Jupiter is recommended because it is a benefic Planet, but choosing a Planet whose nature is more closely aligned with your objective might produce even better results.

without any difficulty. These [183] Spirits will teach you first how, when, and where you can have them, which you will then know from experience, of which we must here remain silent and keep as a profound secret, being restrained by the Seals of Silence. It must be believed that no one has ever been able to have the same happiness as had the Prophet Elijah and several other great men, who were instructed orally. It is true that if this were so, he could not be condemned for impiety, but God wills it to be so, and to be done so in this way, by precious celestial and divine research, man totally takes on the angelic nature. However, you must not aspire after the things of this world, but rather in the place of rest where all the true and faithful Elects will one day find themselves.

Nor did you penetrate further into the sciences of God, as happened to the first of all men, who was condemned to a fatal death. But you can work with Angels and Spirits, who will help you more than enough, so do not look for anything else, and when these Spirits present themselves to you, after you have invoked them, do not you dare to want to delve further into the depths of the inconceivable mysteries of the human race, but by the facts and actions of our operations, you will be able to know and understand all that you wish; do not think either of what these Spirits can do in themselves, but of their forces and powers which they have received from the Supreme Being. This is what must constrain and oblige you to give all the glory and praise which belongs only to God, and you will thank Him unceasingly, both day and night for having favoured you with such a singular Grace, as you can see by your experience of these operations.

It may happen that you have an inclination to work with the Angels. If this happens to you, you will have to fast for a few days, as a sage from Chaldea and another from Persia once did, who made himself seek [184] for nineteen days, on the occasion of this admirable secret, and who neither ate nor drank during all that time; nevertheless he found himself as robust and as strong as he was before.

As long as I am speaking to you through these writings, I will tell you that I did a similar fast for seven consecutive days, and that I took no food substance to fortify me in any way whatsoever,[1] and it seemed to me that a certain melancholy gave me a fearless closed courage to reach this celestial and divine science.[2]

That no one has the ambition nor thinks of going further, than what may be permitted in the ordinary and lawful research of Men at.......[3]

When he has arrived, led and guided by the Angel of Almighty God, let him finish his work, for this is the true way and manner which I have used in utilising this precious and admirable secret which God has kindly granted me, by the singular effect of His divine goodness. I wish to communicate this great and precious secret

---

[1] As long as plenty of liquids are drunk, a fast of 15 days is not that difficult.
[2] You should ensure that you drink adequate liquids during these fasts.
[3] Missing word.

to my friends and beloved disciples, who are desirous of attaining that which is great in these high sciences, and this in the Name, and to the Glory of Almighty God, and to the eternal praise of the Most Holy and Most August Trinity. Amen.

To the greater glory of God.[1]

The End of the [Operation of the] Magical Bell

---

[1] This line is in Spanish "*Sea por la mayor gloria de Dios.*"

[185] How to prepare Parchment for the Operations of our Art

On Sunday before sunrise when the Moon is in conjunction with the Sun, i.e. when there is no Moon, you should take olibanum, mastic, musk, saffron, amber and aloe, all ground to powder. You should have lustral water[1] and willow charcoal which you will light, with whatever [else] the Art may depend on. Then you will light a blessed candle and you will bless your perfumes, and you will say over your parchment the Exorcism below:

> "*Exorcizo te creaturam pergaminis, per virtutem Ely, Eloym, Jod, Jeovah, Sabaoth, Adonay, ut sis pura, munda, sancta, et habeas virtutem vocandy, coercendy que spiritus, et attrahendi dotes Planetarum, stellarum que per Dominum Jesum Cristum; Amen.*"

> "*Benedic[te] Domine creaturam Pergaminis Jstam + Sanctifica + munda + et illustra, ut mihi propitiabilis sit in omnibus operationibus meis. Amen.*"[2]

Then you dip it in a black hen's egg white, well beaten with lustral water, then you will bury it three days in the ground between two blades of fine tin, on which you will put two branches of male Verbena in a cross, then having dug it up at the end of these three days, at an odd hour, you will keep it in a pure and clean place to use it for the operations of the Art.

---

[1] Holy water, originally created in Jewish ritual from the ashes of the red heifer, but here simply water that has been blessed.

[2] "I exorcise you, creature of parchment, by the power of Ely, Elohim, Yod, Jehovah, Sabaoth, Adonay, so that you may be pure, clean, holy, and have the power to call, control the Spirit, and attract the gifts of the Planets, and the Stars through Lord Jesus Christ; Amen.
Bless, O Lord, this creation of parchment, justify + sanctify + clean + and enlighten it, that it may be acceptable to me in all my operations. Amen."

TABLE DU MOUVEMENT PROPRE ET

Particulier des Dix Sphères Célestes

LES DIX SPHERES CELESTES	Signes	Degrés	Minutes	Secondes	Tierces	Quartes	Quintes	Sextiles	Septaines
La 10.ième Sphere, où Premier Mobile Fait son mouvement Propre & Particulier, en une Heure	.	.	15	.	.	.	.	.	.
& en un Jour de 24 Heures Elle Fait	12	.	.	.	.	.	.	.	.
La 9.ième Sphère, où second Mobile, Fait en un Jour	.	.	.	.	4	20	41	17	21
& en un An	.	.	.	20	24	51	3	30	.
& en 49000 Ans	12	.	.	.	4	56	34	.	.
La 8.ième Sphère, Fait en un Jour	.	.	.	.	30	24	49	.	.
En un An	.	.	.	3	5	54	5	.	.
& en 7000 Ans	12	.	.	.	12	3	.	.	.
♄ En un Jour	.	.	2	35	17	4	21	.	.
En un An	.	12	13	34	42	50	27	45	.
En 29 Ans & 163 Jours	12	.	1	22	25	44	1	48	.
& en 30 Ans	12	7	1	25	22	17	34	57	.
♃ En un Jour, avance en un Signe de	.	.	.	4	59	15	27	7	23 30
En un An, de	1	.	.	20	28	59	59	59	1
En 12 Ans & 314 Jours de	12	.	1	24	22	50	57	12	.
& en 12 Ans de	12	4	20	45	46	21	22	1	30
♂ En un Jour de	.	.	31	26	38	40	15	.	.
En un An & 322 Jours de	12	.	2	4	44	57	15	.	.
& en Deux Ans est de	12	22	34	10	27	40	50	.	.
Le ☉ ♀ & ☿ en une Heure est de	.	.	2	27	50	49	3	18	4
En un Jour est de	.	.	59	8	15	37	19	13	56
En un An de 365 Jours est de	11	29	45	39	22	1	59	45	40
& en l'Année de 365 Jours 6 Heures est de	12	.	.	26	26	36	19	44	4
La ☽ En une Heure de	.	.	32	56	27	33	7	57	41
En un Jour est de	.	13	10	35	1	15	11	4	35
& en 27 Jours 8 Heures est de	12	.	9	17	14	15	2	45	13

Figure 15: The Proper and Particular Movement of the Ten Celestial Spheres.

[186] Table of the Proper and Particular Movement of the Ten Celestial Spheres

	The Ten Celestial Spheres	Signs	Degrees	Minutes	Seconds	Thirds	Quarters	Fifths	Sixths
10th Sphere	10th Sphere, or Primum Mobile, the prime mover								
	Proper and Particulier, in one hour			15					
	And in a 24-hour day she passes through	12							
9th Sphere	9th Sphere, or Secondary Mobile makes in one day					4	20	41	17
	And in a Year				20	24	51	3	30
	And in 49000 Years	12				4	56	34	
8th Sphere	8th Sphere, done and a day					30	24	49	
	In a Year				3	5'	54	5'	
	And in 7000 Years	12					12	3	
Saturn ♄	In a day					2	35	17	4	21
	In a Year			12	13	34	42	50	27	45
	In 29 Years and 163 days	12		1	22	25	44	1	48
	And in 30 Years	12	7	1	25	22	17	34	57
Jupiter ♃	And in one day, advance in a Sign of				4	59	15	27	7	33
	In a Year, of	1				20	28	59	59	59
	In 12 Years and 314 days of	12		1	24	22	50	57	12
	And in 12 Years of	12	4	20	45	46	21	22	1
Mars ♂	In a day of			31	26	38	40	15	
	In a Year and 322 days of	12		2	4	44	57	15	
	And in two Years is	12	22	34	10	27	40	50	
Sun ☉	♀ [Venus] and ☿ [Mercury] in an hour is of				2	27	50	49	3	18
	In one day is of				59	8	15	37	19	13

The Ten Celestial Spheres	Signs	Degrees	Minutes	Seconds	Thirds	Quarters	Fifths	Sixths	Sevenths
In one Year of 365 days is of	11	29	45	39	22	1	59	45	40
And in the year of 365 days, 6 hours is	12			26	26	36	19	44	4
In an hour of			32	56	27	33	7	57	41
In a day is		13	10	35	1	15	11	4	35
And in 27 days 8 hours is	12		9	17	14	15	2	45	13

Table 66: The Proper and Particular Movement of the 10 Celestial Spheres.

Table du Cours Propre et Particulier

D'Occident en ORIENT des 7 Planètes, dans les Signes du Zodiaque

Cours Propre de SATURNE en 30 Ans.	
Le 19. Décembre. 1699. il Etait au ♒	le 30. Juin ... en .... 1707 ... à l'écrevice ♋
le 18. Mars .. 1701 .... aux ♓	le 1. Janvier . en . 1708 .... à l' ♋
le 30. Septembre . 1701 ... au ♓	le 21. Juillet .. en .. 1708 ..... au ♌
le 7. Décembre ... 1701 ... aux ♓	le 15. Août .. en ... 1709 ... à la ♍
le 10. Juin ...... 1703 .... au ♈	le 1. Janvier .. en ... 1710 ..... à la ♍
le 13. Août ..... 1703 .... aux ♓	le 29. Septembre . en . 1710 .... à la ♎
le 25. Février .... 1704 .... au ♈	le 26. Octobre . en .. 1711 .... au ♏
le 22. Avril ..... 1706 .... au ♉	le 27. Novembre. en. 1712. ut supra. au ♐
le dernier Décembre. 1708 .... aux ♊	**Propre Cours de MARS de 2 ans en 2 ans.**
le 9. Juin ...... 1711 .... à l' ♋	LE 2. Janvier ..... en . 1704. il était aux ♓
le 20. Juillet .... 1713 ..... au ♌	le 11. Février .... au ♈
le 3. Septembre ... 1715 .... à la ♍	le 23. Mars .... au ♉
le 1. Novembre ... 1717 .... aux ♎	le 4. Mai .... au ♊
le 4. Avril .... 1718 ..... aux ♎	le 17. Juin .... al' ♋
le 10. Octobre ... 1720 .... au ♏	le 2. Août .... au ♌
le 29. Décembre .... 1722 .... au ♐	le 18. Septembre .... à la ♍
le 4. Juin .... 1723 ..... au ♏	le 5. Novembre .... aux ♎
le 30. Septembre ... 1723 .... au ♐	le 1. Janvier ..... en . 1705 ..... aux ♎
le 28. Décembre .... 1725 ..... au ♑	le 27. Janvier .... au ♏
le 6. Avril .... 1728 .... au ♒	le 11. Mai .... aux ♎
le 14. Décembre .... 1728 ..... au ♑	le 30. Juin .... au ♏
le 19. Décembre ..... 1729. ut supra. au ♒	le 31. Août .... au ♐
	le 15. Octobre .... au ♑
Cours Propre de JUPITER en 12. Ans.	le 25. Novembre .... au ♒
LE 27. Novembre ... 1699. il Etait au ♐	le 2. Janvier ..... en . 1706. ut supra. ♓
le 19. Décembre en .... 1700 ...... au ♑	
le 6. Janvier en .... 1702 .... au ♒	**Cours Propre Du SOLEIL en un An**
le 18. Janvier en .... 1703 ..... aux ♓	LE 1er Janvier le Soleil Est au signe du ♑
le 6. Juin en .... 1704 .... au ♈	le 20. Janvier, il entre au signe . du ♒
le 20. Septembre en . 1704 ..... aux ♓	le 19. Février, il entre au signe ... des ♓
le 23. Janvier .. en .. 1705 .... au ♈	le 21. Mars, il entre au signe ... du ♈
le 5. Juin ..... en .. 1705 ...... au ♉	le 21. Avril, il entre au signe .. du ♉
le 14. Juin ..... en ... 1706 ..... aux ♊	le 21. Mai, il entre au signe ..... des ♊

le 22. Juin le soleil entre au signe de l'écrevice ♋	le 5. Octobre Vénus Etait au Scorpion ♏
le 23. Juillet, il entre au signe du Lion ♌	Le 6. Janvier, en suivant ut Supra . au ♐
le 21. Août, il entre au signe de la Vierge ♍	
le 22. Septembre, il entre au signe des Balances ♎	**Cours Propre de MERCURE en un An.**
le 21. Octobre, il entre au Signe du Scorpion ♏	LE 13 Janvier Mercure est au Capricorne ♑
le 20. Novembre, il entre au Signe du Sagittaire ♐	le 9. Février ... il Est au .... ♒
le 22. Décembre, il entre au signe du Capricorne ♑	le 25. Février ...... il Est aux .... ♓
LE 20. Janvier, ut Supra . ♒	le 14. Mars ... il Est au Signe bélier ♈
	le 22. Avril .... il Est au Taureau ...... ♉
Cours Propre de VENUS en un An.	le 4. Mai, il se retrouve au bélier ♈
LE 1er Janvier Vénus Etait au scorpion ♏	& le 13. Mai se trouve au Taureau ♉
le 6. Janvier .... au ♐	le 7. Juin .... aux ♊
le 1. Février .... au ♑	le 13. Juin .... à l'écrevice ♋
le 26. Février ...... au ♒	le 8. Juillet ...... au Lion ♌
le 13. Mars .... au ♓	le 27. Juillet ..... à la Vierge ♍
le 17. Avril .... au ♈	le 29. Août .... au Lion ♌
le 12. Mai .... au ♉	le 10. Septembre .. à la Vierge ♍
le 5. Juin .... au ♊	le 3. Octobre .... aux balances ♎
le 30. Juin .... à l'écrevice ♋	le 20. Octobre .. au Scorpion ♏
Le 24. Juillet ..... au ♌	le 7. Novembre .. au Sagittaire ♐
le 28. Août .... à la Vierge ♍	& le 13. Janvier ut Supra . au ♑
le 11. Septembre ... a la Balance ♎	FIN de la Table du Cours Propre des Planètes.

Figure 16: The Proper and Particular Course of the 7 Planets in the Zodiac.

Steganographia

[187] Table of the Proper and Particular Course, from West to East of the Seven Planets in the Signs of the Zodiac

	The Proper Course of Saturn in 30 Years		
19 December	1699	it was in	♒[1]
18 March	1701	it was in	♓
30 September	1701	it was in	♒
7 December	1701	it was in	♓
19 June	1703	it was in	♈
13 August	1703	it was in	♓
25 February	1704	it was in	♈
22 April	1706	it was in	♉
End of December	1708	it was in	♊
9 June	1711	it was in	♋
20 July	1713	it was in	♌
3 September	1715	it was in	♍
1 November	1717	it was in	♎
4 April	1718	it was in	♎
10 October	1720	it was in	♏
29 December	1722	it was in	♐
4 June	1723	it was in	♏
30 September	1723	it was in	♐
28 December	1725	it was in	♑
6 April	1728	it was in	♒
14 December	1728	it was in	♑
19 December	1729	above at	♒

---

[1] Note that Saturn wanders backwards and forwards through the signs, as do other planets, changing from Direct to Retrograde.

The Proper Course of Jupiter in 12 Years			
27 November	1699	it was in	♐
19 December	in 1700	it was in	♑
6 January	in 1702	it was in	♒
18 January	in 1703	it was in	♓
6 June	in 1704	it was in	♈
30 September	in 1704	it was in	♓
23 January	in 1705	it was in	♈
5 June	in 1705	it was in	♉
14 June	in 1706	it was in	♊
30 June	in 1707	it was in	♋
1 January	in 1708	it was in	♋
21 July	in 1708	it was in	♌
15 August	in 1709	it was in	♍
1 January	in 1710	it was in	♍
29 September	in 1710	it was in	♎
26 October	in 1711	it was in	♏
27 November	in 1712	above at	♐
The Proper Course of Mars in a two-year period			
2 January	in 1704	it was in	♓
11 February		it was in	♈
23 March		it was in	♉
4 May		it was in	♊
17 June		it was in	♋
2 August		it was in	♌
18 September		it was in	♍
5 November		it was in	♎
1 January	in 1705	it was in	☉

27 January		it was in	♏
11 May		it was in	♎
20 June		it was in	♏
31 August		it was in	♐
15 October		it was in	♑
25 November		it was in	♒
2 January	in 1706	as above	♓
The Proper Course of the Sun in one Year			
1 January	The Sun is in the	the Sign of	♑
20 January	it enters	at the Sign of	♒
19 February	it enters	at the Sign of	♓
21 March	it enters	at the Sign of	♈
21 April	it enters	at the Sign of	♉
21 May	it enters	at the Sign of	♊
[188] 22 June	it enters	at the Sign of	♋
23 July	it enters	at the Sign of	♌
21 August	it enters	at the Sign of	♍
22 September	it enters	at the Sign of	♎
21 October	it enters	at the Sign of	♏
20 November	it enters	at the Sign of	♐
22 December	it enters	at the Sign of	♑
20 January		as above in	♒
The Proper Course of Venus in a Year			
1 January	Venus is in		♏
6 January	Venus is in		♐
1 February	Venus is in		♑
26 February	Venus is in		♒
13 March	Venus is in		♓

Steganographia

17 April	Venus is in		♈
12 May	Venus is in		♉
5 June	Venus is in		♊
30 June	Venus is in		♋
24 July	Venus is in		♌
28 August	Venus is in		♍
11 September	Venus is in		♎
5 October	Venus is in		♏
6 January	[Venus] is	following above	♐
The Proper Course of Mercury in a Year			
13 January	Mercury is in	Capricorn	♑
9 February	he is in		♒
25 February	he is in		♓
14 March	he is in	the Sign of Aries	♈
22 April	he is in	Taurus	♉
4 May	he returns to	Aries	♈
& 13 May	he finds	Taurus	♉
7 June		to	♊
13 June		at Cancer	♋
8 July		at Leo	♌
27 July		at Vergo	♍
29 August		at leo	♌
10 September		at Virgo	♍
3 October		at Libra	♎
20 October		at Scorpio	♏
7 November		at Sagitarius	♐
& 13 January		above at	♑
End of the Table of the Proper Course of the Planets			

Table 67: The Proper and Particular Course of the Seven Planets in the Zodiac.

[THE SHEMHAMMAPHORESHIM]

Figure 17: The Ark of the Covenant guarded by two Cherubim.
Done on September 20, 1787, in Paris.[1]

---

[1] This acts as an introductory image of the Ark of the Covenant designed to indicate the Biblical origin of the Shemhammaphoresh.

[189] The SHEMHAMMAPHORASH [OF SOLOMON][1]

> The next book is by Solomon, in which is contained the name of God whom Adam and Moses called Shemhammaphorash, with whom Abraham and Solomon operated and did whatever pleased them.

Solomon son of David, King of Jerusalem, Egypt, Syria and Macedonia, Prince of Babylon,[2] curious about the secret sciences, a lover of the virtues and the knowledge of the most sublime mysteries, the most profound that can be found in the words.[3] He recognised that all the virtues together, the effects, consisted entirely in the words, from which proceeded the great and admirable works of the prophets, which they wished to divide into various books, so that the memory of them might remain eternal.

Hence King Solomon, studied for a long time the virtuous sciences and their miraculous effects, discovered all these virtues and the means of accomplishing all of them he wished for, by this power. He saw many other books in which applying his study he found that Adam, Jeremiah, Noah, Moses, and many other wise men who were secret masters, had made a great mystery about revealing their secrets, one day they were conversing with the most learned people of his time.

One of the elders of great memory and excellent spirit whose name was Cabramael, answered and said to Solomon: "Adam had a Master, and his Master was Rasiel;"[4] and after Solomon had spoken, it was known that it was not possible to achieve what he aspired to, without having a master, on which Cabramael said to him:

> "Do you think [190] to arrive at your goal, to desire without any master, read many books of the ancient sages, and there you will meet a wise, prudent and discreet master, who will be very necessary to you, and when you have read, reread, contemplated and meditated very seriously in your mind, you will have intelligence and long-lasting health, without being troubled or modified."

Solomon responded to Cabramael: "I know now that you are a wise man; consider how the King could know and acquire knowledge of all these things in a short time."

---

[1] The Shemhammaphorash is a list of angels drawn from three verses in Exodus. The full list of these may be found in Tables A23 - A25 of Skinner, *The Complete Magician's Tables*, Singapore: Golden Hoard, 2006. This word is spelt in a number of different ways throughout this book, which have been here standardised as 'Shemhammaphorash.' Modern usage separates the Hebrew words Shem ha-Mephorash, which is sometimes translated as "the explicit Name" (of God), *shem* being Hebrew for 'name,' and *ha* being the definite article. It is *not* the name of a prophet, but a formula that evolved into the names of 72 angels.
[2] Here the author has confused Solomon with Alexander the Great, who did indeed conquer these countries.
[3] More specifically in the invocations.
[4] *Note in the manuscript*: Rasiel was the Angel God gave to Adam.

Cabramael replied, "I want you to know that the truest and shortest way that could be found, was by means of prayers and oraisons," and then he went on to say:

> "One thing you must do: you must open the Ark, but let it be done so secretly that no one can hear or see it, in which are inserted all the virtues and secrets of the ancient Patriarchs and the words of great virtues and powers, by which are given to know not only things past but also things to come."

Solomon replied:

> "Since you have instructed me so well, I give thanks to the most High God, the Creator who reigns from all eternity without beginning, and who lives without end."

And believing the words of the sages, he called the Ark of the Testament before him, in it were found all the Books of Moses, those of Noah, of Jeremiah and the other Prophets, and all that Solomon had sought for so long, among which he found a book with the title Rasiel, which God gave as an Angel to Adam after he was driven out of the Earthly Paradise, or another book with the title Prophet's Shemhammaphorash, which God gave to Adam in the Earthly Paradise [191] and yet another that God gave to Moses on Mount Sinai, when he was struggling to complete the Ternary (a suitable term).[1]

Then Solomon said:

> "I found in the Ark the Rod of Moses, which changed into a serpent and back again, from serpent to rod; I also found three Tables,[2] which Moses had broken because of the idolatry of the people, who were full of sin and iniquity."

At the bottom of the Ark he found a square table, in which were set fourteen[3] precious stones in a golden table, which were compared to the twelve Tribes of Israel, and in the middle one was written and engraved the name of the Most High and Holy Creator. The aforementioned Tables and Books were named Shemhammaphorash, as were the other treatises.

I also found a rather small chest of marble the colour of jasper fading to green, this small chest was painted with twelve figures, and in each figure was written the Seven Names of great virtue of the Creator that he gave to Moses and seven other names that God the Creator gave to Adam in the terrestrial Paradise. These Names must be carefully guarded and hidden in secret, and in the four corners of the Ark, I found twenty-four Rings in which were engraved the virtuous names of God, figured in various colours representing the name of Shemhammaphorash, with its

---

[1] As Trithemius remarked to Ganay, to achieve a perfect understanding of the Emerald Tablet, "the ternary must be completely reduced to unity, for although unity is not a number, every number arises out of it."

[2] It is conventionally thought to be two Tablets.

[3] It should, of course, be 12 precious stones.

figures. And I, Solomon, took a ring, and was astonished to see how it had such virtue and power, for when I said, "Let it rain," it rained, and when I said, "Let it cease to rain," it ceased.

Here begins the SHEMHAMMAPHORASH
His Experiments and how to proceed with them

Solomon said:

> "I found or rediscovered the Shemhammaphorash [192] by means of which Moses stirred up the storms, that divided the Red Sea, that converted the rocks into a spring of water, that he was able to know the secrets of his people, with which he overcame the Kings and Princes who opposed him, and that he did everything he wanted. Shemhammaphorash is a name that Angels and Demons fear, as do winds and men, both living and dead, and all Spirits. Shemhammaphorash is thus named the great pure and ancient[1] secret, and the name of great virtue, which must not be manifested or revealed openly to all, and no one must undertake to operate by means of it, except in great necessity, with fear of God the Creator, with humility and reverence. Shemhammaphorash is the queen and the principle of honesty, the example of a pure, good and honest life, that is, of a man who fears God and his creatures."[2]

Teaching for those who want to Operate[3]

Solomon says:

> "Let him who would operate and put into practice the virtues of Shemhammaphorash, have in himself humility, truth in his words, patience, faith, abstinence, chastity, mercy, and be free from all vice in his body, fearing God, and revering the things He has created, namely the seven planets, from which we receive all good and evil."

Solomon says again:

> "By the hours and by the signs I have consequently recognised and discovered the good and the evil, and I give the proof by the hours of the day of Mars and Saturn, and that he recognised that they were unfortunate, because on the contrary he proved that the hours of the days of Jupiter and Venus are blessed and favourable.

First Consideration

If you wish to Operate, you must consider on which day of the week you wish to operate, for if it is on the day of Sunday, you must choose the first hour which is

---

[1] In the manuscript '*Antren.*'
[2] Christianity lays a lot of stress upon the fear of god.
[3] *Manuscript note:* The virtues that are needed by the operator.

called the hour of the Sun, and this hour begins at the moment of the rising Sun, because Sunday is [193] the first day of the week, and for this purpose you will call upon the Angels of the 4th Heaven, of the four parts of the world, not especially the seven names of the Angels who are in power, among others over the seven colours and the seven words; and if you operate on this day, consider well what has been said. If you wish to operate on the second day, which is that of the Moon [Monday], you will call upon the Angels of the 1st Heaven. If you wish to operate on Tuesday, you should call upon the Angels of the 5th Heaven. If it is Wednesday, you should call on the Angels of the 2nd Heaven; and so on with the other days. You will call the others according to the order of the planets, observing exactly the rules and principles of the Art.

Here begins the order of Operations

First, having prostrated yourself on your knees, you will name the 7 Angels whom you will call from the Seven Heavens and the Seven Planets in the following manner:[1]

> "Capziel, Sapquiel, Samael, Raphael, Denael, Michael, Gabriel, O aforementioned Angels be my help and aid in my Request and in what I intend to operate."

Names of the 7 Heavens

Samayn, Raquio, Sachaquin, Maben, Cebul, Sirabosh, Crature:[2]

The Order of planets can be taken as follows:

---

[1] *Note in the manuscript:* For the nomination of the 7 Angels of the 7 Planets, see the previous manuscript page 127.
[2] The 7 heavens are usually expressed as Araboth, Makon, Ma'on, Zebul, Schechaqim, Raqia and Shamayin.

♄	Sabaday[1]	Is the name of Saturn. It is the highest planet of all. Through it come unfortunate changes on Earth, and all kinds of misfortune. Its day is Saturday, and below it is Zedé or [Zadoch].
♃	Zadoch[2]	Is that of Jupiter. Through this planet we have abundance and justice on Earth. Its day is Thursday, below it is Madin.
♂	Madin[3]	Is the name attributed to Mars. Its day is Tuesday.
☉	Ame[4]	Is the name of the Sun. Its day is Sunday.
♀	Noage[5]	Is the name of Venus. Its day is Friday.
☿	[194] Lucap[e][6]	Is the name Mercury. [Its day is Wednesday.]
☽	Diane[7]	It is the name of the Moon, the planet closest to Earth. It influences all things down here, such as animals, minerals and plants. Its day is Monday.

Table 68: The Order of the seven Planetary Heavens.

By means of the said planets and their Aspects, we obtain all the things we can ask of God with a good reason.

Solomon says that it is necessary to know what the good and bad hours are, and what the good and bad Signs are. He declares that he operated in his experiments at the hour of Sabaday and Madin, and found them very difficult. Then he made his experiments at the hour of Zadoch and Noage, at which he found all that he wished with great ease.

> "I found it," he says, "and tested it in the hour of Lucape [Moon], in which I found it sometimes good and sometimes bad. But when it came to Ame [Sun], I could not go any further. I give, he says, the example of what is Hebrew for Sabaday; means the name Zoïl in Arabic, and in Greek Plenos."

Saturn being the highest planet; its hour is the first of Saturday during which it dominates it as its Lord; this first hour of the day begins at the rising of the Sun but its true rising is when it is by the centre in the Eastern quarter of the Horizon,

---

[1] Shabathai.
[2] Zedek.
[3] Madim.
[4] Shamesh.
[5] Nogah.
[6] Kokab.
[7] Levanah.

at the time of the Equinoxes which form the equal days and night, which will be seen in the Table of Planetary hours shown below, with the explanation and usage for the whole year. The second is dominated by Jupiter, the third by Mars, the fourth by the Sun, the 5th by Venus, the 6th by Mercury, the 7th by the Moon and the 8th by Saturn. And so on in order, for each day of the week.[1]

It should be noted that the astrological hours are unequal, since an hour is not the 12th part of the day. So the diurnal hours are called major, since they increase in Spring and Summer, and the [195] nocturnal are called minor, and on the contrary in Autumn and Winter, with days diminishing, diurnal hours minor, and nocturnal ones major. [When] the Sun is in the opposite points of the Equinoxes, the hours of the day and that of the night are found equal.

Having observed the hours of the planets in any magic experiments you wish, you must also observe the state of the Moon, as explained below.

[Table of Planetary Hours]

♄ ♂ ☽ The hours of ♄ [Saturn] and of ♂ [Mars] and of ☽ [Moon] are excellent for talking to Spirits.

☿ Those of ☿ [Mercury], [are excellent] to discover thefts by means of the Spirits.

The hours of Saturn are appropriate for evoking the souls of the underworld that only died a natural death; and the men of those who would have been killed or caused to die a violent death in the hour of Mars. It is certain that you can make or operate these predictive arts on the proper day, for example to evoke the soul of some deceased person, if you make the experience on the day and hour of ♄ [Saturn], the experience will be better, and it will always be successful if you punctually observe all that is inserted in this part. And if you omit only one of these things you will never be able to achieve it with the Art. And as you wish to have the experience and effect of your operation, you must be attentive to these, because the truth of this Art depends on it.

☉ ♃ ♀ The hours of the ☉ [Sun], of ♃ [Jupiter] and of ♀ [Venus] are fit to prove the experiments for love, grace, requests, and invisibility, as is clearly explained in its place and chapter, having also added what is required in this matter, as well as in the contents of the present book.

♄ & ♂ Likewise, the days and hours of ♄ [Saturn] and ♂ [Mars] in which the ☽ [Moon] is in conjunction, or whether they be seen from her in opposition, are excellent for making experiments of hatred and enmities, trials, vengeance, and discord, having added what is contained [196] in the locations of these different objects.

---

[1] These Planets are in the order of the Tree of Life, and not in the order of the days of the week.

☿ Mercury's hour is to prepare the experiments of laughter and mockery, which appear to us to be admirable and [not] impossible, with the right observance.

☉ ♃ ♀ The hours of the Sun, Jupiter and Venus, are proper to prove the extraordinary experiments which are not contained in any revealed source. These are still more effective in their execution, on the day of each of these planets, by adding what is indicated in each of these experiments.

☽ For the Properties and various effects of the Moon in the Signs. For those things which belong to the Moon, such as the invocation of Spirits, works of necromancy, and the recovery of thefts, for this effect it is necessary that the Moon be in an earthly sign, as are ♉, the ♍, the ♑.

> **Earth** - For hatred, discord, and destruction, [the Moon must be in ♉, ♍, ♑]
>
> **Water** The Moon must be in a water sign such as the ♋, ♏ and ♓.
>
> **Fire** - For love, grace and invisibility, the Moon must be in a fire sign, as ♈, ♌, ♐.
>
> **Air** - For extraordinary experiments that are not constrained to a certain hour, the Moon must be in ♊, ♎, or ♒.

The Effects of the Planets in each of their hours

It should be noted that each magical experiment or operation, must be carried out on the [day of their] planet and in the hour principally which relates to the same [Planet], as for example:

♄ In the days and hour of Saturn, experiments are prepared to call souls from the Underworld, not only from those who have died a natural death as already stated. Likewise, during these days and hours, experiments are also prepared to give good or bad fortune to buildings, to have familiar Spirits in dreams, to cause good or bad success in business, [197] possessions, goods, stables, fruits and the like. To acquire doctrine or theories, to give death and to sow discord.

♃ The days and hours of Jupiter, are for obtaining honours, acquiring wealth, contracting friendships, preserving health, and achieving whatever one desires.

♂ In the days and hours of Mars, one may make experiments touching war, to attain military honours, to acquire bravery and valour, to repel and drive away enemies, and moreover to cause ruin and carnage, cruelty and discords between soldiers, and to wound and give death.

☉ The days and hours of the Sun are very good for perfecting experiences of temporal goods, of hope of gain, of fortune, of divination, for the good grace of Princes, for dissolving enmities, and for making friends.

♀ The days and hours of Venus are for acquiring friendships, recovering benevolence, love, doing happy and pleasant things and for travelling.

☿ The days and hours of Mercury are for doing the operations of the sciences, divination, of eloquence, as also of intelligence, promptitude in business, for prestige, apparitions and for having answers about things to come.

☽ The days and hours of the Moon are for operating the experiments of embassies sent on important business, for travels, navigations, for the reconciliation of love, and for the acquisition of aquatic goods.

♉ One can also operate under the sign of Taurus, touching theft, writings, deceit and all kinds of merchandise. But as these things will perhaps seem to you a little difficult to do and to operate, it will suffice for you only to observe [198] the Moon after Conjunction, but if it is as soon as it emerges from the Sun's rays and begins to appear, then it is well to make all the experiments which tend to trials approaching the construction of something or operations. It is necessary, however, to keep to the operation of one thing. Therefore, at the hour when the Moon is in its crescent until it is full, and when it exists in an even number [of days] from the Sun, it is good to do as said above.

☍ When the Moon is in Opposition to the Sun, and full of Light [i.e. Full Moon], this time is proper for making Experiments concerning war, ruin, discord, and when it is in its course it is good to make all experiments that tend to destruction and ruin. As the Moon moves towards Conjunction with the Sun, it is suitable for experiments for evil, being at this time deprived of light.

♂ Moreover you will inviolably observe not to begin anything when the Moon is in Conjunction with the Sun,[1] for that time is very unfortunate, and you will not be able to achieve the desired effect or any advantage. But for certain, when the Moon is growing, and its Light increases, you may write and prepare such experiments as you please, observing what is necessary to observe.

Moreover, if you wish to speak to the Spirits, it must be especially the day that belongs to Mercury [Wednesday], and the Moon must be in an Air Sign, as has already been said, and be conjoined with the Sun at such a day. See the Table of Direction[2] chart at the head of this Book for what concerns the four Parts of the universe, which are: East, West, South and North.

[199] The Angels of the day of the **Moon** in the first Heaven, which is called Samayn, serving in the four quarters of Heaven.

In the *Northern* Quarter are: Alaff, Unael, Vaalam, Valiel, Valai, Umastayl.

In the 1st Quarter [i.e. *Eastern* Quarter] are namely: Semaniel, Darbiel, Darqueil, Hamum, Hanayel, Betiniel.

The Angels who serve in the *Western* quarter are: Saqueil, Camel, Habayel,

---

[1] The dark Moon.
[2] Figure 5.

Steganographia

Beshanael, Cerabiel.[1]

The Angels of the day of **Mercury** in the 2nd Heaven named Raquio.

The Angels named below serve in the Four Parts of the World, namely:

In the *Northern* quarter are: Tiel, Tael, Venael, Velel, Abino and Beshumel.

Here are those that serve in the *Southern* region: Vel, Pabael, Caluel, Jaquel;

There are only two who serve in the *Eastern* quarter: Siezerays and Metatron.

Those of the *Western* [quarter] are: Magraton, Tamael, Balatron.

The Angels of **Venus** in the 3rd Heaven are for the four Parts of the World, namely

In the *North*: Pomel, Ponalh, Raphael, Bamael and Deremiel.

In the *South* are: Perna, Zadquiel, Chercruel, Stitamael, Samael, Quaphaniel.

In the *West*: Sedquiel, Quadisa, Tatamel, Caniel, Corac, Vanael.

In the *East*: Turiel, Cumel, Babiel, Adriel, Malchiel, Huphalciel.

The Angels of the **Sun** in the 4th heaven serving the four Parts of the World

In the *North*: Sayel, Samel, Veal, Eniel, Magabiel, Saapriel, Matuyel.

In the *South* are the following, namely: Mael, Badiel, Mashasiel, Carsiel, Oriel, Natomiel, Humaliel, Cuiel.

In the *East*: Phansel, Barquiel, Samael, Buaciel, Acelpharbel.

In the *West*: Ruael, Anael, Paluel, Uphlael, Burlat, Succeratus and Cabapaly.

The Angels of **Mars** in the 5th heaven, deputies to serve the four Parts of the World

In the *North*: [200] Ramayel, Ymel, Rachiel, Sirapiel, Mashiel, Sarciel.

In the *South*: Garriel, Yahamel, Guedel, Osuel, Vramiel, Vatustiel.

In the *East*: Tarael, Valaliel, Raguenael, Damel, Calbas, Aelragon.

In the *West*: Lahama, Astagua, Labquin, Sontas, Yayel, Illael, Yrel.

The Angels of **Jupiter**, in the 6th heaven, deputies to serve the four Parts of the World are: Tubal, Sinael and Cebuc.

Say the following from the side of the *North*: "O mighty and powerful God, God without doctrine."

Say the following from the side of the *South*: "O patient merciful God."

---

[1] The Angels of the Southern Quarter are missing

Say the following from the side of the *East*: "To the great God most high and honoured for infinite centuries."

[Say from the side] of the *West*: "O just God, God of clemency, I pray that my request, my work and my labour be accomplished today with Intelligence, you who live and reign for all the Centuries of Centuries. So be it."

The Angels of **Saturn** in the 7th heaven: There is only Shemhammaphorash. None other than him is in the 7th heaven; which is written in the Book of Life.

Oraison

"O God of great virtue, O strong God, O God full and abundant in all grace, blessed be your holy Name, you who give perfection and fulfilment at my request, you who give with largesse to whom it pleases you; be the entire fulfilment of my work, you who are holy and merciful, have mercy on me and may your name Hezerayel be blessed for all eternity. So be it."

Explanation of what is said above in this part:

Firstly, the name Hezerayel is, as it were, God without beginning or end. AGLA is a name of God that the prophets found written on a blade of gold, and whoever bears this divine name with faith shall not die without penance, nor die of sudden death.

[201] Now the names of the Creator, each of four letters, which the prophets found written in precious stones and these holy Names are: Joac, Java, Eloym, Janael. If he wears it engraved on a golden blade or on virgin parchment, which they called Hebrayl, written in letters of gold, he will not die suddenly, nor will he ever lack goods, if he wears it with chastity of his body. Here is another very holy and very high name of God, with and by means of which Joshua stopped the course of the Sun, against nature, as long as it took him to defeat the Gibeonites and throw the 24 kings in disorder and discord. The Angels themselves fear and revere the holy name which is Athionada and these others: Haa, Rashio, Liar *(sic)*. Whoever carries these names written in letters of gold on virgin parchment made of male lambskin, if he is taken prisoner, the prison will not be able to hold him, and it will preserve him from the hands and vengeance of his enemies. The first holy name is Chastet. There is another name that God gave to Moses when he revealed it to him on Mount Sinai which is Ashedron. This name casts out anger and sadness, increases joy and gives all good affections.

In addition to what [we have said] above, it must be known that God the Almighty has chosen from among the holy Angels 12 of the Principals whom he has distributed to the Four Parts of the World, namely 3 to the East, 3 to the South, 3 to the West, and 3 to the North, and these 12 Intelligences make up 12 Orders to which God has given various powers.

[IN THE EAST]

FIRST ORDER[1]

The Intelligence or Prince of the first Order in the quarter of the East is named CHAOR[2] who has his operation and his power on the day of the Sun which is Sunday, it is by him that the beginnings of the birth of children to good or bad [202] end are arranged. He is the Prince of the Celestial Gate on the eastern side, and it is he who distributes his gratuitousness as he pleases to all nascent beings, and by whose power the fecundity of creatures is bound or loosed, as for example to a woman the disposition to conceive, and for trees to bear fruit, or not to bear fruit.

Note: Your Request must be written on virgin parchment prepared according to the Art, taking care not to request anything that does not belong to this Prince of this Order, nor to his Office, but invoking his names which are:

Arivel, Gabriel, Carachiel, Hybel, Heliza, saying

INVOCATION

"I adore the holy Name of God, adorable to all eternity, by which you O Celestial powers and angelic virtues come and obey our Creator. I adjure you, I beg you, and I ask you, by the Holy God, by the True God, by the Living God of all creatures, both visible and invisible, by his Holy and Sacred Name expressed by these four letters: Joth, Beth, Agla, Enaym. Grant the Request I have made to you, and which is of your Office to fulfil, this is what I beg you by the holy and beloved of God, by him chosen and pre-ordained, be present and fulfil my Request. So be it."

THE APPEARANCE OF THE ANGEL

Then the Angel will appear, carrying in his hand a standard with a cross clothed in a cope whiter and brighter than a star, having the form of a very beautiful child, having on his head rose flowers in the form of a crown, so that his star is white and bright with flowers; and this apparition will be in the air.

It must here be observed about the above remark with regard to the virgin parchment, that it is also understood that all depends on it, such as the quill, ink, and all that depends on the Art, which is indicated in our *Clavicles*[3] and H[enry] C[ornelius] Agr[ippa].[4]

[203] SECOND ORDER IN THE EAST

This second Order is called Corona, and the Princes of this Order have power over

---

[1] These Orders also relate to the Almadel, with three Orders allocated to each Cardinal direction.
[2] *Note in the manuscript:* Chaor has its operation on Sunday.
[3] *The Key of Solomon.*
[4] *Three Books of Occult Philosophy.*

Steganographia

all acquisitions of goods. This principal begins with them and the head of this Order has the power to distribute his goods as he pleases, to transfer them into other hands, to give to men as he sees fit, to bring in the revenues, etc.

It is necessary to know that this Order has its operation on the day of the Sun which is Sunday, and the way of operating is similar to the preceding one, it is necessary to be very careful not to ask anything which is not of the Office of this Order, to grant it to you, or that it is against the will of God which could displease him, except only what God grants to men according to the course of Nature.

Observe when doing this operation, it is necessary to call the name of this Order and the name of the Princes who are in it, who are Alpharam, Geon, Gerreon, Armon and Geremon.

Then you invoke them in the aforementioned manner while kneeling, and then they will appear to you as an angel with the others having a rose-coloured garment bearing stars in front and behind with flowers on the head in the form of a crown similar to the colour of country poppies; and as soon as he appears, he will be similar to a very beautiful child of about 3 years of age, having hands and face of a colour tending to red which designates the ardour of a divine love. Then this Prince will begin to speak, and turning to the operator with a friendly look, he will say to him:

D[emand:] "What do you ask of me and for what subject do you call yourselves Princes of my Order?"

R: Response of the Operator: "It is so that my Request may be granted which depends on your Office and vocation."

The angel replies: "It will be done according to your wishes."

It is important to know that this celestial Spirit, which appears in the form of a child [204] and the other Princes of the same Order, are entirely amicable.

The angel said to the operator. "What can I do for you?"

The operator must not be troubled, being armed with courage and faith. Let him ask for the fulfilment of his prayer, according to their Office, and he will obtain it. And when the Angel withdraws, he usually says to the operator: "I am your friend."

You must also know that there are many Princes in this same Order; but that only one ever appears, because at the time of their domination, they are separated from each other, and each of them has his domination [only] for 30 days of the year, and that at the moment of your invocation, only the one who is dominant will be able to appear to you.

Now therefore it must be observed that no Order or Prince is to be called, except in the time of its dominion, in the [relevant] Parts of the World, and this sign is given accordingly to the 12 Celestial signs, which have a correspondence with the 12 Orders; in such a way that the first Order must be called when it is in its dominion, which begins at the entrance of the first Sign at which the Sun dwells at that time, so that when the Sun leaves this Sign and enters another. It is also necessary to call and address another Order, and so on; and consequently during 12 months, one will be able to see the 12 Orders.

In addition to this name of the Living God fixed in the substance of heaven in the form of a character, we must also know that in accordance with the 12 Orders, there are also 12 Names of God that fully express all the essence of the divinity, which are things hidden from evil Spirits or demons.

THIRD ORDER IN THE EAST

This Third Order is called HERMON, and the Princes of this [205] Order have power over friends, brothers, relatives, neighbours, and over the movement of all waters, waters of the sea, that of all rivers, and over the changes of all things from place to place, and over the movement of the Elements, in generation and corruption, and over the celestial movement, namely that of Heaven, of the Stars and their Rays, and especially that which moves with a local movement, and finally preventing, or making things happen as they please.

The Princes of this Order are:

Yathanael, Coynyel, Prymaton, Yashanayel, Helen *(sic)*, and Enshytey.

As soon as the operator has made his Request, the angel will appear and begin to speak, being in the form of a soldier, adorned and of very pure gold, his flesh similar, will seem to you to throw rays the same as gold does, with which he will speak and show the operator great gentleness and friendship, asking him with extraordinary eloquence: "What do you ask of me?"

At the same time, he will communicate freely to the operator with such great [virtue] that throughout his life he will have the power to compel any man whatsoever to love him, moreover he will also receive enlightenment and quite astonishing clarity of mind.

But you must know that this admirable secret is depicted in the *Notory Art* of Solomon;[1] and it is hidden among all wise, prudent and discreet men. It is a most precious secret that is above all the human sciences, the secret Queen of all the encyclopaedic Arts. And a Treasure that is sure and unmistakable and incomparable.

[IN THE SOUTH]

FOURTH ORDER

This Fourth Order is called PARTHEON, and the Princes who are of this Order

---

[1] See Stephen Skinner & Daniel Clark, *Ars Notoria*, Singapore: Golden Hoard, 2019.

have power over all treasures and estates; therefore this fourth Order has been placed in the Southern quarter [206] of Heaven, which by certain natural dignities given to it by the Holy Spirit has the power to infuse the Arts into the minds of men, but principally the arts of rhetoric and grammar.

It is therefore necessary for the operator to make his invocation, which being done, the Celestial Intelligence will appear in azure colour, and will address the operator with a very gentle word, and he will obtain all the things outlined in his Request.

The names of the Princes of this Order are Yrath, Yaram, Armelh, Zaremy, Lux, and Ehiel.

Instruction in the various objects that must be known in order to achieve the accomplishment of the Art.

Firstly it must be known that all these three Orders in Mars and their hours. It must also be known that both the Eastern Orders, and those three which are Southern, must begin from the first day of the Moon, until the 15th [day]. And that the Western and Northern Orders are from the 15th [day] until the end of the Moon, and that as soon as the operator's Request has been granted, the angel withdraws. It is also necessary to know that no Order should be called, except on a clear and serene day and time; and all the time the Eastern and Southern Orders, should be called from the first hour of the day, until noon. And the Western and Northern Orders, from noon, until the end of the day.

FIFTH ORDER

This fifth Order is called EYAM or HEYNY. And the Princes of this Order have of their Office in their power, the movement of the first Heaven or first Mobile, as also to move all animals, each according to its nature and species, to generation to multiply, as also the fish and birds, which all regulate the movements, and by a gift of God, they have the power [207] to infuse the natural sciences, such as physics, medicine and chemistry, in all their parts.

Here are the names of the Princes of this Order:

Altray, Ezei, Zabel, Monoyn, Aurash, and Boulay.

If anyone wishes to operate through the ministry of the Princes of this Order, he must make an Almadel of green wax, and say thrice the names of the Princes of this Order with the invocation, and the celestial Intelligence will appear to him dressed in a very green colour, having flowers on his head, then having made the fumigation under the Almadel, the Angel will say amicably and with an affable air to the operator:

D[emand]. "What do you ask?"

R[esponse]. Then the operator will answer with humility; "May it please your dignity to grant me what is exposed on the holy Almadel."[1]

And immediately the angel will grant his Request.

The operator may also ask for something else, such as to be recommended to God by him, which will be done immediately, and immediately afterwards he will withdraw, leaving an odour like musk.

SIXTH ORDER

This sixth Order is called MEHYM, and the Princes of this Order by God's command have each their Office, and their power is over the state of all the world stirring, moving, exchanging monarchies, empires and all the principalities of the world, from region to region, by a celestial movement and ordination, distinguishing masters and lords, with servants, and filling them with virtues and morals of the most illustrious, reducing subjects under the power of their masters or lords, to change as they will servants into masters and masters into servants; they rule the demons and subdue them and defend men from their illusions, they have [208] the power to infuse [them with] three sciences, namely music, logic and philosophy. The names of the Princes are thus:

Horos, Visseros, Onay, Ornelh, Yaresh, Alay.

He who wishes to operate with this Order must make an Almadel of violet wax, and govern himself in the same manner as in the other Orders; this being done, let him name the Princes of this Order and say his Invocation, and shortly afterwards the Angel will appear on the Almadel in the form of a Seraph having six intermingled wings of various beautiful colours. Then the operator will make his fumigation as already said, above on the Almadel, with incense and mastic. Then the Angel will speak and give the operator what he asks for, then withdrawing he will leave a great odour in the air as if it were balsam or cinnamon.

[IN THE WEST]

SEVENTH ORDER

This Order is called GOFFOR. It is the first Order on the Western side and the Princes of this Order have power over the friendships and enmities of all creatures, over wars, battles, disputes, and outrages especially over armies. They may cause arms to be borne in all parts of the world, and nothing good or evil can happen without their ordination or permission; they have by a gift of God the power to infuse the minds of men with astrology, geometry and arithmetic. The Princes [of this Order] are named as follows:

Ay, Albayn, Roel, Albanay, Ratan, Corozay.

If anyone wishes to operate by means of this Order, he must make a holy Almadel

---

[1] This is where the written Request has been placed.

with columbine wax,[1] the candles and candlesticks likewise, as prescribed, and after calling the Angels and Princes of this Order, the Angel will appear with a [209] splendid, pleasing face with fringes on her thigh, holding a sceptre. Then the operator must fumigate with *thimiame*[2] and incense under the Almadel.[3] And then the Angel will appear and speak to the operator and grant him his request, as far as it is within his power and Office. And when the Angel retires, he leaves a great and sweet odour, like that of lilies and laurels.

EIGHTH ORDER

This Order is called EROY, and the Princes of this Order have power over all kinds of pacts and agreements that are made between creatures, that force them under rigorous penalties to observe the agreements made with men, and those of men with the demons, and permit or punish one or the other, or both together, and as it pleases them by God's command they have power over souls, they govern them and direct them to a good end. They are arbiters of the life and death of all creatures, and by an effect of their dignity, they have the power to infuse [in their minds] Theology, Geometry, and Metaphysics. Here are the names of the Princes of this Order:

Amayn, Anay, Gelomissus, Gedobany, Isaramana, Eloumish.

If the operator wishes to operate by this Order, he must make the Almadel as prescribed, of white wax, and the candles and candlesticks likewise. Having called the Princes of this Order and furnished his Request on the Almadel, the Angel will appear in the form of a white dove, having made the fumigation with frankincense and mastic, the dove will be seen wearing on its head a crown of twelve precious stones, and having in its mouth eleven sub-servants,[4] a sign of the cross entwined with a golden thread, and having asked the operator what his Request is, the Angel will grant him his Request, and on his departure he will leave in the air a strong, sweet and very pleasant odour, like that of lily and balm.

[210] NINTH ORDER

This Order is called SAPHERON or SAPHOR and the Names of the Princes who reign there are as follows:

Zaan, Zabut, Zadanay, Arphel, Alxhancy, Zadam.

They have power over the generation of animals, and the mixing of the Elements, they carry men from religion to religion, swiftly, and have dominion over all kinds of movements. If you wish to operate through the ministry of the Princes of this

---

[1] Multicoloured.
[2] Rx: *Thimiama*: cozumber – 3, aloeswood, ambergris – 3 denarii, confita, camphor, musk – 1 denarius.
[3] The Almadel consists of a wax layer punctuated by holes, with the incense burner below it.
[4] *Sou-bec*.

Order, you must make the Almadel of green wax and lucid [clear] wax in equal parts, and the candles and candlesticks in the same way. Fumigation must be done with musk, saffron and frankincense. And the Angel will appear in the form of an eagle of a Celestial colour, and he will grant the operator what he desires.

[IN THE NORTH]

TENTH ORDER

This Order is called RAZAN, and the Princes of this Order are called:

Antypin, Anab, Beyt, Salut, Patience *(sic)*.

And by an effect of the dignity with which God has established them, they have power over the temporal dignities, those of the natural Spirit and the virtues which God had given to Adam in the state of innocence which he still gave to human nature at the time of the passion of Jesus Christ our Saviour, and some others [which] human senses have never known how to understand, and will never understand. This Order is attributed to the beginning of the North quarter. And if anyone wishes to operate by the ministry of the Princes of this Order, the Almadel and fumigation must be made, and the Angel will appear in the form of a lamb with various red marks and will grant the operator all that he desires.

ELEVENTH ORDER

This Order is called ZARVISH or ZARVIESH.

The names of the Princes of this eleventh Order are as follows:

[211] Alphanes, Alphanay, Azer, Surnesh, Almeos, Saphrayn.

You must make the Almadel of cinnamon-coloured wax, being in a pure and clean place and separated from all garbage, after you have made and recited the Invocation and you have placed the Request on the Almadel. The Angel will appear to you in the form of a young man carrying before him a standard marked with a cross, and according to his Office he exercises the judgments of God over men, according to the pulpit or the world, he makes the man of good spirit, and if he is questioned on some articles of piety as on the Incarnation of Jesus Christ, he will declare to you the mystery of it, which is hidden from all the rest of men.

TWELFTH ORDER

This twelfth and final Order is called ELIZAY, and the Princes of this Order are named as follows:

Salushiel, Alymos, Alibyn, Lubirael, Ana or Anay.

The Almadel must be made of white wax added to green and red, in equal parts. Make the invocation, place it on the Almadel and fumigate it, after which the Angel will appear to the operator. It should be noted that the Princes of this Order are very high in dignity, being of the hierarchy of the Dominations; they hold

Lucifer in a chain and violently compel all Spirits to observe God's orders and commandments if they are called upon to do so, they govern God's elect and preserve them from evil Spirits, the demons fear them greatly because they are tormented by them every day. On Judgement Day, these Princes will call together all the Nations of the Four Parts of the Earth, and the principal Angel of this Order will appear in the form of a soldier, holding an olive branch in his hand.

[212] ADJURATION

"O Princes who are constituted in this Order and chosen by God, I adjure you and beg you by the name of SADAY, of the Living God, by that of Helezon[1] and by that of Athanatos, by that of Esquiros[2] whether it pleases you or happy angel Prince and advised by that of Adonay to have pity on this very humble creature, to review my prayer, to accept it, to grant me a happy success."

Note: It must be observed that in all the operations, and any Order prescribed above, an Almadel must be made of wax of the colour prescribed for each Order.

---

[1] Eleison
[2] Ischyros.

Steganographia

[THE ALMADEL]

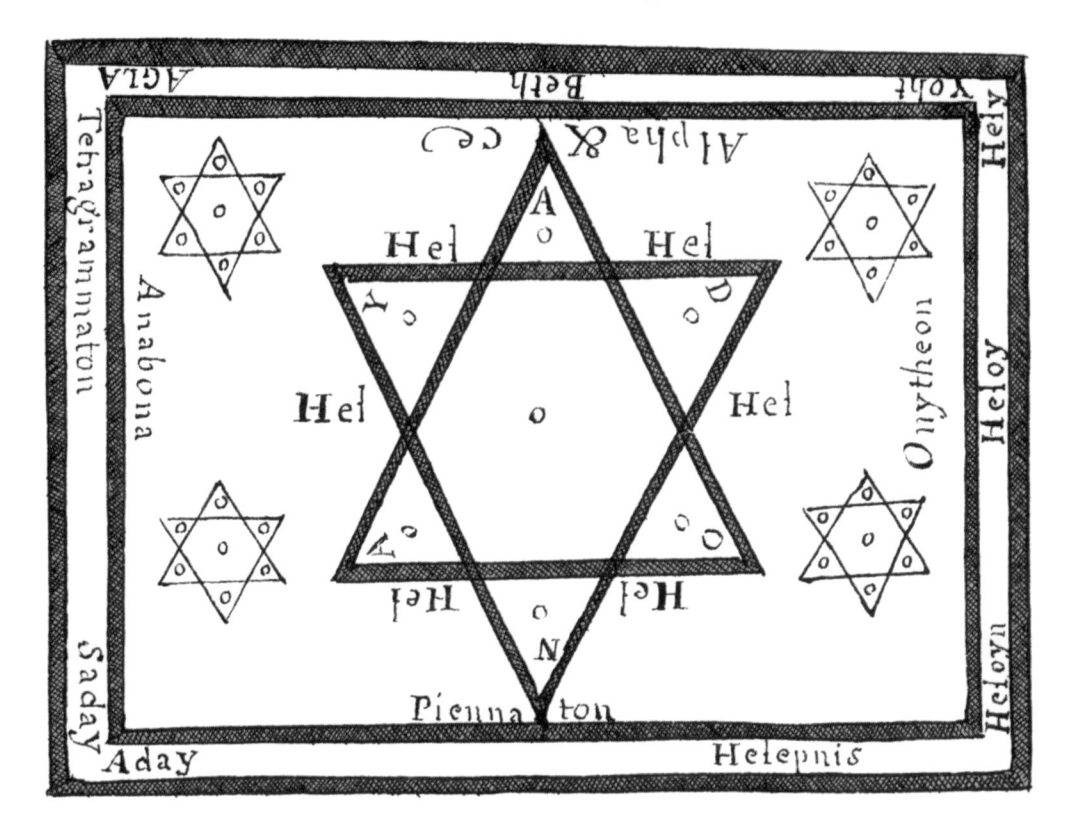

Figure 18: Figure of the Holy and Precious Almadel.[1]

[213] The Almadel is a small wax tablet half a foot square, two *écus*[2] thick or so, which must be pierced with as many holes as there are angles that meet in the figures, which holes are represented by as many o's as you see in the figure above.[3]

CANDLESTICKS AND THE CANDLESTICK HOLE

You need to know that you need four candlesticks made of wax, but so skilfully that two parts are above the height of the Almadel, and the third part is underneath, so that there are a few ledges in each candlestick, corresponding from one to the other in equal proportion to be able to place Solomon's Holy Almadel on it.

The four candles must be made of the same wax. At the top of the candlestick, there must be a hole to hold the candle.

---

[1] Note the small circles which are meant to represent holes, which allow for the passage of incense from the burner located below the Almadel. See manuscript page 214.
[2] A common French coin bearing the coat of arms of France. The Almadel would therefore have been approximately two millimetres thick.
[3] Figure 18.

OF THE SEAL AND HANDWRITING
To Form the Demand

Care must be taken not to light any of the Candles, except positively at the time of making the Request, and when the Almadel is made and composed, a seal must be made on it in which will be engraved in reverse the names Heloyn, Adonay, as can be seen in the figure, with a needle of silver or pure gold, and at the time of the operation, put your Request on the Almadel, in a clean place and separated from all dirt and garbage. Light the candles and invoke the names of the Angels of the first Order, who are:

Arivel, Gabriel, Carachyel or Barachiel, Hybel or Libes, Heliza.

Say now the invocation on [manuscript] page 202: "I adore the holy Name, etc."

[214] OF ASHES

The operator must have a well-polished earthenware vase into which he will place hot ashes; But it must not be too hot lest they melt the wax, and [he should] place this vase under the Almadel, put in its ashes four grains of mastic so that the odour and smoke pass [through] the small holes of the Almadel and can rise into the air, in front of the Angel descending from heaven who will appear to you and satisfy your Request. The operator must be dressed in the same colour as the Almadel, the candlesticks and the candles.[1]

End [of the Almadel]

---
[1] These colours of the wax candlesticks and the Almadel itself change according to the season.

THE FOUR REGIONS OF THE FOUR ELEMENTS

Region of FIRE	That of AIR	That of WATER	That of EARTH
Emperor is Gargatel	Raphael, Prin[ce]	Gabriel, Gra[nd] Pri[nce]	Tarquael, Emper[or]
It is Camael or Michael	Honey, Prince	Samael, Prince	Anael
Tariel, Prince	Seraphiel, Prin[ce]	Madiel, Prince	Uriel, Gr[and] Pri[nce]
Tubiel, Prince	-	Mael, Prince	Cassiel, Prince
Gaviel, Prince	-	-	Sachiel, Prince
Ruel [Prince]	-	-	Asasiel, Prince

Table 69: The Four Elements and their presiding Angels who preside over them.

♈	♉	♊	♋
Mulchidiel	Asmodel	Ambriel	Muriel
♌	♍	♎	♏
Verchel	Hamatiel	Zuriel	Barbiel
♐	♑	♒	♓
Adnachiel	Humiel	Gabriel	Barchiel
Fire signs	**Earth Signs**	**Air Signs**	**Water Signs**

Table 70: Twelve Signs of the Zodiac, with their Angels or Intelligences who presides over and govern them.

Steganographia

[215] THE SHEMHAMMAPHORASH OF ADAM

How the SHEMHAMMAPHORASH of Adam works

Anyone wishing to begin the operation must name the names of the Angels of the seven celestial planets, then the week, day, metal, colour and their characters. These are reported above on [manuscript] pages 127 and 193.

	Names of days	Planets	Colours	Names of Angels	Responding to Metals	To Planets
1	Sunday	Sun	Yellow	Raphael	Gold	☉
2	Monday	Moon	White	Gabriel	Silver	☽
3	Tuesday	Mars	Red	Samael	Iron	♂
4	Wednesday	Mercury	Grey	Michael	Quicksilver	☿
5	Thursday	Jupiter	Black[1]	Sanqueil or Sachiel	Tin	♃
6	Friday	Venus	Green	Anael	Copper	♀
7	Saturday	Saturn	Black	Capriel	Lead	♄

Table 71: Days, colours, angels and metals of each Planet.

Do not forget to invoke the Angel who governs France, ASCHEL.[2] These Angels should be invoked individually or in general.

FIRST CONJURATION

"ISTI Angeli adjurotes mei in mea petitione quam volo petere[3] O Raphael, Gabriel, aid my Request."

Names of the Angels serving in Heaven, who are the true Ministers [216] of the planets and Parts of the World:

Samaïer, Raquia, Saaquius, Mahon, Zebal, Arboé.[4]

When you wish the Elements to do your will, you should pronounce these names

---

[1] Should be blue, as black more correctly corresponds to Saturn.
[2] That should be adjusted for the country you are invoking in, if it is not France.
[3] "These angels are my advocates in my petition for what I wish to request."
[4] These are a slightly corrupt version of the Hebrew names of the Heavens.

to the Four Parts of the World:

1st. In the First Heaven in the East are: Gabriel, Gabroel, Adrael, Madiel, Madiael, Ramiael, Donael.

In the Second Heaven in the West are: Alfon, Sachiel, Zaniel, Hurosel, Batavael, Lerpalier.

In the Third Heaven in the South are: Duramel, Drabiel, Baminq, Anael, Mihumel.

In the Fourth Heaven in the North are: Elael, Vealier, Vealdin, Dael, Dalus, Urias, Thay.

2nd. In the Second Heaven in the East are: Cumiel, Mathein, Bethobaat, Ouvet, Sabriat.

In the West are: Gestas or Yestas, Raye, Initraton.

In the South are: Colbiel, Liel, Braterel, Inissia, Nelia, Balier.

In the North [are]: Yereel, Yrael or Yraeel, Jomael, Numael, Beaeiel or Beameil, Zyany.

3rd. In the Third Heaven in the East are: Sangel, Qudissy, Traumel, Trariel, Tapael, Amael.

In the West [are]: Amiel, Turiel, Rabiel, Stadiel, Molus, Hufaltuel.

In the South are: Prava, Sadiel, Hemel, Fatamel, Samael, Samuel.

In the North are: Reamiel, Penech, Raphael, Ramiel, Deramiel.

4th. In the Fourth Heaven in the East are: Damael, Trabiel, Bauliel, Tagaguel, Talichas, Atragon.

In the West are: Lacave, Assagua, Lapara, Sohermeas, Ybael, Yastiel, Yyel.

In South are: Sariel, Maamiel, Hadiel, Hosael, Vaanel, Vecartiel.

In the North are: Bachimeel, Haymniel, Bachiel, Seraphiel, Mathiel, Lerael.

5th. In the Fifth Heaven in the East are: Saniciel, Tacquel, Santiel, Raaciel, Ariel, Scarbiel, Monatrabae[l].

In the West are: Atael, Pabel, Uflael, Droat, Sinitater, Tupa.

In the South are: Aael, Badiel, Naffiel, Tartiel, Ariel, Noromiel, Hamalquiel.

In the North are: Hayel, Ariel, Vaaquel, Morgabriel, Sarpiel, Moniel.

6th. In the Sixth Heaven in the East, the following Oraison must be said:

"Great God who deserves to be worshipped by all and in all ages, I pray thee by thy Holiness and by thy power, that [thou] will presently grant me my Request, and perfect my work, through thee who liveth and reigneth everywhere for all the Centuries of Centuries. Amen."

At the West say the following:

"God, knowing, clear, and just, I pray to you in your holiness and by your power that you will presently perfect my request and my work through you who lives and reigns for all the Centuries of Centuries. Amen."

At the South, we will say the following:

"Holy and knowing and full of mercy I pray to you by your holiness and by your power, that you may want presently [217] to perfect my request and my work, you who live and reign everywhere for the Centuries of Centuries. Amen."

And at North, we say the following Oraison:

"Strong and Mighty God without end, I pray to you by your Holiness and power, that you may want me at present to perfect my Request and my work, you who live and reign through all the Centuries of Centuries. Amen.

Here is the way to use the
SHEMHAMMAPHORASH
OF THE FIGURE

The next table is the Shemhammaphorash,[1] where are the greatest names of God, and in the middle of the table is the greatest name, the four letters: and at the 4 angles are the four Names of the Creator explained. At the sides are the four Names of the Angels by which the Four Parts of the World are governed and at the angles of the side inside close to the name of God, are the four Names and in each is contained two letters. It should be noted that each angle has a name.

When it is time to operate, this table should be made with eyes raised to heaven, and God should be prayed to with the table lowered in the middle and at the four angles. This figure must be perfumed with good odours and anointed with virgin oil. It must be made as cleanly and quickly as possible. This table and figure will be made on virgin parchment made from young deer skin, with Instruments made according to the Principles of the Art.

[219] The Hebrew, Greek, Arabic and Latin letters are [represented by] A B C.[2]

---

[1] See Figure 18 which shows the wax Almadel, which will be supported by 4 candles. The author has confused the Almadel with the Table of Practice (Figure 19).

[2] i.e. the full alphabet of these four languages should be written on the sides of the Figure, one language per side.

They are written around the Figure of the Table as it will be represented hereafter in the said figure, and you will do the same in the upper part of the table where it is written. And you will write A B C in Greek [letters] where it is written Eloy. You will write A B C in Arabic. And above in the right part, A B C in Latin. On the left, where "alla"[1] is written, you will write A B C in Hebrew [letters].

So here is the Shemhammaphorash called Alego *(sic)*.

If you do not have this precious book with you when you find yourself in some peril and besieged or surprised by your enemies, you should at least have these four words written on virgin parchment: Leffar, Dagy, El, Cesegat. Then throw it [the words] towards heaven seven times during the day and once at night, reciting the following prayer.

ORAISON

"Lord, blessed be thou, who has given power to men by means of thy holy Names, and who hast given thy blessing to all creatures, thy name in Thee, in him and thy name, and thy name was before all things, and thou shalt ever be great and admirable over all things, all things serve and adore thee, thou art Almighty over all things, and thou art sufficient over all things, therefore by thy holiness, by thy holy Name, which thou hast made known to thy creatures, O Lord, by thy virtue, by the virtue of thy holy Name which I have named, though I am unworthy of it. Please help me now in this work. Answer my prayer by your holy Name and by your almighty power, do not frustrate me of my hope, which I have in your great goodness."

"Et Non Frustrabitur eam, Amen.[2]

[220] If you have the Book and the Sign where is the Holy Name of God, you will have to stand as secretly as possible, and do as said above, having your hands raised towards the Four Parts of the World with the paper whereon will be written the Holy Names such as follows:

"Arrive O Michael from the East, O Gabriel from the West, O Raphael from the South, O Uriel from the North, O Septimiel from on High. Help me in this hour, I who am called N,[3] so that I may have full and complete satisfaction."

You will hold your paper in the hour that you do your work and then you will have all satisfaction. Moreover it is necessary to observe that you have a pure conscience and clean every time that you want to operate: wash well, and wear white linen, and to perfume the place where one writes.

Moreover, you must be careful not to do anything out of derision [lest] some

---

[1] Allah.
[2] And he will not frustrate him.
[3] Your name.

damage befall you, but if you are armed with firm confidence, you will be able to obtain with all assurance the effect of your Requests. By this means you will know things past and future, and you will have the power to remove hidden and enchanted treasures, you will be exempt from all evils; one will even be able to calm storms on the sea and on the Earth, no beast will be able to harm you, and you will produce by its means, very great wonders in nature, without any doubt.

For the Grand Intelligence, there will be represented the Figure of the Table, as it should be, with the arrangement of the names of the good Angels, and the dreadful name of the great God.

Prayer to be said over the Figure

"*Propheta Zerimia or Lerimia peccavit Domine super numerorum aranae maris fecit iniquitates super iniquitates et per multitudinem non passus caput in altum Attollere Eve Domine* [221] *pecata mea agnosco tu Domine Fecisti misericordiam propter ne peccatorem non propter Justos Abraham, Isaa[c] & Jacob miserere mei Domine et fac misericordiam eam servo tuo.*"[1]

---

[1] The prophet Jeremiah or 'Lerimia' sinned Lord over the numbers of the 'spiders' of the sea, he did iniquities upon iniquities and did not suffer through the multitude. Lift up your head on high Eve, O Lord I acknowledge my sins to you. O Lord has shown mercy for the sake of the sinner, not for the sake of the righteous Abraham, Isaac and Jacob have mercy on me O Lord, and have mercy on me your servant.

The 12 Altitudes of Solomon[1]

Each quarter of the sky has its own Altitude, that is to say its Angel.

The Eastern Angel is called LHOS or AHAVOR. It has its power and domination on the day of the Sun. This Altitude disposes of the nativity of children and journeys, towards a good or bad end.

The Way to Operate by this Altitude is thus:

You take the Almadel of Salomon, which is a piece of White Wax and well clean, containing half a foot square, and at each angle there must be a hole, you must write on it with a Silver Needle (arranged according to the Art) at each angle the following.

At the First corner you write: ADONAY, ELION, PIUS.

On the Second: ELION, ALOY, ELY.

On the Third: JOTH, OTHE, AGLA, YAVA.

On the Fourth: TETRAGRAMMATON, SADAY, YA.

And between the Square Angles, the Signs of Solomon must be written and traced.

The first way of the Almadel, its form and figure, is shown below.

---

[1] Altitude or 'Chora' is a Spirit location, sometimes translated as 'heaven.' This terminology indicates that this material is derived from the grimoire called *The Art Almadel*, which is the source for much of the remaining pages of Book IV. For the full text of the *Almadel* see Skinner & Rankine, *The Goetia of Dr Rudd*, Singapore: Golden Hoard, 2007, pp. 342-347.

[222]

FIGURE DE L'ALMADEL
DE SALOMON.

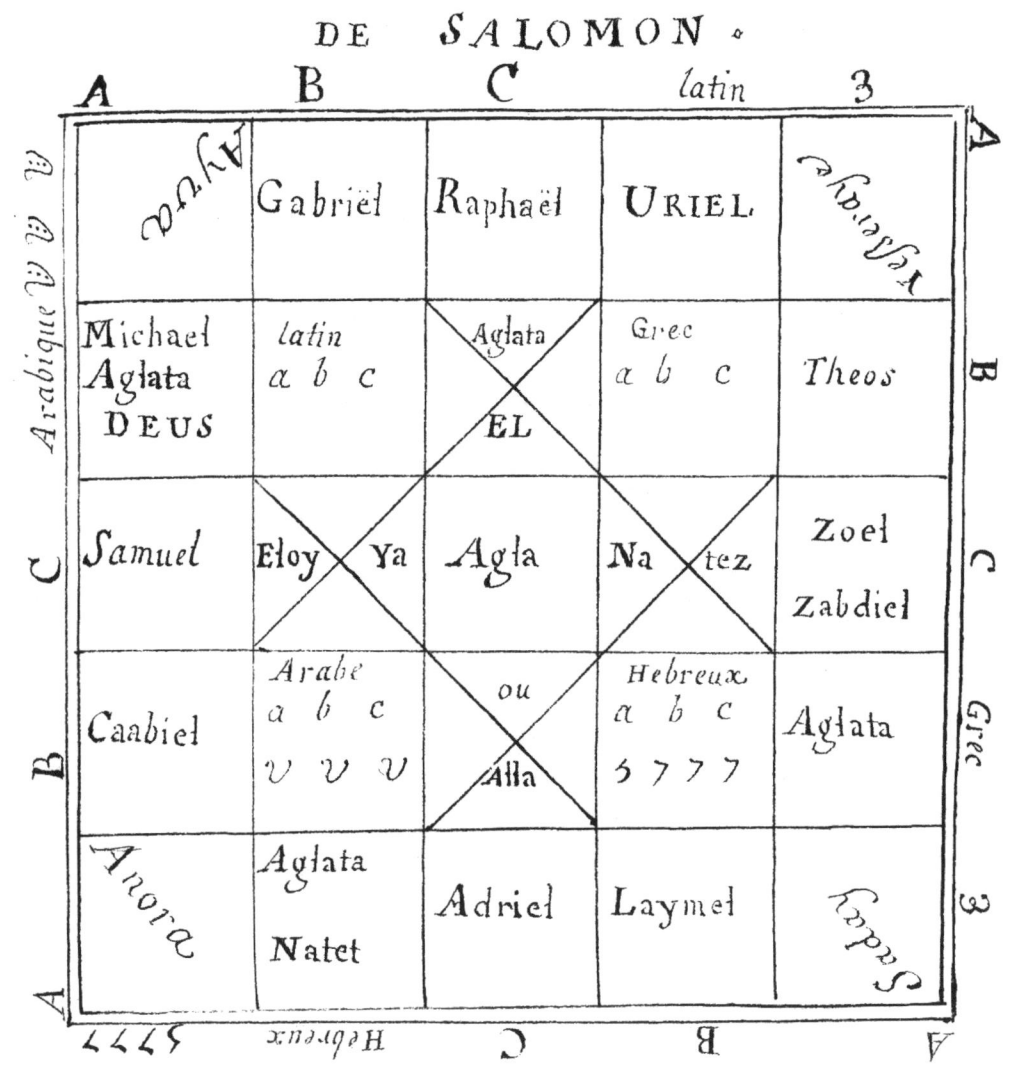

A	B	C latin	3
	Gabriël	Raphaël	URIEL	
Michael Aglata DEUS	latin a b c	Aglata EL	Grec a b c	Theos
Samuel	Eloy Ya	Agla	Na tez	Zoel Zabdiel
Caabiel	Arabe a b c v v v	ou Alla	Hebreux a b c 5 7 7 7	Aglata
Anora	Aglata Natet	Adriel	Laymel	

(Side labels: Arabique, B, C on left; B, C, Grec, 3 on right; top corners A...A; bottom: Hebreux, C, B, A; bottom-left: 5777)

Voyez aussi lALMADEL ci-devant page 212.

Figure 19: Design for the Almadel of Solomon, which is really a Table of Practice.[1] The 4 alphabets in which magical texts have been written should be on the sides.

---

[1] *The comment at the bottom:* "See also the ALMADEL on [manuscript] page 212." This diagram does not show any similarity to the diagram on manuscript page 212. The Almadel on manuscript page 212 is a three-dimensional object with holes for the reticulation of incense smoke, and a lot closer to the traditional Almadel than Figure 19. This diagram, Figure 19, is instead a simplified version of the Table of Practice seen in a number of grimoires including the *Summa Sacre Magice*.

[223] MAKING THE ALMADEL

You will make four candlesticks of the same material as the Almadel, they will be made so artistically that two parts are above the Almadel, and the remainder underneath, and that each candlestick has its own Almadel, you should have four candles to put in the candlesticks. You must also have a plate or seal of gold or pure silver, on which will be engraved the following words:

Usmodo, Helon, Adonay.

which you will put on the Almadel.

Write your request on a blank parchment, prepared according to the Art. Be careful not to ask for anything other than the power and Office of the Altitude you wish to invoke. Put it on the Almadel and pronounce the Invocation of the Prince of this Altitude, and of the Angels, after you have lit your candles.

[East]

First. Names of the Angels of the First Altitude of the Eastern Quarter

Arimiel, Sabriel, Darachie, Libes, Elisau.

Then you will recite the following:

Invocation and Conjuration to the Holy Angels

> "I worship the Holy One, the adorable God, forever by which O you Heavenly powers, live and humble your creature. I adore and pray to the Almighty Living God of creatures, both visible and invisible, also by his diadem and crown of his head, and by the Holy Almadel of Solomon, and by the name feared by all creatures [224] celestial, terrestrial, and infernal, which is written by these four letters: Jod, He, Vau, He. In order that you fulfil my request which I have placed on the Almadel, and that you O glorious ornament that God has raised above others contribute by your power to fulfil my request. I beseech you saints and Angels who are in this elevated Altitude of God by the name SADAY, of the living God ELION, Athanatos, Usios, IHS, first counsellor of Anathelas *pax meu Vita Adonay, Quatenuie misichu mili Dei Creatura prime*,[1] of this Altitude SITHEOS, receive my Request and by the virtue of this name of God Alpha and Omega, Elion, Athanatos, Emmanuel, Usim; please perfect and carry out this Request."

This invocation or conjuration must be recited three times in succession, with all humility, devotion, purity, etc. as the Art requires in such circumstances. There must appear to you an Angel carrying a Standard in his hand, a white Cross, a robe of the same, and on his head flowers in the form of a crown, he will be in the air above the Almadel. Take care to have a vase under the Almadel where there

---

[1] Peace be upon my life Adonay, how much I miss God's thousand first creatures.

will be perfumes.

Demand. The Angel will speak to you, saying: "What do you ask of me?"

Response. "O Angel of God and Creator of all things, is it to fulfil the Request which is on the present Almadel, or else to grant me that which depends on thy power for my utility, the glory of my God, and the salvation of my soul, Amen."

Take care to place 3 or 5 candles, and say the invocation as described above, repeating it three times in succession, and with as much purity, faith and accuracy as possible.

[225] Second. Names of the Angels of the Second Altitude of the Eastern Quarter

This Altitude is called Crown. Its Prince has power and authority over acquisitions, trades, and games. It is necessary to operate as it is said above, on the day and hour of the Sun. You must have pink wax.

These are the names of the Angels who are thus, namely

Alphaim, Heon, Heocum, Orin, Gevemach.

The Angel will appear to you in the colour of rose with a crown of flowers and in the shape of a beautiful child of three years old. He will question the operator, and he will be given the answer as it is here before. It must be further known and noticed, that each Sign must be invoked by the Dominant, that is the Angel or Intelligence of each Sign, as they are represented herein before on [manuscript] page 214, and each has a name of God by which the Intelligence must be invoked. The Names of God, and the Names of the Intelligences or Angels are written in the Almadel. They must not be confused with each other.

[Third.] Names of the Angels of the Third Altitude of the Eastern Quarter

This Altitude is called Hermon, its Prince has power and might over friendship and benevolence, and over the movements of sublunary things. It requires yellow wax.

The Names of the Angels are: Fortitude, Patientia, Pacaniany, Cicuriel, Prant, Saton and Hote.

The Angel will appear covered in golden weapons, revealing to you secret and hidden things. Here are the Properties of this Third Altitude.

[South]

[226] First. [Names of the Angels of the First] Altitude of the South.

This Altitude is called FORTUNE, its power is over treasures and earthly goods.

The wax used to make the Almadel must be of the colour azure.

The Names of the Intelligences or Angels are Yareth, Yava, Arirech, Tanaï, Ralux.

The days to perform these operations are Tuesdays, both the aforementioned Eastern and Southern, which must be performed when the Moon is new, and in its crescent, and when it is in good aspect with Jupiter or Venus, and the weather is clear and serene. As for the hour, it is from sunrise to noon.

At other times for the western and northern parts, it is at the time of vespers, that is to say at the setting sun.

Second. Names of the Angels of the Second Altitude of the South.

This Altitude is called EJAR, the power and might of the Prince of this Altitude extends over generation and the sciences.

Here are the Names of the Intelligences which are under the domination of this Prince: Alnay, Ercy, Alabe, Moracy, Annach, LAnay.[1]

The wax must be green, and the operation will be carried out as usual.

Third. Names of the Angels of the Third Altitude of the South.

This Altitude is called NOYNT. The Princes of this Altitude have their power and might over Empires. Here are the Names of the Intelligences subject to them: Hercos, Baffieros, Omay, Oralby, Vitae, Ivath, Ajay.

The wax must be violet, and the operation will be carried out as usual.

[West]

First. [Names of the Angels of the] The First Altitude of the West which is called SEPHOR.

Its power and might are over battles, friendships and contentions.

This is followed by the Names of the Intelligences that depend on this Altitude.

[227] Ay, A, Laym, Hozel, Abuy or Abauy, Yatan, Larozay.

The wax must be grey, the operation will be done in the ordinary way.

Second. Names of the Angels of the Second Western Altitude.

This Altitude is called EXON. It has its power and might over promises and things that are safe towards God, and towards demons, and over souls that are separated from bodies, over death and life, metaphysics, as well as negromancy.

Here are the Names of the Intelligences of this Altitude: AMayn, ARas, Any, GElon, Vero, GAdebamay, ZAcarthana and ELxoniut.

The wax must be tan. The operation [will be done as] usual.

---

[1] Double capitalisation of the first two letters has been left in place from this example to the end of manuscript page 232. Elsewhere it has been normalised.

Third. Names of the Angels of the Third Western Altitude.

This Altitude is called SAPH and NOA. And [its Prince] has the power to transport from one place to another, and other supernatural abilities.

Here are the Names of the Intelligences of this Altitude which are first: SAPH and NOA. Then are RAya, ZAbin, ZAdanay, ARphel, ARphanay, ZAday.

The wax used to make the Almadel must be green. For the operation, it will be done as usual.

[North]

First. [Names of the Angels of the First] Altitude of the Northern Quarter.

This Altitude is called BAZARD. The power of the Princes of this Altitude is over the dignities and virtues.

Here are their Names: ARphy, ANab, Boüs, ANy, PAtram, h, y, r, p, d.

The wax must be diaphanous in colour, and the perfumes will be aloes, pepper, etc. The operation will be carried out as usual, always following and observing the principles of the Art.

[228] Second. [Names of the Angels of the] Second Northern Altitude.

This Altitude is called ZANNEK. And its Princes have power over health, and they enlighten the mysteries of our law and of the saviour Jesus Christ.

Here are their Names: Alphamos, AZir, Zarneoch, Alymery and Saffray.

The wax must be brown and the operation [done] as usual.

Third. [Names of the Angels of the] Third [Northern] Altitude which is named Eleïson or Eleïsan. The Princes of this Altitude are Almos, Labries, Ana, Anay.

To form the Almadel of this Altitude, we need white, green and red wax, as much of one as the other, to make equal parts of this matter. Observe that these Spirits and Intelligences are of the Order of the Dominations and therefore, [they] are dominators, they bind the demons and compel them to obey God, etc.

JE[H]OVA is one of the great Names of God, which, when pronounced with respect before a crucifix, brings relief from the necessities of human life.

J. p. s. j. v. x. x. These letters are called Yesseraye. Namely: He, He, Y, I, I am God without beginning and without end. With these words, you will speak to the Angels, from whom you will have very great satisfaction with what you wish, provided that it is for the glory of God, and for your advantage, etc.

When you wish to assemble the Spirits, the winds and the demons, you must say the following words: ADONAY, CADOS, ADONAY, ANNORA.

When you want to untie Spirits or animals say the following:

"LAnginian, Lavat, Zerin, Lause, Lagin, Laval, Guiry, Lavagata, Lavarotin, Layfasin."

[229] When you want to bind the seeds,[1] say the following words:

"Liehan, Lealguava, Leafan, Molvaral, Leberal, Lebaron, Layassalos, Letaymiry, Letagton or Lethagton, Lethaforin."

The Names that follow are of great virtue when you want to destroy, etc.

These Holy Names were given by God to Adam to serve him, etc. They can also serve you.

THE 72 GREAT NAMES OF GOD

ADONAY, Cados,[2] Hebraël, Eloy, El, Ya, On, Even, Yaly, Helin, Delis, Zathy, Recathael, Hela, Agiel, Ajont, Sacradont, Hezul, Hela, Heltagin, Delyony, Pramon, Alinar, Pancyn, Alion, Cathimal, Mammus, Ovela, Delatan, SADAY, Omel, Doulh, Jhef, Aglata, Auriel, Phaneton, Orion, Seraje, Patrion, Utayr, Iraph, Salpy, Culusa, Safera, Ritan, SADAY, Ymiel, Zabatim or Labatins, Alla, Ya or La, Zafont or Lafont, Via, Taulifevor, Aglata, Za or La, Sy, Ty, El, Py, El,[3] Putry, Teron, Cefaragin.

AGLA is a name of God invented by the prophets, and [should be] engraved on a golden blade and carried on one's person, he who wears it will be exempt from sudden death. Whoever carries in writing on velvet parchment the following names, with firm confidence, can be assured of having no want of anything: Yat, Yava, Eloy, Yava. Whoever bears the following names cannot be defeated by his enemies: Mepheney and Phatosy. When you want to profit from doing your will, devoutly say the following: Cornithé, Mon, Sadalay, Trechomas, Zeprin or Leprin, Agata, Bithel, Yoel. The Elements are linked by the word Theomigain. The following word, written on an apple and thrown between two enemies, will instantly reconcile them: Haon, or Haou.

[230] By the name Hateny geon, the Elements and the firmament will be mute and obey you.

The following names and words are to be written at the beginning of your work when you want to operate, recite them with faith and devotion, and you will immanently be granted [your desires].

Thiegans, Cazas, Agas, Yava, DEUS, Israël, Oluyl, Dubay, Geales, Luy, Canie, Mathy, Deffa ou Dena, Bethiun."

---

[1] *Semences* also means 'semen' as well as seeds.
[2] Kadosh = holy.
[3] El appears twice.

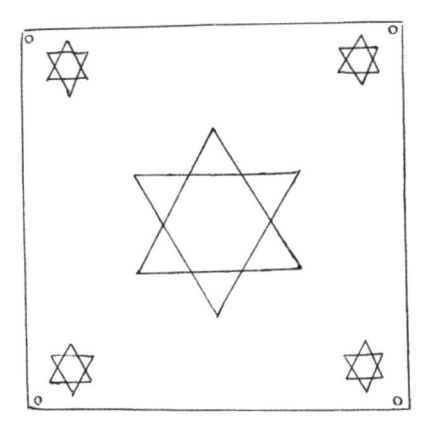

Figure 20: A simple Almadel of Solomon.

End of the Shemhammaphorash of Adam

[231] THE SHEMHAMMAPHORESH OF MOSES

Moses spoke the following words as he ascended Mount Sinai. If you recite them with devotion, you will get what you want.

> * "MEY, Aafy, Zié ou Lié, Zaré ou Laré, Dugé, Bué, Hazé, Ecremia, Ya, Mié, Yama, Aledacy, Bujé, Raha, Yabé, Atha, Robé, Sesgalé, Meta, A, Amé, Rey, Zeby or Leby, Avey, Yby, Yré, Theby, Zalié or Lalié, Zerbaté or Lerbaté, Tadé, Zeghié or Leghié, Yhe, Oyera, Ratoye, Try, Hy, Sasaguin, Yme, Safé, Yméé, Yela, Habé, Velé, Hela, Quego, Rang, Haabe."

He also repeated the following:

> "ZAbogny or LAbogny, Tant, Zayraré or Layraré, Mamuë, Dezarae, Petita, Catafigé, Acaptena, Jegay, Pediloy, Satfia."

The following words are very effective for obtaining what you ask for with good intentions. Fast three days in a row and be pure and clean: it was on the basis of these words that Solomon built a Temple to God.[1]

> "* ZEzabel or Rezabel, Cacua, Sayat, Helamo, Oraan, Elehaa, Za or La, La, Hu, Abach, Avele, Azaya, Aledo, Zocue or Locue, Hyeha, Yzale, Marbra, Ylayé, Araya, Alainné, Zeona or Leona, Elago, Ziea or Liea, Eao, Phale, Melae, Ye, Ye, Molach, Hahava, Net, Hee, Yzele."

Moreover, Moses spoke these words when he opened the [232] crossing of the Red Sea. You can say them whenever you want to get into someone's good graces, armed with faith, piety and devotion.

> "REpy, Sachonety, Paronit, Yt, Ymor, Hegaroh, Higayron, Semigaron, Nucun, Micodafaos, Castas, Yaccus, Yecon, Ignaraba, Nanth, EZatuf."[2]

The prophets pronounced the following words when they wanted to prophesy, and Moses used them to destroy the serpents; you can say them whenever you want to operate.

> "SADAY, Bay, Bezesel, Aty, Comy, Yzy, Cha, Yeynt, Gnosol, Acadis, Bamehuin, Voha, Ey, Aha, Eya, Eye, Ey, Eye, Hay, Ha, Hay, Ha, Hay, Ha, Hay, Ey, Ey, Ey, Ha, Ya, Ael, Es, El, Hay, Hau, Hau, Hau, Va, Va."[3]

The following Names obtain what is desired, when said and recited with faith and devotion. They dispel all charms and enchantments, and ward off all evils.

> * "YAVA, Yava, Diae, Abisis, Hygane, Ya, Ya, Aloqui, Gel, ADONAY, Sabasty, Ehye, Aser, Ehye, Titgos, Yava, Eloym, Ya, Vert, Venant, Ay,

---

[1] I think it cost Solomon a lot more effort than just a short fast.
[2] This is the last example of double capitalization left in the text, as an example of cryptography. From here on the double capitals have been normalised.
[3] This has obviously been the spelling out of various combinations of Yod, Heh, Vau, He.

Maræcas, Asma, Myas, Hy, He, Ha, ADONAY, Yant, Arihamel, Gayas, Matæ, Puyoe, Yava, Yæ, Yavæ, Ya, Ya, He, Hau, He, Hya, Eveth."

When you find yourself in great necessity and needing to do something extraordinary, but that it be for a good end, you recite the following names with faith and devotion.

* "SADAY, Auxoræ, Elon, Pheneton, Eloy, Ebreil, Messias or Memas, Prophetas, Hæ, Yava, Elion."

You can add the following:

*"VERVA et magnes vivis, et fortes potens, et pius Sancus, et mundus, est plenes, tolius, bonitatis tu Benedictus Dominus [233] et Benedictus Nomen tuum incomplector comple petitionem meam tu factor fac me addivere ad ferient mei operis tu Sanctus et misericors miserere mei nonem tuum; Yesseraye Sic Benedictum in omni tempore. Amen.[1]

To avoid slavery and prison, we can recite the following three words with faith and confidence, as Joshua pronounced them when he stopped the course of the Sun.

"JOCHION, ADAY, BACHAR"

END OF THE SHEMHAMMAPHORASH OF MOSES
LAUS DEO

The Key is above, besides look at the book *Enchiridion*.[2]

---

[1] VERVA and great, living and strong, powerful and pious holy, and world, is full, of your goodness, Blessed Lord [233] and your Blessed Name, incomplete, complete my request, you are the maker, make me, add to my work, you are holy and merciful, have mercy on me, your name; Yesseraye here blessed at all times. Amen.

[2] The *Enchiridion of Pope Leo III* was first heard of in 1584 when it was published in French. It was later reprinted a number of times It is a heavily religious grimoire which was probably known to Trithemius as a manuscript, with references to St. Cyprian, King Abgar of Edessa, Charlemagne, Agrippa and the Gospel of St. John.

ANNOTATIONS

Containing the imprecations of men that naturally imprint their forces on external things, and which teach how the spirit of man attains by a degree of dependence on the Intelligible world, and becomes similar to the more sublime Spirits and Intelligences.

The souls of Celestial bodies give their virtues to their bodies, which are then communicated to this Sensible World, for the virtues of the terrestrial globe have no other cause than a celestial one. Therefore, he who wishes to operate by the force of these souls, makes his invocation in the presence of the Superiors, by mysterious words, applying one thing to another, by joining to it a certain formula of ingenious words, he therefore applies one thing to another, with a natural force, by certain mutual conveniences between them, by which things come of themselves, or when [234] we force them. This is what makes Aristotle say, in Book Six of the *Mystical Philosophy*;[1] when someone by ligature or binding wants to invoke the Sun or one of the other Stars,[2] praying that they cooperate in the work he desires, the Sun or the other Stars do not hear his prayer, but in some ways set themselves in motion according to certain liaisons and natural harmony, with which the parts of the world are subordinated and conspire together to make their great union; just as in the human body, one member is set in motion, receiving motion from another; and in an instrument one string touched or is set in motion, gives motion to another. In the same way, when someone gives movement to some parts of the world, the other parts are also set in motion, and receive the movements of the first: hence the knowledge of the dependence of the things that follow one another and the foundation of all marvellous operations which is necessarily required to put into execution the power to attract the Heavenly virtues. Now then, the words of men are certain natural things; and as the parts of the world naturally attract one another, so does the operator invoking by words, operates them by Nature's own forces, driving certain things by love from one to another, or attracting it because of the aftereffect of one thing on another, or repelling it because of the antipathy of the one to the other, according to the contrariety, diversity and multitude of virtues, which although contrary and different, are nevertheless a part of the operation, sometimes also forcing things to a species of superiority by celestial virtue: if therefore some men feel the impression of some ligature or bindings, he does not feel it [235] according to the reasonable soul, but according to the sensual [soul], and if it suffers in any of its parts, it is according to the animal soul, of this lower world; for words cannot attract the soul; which withholds its knowledge from reason, and which has the understanding, and which nevertheless conceives this impression, and this force by the sense, inasmuch as by the influence of the Stars and by the concurrence of

---

[1] Probably Aristotle's *Metaphysics*.
[2] Planets.

the things of the world, the animal spirit of man is touched beyond its first or natural disposition; in the same way that a son engages his father in works, even in spite of himself, to preserve and nourish him, however tired he may be, and that the desire to dominate throws us into anger, and engages us in other works to enlarge ourselves, and that the indigence of nature and the fear of poverty make us wish and desire riches, and that the beauty of a lady who sees herself adorned with an ornament by some brilliant costumes are a spur to concupiscence, and that the harmony of a skilful musician gives rise to various passions in his auditors, some of whom give in to the harmony of the music, others conforming by their gestures to those of the musician, even in spite of themselves, because their sense is captivated, because reason has no attention to these sorts of things, but the common vulgar person admires none of these species of fascination, and of ligature, nor does he hate them, because they are common; but he admires other natural ones, because he ignores them, and they are extraordinary to him: which is why the common man errs, believing that this is above, and even against nature, and that which comes from nature, and is made according to its laws.

It must therefore be known that each superior sets in motion his next inferior in rank and degree, not only in the order of bodies, but also in the order of Spirits; [236] this is how the Universal Soul of the world sets in motion the particular souls; and the reasonable soul acts upon the sensitive soul, and the sensitive upon the vegetative, and each part of the lower world receives the impression made upon it by the Heavens, according to its nature and aptitude, as one part of the body of the animal makes impression upon the other, and the superior world of Intelligences acts upon and gives motion to all that is under it, because it contains all the same beings from the first to the last, as the inferior worlds, consequently the Heavenly Bodies give motion to the bodies of the Elemental World, mixed, corruptible and sensible, from the concave to the centre, by means of the superior perpetual and spiritual essences dependent on the first understanding, which is the acting understanding, and also on the virtue that God has given through his word, it is this word that the Chaldean philosophers of Babylon call the 'cause of all causes,' since it is this word that produces the entities, and even the active understanding, which is only second to it, and this because of the union of this word with its first author, who truly produces all the beings of the universe. The verb, then, is the image of God; the active understanding is the image of the verb, the soul is the image of the understanding, and our word is the image of our soul, by which it naturally acts on natural things, because nature is its workmanship, and each of these things perfects what follows after it, as the father makes the son, and there is no posterior without a prior; for things are dependent on one another, with a certain regulated dependence, so that when the posterior corrupts, there is a return to the first nearest until it reaches the Heavens; then to the Universal Soul, afterwards to the agent understanding, where all other creatures have their existence; [237] and which itself has its existence in the principal author who is the Creator Verb to whom all things return as to their principle. It is therefore necessary that our soul, wishing to do some marvellous works in the things of this lower world, contemplate its principle, so that it may fortify it, enlighten it, and give it the strength to act through all the degrees from its first author, to itself; we have therefore endeavoured to make us contemplate the souls of the Stars, more than the bodies; more than the celestial Intellectual World, more than the celestial corporeal, since this one is more noble, whatever this one is to be considered, that it is at the entrance of the other, and that the influence of this superior cannot continue its route without crossing it, as in the middle.

FOR EXAMPLE

The Sun is the king above all the Stars [planets], because his soul is more capable of this Intelligible Splendor; therefore he who wishes to attract the influence of the Sun, must contemplate the Sun, not only by the contemplation of the external Light, but also by the interior, and no one can do this without returning to the very Spirit of the Sun, and without becoming like him, and understanding and seeing with the eye of the understanding his intelligible light, as the sensible light by the eye of the body, for the latter will be filled with the splendour of the former, and will also receive in itself its light, which is the hypotype communicated by the superior sphere, where being clothed with its illustration, is truly like to it, and as it is carried and aided from a height, it will obtain at the will of its understanding this sovereign clarity, and the favour of all the other souls who are participants of it: And when he [238] will have drawn the light of the sovereign degree, then his soul will approach perfection, and will become similar to the Spirits of the Sun and will reach the forces and illustrations of supernatural virtue, and will make use of their power if he has found creed in the first author. Above all, one must ask the first author for help and assistance, and this not only by mouth, but also with deep humility, sentiments of piety and religion, and with a suppliant Spirit, praying very abundantly without ceasing, and making his prayers whole, so that he may enlighten the understanding and turn away from souls the darkness that takes over because of the body.

[THE END]

APPENDICES

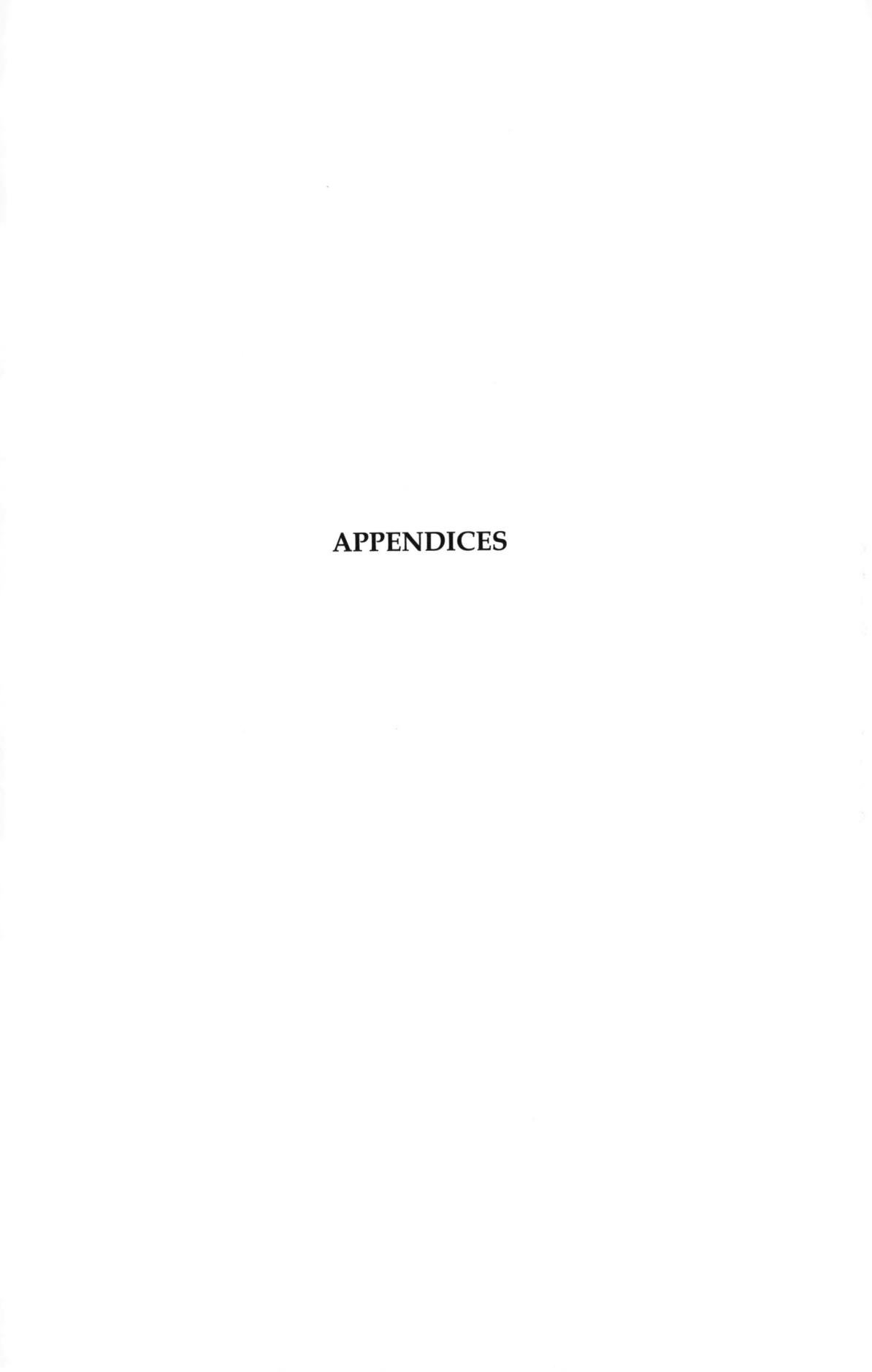

Appendix 1 - *Theurgia-Goetia*

Good and Evil Aerial Spirits of the Compass from *Theurgia-Goetia* (*Lemegeton* Book II).[1]

No.	Emperors Ruling	Dukes	Direction	Commands	Some Spirits/Dukes Commanded
1	Carnesiel	PAMERSIEL	E	1000 Spirits for Day	Anoyr, Madriel, Ebra, Sotheans, Abrulges, Ormenu, Itules, Rablion, Hamorphiel, Itrasbiel, Nadres
2		Padiel	E by S	10000 Spirits for Day / 20000 Spirits for Night	[not given, as 'Padiel rules all Spirits']
3		Camuel	SE	10 Spirits for Day	Orpemiel, Omyel, Camyel, Budiel, Elear, Citgara, Pariel, Cariel, Neriel, Daniel
				10 Spirits for Night	Asimiel, Calim, Dobiel, Nodar, Phaniel, Meras, Azemo, Tediel, Moriel (s), Tugaros
4		Aseliel	S by E	10 Chief Spirits for Day	Mariel, Charas, Parniel, Aratiel, Cubiel, Aniel, Asahel, Arean,
				20 Chief Spirits for Night	Asphiel, Curiel, Chamos, Odiel, Melas, Sariel, Othiel, Bofar
5	Caspiel	BARMIEL	S	10 Dukes for Day	Sochas, Tigara, Chansi, Keriel, Acteras, Barbil, Carpiel, Mansi
				20 Dukes for Night	Barbis, Marguns, Carniel, Acreba, Mareaiza, Baaba, Gabio, Astib
6		Gediel	S by W	20 Chief Spirits for Day	Coliel, Ranciel, Agra, Naras, Mashel, Anael, Sabas, Bariel, Aroan
				20 Chief Spirits for Night	Assaba, Reciel, Cirecas, Sariel, Sadiel, Aglas, Vriel,
7		Asiriel/Asyriel	SW	20 Dukes for Day	Astor, Ariel, Maroth, Carga, Cusiel, Omiel, Buniel, Malguel, Budar
				20 Dukes for Night	Rabas, Amiel, Aspiel, Areisat, Cusriel, Faseua, Hamas
8		Maseriel	W by S	12 Dukes for Day	Mahue, Roriel, Zeriel, Atniel, Patiel, Assuel, Aliel, Espoel, Amoyr, Bachiel, Baras, Eliel,
				12 Dukes for Night	Vessur, Azimel, Chasor, Arach, Maras, Noguiel, Sarmiel, Earos, Rabiel, Atriel, Salvar
9	Amenadiel	MALGARAS	W	30 Dukes for Day	Carmiel, Meliel, Borasy, Agor, Oriel, Misiel, Barfas, Arois, Raboc, Aspiel, Caron, Zamor, Amiel
				30 Dukes for Night	Casiel, Babiel, Cabiel, Udiel, Aroc, Dodiel, Cubi, Libiel, Aspar, Deilas, Basiel
10		Darochiel	W by N	Dukes before Noon of the 24 Dukes for Day	Magael, Artino, Efiel/Artino, Maniel/Efiel, Suriel/Maniel, Carsiel/Suriel, Carsiel, Fubiel, Carba, Merach, Althor, Omiel
				Dukes after Noon of the 24 Dukes for Day	Gudiel, Asphor, Emuel, Soriel, Cabron, Diviel, Abriel, Danael, Lomor, Casael, Busiel, Larfos
				Dukes before Midnight of the 24 Dukes for Night	Nahiel, Ofisiel, Bulis, Momel, Darbari, Paniel, Cursas, Aliel, Aroziel, Cusyne, Vraniel, Pelusar

---

[1] Table M20 from Skinner, *Complete Magicians Tables,* Singapore: Golden Hoard, 2006. The listing and spelling of the Lesser Dukes and Spirits of the *Theurgia-Goetia* corresponds to Sloane MS 3825, not the spelling in the *Steganographia*.

Steganographia

No.	Emperors Ruling	Dukes	Direction	Commands	Some Spirits/Dukes Commanded
				Dukes after Midnight of the 24 Dukes for Night	Pafiel, Gariel, Soriel, Maziel, Cayros, Narsiel, Moziel, Abael, Meroth, Cadriel, Lodiel
11		Usiel	NW	40 Dukes for Day	Abariel, Ameta, Arnin, Herne, Saefer, Potiel, Saefarn, Magni, Amandiel, Barfu, Garnasu, Hissam, Fabariel, Usiniel
				40 Dukes for Night	Ansoel, Godiel, Barfos, Burfa, Adan, Saddiel, Sodiel, Ofsidiel, Pathier, Marae, Asuriel, Almoel, Las Pharon, Ethiel
12		Cabariel	N by W	50 Dukes for Day	Satifiel, Parius, Godiel, Taros, Asoriel, Etimiel, Clyssan, Elitel, Aniel, Cuphal
				50 Dukes for Night	Mador, Peniel, Cugiel. Thalbos, Otim, Ladiel, Morias, Pandor, Cazul, Dubiel
13		RASIEL	N	50 Dukes for Day	Baciar, Thoac, Sequiel, Sadar, Terath, Astael, Ramica, Dubarus, Armena, Albhadur, Chanael, Fursiel, Betasiel, Melcha, Tharas, Vriel
				50 Dukes for Night	Thariel, Paras, Arayl, Culmar, Lazaba, Aleasy, Sebach, Quibda, Belsay, Morael, Sarach, Arepach, Lamas, Thurcal
14	Demoriel	Symiel	N by E	10 Dukes for Day	Asmiel, Chrubas, Vaslos, Malgron, Romiel, Larael, Achot, Bonyel, Dagiel, Musor
				10 Dukes for Night	Mafrus, Apiel, Curiel, Molael, Arafos, Marianu, Narzael, Murahe, Richel, Nalael
15		Armadiel	NE	15 Dukes	Nassar, Parabiel, Lariel, Calvarnia, Orariel, Alferiel, Oryn, Samiel, Asmaiel, Jasziel, Pandiel, Carasiba, Asbibiel, Mafayr, Oemiel
16		Baruchas	E by N	15 Dukes	Quitta, Sarael, Melchon, Cavayr, Aboc, Cartael, Janiel, Pharol, Baoxas, Geriel, Monael, Chubo, Lamael, Dorael, Decaniel

Table 72: Good and Evil Aerial Spirits of the Compass from *Theurgia-Goetia*.

	Direction	Emperors	Commands	12 Chief Dukes
F	South	Caspiel	200 Great Dukes 400 Lesser Dukes 1,000,200,000,000 Ministering Spirits Attended by 2660 Lesser Dukes	Ursiel, Chariel, Maras, Femol, Budarim, Camory, Larmol, Aridiel, Geriel, Ambri, Camor, Oriel
A	East	Carnesiel	1000 Great Dukes 100 Lesser Dukes 50,000,000,000,000 Ministering Spirits 60,000,000,000,000 attendant Dukes	Myrezyn, Ornich, Zabriel, Bucafas, Benoliam, Arifiel, Cumeriel, Vadriel, Armany, Capriel, Bedary, Laphor
W	West	Amenadiel	300 Great Dukes 500 Lesser Dukes 40,000,030,000,100,000 Ministering Spirits Attended by 3880 Servants	Vadros, Camiel, Luziel, Musiriel, Rapsiel, Lamael Zoeniel, Curifas, Almesiel, Codriel, Balsur, Nadroc
E	North	Demoriel	400 Great Dukes 600 Lesser Dukes 70,000,080,000,900,000 Servants Attended by 1140 Servants	Arnibiel, Cabarim, Menador, Burisiel, Doriel, Mador, Carnol, Dubilon, Medar, Churibal, Dabrinos, Chamiel

Good and Evil Aerial Spirits (Emperors) from *Theurgia-Goetia* (*Lemegeton* Book II).[1]

Table 73: Good and Evil Aerial Spirits (the Emperors) from *Theurgia-Goetia*.

---

[1] Table M21 from Skinner, *Complete Magicians Tables,* Singapore: Golden Hoard, 2006.

No.	Emperor Ruler	Wandering Princes	Direction	Commands	Commands
1	Carnesiel Amenadiel Demoriel	Geradiel	ESE SE by E NNW NNE?	18150 Servants	[not given]
2	Carnesiel Demoriel	Buriel	SE by S NNE NE by N	12 Dukes for Night 880 Servants	Merosiel, Almadiel, Cupriel, Sarviel, Casbriel, Nedriel, Bufiel, Futiel, Drusiel, Carniel, Drubiel, Nastros
3		Hidriel / Hydrial	SE by S SSE NE by N NE by E	100 Great Dukes 200 Lesser Dukes	Mortaliel, Chalmoriel, Pelariel, Musuziel, Lameniel, Barchiel, Samiel, Dusiriel, Camiel, Arbiel, Lusiel, Chariel
4	Amenadiel	Pirichiel	NW by W NW by N	8 Knights	Damarsiel, Cardiel, Almasor, Nemariel, Menariel, Demediel, Hursiel, Cuprisiel
5		Emoniel	NW by N NNW	20 Dukes	Ermoniel, Edriel, Carnodiel, Phanuel, Dramiel, Pandiel, Vasenel, Nasiniel, Cruhiel, Armesiel, Caspaniel, Musiniel
6	Carnesiel Caspiel Demoriel	Icosiel	SSE SSW NE by E ENE	100 Dukes 300 Companions	Machariel, Psichiel, Thanatiel, Zosiel, Agapiel, Larphiel, Amediel, Cambriel, Nathriel, Zachariel, Athesiel, Cumariel, Munefiel, Heresiel, Urbaniel
7		Soleviel	ESE SSW SW by S ENE	200 Dukes 200 Companions	Inachiel, Praxeel, Moracha, Almodar, Nadrusiel, Cobusiel, Amriel, Axosiel, Charoel, Parsiel, Mursiel, Penador
8	Caspiel	Menadiel	SW by S SW by W	20 Dukes 6 Chief Dukes 100 Companions	Larmol, Drasiel, Clamor, Benodiel, Charsiel, Samyel
				6 Lesser Dukes	Barchiel, Amasiel, Baruch, Nedriel, [2]Curasin, Tharson
9	Caspiel	Macariel	SW by W WSW	40 Dukes	Claniel, Drusiel, Andros, Charoel, Asmadiel, Romyel, Mastuel, Varpiel, Gremiel, Thuriel, Brufiel, Lemodac
10	Caspiel Amenadiel	Uriel	WSW WNW	10 Dukes 100 Under Dukes	Chabri, Drabos, Narmiel, Frasmiel, Brymiel, Dragon, Curmas, Drapios, Hermon, Aldrusy
11	Amenadiel	Bidiel	WNW NW by W	20 Chief Dukes 200 Other Dukes	Mudirel, Cruchan, Bramsiel, Armoniel, Lameniel, Andruchiel, Merasiel, Charobiel, Parsifiel, Chremoas

Table 74: Good and Evil Aerial Spirits (Wandering Princes) from *Theurgia-Goetia*.

---

[1] Table M20a from Skinner, *Complete Magicians Tables,* Singapore: Golden Hoard, 2006.
[2] Total = 4 Emperors + 11 Wandering Princes + 16 Aerial Spirits (Dukes) = 31 Spirits, as in Book I of the *Steganographia*.

Appendix 2: Trithemius' letters embedded in the *Steganographia*.

These letters are a on a number of ordinary subjects ranging from Christian piety, to the recommendation of specific persons for employment, or requests for information, but do not have any magical or cryptographic content. As an example we have selected one letter in which Trithemius attempts to shame a soldier into returning books that he had borrowed, a translation of an example letter found in the Latin text of Book II, Chapter VII.

Johannes Trittenheim Abbot of Spain greets the valiant soldier Henry of Bunano, with the most studious philosophical greetings he says:

"I would have lent you my books on the condition of restoring them, my dearest soldier Bunane: but behold, you have not restored at all those which you ought to have returned in short order. You are proceeding contrary to the law which the Catholic faith has sanctioned concerning the promise: do not postpone what you have promised to pay to all: it is not fitting for a good and honorable man, born of older nobles, to violate your promise. But you had promised to restore it with the utmost care. It is as if it is the lightest promise to defer to Greek Calends.[1] Have I not waited long enough with great benevolence? It is most shameful to promise the greatest and to pay the least. Good faith adorns a soldier. It is a graver crime to deny a promised promise; now the constitution of the Christian law commands you to keep a promise, to repay a loan: and what you desire to be done to yourself, you must also willingly do to others. I will send out my books, which I had adapted to your request, and I will release the longer excuses which you sent to the Greek Calends instead. You hold my mind in short.[2] Consider your honorable name part of the race of Buna Wensium:[3] send me my volumes."

- *Farewell from Spain. The ninth of April in the year of the Lord MD.*[4]

---

[1] A light promise that will never be satisfied, as the Greeks did not measure time by Calends.
[2] I await your reply.
[3] Good wishes.
[4] 1500.

Appendix 3: Planetary Hours

Sunset marks the start of the 12 night hours, and sunrise marks the start of the 12 day hours. This means that night hours will be longer or shorter than day hours, depending on the season. In summer day hours will be longer, but in winter night hours are longer. Planetary hours are of an elastic length, unlike clock hours, and depend entirely upon sunset and sunrise times. If you want to be very precise about them, you can check the official time of sunrise and sunset in your local newspaper, or you can check sunset yourself by using the ancient test that sunset has occurred 'as soon as three stars become visible.'

The determination of Planetary hours is most important for any magical operation. The length of the hours of the day are determined by dividing the number of minutes between dawn and sunset into 12 equal parts. Likewise, the hours of the night are derived by dividing the time in minutes from sunset to sunrise into 12 equal parts. Obviously as the seasons change so will the length of these hours. Only on two nights of the year will all the hours be of equal length, and 60 minutes in duration, and this is at the time of the two Equinoxes (which literally means 'equal night'). In this text they are referred to as 'uneven hours' which means precisely that.

Planetary hours, being tied to the actual movement of the sun are therefore much more 'natural,' and therefore magical than clock hours which are determined by a man-made device. In past times, when many more men and women worked in agriculture, if meant that summer days were much longer, when more work needed to be done. During winter however the shortness of the day naturally matched the lesser demands of the fields.

Appendix 4: The Angelic Rulers of *De Septem Secundeis*

Although he was thinking about the division of history into ages ruled by angels before 1500, Trithemius wrote *De Septem Secundeis* ('The Seven Secondary Causes') in 1508.[1] His doctrine of planetary cycles defined as periods of 354.33 years ruled by planetary angels ultimately derives from Peter d'Abano. Despite the thirteenth-century d'Abano being usually thought of as a physician, he was deeply interested in magic, for which he suffered under the Inquisition several times. He laid out his theory of planetary ages in his brilliant *Conciliator differentiarum philosophorum et medicorum*. The names of the first two angels in d'Abano were however different from those used by Trithemius. d'Abano used the more familiar Cassiel [Saturn] and Sachiel [Jupiter] rather than Trithemius' Orifiel and Zachariel.

According to Trithemius, the world was created 5206 years before Christ. The seven angels (the 'Secondary Intelligences' of the title) are given distinct identities in the third book of the *Steganographia*. The text of *De Septem Secundeis* covers history before Trithemius, and then with less detail up to November 1879, at which point Gabriel hands over his rule to the Sun, whose rulership survives until 2033. This means we are currently in the 21st cycle, under The Sun and its angel Michael.

No.	Planet	Angel	Begins	Year *Annus Mundi*	Year CE
1	Saturn	Orifiel	15 March	1	
2	Venus	Anael	24 June	354	
3	Jupiter	Zachariel	25 October	708	
4	Mercury	Raphael	24 February	1063	
5	Mars	Samuel	26 June	1417	
6	Moon	Gabriel	28 October	1771	
7	Sun	Michael	24 February	2126	
8	Saturn	Orifiel	26 June	2480	
9	Venus	Anael	29 October	2834	
10	Jupiter	Zachariel	28 February	3189	
11	Mercury	Raphael	1 July	3543	
12	Mars	Samuel	2 October	3897	
13	Moon	Gabriel	30 January	4252	
14	Sun	Michael	1 May	4606	

---

[1] An English translation of this was published and made popular by William Lilly in 1647.

No.	Planet	Angel	Begins	Year *Annus Mundi*	Year CE
15	Saturn	Orifiel	30 September	4960	
16	Venus	Anael	31 January	5315	109 CE
17	Jupiter	Zachariel	1 June	5669	463 CE
18	Mercury	Raphael	2 November	6023	817 CE
19	Mars	Samuel	3 March	6378	1171 CE
20	Moon	Gabriel	4 June	6732	1525 CE
21	Sun	Michael	November	7086	1879 CE
22	Saturn	Orifiel	March	7440	2233 CE

Table 75: Angelic and Planetary rulers of Trithemius' Ages.

Appendix 5. Calculating the current quarter days for timing.[1]

Trithemius begins his explanation in Book III with Saturn who began the whole angelic rulership cycle. Fortunately, the ruling planet now, in the early years of the 21st century is the Sun, which moves a lot faster than Saturn. Remember that each day, and each night, is divided into 12 Planetary hours, which change in length from winter (shorter than a clock hour) to summer (longer than a clock hour). Only on two days a year are they exactly 60 minutes, the two Equinoxes. On every other day we have to calculate them. Let us take the same date as used by Trithemius, April 28th, but for the year 2023 rather than 1500. Our calculation is therefore for a different year and a different 'planet,' and a different city, London.

To begin we need to find the exact time of sunrise and sunset on April 28th 2023. Sunrise was 5:38 am, and sunset was 20:20 pm, which means that the length of daylight hours is 14:39 hours. Each Planetary hour is, therefore, a twelfth of that, or 1 hour 13.5 minutes. Using this Planetary hour interval we can calculate the beginning and end of each quarter of the day, as each 3 Planetary hours or 3 hours 40 minutes clock time is a quarter day.

1st quarter = 5:38 am to 9:18 am
2nd quarter = 9:19 am to 1.00 pm
3rd quarter = 1.00 pm to 4:40 pm
4th quarter = 4:40 pm to 20:20 pm

If we are dealing with the angels of the Sun, for example, their quarters become:

1st quarter = Michael, angel of the Sun
2nd quarter = Pafael, first sub-angel
3rd quarter = Vanriel, second sub-angel
4th quarter = Zabdiel, third sub-angel

---

[1] In Book III.

Appendix 6. Comparison with the Spirit Register of the *Theurgia-Goetia*.

The following table shows the differences between the Spirit Registers of the *Steganographia* and *Theurgia-Goetia*.

The order in the *Steganographia*	The order in the *Theurgia-Goetia*[1]	Title	Direction provided by the *Theurgia-Goetia*
	Carmaesiel	Emperors[2]	East
	Caspiel		South
	Ameradiel		West
	Demoriel		North
Pamersiel	Pamersiel	Dukes	East.
Padiel	Padiel		East by south
Camuel	Camuel		South east
Aseliel	Aschiel		South by east
Barmiel	Barmiel		South
Gediel	Gediel		South by west
Asiriel	Asyriel		South west
Maseriel	Maseriel		West by south
Malgaras	Malgaras		West
Dorothiel	Darochiel		West by north
Usiel	Usiel		North west
Cabariel	Cabariel		North by west
Raysiel	Rasiel		North
Symiel	Symiel		North by east
Armadiel	Armadiel		North east
Baruchas	Baruchas		East by north
Carnesiel		Emperors[3] or Princes	East
Caspiel			South
Amenadiel			West
Demoriel			North
Geradiel	Garadiel	Wandering Dukes	No specific direction
Buriel	Buriel		
Hydriel	Hydriel		
Pyrichiel	Pyrichiel		

---

[1] Skinner & Rankine, *Goetia of Dr Rudd,* Singapore; Golden Hoard, 2007, pp. 212-306.
[2] The *Theurgia-Goetia* has made the sensible decision to move the 4 Cardinal Princes to the front of the book rather than leaving them half way through.
[3] See above at top of column for these four Emperors in the *Theurgia-Goetia*.

The order in the *Steganographia*	The order in the *Theurgia-Goetia*[1]	Title	Direction provided by the *Theurgia-Goetia*
Emoniel	Emoniel	Wandering Dukes	
cosiel	Icosiel		
Soleviel	Soleviel		
Menachiel	Menadiel		
Macariel	Macariel		
Uriel	Uriel		
Bydiel	Bidiel		

Table 76: The Spirits of the *Steganographia* and the *Theurgia-Goetia*.

Bibliography

Manuscripts

Biblioteca Nacional de Espana MS 7988. *Steganographia nec non Clavicula Salomonis.*

Bibliotheca Philosophica Hermetica MS 277. *La Steganographie*, 27 February, 1784. [Although relatively late, this appears to be more complete than many of the Latin manuscripts and their printed editions.]

Bibliothèque Nationale MS 7869, f. 75r-80v. *Fragmentum epithalamii soluta oratione scripti.*

British Library Sloane MS 3670, *Libri experimentorum Johannis Trithemij.*

British Library Sloane MS 3824, f. 121-130, *Trithemius Redivivius.* [a small extract.]

Hochschule-und-Landesbibliothek MS Fulda 100 C 16. *Steganographia*, 1588. [One of the most beautiful Latin manuscripts of the *Steganographia.*]

National Library of Scotland Adv. MS 18.2.12. *Steganographia*. 16th century.

National Library of Wales. Penarth MS 423D. *Steganographia.* [This is a copy of Dr John Dee's copy of the *Steganographia*]

Oxford Bodleian Library MS Auct. D. 2. 17. [An example of Trithemius' handwriting.]

Royal Library Copenhagen (Black Diamond) MS Thott 843 quarters. *Steganographia* 17th century.

Somerset Heritage Centre MS DD/L/2/51/16. *Steganographia*. 17th Century.

Vatican Library MS Reg. lat. 1344 *Steganographia.*

Washington University book microfilm Z103 T84S 1618a. *Steganographia.*

Manuscripts relating to Pelagius

Bibliothèque Nationale MS lat. 7486A, f. 1r: *Magistri Pelagii heremite sanctissimi, ad Libanium suum in philosophia naturali discipulum epistola in opus subjectum Peri anacriseon ton hypnoticon feliciter initium capit ad laudem Dei.*

Bibliothèque Nationale MS lat. 7869, f. 75r-80v. - *Fragmentum epithalamii soluta oratione scripti. Compositio Tabula veritatis magistri Pelagii [...] ad discipulum suum Libanium Gallum.* 19 tracts, of which 12-16 most relevant.

British Library Harley MS 181, f. 75r, *De arte crucifixi Pelagii Solitarii, doctrina non vulgaris.*

British Library Sloane MS 3846, f. 182r, *De arte crucifixi Pellagii, doctrina non vulgaris.*

Leipzig University Library Cod. mag. 13, *Pelagii Eremitae II Bücher von Erkandnus und Nahmen seines guten Engels.*

Leipzig University Library Cod. mag. 25, *Magistri Pelagii Eremitae in insula Majoricarum...Libano*

Gallo.

Leipzig University Library Cod. mag. 26, *Drey Bücher Pelagii*...

Österreichische Nationalbibliothek. Cod. 10477. Pelagius de Mallorca. *Ad Libanium Gallum de somniorum interpretatione libri tres*, 1465.

SLUB Dresden MS N.93 *Pelagij Eremitae drey Bücher.*

Vrijmetselarij Museum Kloss MS 1210-B - *Magistri Pelagii Eremitae in Insula Majoricarum, Circulus seu Tabula veritatis, proscribente cam discipulo suc magistro Libano Gallo.*

Books

*Key texts have been asterisked *

Trithemius, Johannes. *Steganographia* . Frankfurt: Matthias Becker, 1606.*

Trithemius, Johannes. *Steganographia* . Frankfurt: Johannes Saurius, 1608.

Trithemius, Johannes. *Steganographia* . Darmstadt: Auleandrus, 1621.

Trithemius, Johannes. *Steganographia* . Nuremberg: Heidel, 1721.*

Other books by Trithemius

Trithemius, Johannes. *Annales Hirsaugienses*. St. Gallen: Joannes Georgius Schlegel, 1690.

Trithemius, Johannes. *Antipalus Maleficiorum*. Mainz: Lippius, 1605; reprinted India: Pranava Books, c. 2010. *

Trithemius, Johannes. *Clavis Steganographiae*. Frankfurt: Joannem Bernerum, 1621.

Trithemius, Johannes. *De Septem Secundeis, id est Intelligentiis*, Nurnberg, 1522.*

Trithemius, Johannes. *De Septem Secundeis*. Frankfurt: Cyriacus Jacobus, 1545.

Trithemius, Johannes. *De Viris Illustribus Ordinis Sancti Benedicti*. Cologne: Calenius, 1575; Maintz: Albinus, 1605; translated as *Illustrious Authors of the Order of St Benedict*. Eugene: Wipf & Stock, 2023.

Trithemius, Johannes. *In Praise of Scribes (De Laude Scriptorum)*. Edited by Klaus Arnold, translated by Robert Behrendt. Kansas: Coronado Press, 1974.

Trithemius, Johannes. *Liber de Octo Questionum*. Mainz: Johannes Albinus, 1601.

Trithemius, Johannes. *Opera Historia*. Frankfurt, 1601.

Trithemius, Johannes. *Opera Pia et Spiritualia*. Mainz, 1604.

Trithemius, Johannes. *Polygraphia*. Paris, 1561 [French].

Trithemius, Johannes. *Polygraphia*. Strasburg. 1600.

Trithemius, Johannes. *Polygraphiæ libri sex*. Basel: Johann Haselberg, 1518.*

Trithemius, Johannes. *The Magical Amulets of the Ancient Sages* and *Bibliotheca Necromantica*. Trans. Robert Nixon. Keighley: Hadean, 2023.

Trithemius, Johannes. *Veterum Sophorum Sigilla et Imagines Magicae*. 1612.

Secondary Sources

Agrippa, Heinrich Cornelius. *Three Books of Occult Philosophy by Henry Cornelius Agrippa of Nettesheim.* Translated by James Freake [French]. Edited and annotated by Donald Tyson. Woodbury: Llewellyn, 2007.

Arnold, Klaus. *Johannes Trithemius (1462-1516).* Würzburg: Schöningh, 1971, 1991, 2018. [pp. 228 et seq. has an almost complete Trithemius bibliography.]

Arnold, Klaus. *Additamenta Trithemiana: Nachträge zu Leben und Werk des Johannes Trithemius,* 1975. [*Proemium* and chapter headings of Trithemius' *De Demonibus.*]

Ashen Chassan, Frater. *Gateways Through Stone and Circle: A Manual of Evocation for the Planetary Intelligences.* Timmonsville: Nephilim, 2013.

Bailey, J. 'John Dee and Trithemius' *Steganography*' in *Notes and Queries,* May 1879, pp. 401-402, 422-433.*

Beaumont, John. *An historical, physiological and theological treatise of spirits: apparitions, witchcrafts, and other magical practices. Containing an account of the genii ... With a refutation of Dr. Bekker's World bewitch'd; and other authors...,* London: Browne, 1705.

Brann, Noel L. 'Conrad Celtis and the "Druid" Abbot Trithemius: an Inquiry into Patriotic Humanism' in *Renaissance and Reformation.* New Series 3, No. 1, 1979, pp 16-28.

Brann, Noel L. *The Abbot Trithemius: (1462-1516): The Renaissance of Monastic Humanism.* Studies in the History of Christian Thought, Vol. 24. Leiden: Brill, 1981.

Brann, Noel L. *Trithemius and Magical Theology: A Chapter in the Controversy over Occult Studies in Early Modern Europe.* SUNY Series in Western Esoteric Traditions. Albany: SUNY, 1999. *

Boxer, Alexander. *A Scheme of Heaven: Astrology and the Birth of Science.* London: Profile, 2020.

Boxer, Alexander. *Steganographia and other occult writings of Johannes Trithemius (1462-1516).* Trithemius.com.

Caramuel y Lobkowitz, Juan. *Steganographia nec non Claviculae Solomonis Germani Joannis Trithemii....* Cologne: Egmondanis, 1635. [Interpreted with reference to Kabbalah, theology, Hebrew, and natural magic.] *

Couliano, Ioan. *Eros and Magic in the Renaissance.* Chicago: University of Chicago, 1987, pp. 162-175.

de Mendonça Jr, Francisco de Paula Souza. 'In the Wings of Asiriel: some reflections over an Excerpt of Trithemius' Steganographia' in *Studia Hermetica Journal,*

Issue I, no. 2, 2011.

Falconer, J. *Cryptomenysis Patefacta, or the Art of Secret Information disclosed without a Key,* London: Brown, 1685. [primarily on cryptography.]

Frater Archer. *Black Abbot White Magic: Johannes Trithemius and the Angelic Mind.* London: Scarlet, 2020. *

French, Peter. *John Dee, the World of an Elizabethan Magus.* London, 1972.

Heidel, Wolfgang Ernest. *Johannis Trithemii Steganographia…Vindicata Reservata et Illustrata.* Mainz: Zubrodt, 1676; reprinted India: Skilled Books, c. 2010.

Kahn, David. *The Codebreakers: The Comprehensive History of Secret Communication from Ancient Times to the Internet.* New York: Scriber, 1996.

Kircher, Athanasius. *Polygraphia nova et universalis.* Rome: Varesius, 1663.

Kolata, Gina. 'A Mystery Unravelled, Twice' in *The New York Times*, April 14, 1998, pp. F1, F6.

Kuper, M. *Johannes Trithemius, der Schwarze Abt.* Berlin: Zerling, 1998.

Laycock, Donald. *The Complete Enochian Dictionary.* Preface by Stephen Skinner. London: Askin, 1994. Newburyport: Weiser, 2023.

McLean, Adam (Ed.) Translated by Fiona Tait & Christopher Upton. *The Steganographia of Johannes Trithemius* [Books I & III], Edinburgh: Magnum Opus Hermetic Sourceworks No. 12, 1982.

Page, Sophie. *Magic in Medieval Manuscripts,* London: British Library, 2004.

Peterson, Joseph. 'The Art Theurgia-Goetia' in *The Lesser Key of Solomon: Lemegeton Clavicula Salomonis.* York Beach: Weiser, 2001, pp. 57-108.

Rankine, David. *The Grimoire Encyclopaedia.* Keighley: Hadean, 2023.

Reeds, James A. 'Solved: The Ciphers in Book III of Trithemius' *Steganographia.*' in *Cryptologia* 22 (October, 1998): pp. 291-313. *

Schott, Gaspar. *Schola Steganographica.* Würzburg: Jobus Hertz, 1680.

Selenus, Gustavus (Duke of Braunschweig-Lüneburg). *Cryptomenytics et Cryptographiæ libri IX.* Lüneburg: Stern, 1624. [partially translated by J. W. H. Walden in McLean (1982)] *

Sherman, William H. *John Dee: The Politics of Reading and Writing in the English Renaissance.* Amherst: University of Massachusetts Press, 1995.

Shumaker, Wayne. *Renaissance Curiosa.* Medieval and Renaissance Texts and Studies, 8. Binghamton, NY: Center for Medieval & Early Renaissance Studies, 1982, Chapter 3, Johannes Trithemius and Cryptography. *

Sigismund of Seeon. *Trithemius sui ipsius vindex sive Steganographiae.* Ingolstadt:

Ederiano, 1616. [Interpreted as a work on magic rather than cryptography.]

Silbernagel, Isidore. *Trithemius: Eine Monographie*. Landshut: Wölfle, 1868. [Useful biography.]

Skinner, Stephen. *Complete Magician's Tables*. London/Singapore: Golden Hoard, 2006; rpt. Llewellyn, Woodbury, 2007, 2011. Fifth expanded edition, Golden Hoard, 2015, 2017, 2021.

Skinner, Stephen and David Rankine. 'Theurgia-Goetia' and 'The Art Pauline' in *The Goetia of Dr Rudd*, Vol. 3, SWCM. London: Golden Hoard, 2007. pp. 212-325, 382-386. *

Thorndike, Lynn. A *History of Magic and Experimental Science*, Volumes I-VIII. New York: Columbia University Press, 1923-1958, Vol. IV, Chap. 60; Vol. V, p. 131.

Van der Laan, J.M. and Andrew Weeks, eds. *The Faustian Century: German Literature and Culture in the Age of Luther and Faustus*. Rochester, New York: Camden House, 2013.

Vigenère, Blaise de. *Traicté des Chiffres ou Secrètes Manières d'Escrire*. Paris: Abel l'Angelier, 1586.

Walker, D.P. *Spiritual and Demonic Magic: From Ficino to Campanella*. Studies of the Warburg Institute, 22. London: Warburg Institute, University of London, 1958, pp. 86-89.

Weyer, Johann. *De praestigiis daemonum…accessit pseudomonarchia daemonum*. Basel: Officina Oporiniana, 1583. *

Wilkins, John (Bishop of Chester). *Mercury, or the Secret and Swift Messenger: shewing, how a man may with privacy and speed communicate his thoughts to a friend at any distance*. London: Norton, 1641, 1694; Delhi: Gyan, 2022.

Yates, Francis. *Giordano Bruno and the Hermetic Tradition*. London, 1964.

Yates, Francis. *The Occult Philosophy in the Elizabethan Age*. London, 1979.

Zambelli, Paola. *White Magic, Black Magic in the European Renaissance from Ficino, Pico, Della Porta to Trithemius, Agrippa, Bruno*. Leiden: Brill, 2007. especially pp. 73-112.*